ACCORDING TO OUR HEARTS

ANGELA ONWUACHI-WILLIG

According to Our Hearts

RHINELANDER V. RHINELANDER AND
THE LAW OF THE MULTIRACIAL FAMILY

Yale

UNIVERSITY PRESS

NEW HAVEN & LONDON

Yale University Press books may be purchased in quantity for
educational, business, or promotional use. For information, please e-mail
sales.press@yale.edu (U.S. office) or sales@yaleup.co.uk (U.K. office).

Set in Scala type by Integrated Publishing Solutions.
Printed in the United States of America.

Library of Congress Cataloging-in-Publication Data

Onwuachi-Willig, Angela.
According to our hearts : Rhinelander v. Rhinelander and the law of the multiracial family /
Angela Onwuachi-Willig.
p.   cm.
Includes bibliographical references and index.
ISBN 978-0-300-16682-8 (cloth : alk. paper)   1. Rhinelander, Leonard Kip—Trials,
litigation, etc.   2. Jones, Alice Beatrice—Trials, litigation, etc.   3. Trials (Divorce)—
United States.   4. Race discrimination—Law and legislation—United States.   I. Title.
KF228.R47O59 2013
346.74701'66—dc23
2012044511

A catalogue record for this book is available from the British Library.

This paper meets the requirements of ANSI/NISO Z39.48-1992
(Permanence of Paper).

10 9 8 7 6 5 4 3 2 1

This book is dedicated with much love and gratitude to my husband, Jacob Willig-Onwuachi, and our children, Elijah, Bethany, and Solomon. This book also is dedicated to the memory of my sister, Cordillia (Onwuachi) Guerrero, whose own family experiences have served as added inspiration for this book.

CONTENTS

ACKNOWLEDGMENTS

I AM GRATEFUL TO SO MANY PEOPLE for their help with this project. I am most grateful to my wonderful family, my husband Jacob Willig-Onwuachi, and our three children, Elijah, Bethany, and Solomon. They inspire me every day and have taught me so much about life, including much of what is in this book. I also give thanks to Jacob for many related conversations and discussions and for his comments on my work.

I also am thankful for the love and support of my mother, Veronica; my sister, Bridget; my brothers, Emmanuel and James; my in-laws, David and Susan Willig; my grandparents-in-law, Ethel and Richard Stuckman, and Robert Onkka; my brother-in-law, Ernest Guerrero; my niece, Rosie; my nephew, Sidney; my brother-in-law, Isaac Willig; and my sisters-in-law, Chantana Struckman and Petrina Willig.

I give great thanks to Michael O'Malley, the former editor at Yale University Press who inquired about this project and made this book possible. I am especially grateful for his belief in and great enthusiasm for the project. I also am very grateful to my editors, Andrew Frisardi, William Frucht, and Dan Heaton, and to editorial assistant Jaya Chatterjee, who assisted with this project in so many ways. Thank you so much for all of your hard work on this project.

Research for this book could not have been completed without the support of Charles and Marion Kierscht. Dean Gail Agrawal, Dean Carolyn Jones, the Provost's Office at the University of Iowa, and the Office of Research at the University of Iowa also provided invaluable support for this project. I am deeply indebted to these individuals and offices, especially to Charles and Marion Kierscht, two wonderful people who have so graciously allowed their name to be connected to my work in title.

University of Iowa Law Librarians Ted Potter and John Bergstrom also provided invaluable research assistance. I also give great thanks to former Dean and Associate Dean Rex Perschbacher and Kevin Johnson, Law Librarians Peg Durkin, Susan Llano, and Erin Murphy at the University of California, Davis School of Law for their research support and funding. This project would not have even started without the help of Peg Durkin, who worked to provide funding and helped me secure a copy of the *Rhinelander* transcript.

I also thank my colleagues at the University of Iowa College of Law and my former colleagues at the University of California, Davis School of Law for their general support. Of course, I miss my dear colleague from Iowa, David Baldus, who, simply through his spirit and warmth, always added much to my work on all projects.

This book also could not have been completed without my survey and interview participants, whom I cannot name, but who are each dear to me. I am appreciative of the time that they took out of their busy schedules to assist me with this project. In so many ways, their experiences have made this book come alive.

My former research assistants, Jonathan Brayman, Christie Canales, Tai Duncan, Amber Fricke, and Berneta Haynes also contributed greatly to this project. I am eternally grateful to them for their hard work and enthusiasm, and I am particularly grateful to Amber Fricke and Berneta Haynes, who provided tremendous help during and near the end of this project. My former assistants Mary Sleichter and Kati Jumper and temporary assistant Jeremiah Stai also provided help on this book.

I also give thanks to my writing group at my second academic home as a "faculty member," Grinnell College: Shanna Benjamin, Karla Erickson, Lakesia Johnson, and Michelle Nasser. These women really saw me through the end of this project, and I could not have finished the book without them. Their encouragement (and "pomming") kept me going in the final months. I also am thankful to Dean Paula Smith of Grinnell College and Grinnell College Librarian Richard Fyffe for providing me with a space on campus to work on this book and for all other assistance with this project. Many others provided assistance for which I am thankful. I especially thank Marna Montgomery, Sheryl Bissen, and Retta Kelly for their help.

Of course, I am incredibly grateful for the help and advice of my fabulous mentor, Dean Kevin Johnson of the University of California, Davis School of Law, who made my career possible in so many ways, and who has always supported my creative work. I also give great thanks to Nancy Levit, University of Iowa President Emeritus Sandy Boyd and Dean Emeritus Bill Hines for their advice and mentorship. I owe special thanks to some dear friends, who have suffered through hearing me talk about this book (far too much) for far too long, who read and commented on parts of my drafts, and who provided much-needed emotional and intellectual support along the way: Mario Barnes, Jacquelyn Bridgeman, David Cook Martin, David Coster, Michele Goodwin, Aya Gruber, Jennifer Holladay, Trina Jones, Kevin Kopelson, Robin Lenhardt, Melissa Murray, Camille Gear Rich, Kesho Scott, Jessica Silbey, Catherine Smith, and Peggie Smith.

So many others have contributed tremendously to this project by reading and commenting on chapter drafts, talking through ideas with me, writing great articles and books for me to cite and use in this book, providing wonderful ideas, and/or encouraging me along the way. To all of you, I am very thankful: Kerry Abrams, Ifeoma Ajunwa, Laila Amine, Annette Appell, Rick Banks, George Barlow, Elizabeth Bartholet, Rabia Belt, Randy Bezanson, Arthur Bonfield, Christopher Bracey, Tonya Brito, Alfred Brophy, Paul Butler, Mary Campbell, Jennifer Chacón, Anupam Chander, Guy Charles, Miriam Cherry, Frank Rudy Cooper, Marcella David, Cullen Davis, Richard Delgado, Ann Estin, Dresden Farrand, Barbara Flagg, Mary Louise Frampton, Liz Glazer, Timothy Glynn, Lawrence Goldstone, Laura Gomez, Ariela Gross, Lani Guinier, Meredith Harbach, Jill Hasday, Emily Houh, Herb Hovenkamp, Kristin Johnson, Nick Johnson, Bernie Jones, Randall Kennedy, Linda Kerber, Susan Kuo, Al Lacson, Marina Lao, Holning Lau, Cynthia Lee, Adriane Lentz-Smith, Evelyn Lewis, Benjamin Means, Solangel Maldonado, Judge Karen Nelson Moore, Rachel Moran, Adele Morrison, Odeana Neal, Osagie Obasogie, Chief Judge Solomon Oliver, Rigel Oliveri, Hari Osofsky, Imani Perry, Twila Perry, Todd Pettys, Marc Poirer,

Judge Robert Pratt, Mae Quinn, Song Richardson, Alice Ristroph, Darren Rosenblum, Laura Rosenbury, Bertrall Ross, Paul Secunda, Sacha Somek, Madhavi Sunder, Rose Cuison Villazor, Gerry Wetlaufer, Diana Williamson, Francille Wilson, Adrien Wing, Marcia Yablon-Zug, and Rebecca Zietlow. I give my sincerest apologies to anyone whom I may have inadvertently left off of this list. I am grateful for your assistance, too.

Additionally, I must thank several institutions, which hosted lectures, workshop presentations, and conference presentations where attendees helped me to strengthen this book through questions and comments. These institutions are the Emerging Family Law Scholars Workshop (at the University of Colorado School of Law); the Southeast/Southwest People of Color Legal Scholarship Conference (at the University of South Carolina School of Law); the University of Houston Law Center Speakers Colloquium; the Law and History Colloquium at University of Southern California, Gould School of Law; the Race, Law, and Socioeconomic Class Conference at the University of California, Irvine School of Law; the Iowa Legal Studies Workshop; the Lutie A. Lytle Black Female Law Faculty Workshop (at both the University of Kentucky College of Law and Texas Southern University, Thurgood Marshall School of Law); the Brigitte M. Bodenheimer Lecture Series at the University of California, Davis School of Law; the Thelton Henderson Center for Social Justice at the University of California, Berkeley School of Law; and law faculty workshops at Denver University, Sturm College of Law; Washington University-St. Louis School of Law; Seton Hall University Law School; Marquette University Law School; George Washington University Law School; Cumberland School of Law, Samford University; and the University of Alabama School of Law.

Parts of this book previously appeared in two of my articles: *A Beautiful Lie: Exploring* Rhinelander v. Rhinelander *as a Formative Lesson on Race, Identity, Marriage, and Family,* 95 Cal. L. Rev. 2393 (2007); and *A House Divided: The Invisibility of the Multiracial Family,* 44 Harv. C.R.-C.L. L. Rev. 231 (2009) (co-authored with Jacob Willig-Onwuachi, Grinnell College).

Finally, thank you to everyone who ever whispered an encouraging word to me as I was writing this book, from my doctor to my next door neighbor.

These thanks are all truly from my heart.

ACCORDING TO OUR HEARTS

Introduction

MY HUSBAND, JACOB, AND I MUST HAVE been told "You have to see *A Bronx Tale*" ten times before we actually figured out or, rather, saw why. Often, when given this recommendation, Jacob, a white man, and I, a black woman, would respond, "Really? What's the movie about?" Usually, the reply was something along the lines of: "You just have to see it."

Then one day, as Jacob and I were using the remote control to flip through television channels—one of our favorite pastimes—we came across the movie and it all became clear. Released in 1993, *A Bronx Tale* chronicles the story of Calogero Anello, an Italian American teen who grows up in the Bronx during the 1960s and finds himself caught between the worlds and lessons of his father, Lorenzo Anello, a hardworking and honest bus driver played by Robert De Niro, and Sonny LoSpecchio, a powerful local mobster, played by scriptwriter Chazz Palminteri, who takes Calogero under his wing.[1] In the midst of the racial turmoil of the 1960s, Calogero finds himself falling in love with Jane Williams, a young African American girl who attends his high school and proclaims to him, "I like Italians."[2]

Jacob and I chuckled the first time that Jane was introduced in *A Bronx Tale*—the lightbulbs quickly going on in our heads. Nevertheless, we loved the movie. After all, who doesn't love De Niro, much less a film directed by De Niro? Who doesn't love a good love story, especially one in which you can see yourself reflected in the characters? *A Bronx Tale*—or rather its story— had a significant impact on us, making us lifelong fans of Palminteri and even bigger fans of De Niro. Although the movie had its tragic parts, ending with the death of LoSpecchio and several of Calogero's friends, those tragedies did not center on the interracial relationship between Jane and Calogero, as do so many films that concern interracial love. Not only was Jane a "great one" (a reference by LoSpecchio to her action in reaching over to unlock the car door for Calogero), but Calogero and Jane's love story was also a great one. De Niro, who just a few years earlier had come out of a long-term interracial marriage with black actress Diahnne Abbott, and who, at the time, was in a long-term relationship with black model Toukie Smith, clearly brought his own personal experiences to bear quite nicely in directing the film.

Back in 1993, Jacob and I were college sweethearts, dating and not yet married. Ever since, we have continued to receive recommendations from people about stories concerning interracial couples and, in some cases, potential couple-friends for us to cultivate. To many, our being in an interracial relationship becomes the most salient part of our identity as a collective, such that they do not see our relationship as influencing simply our selection of movies but also our friends, regardless of any other similarities or differences. The stories that have been recommended to us, however, have never resonated with us like *A Bronx Tale*. They never proved to be as powerful, compelling, or well structured.

So when I first discovered the story of Alice Beatrice (Jones) Rhinelander and Leonard Kip Rhinelander—two New Yorkers who are the focal point of this book—my attraction to them and their story came as a surprise. I learned of *Rhinelander v. Rhinelander* and thus the Rhinelanders themselves through a good friend, who, in turn, had uncovered these treasures in the way that so many of us encounter real-life narratives of romance and heartbreak: through her own good friend, Jamie Wacks (with whom I later discussed the case and the story).

At that time, Jacob and I were married with one child, and I was working at a law firm in Boston. Jessica Silbey, a former classmate, a co-worker at the firm, and the Jewish godmother to my child, stopped by my office and inquired, "You ever heard of this *Rhinelander* case?" Jessica knew that I, a black woman, was married to a white man, but more importantly, she knew that I was a sucker for love stories. When I responded to her question with a "no," Jessica furrowed her eyebrows, sat down in my guest chair, and bared the basic facts of the case to me. As I researched the case further, I learned even more details.

Alice Beatrice Jones, a working-class woman of racially ambiguous heritage, and Leonard Kip Rhinelander, a wealthy white blueblood, met and quickly fell in love during the fall of 1921. Their romance blossomed over a three-year period, including a year-and-a-half period of long-distance separation that Leonard's father, Philip Rhinelander, had engineered to keep them apart. During that time, Alice and Leonard regularly wrote love letters to each other—many of which would later become evidence at the trial. Eventually, Alice and Leonard reunited and married on October 14, 1924. But less than two months later, on November 26, 1924, Leonard filed for annulment of his marriage to Alice on the grounds that Alice had misrepresented her race to him. According to Leonard, their marriage needed to be declared null and void because Alice committed fraud, not only by failing to inform him that she was of "colored blood," but also by directly telling him that she was white.[3] Alice's parents were immigrants from England, but her mother was white, and her father was, from what anyone could tell, either of black and white parentage or white and South Asian parentage.

According to legend, Leonard and Alice were actually madly in love, with Leonard filing the lawsuit only because of his father, who refused to accept their relationship. Instead of fighting against his father and losing all connection to his family and its money, Leonard told Alice to fight the case to ensure that they could be together as husband and wife.

But Alice surprised everyone when she did not attempt to prove her whiteness, the only way in which she and Leonard could have socially remained together as husband and wife. Instead, Alice admitted that she was of colored descent and argued that Leonard was aware of her race before the marriage.[4] This strategy signified certain death for the marriage of the newlyweds. If Leonard won and was granted an annulment, the Rhinelander marriage would forever be erased from the books, as though Alice and Leonard had never been acquainted. And if Alice won, which, at the time, seemed impossible given the vast differences in both their class and their race statures, she could never live with Leonard again as his wife. A victory for Alice at trial required a finding not only that she was "colored," but also that Leonard knew that she was not "purely" white. Although New York law did not officially ban interracial marriages between black people and white people, racial endogamy was taken for granted in marriage, particularly in middle- or upper-class marriages. No one questioned whether race, or rather knowledge of race, was material to the decision of marriage.[5] Socially speaking, although the Harlem Renaissance had begun to change the racial landscape of 1920s New York society, within the world that Alice and Leonard were inhabiting, a poor and colored Alice could never be the wife of the wealthy, prominent, and white Leonard. Even if Leonard lost his claim for annulment, the couple would still have to obtain a divorce.

The trial of the Rhinelanders proved to be shocking: from racy love letters, to tales of premarital lust and sex, to the inclusion of blackface performer Al Jolson as a trial witness, to the exhibition of Alice's bare breasts and legs in the courtroom to prove that Leonard, who had seen her naked before marriage, would have known that she was colored at the time of their nuptials. Most scandalous, however, was the trial's end. The jury returned a verdict for Alice, the young defendant who never testified at trial. The jurors declared both that Leonard knew (or at least should have known) of Alice's racial "shame" prior to their marriage and that he married (or at least would have married) her regardless of her race. As the New York Times reported, the jury "declared by their verdict that the fervid love for the dark-skinned Alice Jones which characterized all of Rhinelander's letters would have been declared even though he had known at the time that she was not white, and that whatever his doubts were before his marriage his affection was greater than the bar of race."[6] Reminiscent of the biblical story of David and Goliath, Alice, a colored chambermaid and the daughter of a New York taxicab driver, had defeated Leonard, a white fixture on the New York Social Register and a descendant of the Huguenots. A few years later, the Rhinelander marriage ended—as it had to socially—by divorce in Las Vegas, the only remaining legal means for their separation after Alice's victory at trial, and later on appeal.[7]

Once I learned about the Rhinelanders, I found myself captivated by their tale. The story's ending—a verdict in Alice's favor—mesmerized me. I could not believe that a working-class colored woman (at least as defined by the rule of hypodescent or the one-drop rule, which is the notion that one drop of black blood makes one black) had actually won a trial against a wealthy, white man in 1920s New York. I was impressed by what I viewed as Alice's strength in "choosing" not to litigate her whiteness—to not try to prove that she was white. As Professor Ariela Gross explains in her book *What Blood Won't Tell: A History of Race on Trial in America,* trials in which individuals had to prove their white racial identity occurred regularly from their start during the late eighteenth century and until well into the twentieth century.[8] In some of these trials, proving that one was white meant the difference between slavery and freedom. In such cases, it was not uncommon for the examinations at trial themselves to demean litigants who worked to prove their right to freedom by putting their very bodies on as exhibits. For instance, in discussing the trial of Alexina Morrison—a female slave who ran away from her master, fought to prove her whiteness in the courtroom, and won at trial—Gross proclaims, "[T]he white men in the courtroom treated Alexina Morrison in ways a white woman of the time . . . would never have been treated, publicly disrobing her and touching her body, enacting the rituals of the slave market."[9] For other individuals, proving one's whiteness in these racial trials meant the ability to retain the privileges of white citizenship, such as a good education for one's children—privileges that could easily be threatened with just one accusation of what was commonly viewed as tainted black blood. Here, for Alice, litigating and proving her whiteness would have meant the resuscitation of her marriage to Leonard and, more so, the recognition of her marital family's belonging in the larger community or, as Professors Jennifer Gordon and Robin Lenhardt would say, their very citizenship.[10] With this history of racial trials in mind, I viewed Alice's position at trial as one of great courage. I thought, "What courage it must have taken for her to stand up to the Rhinelander family and name in that fashion!" It was on this portion of Alice and Leonard's narrative that I focused initially. I did not concentrate on their failed love story. Rather, my mind filled with questions such as, "How did Alice accomplish the impossible by winning at trial?" and, "Why did she win at trial?"

For years after, I became preoccupied with the Rhinelanders' lives. When I left legal practice nearly two years later to become a law professor, I found myself wanting to learn more about the Rhinelanders—their story, their love, their love's demise, and Alice's legal success. Slated to teach both family law and critical race theory, I considered how the case could unearth important concepts in each course. I began to acquire materials about the case shortly after I arrived at the University of California, Davis School of Law in July 2003. I started with the trial transcript, exhibits, and a few appellate documents—quite a score for me. The *Rhinelander* case had remained relatively unknown until the turn of the century, when Earl Lewis, then a professor at the University of Michigan, and his then-graduate student, Heidi Ardizzone, used local newspapers to write about the Rhinelanders in their illuminating and insightful book, *Love on Trial: An American Scandal in Black and White*. In part, *Rhinelander*'s obscurity was due to the fact that it remained buried in newspaper articles for decades. In fact, for many decades, scholars, including Lewis and Ardizzone, who wrote the first book about the case, had not discovered the whereabouts of the trial transcript for *Rhinelander* and its court materials in the Association of the Bar of New York City Library. Unbeknown to them, however, Jamie Wacks, a friend of my friend Jessica Silbey, had discovered these treasures on her own in the New York City Library during her time as an undergraduate student at Harvard University. Wacks is the person who told me where to find the Rhinelander materials.

Yet, even as I began to gather newspaper articles and other writings about the case, they largely collected dust in my office. As the years passed, my reaction to Alice and Leonard's story changed. I began to pose a different set of questions, concentrating, this time, on their failed relationship as well as on Alice's verbal silence at her own trial. Were Alice and Leonard still in love by the time of the trial, during the trial, and even after the trial? After the jury trial, Alice hesitated when journalists asked, "Would you go back to your husband?" but, just seconds later, she agreed that her relationship with Leonard had been "a beautiful love affair."[11] Was Leonard really just following his father's wishes? The black press, particularly the *Chicago Defender*, had implied as much, reporting that the "young Rhinelander would never have signed an annulment complaint of his own free will."[12]

I started to think, too, about paths not taken. Did Alice and Leonard ever think to run away together? Before the trial, the *Chicago Defender* alluded to plans by Alice and Leonard to move away and live together in Europe.[13] Did

Alice have any say in revealing her body at trial? The fact that she never verbally testified at trial could suggest no. Did Alice fall out of love with Leonard as she became a spectacle on display—with her bare chest—within the courtroom? The trial record reported that Alice wept as her bare body parts were inspected by the all-male, all-white, and all-married jurors.[14] Why did Alice not litigate her whiteness so that she and Leonard would at least have a chance of living together as husband and wife? After all, early reports from Alice's first, lead attorney, former Judge Samuel Swinburne, indicated that Alice's "main objective would be to prove that she was white."[15]

From 2003 to 2006, I hardly looked at my documents concerning *Rhinelander.* But I never fully appreciated why I avoided these historical papers during this period until I began to write an essay about the case, "A Beautiful Lie: Exploring *Rhinelander v. Rhinelander* as a Formative Lesson on Race, Identity, Marriage, and Family."

As I wrote my essay, I realized that the story of the Rhinelanders dampened my spirits, rather than lifted them. Even though Alice had, to some extent, won a racial victory of sorts, I found her narrative to be depressing. It was a tale of losing by winning and a story of lost intimacy, love, and devotion in a world with plenty of room but, sadly, no space within which Alice and Leonard could be lovingly and openly together.

I began to tell myself that the story of the Rhinelanders was no longer relevant. Although I recognized that the U.S. Supreme Court's 1967 decision in *Loving v. Virginia,* which held that antimiscegenation statutes violate citizens' rights to equal protection and due process,[16] had not altered all social, and even legal, reactions to interracial couples, I convinced myself that race and the implications of passing, whether voluntary or involuntary, were a thing of the past in marriage.

But not too soon after I began to write my essay, I met a modern-day Alice, or rather, I discovered that I already knew one. While at a conference, I met another black female attorney—I will call her "Mary"—who asked me if I knew her cousin—whom I will call "Sara"—who lived in my town and who I had always assumed was white. I must have looked surprised at Mary's announcement, because Mary, whose skin color was a tad lighter than milk-chocolate brown, smiled broadly and proclaimed, "Yes, Sara is my blood cousin. I was just checking on her." I learned later during my conversation with Mary that she was curious to know if Sara ever passed, taking my pause and shock as a yes. Mary and her black extended family had yet to meet Sara's new boyfriend, a white man who Mary had heard through family grapevines possessed "husband potential." I, however, had met the boyfriend before, and I wondered, "Did he know? If not, what would he do if he found out? Would it matter to him at all?" Mary also asked me those same questions. It was then and only then that I began to recall the other modern-day Alices in my life—from college, in law school, and even at work. Like Alice, who did not hesitate to introduce Leonard to her father, her darker sister Emily, and Emily's husband, Robert, who was readily identifiable as a black man by skin color—all signs that Alice was not trying to hide her racial heritage from Leonard—none of my modern-day Alices actively passed as white. They did not deny their racial backgrounds or try to hide them at all. They simply did not go out of their way to correct people's assumptions about their race, assumptions that people may or may not have expressed openly to them, just as I had never expressed my assumption about race to Sara. Much like with Alice, people imposed a racial identity upon them without ever explicitly asking them about their own identifications.

It was at that time that I also began to think more broadly, not only about how society frames individuals in terms of race, but also about how both law and society work together to define families and their rights and opportunities by race—especially when those families are multiracial. I knew at that moment that my future exploration of the *Rhinelander* case and its lessons would have go deeper. It would have to delve into the lives of real people who have found or who find themselves traversing lines of race, color, and family.

This book project became that future exploration, which I began by surveying and conducting follow-up interviews with twenty-one interracial, black-white couples. Sixteen of these couples are opposite-sex couples, while five are same-sex couples. Their relationships span from five years to nearly thirty-one years. The individuals in the couples range in age from thirty-two years old to sixty years old. They live in all regions of the country—West to Midwest to East to South—in cities like Laramie, Wyoming; Urbandale, Iowa; Brooklyn, New York; and Lawrenceville, Georgia, and they grew up in areas that are diverse to nondiverse, with some attending racially integrated schools and others racially segregated schools. All of the individuals in the couples have completed at least some education in college, and the couples are all middle class to upper middle class, which makes for a very privileged group. However, the fact that this group is privileged is not so strange, as studies have shown that individuals in interracial marriages and unions tend to be well educated, regardless of their race.[17] In fact, I suspect that such privilege makes my surveyed couples' experiences with discrimination and microaggressions, meaning the daily "indignities, whether intentional or unintentional, that communicate hostile, derogatory, or negative, racial . . . slights and insults to the target person or group,"[18] all the more meaningful. After all, one could argue that, if this group of socioeconomically privileged, black-white couples is experiencing microaggressions and discrimination based on race and family, then their less fortunate peers, in terms of socioeconomic status, certainly must be. Additionally, nearly all of my surveyed heterosexual couples are black female–white male couples, even though black male–white female couples are more than twice as present as black female–white male couples in the United States. Such disproportionate representations in my study are in part the result of using a "convenience sample," in which I identified interviewees through my own personal contacts and through previous survey participants, and in part the result of which invited couples actually decided to complete the survey and engage in interviews. But, again, given the history of harsher punishments and discrimination against black male–white female couples as compared to black female–white male couples (discussed in more detail in Chapter 5), the experiences of my surveyed, heterosexual couples are still critical because the effects or level of the discrimination and microaggressions felt by black male–white female couples and their families are likely to be at the same level as or, arguably, at an even worse level than those endured by black female–white male couples and their families.

Overall, much like my former "neighbor" Sara had informed my understanding of Alice and the ways in which Alice may or may not have been voluntarily passing, and certainly my understanding of the ways in which racial assumptions were imposed upon Alice as an individual, these couples have informed my own personal and academic understanding about the spaces in which multiracial couples and families live and work and play. As you will see throughout this project, these couples' experiences in their homes, in their jobs, with their children, and with their families have added tremendously to this book and its understanding of the role that law and society play in both creating a space and leaving no space for those, who as Professor Heather Dalmage writes, are "tripping on the color line."[19]

As I worked on this book project, what I learned is that the many lessons that can be absorbed about multiracial individuals and families do not just end with formal "subjects" like Alice or the black-white couples I surveyed. They come daily, and often at unexpected moments. For example, a few years after I had learned about my real-life Alice's—Sara's—racial background, a biracial, black-white student in one of my law school seminars wrote eloquently about her own involuntary passing. With blond, straight hair and a complexion as light as my husband's, Cara,[20] in part because of her appearance and in part because she had been adopted by a white family, was often presumed to be white. In describing the burdens of inactive passing, she wrote: "My skin was pale, I passed as white, but I wasn't. . . . [P]assing as white carries its own burdens. Yes, I can pass as white and avoid discrimination based on race. Yes, I exercise white privilege even without consciously intending to do so. Passing carries a negative side to it as well, including the difficulty of denying part of my self-identity and anger when marginalized by discussions on both sides of the racial divide—minority and majority."[21]

Cara's paper helped me more fully appreciate the contemporary as well as the historical significance of *Rhinelander v. Rhinelander*. In many ways, *Rhinelander* is not just about a legal battle between Alice and Leonard or even the Rhinelanders and the Joneses. It is about society's contradictory concepts of race as purely biological and yet also performative. It is about the ever-shifting, but also stagnant, role of race in defining identity, love, marriage, family, housing, and work as well as the continuing ways in which multiracial families are deprived of defining, for themselves, their own familial identities.

For instance, *Rhinelander* presents several important lessons about race, personhood, and identity with respect to individuals. First, *Rhinelander* demonstrates how race in our society is defined not only by a person's perception of herself, but also perceptions of her by others, including family members. For example, my seminar student, Cara, provided this description of her adopted white father's view of her racial identity: "My father is a good man. Unfortunately, when it comes to race, he also has broken my heart. I don't think he sees me as biracial. I think he sees me as white, in part because this is his default view, in part because I look white, and in part because I was raised by white parents. Even when he does acknowledge my biracial background, obviously I'm not like those *other* mixed race people."[22]

Cara's comments expose how race, although a social construct, is not so easily determined by individuals themselves. Here, Cara's father engaged in an interpretive act that acknowledged part of who she is but still dismissed and demeaned another part, disregarding the significance of her being biracial. All the while, he left his own racism intact, wounding his daughter. Similarly, comments from Julie and Barry, a black male–white female couple whom I surveyed, also revealed the powerlessness that people can feel over defining their racial identities or those of their loved ones. For instance, in response to a question about whether they had discussed how they wanted their four-year-old, biracial son to identify racially, the young couple simply stated, "We didn't think of it as something that we could control but Barry assumed that he would be black."[23]

It is in this light that I came to view Alice's victories in litigation as tragic, personal losses. Although Alice was able to defeat Leonard's suit for annulment within the courtroom, she suffered a personal loss in terms of her own self-identification. Alice purportedly identified as a white, not a colored, woman. Several stories from Alice's acquaintances indicate that she either identified herself as a white woman or at least intended to pass as one. For example, Jane Dunham, Alice's former supervisor at Travers Island Clubhouse of the New York Athletic Club, stated that Alice began to sob and denied that she was colored after inspectors in the clubhouse laundry area listed her as "mulatto" in their report.[24] Similarly, Ira Morris, a black man who reportedly went out with Alice once, noted that his relationship ended with Alice when "she told him she was 'white' and would have nothing further to do with him."[25] Furthermore, either Alice identified herself as white on her marriage certificate, or the city clerk (with or without asking her) identified her as white. Additionally, it is undisputed that

Alice either purposely passed as or actually identified as a white woman, as well as Leonard's wife (before their marriage), when she slept with him in a hotel on two separate occasions and when she and Leonard traveled together throughout the Northeast and stayed in numerous hotels within the region. Without doing so, she could not have stayed in those hotels as Leonard's "wife." In fact, some have speculated that Alice never testified at trial because her trial attorney, Lee Parsons Davis, feared that she would proclaim a white identity instead of a colored one.[26] Alice was even rumored to have considered "a legal battle [after the trial] to clear her name of the allegation she has negro blood in her veins."[27] The mere possibility that Alice might have considered "reversing" her own symbolic raced and classed victory in the legal system to obtain and preserve legal whiteness, even after her marriage had ended, is astounding.

Yet, despite the fact that Alice may have identified as white herself and that her marriage was at stake and could be saved only by trying to prove her whiteness, Alice's own account of who she was did not factor into the greater scheme of the trial and, more importantly, in the law. Assuming that the newspaper accounts and rumors are true and Alice identified herself as a white person, then she lost, through her attorneys' choice of a trial strategy, the ability to define herself racially, or at the very least to declare her self-identified race to the public. The ethical implications of the decisions by Alice's attorneys are unclear. It may have been that Alice's attorneys silenced her at trial because they could not see her as anything other than colored and thus worried that she would commit perjury on the stand if she announced any other racial identity. Or it may have been that they completely stripped Alice of her voice by not seeking her approval or input regarding decisions about her defense.

What is clear, however, is that both the legal and social notion of whiteness as a pure state of being that can be tainted by just one drop of black blood marked Alice not just as unsuitable for social recognition as a Rhinelander, but also as unsuitable for recognition as a mere white person. Alice, like so many people of multiracial descent today, resided and lived in a society that recognized only the dual world of white and nonwhite, albeit with variations of nonwhiteness. Although Alice, through her own self-definition, was arguably not challenging hierarchies of race, but rather reifying them by trying to rise higher within those established and oppressive hierarchies through her possible racial identification as white or through a form of passing, one has to admit that there was a certain sadness in her powerlessness to define herself, both publicly and privately. That harm did not rest solely in Alice's inability to claim whiteness, but rather in the accepted notion of whiteness as so pure and blackness as so tainted that just one drop of blackness negates the whiteness. That the same argument was also applied to Alice's family because of its multiraciality, and then could be used against her at trial as evidence, only demonstrates the strength of the one-drop rule.

Today, despite the gains of the civil rights movement, both the social and legal power behind the one-drop rule remains strong. For example, as late as 1985, a Louisiana woman was denied her request to change the racial identification on her birth certificate from black to white, despite the fact that she had lived her entire life believing that she was white and was only 3/32 black.[28] Furthermore, as scholar Amos Jones has explained, even today, the historical process of defining race in the United States has not permitted biracial individuals, who may be just as much white as they are black, to claim that they are white, while fully allowing them to assert a black identity. President Barack Obama stands as one good example. Although Obama, who is half white and half black, "can easily and without challenge say that he is black . . . [he cannot] stand before a national audience and declare without ridicule that he is white."[29] More recently, Academy Award–winning actress Halle Berry, who is biracial but identifies as black, announced her belief in the "one-drop theory." Referring to her daughter Nahla, the child of Berry's relationship with white, male model Gabriel Aubry, Berry declared, "I feel she's black. I'm black and I'm her mother, and I believe in the one-drop theory."[30]

Additionally, on an individual level, *Rhinelander* exposes the manner in which the powerlessness to completely define one's own identity can result in the misuse of the body—the physical representation of one's being—especially among black women. For example, during the *Rhinelander* trial, Alice's lead attorney, Lee Parsons Davis, offered what he viewed as the strongest evidence of Leonard's premarital knowledge of Alice's racial background: Alice's bare body, a body that Leonard had fully viewed when

Fig. I.1. Justice Joseph Morschauser did not permit photographers to see Alice
as she revealed her breasts, shoulders, and legs to the jurors in the *Rhinelander*
case. However, Emile Gavereau, editor of the *New York Evening Graphic,* ran what he
viewed as the next best thing: a composite photograph of the scene. Gavereau and
Harry Grogin, who was the paper's assistant art director, set up a mock courtroom
scene with a chorus girl, instead of Alice; retouched the picture; and then placed
the actual faces of those involved in the trial onto posed bodies. The *Evening
Graphic* published the composite photograph, with the headline "Alice
Disrobes in Court to Keep Her Husband," on November 25, 1925.

he and Alice had engaged in sexual intercourse on numerous nights. In a
scene that, in some ways, must have been reminiscent of a slave auction,
Davis made Alice's body a physical exhibit before the jury in the trial justice's chambers. The presentation of Alice's breasts, shoulders, and legs
was intended to allow Leonard "to identify the color of her skin,"[31] and to
reveal the obviousness of Alice's race based on skin color to the all-white,
all-male, and all-married jury (see fig. I.1). The court record described the
event as follows:

> The Court, Mr. Mills, Mr. Davis, Mr. Swinburne, the jury, the plaintiff, the
> defendant, her mother, Mrs. George Jones, and the stenographer left the
> courtroom and entered the jury room. The defendant and Mrs. Jones then
> withdrew to the lavatory adjoining the jury room and, after a short time,
> again entered the jury room. The defendant, who was weeping, had on her
> underwear and a long coat. At Mr. Davis['] direction she let down the coat, so
> that the upper portion of her body, as far down as the breast, was exposed.

She then, again at Mr. Davis' direction, covered the upper part of her body and showed to the jury her bare legs, up as far as the knees. The Court, counsel, the jury and the plaintiff then re-entered the court room.[32]

Unlike in other instances, Davis did not engage in extensive questioning about this "piece" of evidence. Instead, he left the jury with the legal notion of *res ipsa loquitur*—the notion that "the thing speaks for itself." Davis asked Leonard if he had seen all of the parts of Alice's body that were shown, and Leonard replied that he had seen everything but her legs in the inspection room. At which point, Davis asked Leonard one question: "Your wife's body is the same shade as it was when you saw her in the [Hotel] Marie Antoinette with all of her clothing removed?"[33] Leonard responded, "Yes."[34] Thereafter, as though the color of Alice's body was determinative on the issue of race, Davis ended with, "That is all."[35]

As the *Rhinelander* court record indicates, Alice internalized the shame borne upon her, crying as her body was exposed and her identity was stripped from her. Alice, however, was not the first woman of African descent to endure such a forced public display, nor was she the last. Nearly seventy years earlier, in 1858, a dark-skinned Sojourner Truth attended the National Women's Suffrage Convention in Akron, Ohio, where she delivered her "Ar'n't I a Woman?" speech, only to encounter a similar demand to expose her bare body as proof of her sex, rather than her race. As Dorothy Sterling explicated, during this era "women did not even dare to bare their ankles,"[36] but the men who opposed Truth, such as Dr. T. W. Strain, demanded that Truth submit her breasts for visual examination by a group of women to ensure that she was not a man. When Truth questioned the basis for the men's doubt about her femaleness, she heard in response, "Your voice is not the voice of a woman, it is the voice of a man, and we believe you are a man."[37] Truth replied "that her breasts had suckled many a white babe, to the exclusion of her own offspring and she quietly asked them, as she disrobed her bosom, if they, too, wished to suck!"[38] Then, Truth revealed her breasts to the entire congregation, male and female. Only unlike Alice who was without voice and completely full of shame, Truth rejected any sense of humiliation or disgrace, proclaiming instead to her audience, "It is to your shame, not mine, that I do this."[39]

In 2009, approximately eighty-five years after the display of Alice's breasts at trial and more than 150 years after Truth's baring of her breasts at a convention, Caster Semenya, an eighteen-year-old world-class, black female athlete from South Africa, underwent a controversy analogous to Truth's concerning her identity as a woman. Protests about Semenya from other athletes led the International Association of Athletics Federations (IAAF) to require Semenya to submit to a public sex test. Italian 800-meter runner Elisa Cusma Piccione referred to Semenya as a man, and reminiscent of Davis during the *Rhinelander* trial, Russian runner Mariya Savinova told journalists about Semenya, "Just look at her," as though "the thing spoke for itself."[40] One political group in South Africa supported Semenya, declaring that the IAAF's decision to require testing, even in the face of Semenya's own identification as a woman, "feeds into the commercial stereotypes of how a woman should look, their facial and physical appearance, as perpetuated by a backward Eurocentric definition of beauty."[41] Ultimately, much like Alice had to submit to inspection by eye in the courtroom, and Truth had to exhibit herself before an audience of suffragists, Semenya was forced to submit to a test that involved a physical medical evaluation and included reports from a gynecologist, an endocrinologist, a psychologist, an internal medicine specialist, and an expert on gender.[42] Apparently, for Semenya, who is intersex—meaning there is a discrepancy between her female external genitals and her internal genitals—the "thing did not speak for itself." Only later, when IAAF officials declared Semenya a woman, did Semenya have the opportunity to declare victory like Alice.

Truth and Semenya's utility as exhibits during their controversies revolved around sex, but the relevance of Alice's experience as a piece of evidence is not limited to gender trials alone. Biracial individuals undergo the microaggression of miniracial trials frequently with questions such as, "What are you?"[43] Like Alice did during the 1920s, biracial individuals today unsettle societal understandings of race as fixed, clean, and unambiguous. As author Angela Nissel explained during an interview regarding her book *Mixed: My Life in Black and White,* "I think that many Americans become tongue-tied when it comes to race, and that uneasiness is multiplied when talking to someone whose race they can't discern."[44] So often, people want to be able to place people racially. For example, in describing how some strangers react to her biracial daughter, one of my interview subjects, Edith, a black woman who is married to a white man, noted, "Most [strangers] seem to presume that she is biracial, and some actually inquire as to her racial make-up by asking, for example, 'What is she mixed with?'"[45]

Indeed, Professor Osagie Obasogie's groundbreaking research on how the blind "see" race demonstrates the significance, not just of race as a way of compartmentalizing people, but specifically of the idea of visual race and perceived clear-cut, visual categories of race in our society. Essentially disproving the notion that blind people's understanding of race is less significant than those who are sighted, Obasogie found not only that our "visual understanding of race stems from social practices that train people to think about race visually regardless of their ability to see," but also that blind people considered knowledge of other people's races to be very important in their interactions, particularly with dating and mating.[46] For instance, one blind, white man recalled a decision by one of his white, male friends, who had unknowingly begun to date a black woman but then "broke it off" when "somebody told him that she was black."[47] Along those same lines, one blind, black man described how race can serve as a filter for blind people in deciding whom to pursue, noting: "A lot of my black blind friends have sort of a joke because when someone doesn't know our race— especially the male—they'll find some way to reach out and touch our hair. People want to know, and that's the one [racial clue] they can always get. . . . People always come up with some kind of way to [touch our heads]. They'll massage you or do something. . . . I think [this happens] mostly in dating. . . . I go to a lot of the conventions now, the national conventions [for the blind]. And there are people trying to meet somebody [to date]. You can see that they're kind of pursuing somebody [that they find attractive]. And they'll go for the hair and then they'll change their mind."[48] In sum, even when race cannot be seen, individuals feel unsettled when the race of others is not clear to them. They crave a certainty that race can always be discerned, if not visually then palpably. Racial trials of "What are you?" persist, particularly for those, like Alice, who have a multiracial background.

More so, as I have learned from studying the *Rhinelander* case, living within my own multiracial family, and surveying and questioning other individuals in multiracial families, this same type of unsettled reaction applies to multiracial families, not just multiracial individuals. For example, one woman I interviewed, Janice, a white woman who is in a civil union with her black female partner and who has a monoracial, black child with her partner, described her hurt after her stepmother asked, "How do you feel being the only white person in a black family?" What hurt Janice about her stepmother's question was not that her stepmother applied the one-drop rule to her family (much like both Leonard's and Alice's attorneys did with her family), but that her white stepmother felt the need to racially categorize her family at all, or, more importantly, that her stepmother saw her as being outside of her family because of race. After all, Janice's family was just her family to her; Janice never thought of herself as the only white person in a family of color.[49]

Overall, *Rhinelander* provides critical insights into the place, or rather the marginality or what I like to call the "placelessness," of multiracial families, specifically black-white families, in our past and present society. This book, *According to Our Hearts,* explores the social and legal meanings of the *Rhinelander* case by examining and analyzing its various lessons regarding law and society's joint role in framing the normative ideal of family as monoracial. In so doing, this book focuses on two means by which law and society define this ideal: (1) by failing to acknowledge the existence of interracial couples and thereby rendering them invisible in law and life; and (2) by punishing racial transgressors—those who are in interracial marriages or who break the norms of monoraciality through transracial adoption or the merging of black and white single-race families through remarriage.[50]

In examining the insights that *Rhinelander* provides into law's past and continuing role in defining the ideal family as monoracial, this book focuses its attention on black-white couples—those couples that racially identify in the same way that Alice and Leonard were ultimately viewed by the public. Black-white couples are also the interracial couples that severely lag behind others in the United States in terms of their actual raw numbers and percentages. In making these examinations, this book studies the trial of Alice and Leonard as a representation of the simultaneously tragic and inspiring story about race and race relations in the United States by analyzing cases, comments, and experiences that teach us about hierarchies among interracial couples that leave black-white couples, and specifically black female–white male couples, at the bottom; societal perceptions regarding race and its place in the essence of marriage; societal forces behind discrimination by association; the invisibility of the multiracial family in antidiscrimination law; and a continued, though different, form of resistance to families who challenge the color line. In sum, *According to Our Hearts* is the first comprehensive study of what I call "the law of the multiracial family."

According to Our Hearts consists of two parts. The first part of the book draws from the trial transcript and appellate record to provide a narrative account of the *Rhinelander* tale, beginning with the initial meeting of Leonard Kip Rhinelander and Alice Beatrice Jones and ending with reports of Alice and Leonard's lives after the verdict. It also includes an analysis of what that verdict taught us, then and even now, about race and racism.

Chapter 1, "A Beautiful Affair," details the love story of Alice and Leonard and the beginning of the end of their love story—Leonard's decision to file and his actual filing for an annulment of their marriage. The chapter starts with the chance meeting of Leonard and Alice's younger sister, Grace, on a road in New Rochelle, New York. It then proceeds to Leonard's and Alice's own meeting and courtship. Finally, it ends with Alice and Leonard's secret marriage and the filing of Leonard's claim for annulment as well as Alice's response.

Chapter 2, "Openings and a Closing: Shutting the Door on Reconciliation," describes the opening statements of both parties at the trial. First, this chapter presents the trial strategy and arguments of Leonard, or perhaps more accurately, of his attorneys in attempting to tarnish Alice's reputation with the social crimes of both failing to understand her place as a working-class, colored woman and trying to rise above that place through deceit and trickery. Second, this chapter presents the defense strategy of Alice's legal team in their efforts to convince the jury that it was Leonard, not Alice, who should be punished for racial transgressions.

Chapter 3, "Testimonies," describes the evidence that each party set forth in presenting their case to the jury. Specifically, this chapter details the evidence that Leonard's attorneys used to try to prove their argument that Alice used sex to gain control over a mentally weak Leonard and make him her "love slave," and that Alice's alleged deceit was the product of her desire to gain access to Leonard's wealth and status.[51] Thereafter, this chapter homes in on the evidence that Alice's attorneys used to prove these three claims: that (1) Alice's race was so obvious that only those who were literally blind could not see it; (2) Leonard's knowledge of Alice's race could easily be inferred from his willingness to cross clear boundaries of race, not just with Alice, but also with others, such as Alice's black brother-in-law, Robert, and niece, Roberta; and (3) given his wealth and status, Leonard, as "a normal man with [a] normal sense of perception,"[52] should be punished for his acts of racial betrayal.

Chapter 4, "A Verdict against the Heart," reviews the end of the *Rhinelander* trial, beginning with the parties' closing arguments. Thereafter, it describes and discusses the surprising jury verdict in favor of Alice. It also includes reports of public reaction to the verdict and the legal and social consequences that flowed from that verdict for Alice and Leonard. Finally, this chapter details how the verdict was, in addition to being a victory, also a loss for racial equality. After all, as one juror noted, "If we had voted according to our hearts the verdict might have been different."[53]

The second part of *According to Our Hearts* utilizes facts from the *Rhinelander* case as a springboard for analyzing the contemporary legal and social challenges that black-white couples and their families face in society. In particular, this part of the book examines how race, racism, and law work together to define the normative ideal of family as monoracial (and heterosexual) through an examination of general prejudice against interracial couples, in particular, black-white couples; the challenges posed to interracial couples through the language of housing discrimination and other antidiscrimination statutes; discrimination by association cases in the employment arena; the regulation and legally facilitated use of race in adoption cases; and the determinations of racial identity in a wide variety of cases.

Chapter 5, "Understanding the Black and White of Love," explicates this book's focus on black-white marriages, highlighting *Rhinelander*'s lessons about the status of black-white intimate relationships, and specifically black-white marriages, as the ultimate taboo in American society. Comparing statistics and studies that examine the frequency of black-white intimacy as compared to other cross-racial intimacies, this chapter scrutinizes the particularly low status of black-white marriage and commitments among couples, both same-sex and opposite-sex. More so, this chapter engages in

a gendered investigation of black-white relationships, analyzing and inter-
preting the especially low numbers of black female–white male partnerships as compared to black male–white female unions. Finally, this chapter
explores the one legal question that was never considered during the *Rhinelander* case, despite the fact that the state of New York did not ban interracial marriages: is knowledge of race sufficiently material to serve as a legal
basis for annulment? Or more specifically, under the heightened standard
applied to most annulment cases in our current society, does knowledge of
race go to the essence of marriage?

Chapter 6, "Living in Placelessness," highlights, identifies, and analyzes
the many privileges that attach to monoraciality among intimate couples in
our society. In so doing, it focuses in particular on the privileges regarding
housing and residence and examines the contemporary legal and social
challenges faced by interracial couples and their children within the context of housing. Specifically, this chapter studies how both our segregated
residential patterns and housing discrimination laws work to reinforce the
general placelessness and invisibility of the multiracial family in our society. The chapter then utilizes *Rhinelander v. Rhinelander* as a bridge to examine how the assumption of monoraciality among married and committed
couples in housing discrimination statutes results in an expressive harm
to interracial, heterosexual couples who are discriminated against on the
housing market because of their interraciality as a couple,[54] as opposed to
the race of just one member of the couple. Finally, it exposes how this hole
in antidiscrimination law solidifies a normative ideal of marriage that is not
only heterosexual but also monoracial.

Chapter 7, "Collective Discrimination," analyzes the ways in which people in interracial marriages are punished in our society, both as individuals
and as a collective. In many ways, this chapter examines how marriage is
used to give status, take away status, or not give status in the workplace.
Much like Leonard, those who engage in interracial marriage today can face
harsh consequences for crossing racial lines of intimacy, consequences that
essentially can have the effect of discouraging interracial marriage. For example, this chapter looks to a section of employment discrimination law
that involves third-party punishment by co-workers against white racial
transgressors: discrimination by association cases. Although a number of

circuits have recognized these plaintiffs' claims of discrimination (which were initially denied due to lack of standing or ability to assert a claim), not all of the circuits have officially recognized these cases, and as late as 2008, the Second Circuit addressed this legal issue for the first time. Moreover, even as courts recognize the viability of the plaintiffs' legal claims, they are often resistant to recognizing and fully understanding the unique forms of discrimination that occur against individuals involved in interracial relationships in employment. Because of civil rights doctrine's focus on the individual, what gets lost in these cases is how law and social norms regulate not only the individual, but also the collective—here, the family.

Finally, Chapter 8, "Reflections in Black and White, and Where We Go from Here," concludes this book by culling together musings from black-white, married, and committed couples and their children about the *Rhinelander* case, its significance, and the reality of the case's lessons in their own lives in terms of identity, race, and family. It also considers the lessons we can learn from *Rhinelander* about the multiracial family and from the multiracial family about current social attitudes toward them as well as about gaps in the law. In so doing, this chapter explores how being part of a collective may shape racial identity and, in fact, may affect or should affect legal analysis in certain antidiscrimination cases. Then, after highlighting broad theoretical deficiencies in doctrines designed to address discrimination but that actually hinder interracial interaction in our society, it ponders one very modest, potential change that may work to better capture the identities of multiracial people and their families and that may more easily reach the harms that are currently disregarded and unacknowledged by the law: the addition of the term *interraciality* as a protected category in current antidiscrimination law statutes. In all, this chapter, and this book, work to remind us about the *Rhinelander* case; its significance, both historically and presently; and the reality of its lessons in the lives of today's multiracial families.

PART I

1

A Beautiful Affair

THE FAIRYTALE ROMANCE OF THE WORKING-CLASS Alice Beatrice Jones and the wealthy Leonard Kip Rhinelander began against the backdrop of 1920s New York society. During this era, formal Jim Crow laws did not exist in New York, but strong beliefs in the inferiority of blacks prevailed. The fear of passing blacks polluted the air among white citizens.[1] Some whites feared the very idea of being surrounded by blacks who passed as white. This fear caused many whites to cling even more dearly to the idea of race as biological, clear, and visible.

Additionally, racial segregation in homes persisted. As Professor Michael Klarman has explained, segregation in New York neighborhoods increased dramatically during the 1920s even in the absence of residential segregation ordinances and even in the face of a growing black population due to migration from the South.[2] Blacks and whites also remained segregated within the workplace and by profession. For example, unlike a significant number of white women, black women rarely had the luxury of staying home to take care of the household. Instead, they, like Alice and her sister Emily, often worked as domestics, caring for the homes of white women in addition to their own. More so, unlike black women, white women remained largely under the "protection" of the virtue of womanhood,[3] a protection that Alice very briefly enjoyed during those few public moments that she and Leonard shared when they passed as husband and wife.

Politically and culturally, however, the 1920s brought a sea change for blacks as well as for women of all races within the state of New York. A number of strong, black leaders such as Marcus Garvey, who founded the Universal Negro Improvement Association (UNIA) in 1917, emerged during this period. Along with those leaders came a powerful political voice for blacks that spanned into the 1920s and beyond. Also in 1917, Edward A. Johnson became the first black man to win a seat in the New York state legislature. Racial victories like the creation of the UNIA and Johnson's election as a state legislator were followed by a huge victory for women, who received the right to vote in 1920.[4]

Finally, while social and physical segregation persisted in many corners of New York society, the culture of the Harlem Renaissance had just begun to slowly soften those very racial borders. The Harlem Renaissance was a time in which "the black ghetto became an attraction for a varied assortment of white celebrities[,] just plain thrill-seeking white people," and white citizens who were "defying the mores of their upbringing by associating with Negroes on a socially equal level."[5] Additionally, white women began to free themselves from the images and restraints of the model of the Victorian woman by becoming flappers, a group of women who, through their behavior, challenged the notion that women should not drink, smoke, expose themselves, or have sex out of wedlock.

Neither Alice nor Leonard was a part of these emerging worlds of flappers or Harlemites, but their love began and grew under the shadow of these changes. These changes would be reflected in their relationship, which involved premarital sex in a decreasingly Victorian era and the crossing of racial lines among lovers and friends.

In this chapter, I chronicle how *Rhinelander v. Rhinelander* came to be. In so doing, I detail the story of Leonard's courtship of Alice, the Rhinelander marriage, and ultimately Leonard's betrayal of Alice through his filing of a lawsuit for annulment of their marriage. First, I recount the story of Alice and Leonard's first meeting, their three-year romance, and their marriage ceremony. Thereafter, I describe the beginning of the end for the Rhinelanders and their love story—Leonard's filing for annulment. Finally, I describe Alice's responses in her formal Answers to the court to Leonard's claims as well as the public's speculations about the real forces behind the *Rhinelander* lawsuit.

In the Beginning

Relations between the Rhinelander family and the Jones family began not with Alice and Leonard but instead with Leonard and Alice's younger sister, Grace Jones. In late September 1921, Grace met Leonard on a road near her family home in New Rochelle. On that day, Leonard and two of his friends, including the older, married Carl Kreitler, had become stranded as a result of troubles with Leonard's car. Around that same time, Grace was taking a walk in her neighborhood and spotted the men on the side of the road. Carl, seeing Grace on a walk by herself, called her over to the car, and Grace stopped to talk to the men as they worked on the vehicle.

Once Leonard and his friends were able to get his automobile restarted, Grace accepted their invitation to go for a ride, first within the town of New Rochelle and then to Port Chester. Clearly aware of how such behavior would appear to a public audience, Grace explained her decision to join the men in the car at trial. She testified, "Well, I said it didn't look very nice for me to get in the car with three young men. . . . I said . . . if they promised to be like gentlemen I would do so and go."[6]

When the foursome eventually returned to New Rochelle, Carl and Grace took off together, riding away in the car alone while Leonard and the other young man remained in town. After approximately an hour, Carl brought Grace back to New Rochelle, where he and she picked up Leonard and his remaining acquaintance before taking Grace home that evening.

A few days later, Leonard returned to New Rochelle to visit Grace, but this time he came without Carl. According to Leonard's testimony at trial, he came back to New Rochelle to give Grace a message from Carl. However, time soon revealed that Leonard, who fancied Grace, had his own plans. That night, at Leonard's suggestion, Leonard, Grace, Alice, and another male friend went to the local theater. There, according to Grace, Leonard improperly placed his hand on her knee. Leonard also gave Grace a star sapphire ring with four little diamonds before leaving to go home.

Just a couple of days later, Leonard and Carl returned to visit the Jones sisters at their home in New Rochelle, but Elizabeth Jones, the mother of the two women, interrupted the sisters' meeting with the two suitors. Elizabeth also forced Grace, who was already dating another man—who also was white—to give the star sapphire ring back to Leonard. At that point, Leonard shifted his attentions toward Alice and began to visit the home of the Jones family nearly every night to see her. According to Leonard's trial attorney, former judge Isaac N. Mills, "there [could have been] no doubt from the evidence that [Leonard] then considered both Jones young women to be loose and immoral, and that he went there solely with a view of having illicit relations with them."[7] Later, during his trial testimony, Leonard himself admitted to a plan to ultimately engage in sexual intercourse with Alice without the purpose of marriage.

Three months thereafter, on December 22, 1921, Leonard received his first opportunity to fulfill this plan for sex. That night, Ross Chidester, a white chauffeur for Philip Rhinelander, began to drive Leonard and Alice from New Rochelle to New York City for a theater show. During their ride to the city, Alice informed Leonard that she planned to stay in a hotel in the city that evening. Leonard quickly asked if he could accompany her to the hotel. After twenty minutes of begging, Alice relented. Chidester drove the then eighteen-year-old Leonard and twenty-two-year-old Alice to the Hotel Marie Antoinette, a hotel whose namesake was herself accused of many sexual improprieties. When they arrived at the hotel, Leonard went in and registered for a room under the names of Mr. and Mrs. James Smith of Rye, New York. Alice remained in the car with Chidester. Over the next five days, including Christmas, Alice and Leonard stayed at the hotel, engaging in repeated sexual intercourse. Leonard left the hotel only once when he departed to have Christmas dinner with his family.

A month later, on January 22, 1922, Alice and Leonard returned to the Hotel Marie Antoinette, registering again as Mr. and Mrs. Smith. This time, the couple stayed at the hotel for two weeks, engaging in sexual intercourse throughout their visit. Leonard even gave Alice baths on occasion. Eventually, an attorney at Bowers, Sand, and Gerard who worked for Leonard's father, Philip, came to the hotel to remove Leonard.

Thereafter, the Rhinelander senior, Philip, worked hard to separate his son Leonard from Alice. First, Philip sent Leonard with chaperones on extended trips to locations such as Atlantic City, Cuba, Bermuda, San Francisco, Hawaii, and Washington, D.C. Then, Philip registered Leonard as a

Fig. 1.1. Roy Mills, right, the son of Leonard's counsel, Judge Isaac N. Mills, and associate counsel for Leonard Kip Rhinelander, is reading the letters of Alice Jones Rhinelander. Throughout the trial, the courtroom was packed with curious spectators, many of whom wished to hear the words written in the couple's love notes. ©Bettmann/Corbis

student at an open ranch school in Arizona, where Leonard remained from October 1922 until April 1924.

But even during this year-and-a-half separation, Alice and Leonard remained close. They wrote letters to each other frequently. Alice wrote a total of 426 letters to Leonard during this period. Many of the letters between Alice and Leonard eventually became evidence in the trial and revealed all of the couple's secrets of lust, love, and marriage (see fig. 1.1). They also revealed secret "talents" of the two lovers, particularly Alice's efforts to write love poems. For instance, one letter revealed this poem by Alice, a poem the *New York Times* described as being "poetry with a truly negro rhythm": "Kisses, dear, from you, can cheer me when I'm blue. Your gentle lips have always thrilled me through; I need caressing, too; There's happiness I can't express. In each kiss from you."[8]

In the end, Philip could not keep Alice and Leonard apart. In May 1924, Leonard turned twenty-one and essentially became a free man. Now of age, Leonard was free to leave his open ranch school. As Leonard himself once wrote to Alice during their forced separation, "But, sweetheart, it won't remain that way always. No, *when I become of age and can do what I like,* I will never leave you and you and I can be together just as long as you want me."[9]

After turning twenty-one, Leonard traveled directly to see Alice in New Rochelle, even before he went to see his father. Within a few months of turning twenty-one, Leonard also received the means to become financially independent from his family. He received $280,000—the equivalent of $3.7 million in 2011—from the estate of one of his grandparents. Indeed, Alice often expressed to Leonard how much she wanted him to be independent from his father. For instance, in one letter to Leonard—a letter with Alice's trademark misspellings and grammatical mistakes—she wrote, "But I wished you was more independent like me. If you only had a good trade, and you would not after look forward, for your father's help."[10]

Finally, on October 14, 1924, Leonard made the ultimate commitment to Alice. He married her in a secret ceremony performed by New Rochelle Mayor Harry Scott. After their wedding, the newlyweds did not live in the type of luxurious home expected for a Rhinelander. The couple did not live in a home like the one that housed Leonard's family at 18 West 48th Street. Rather, they secretly lived in the Jones family's very modest and small home at 763 Pelham in New Rochelle. Even before the Rhinelander marriage became news, Leonard's life of privilege and access had changed dramatically. Leonard traveled back and forth between his father's house and that of the Joneses in order to conceal the marriage. Although Leonard later rented a small, nearby apartment for him and Alice on the sixth floor of Pintard Apartments, 650 Main Street, in New Rochelle, the newlyweds barely had any time to enjoy it, as the news of their cross-class, cross-race marriage broke just a few days after they had signed the lease.

The marriage of Alice and Leonard elicited a large number of responses from their friends and family members. For example, some friends viewed the couple's romance as a perfect love story, free of ill motive and future doom. Katherine Wilson, a white friend of Alice, declared, "Alice married young Rhinelander for love. . . . They both loved each other. She was in love with her husband long before she knew he had money."[11] Indeed, Alice herself would later prove as much when she responded to questions about the addition of her name to the social register of *Gotham's 100* after Leonard filed his annulment lawsuit. In response to a reporter's inquiries, Alice denied any desire to become a part of New York society, stating: "I don't want my name in that book. . . . I don't want to be one of the 100. I didn't marry Leonard to get my name in any book. I married him because I love him. If the Social register should continue my name year after year, would that add anything to my happiness? . . . What is society, anyway? There isn't a single wholesome thing in the life of the so-called 100 as far as I can see. We don't want to be listed among the Rockefellers and the Vanderbilts and the rest of that ilk."[12]

However, others still viewed the Rhinelander marriage as doomed from the start. Alice's own father, George Jones, reportedly tried to stop the marriage. The *Chicago Defender* quoted Judge Samuel F. Swinburne, a fellow church member and the attorney of the Jones family, as saying, "Mrs. Rhinelander's father called on the young man many times before the wedding and pleaded with him not to marry his daughter. He told him that he had his daughter's interests at heart in making his pleas, saying that such an alliance must come to a bad end."[13] According to one other report, George had told Leonard "that he and his family were English working people and that there was a social gulf between his daughter and Rhinelander which could not be bridged."[14]

The Beginning of the End: The Filing of the Lawsuit

On November 13, 1924, George Jones's predictions began to ring true. Scandal arose when a story with the title "Rhinelander's Son Marries Daughter of a Colored Man" ran in the *Standard Star* of New Rochelle. Thereafter, reporters swarmed the house of the Rhinelander newlyweds in an attempt to uncover the mystery of Alice's race and the cross-class marriage of a member of one of New York's most elite families.

Just a few days later, on November 18, 1924, Leonard's attorney, Leon Jacobs, visited the Jones family home to inquire about the marriage. Jacobs, whose office was housed in Philip Rhinelander's suite, returned two days

Fig. 1.2. Seated on the couch is a fair-skinned Alice Rhinelander. © Bettmann/Corbis

later on November 20, 1924, taking a reluctant Leonard with him in a limousine. As Leonard testified during trial, he did not want to leave his wife on that day (see fig. 1.2). According to his trial testimony, Leonard continued to believe Alice's alleged claims of whiteness until Jacobs showed him Alice's birth certificate, which identified her as "black."

Leonard, however, would eventually succumb to his father's pressures and file for an annulment of his marriage to Alice. The reasons why Leonard gave up his relationship with Alice are unknown and, to many, inexplicable, especially given his own independent wealth at that time. However, as many spectators later saw at his trial, Leonard was not the type of young man who could easily challenge his father. In fact, according to his attorneys, Leonard had grown up with a stuttering problem that left him, in some instances, without confidence. Despite receiving encouragement from Alice to become more independent, Leonard never did. Perhaps, for Leonard, a young man who had lost his mother at a young age and then his brother in the war, giving up the one parent who had raised him was simply too much to sacrifice for the sake of love.

In any event, less than two weeks after the first news story on the Rhinelander marriage broke, the saga of the *Rhinelander v. Rhinelander* case began. On November 26, 1924, the newly married Leonard Rhinelander filed a lawsuit for annulment of his marriage to Alice. In his Complaint, Leonard alleged that Alice had committed marital fraud upon him by representing to him that she was not of any colored blood, that she acted with the intent to induce him to marry her, and that he would not have married her had he known that she was of colored blood. The Complaint left Alice distraught and sad. The *New York Times* noted that Judge Samuel Swinburne—then Alice's primary attorney—described Alice as "suffering extreme nervousness and weep[ing] a great deal as a result of her husband's action for annulment."[15]

On December 4, 1924, Alice filed her Answer to the Complaint. She denied each and every allegation of wrongdoing. A few days later, on December 14, 1924, Leonard amended his Complaint to include separate assertions that Alice was of colored blood, that he discovered Alice's racial background as a colored woman only after the marriage, and that he entered into the marriage with Alice under the belief that she was fully white. Leonard's First Amended Complaint read as follows:

Amended Complaint

The amended complaint of the plaintiff alleges:

 I. That the plaintiff and the defendant, at the time of the commencement of this action, are both residents of the state of New York.
 II. That on the 14th day of October, 1924, in the City of New Rochelle, County of Westchester, State of New York, the plaintiff and the defendant were married.
 III. That the consent of said plaintiff to said marriage was obtained by fraud; that prior to said marriage the defendant represented to

and told the plaintiff that she was white and not colored, and had no colored blood, which representations the plaintiff believed to be true, and was induced thereby to consent to said marriage, and entered into said marriage relying upon such representation.

IV. On information and belief, that in truth and fact the said Alice Jones, also known as Alice Jones Rhinelander, was colored and with colored blood.

V. On information and belief, that the said Alice Jones, also known as Alice Jones Rhinelander, had colored blood in her veins.

VI. On information and belief, that the said representation was wholly untrue and at said times known by the said defendant to be untrue and that she made the same with the intent to deceive and defraud the said plaintiff and thereby to induce him into said marriage.

VII. That the said plaintiff did not until after said marriage discover that the said representations were untrue.

VIII. That said plaintiff entered into said marriage in the full belief that said defendant was white and without colored blood.

IX. That the said plaintiff and defendant have not at any time before the commencement of this action, with full knowledge by the plaintiff of said facts constituting the said fraud and false representations or with full knowledge by him that the defendant was not entirely of white blood and ancestry, voluntarily cohabited as husband and wife.

Wherefore the plaintiff prays for judgment that said marriage be annulled and said marriage contract declared void, and for such other and further relief as to the Court may seem just, together with the costs and disbursements of this action.[16]

Additionally, in his Bill of Particulars, Leonard specified exactly how Alice had deceived him. He alleged that she repeatedly gave false statements about her race between May 1924 and October 14, 1924, the date of their marriage. He further claimed that the alleged fraudulent statements to him included critical assertions, not only by Alice but also by her mother, on September 15, 1924, when Alice and her mother purportedly lied to Leonard about Alice's race in response to his questions about Alice's sister Emily's marriage to a colored man, Robert Brooks. Specifically, Leonard wrote in relevant part: "Plaintiff had become informed of the fact that Emily, a sister of the defendant, had married a colored man, and was residing with him as his wife in said City of New Rochelle or its immediate neighborhood, and this fact led him in some way to introduce to the defendant the subject of her parentage and blood, and she thereupon at said time and place made to him the said statements and representations, and that she, after the subject had been thus introduced, repeatedly, of her own accord, spoke to plaintiff of said matter and in substance repeated her said statements and representations."[17]

On January 20, 1925, Alice responded to Leonard's Amended Complaint. She denied every allegation of fraud and intent to deceive and denied any knowledge or information sufficient to form a belief about her racial background. At this point, Alice did not claim her background as a colored person, nor did she deny it. She simply claimed to be uninformed about her race, an action which suggests that, perhaps at this juncture, she had not ruled out litigating her whiteness. Her Answer read as follows:

Answer to the Amended Complaint

The defendant answering the amended complaint alleges:

First—She denies each and every allegation contained in the paragraphs of subdivisions of said complaint numbered respectively III, VI, VII, VIII, and IX.

Second—She denies that she has any knowledge or information sufficient to form a belief as to any of the allegations contained in the paragraphs or subdivisions of said complaint numbered respectively IV and V.

Wherefore, the defendant demands judgment that the complaint be dismissed with costs.[18]

The Complications of Legal and Social Meaning

At the time that Leonard brought his lawsuit against Alice, New York law did not ban interracial marriages between blacks and whites. Thus, Alice and Leonard's marriage was not automatically void or impossible by law. However, New York case law provided that "every misrepresentation of a material fact, made with the intention to induce another to enter into an agreement and without which he would not have done so, justifie[d] the court in vacating the agreement."[19] No one disputed whether this basic legal rule applied to the Rhinelander marriage, because it clearly did. More importantly, despite no legal ban on interracial marriages in New York, no one contested whether misrepresentation about race constituted a material fact that allowed for annulment. Given the importance of racial classifications and the corresponding status of the classifications in society, the judge as well as the parties in the *Rhinelander* case readily accepted prenuptial knowledge (or, rather, lack of knowledge) about Alice's race to be so crucial to the understanding of the marital contract that fraud about it could result in an annulment. In other words, the primary basis for recognizing knowledge of Alice's race as a material fact was racial prejudice and social opprobrium of interracial intimacy. Indeed, Leonard's attorney, Judge Isaac N. Mills, a former state senator, district attorney of Westchester County, and judge, proclaimed the following about the issue of race as a material fact in Leonard's brief on appeal: "The feeling against [interracial] marriage is very strong among American white people. In twenty-eight states of the Union such a marriage is prohibited by statute law."[20] During the *Rhinelander* trial, even Alice's attorney, Lee Parsons Davis, made his own statement about the impropriety of interracial intimacy, stating, "I have my views that blacks have just as much right to live as whites, although I don't know that I believe in mixing the blood."[21]

Furthermore, although the state of New York had not followed many southern states in adopting the rule of hypodescent, more commonly known as the one-drop rule, many whites in New York agreed that any taint of colored blood removed a person from the class of white citizens. In essence, because of long-held beliefs about racial genetics and community expectations about social barriers of race in 1920s New York, knowledge of a spouse's race was widely considered among whites to be as central to marriage as the ability to consummate it. It was with this thinking and these very beliefs that the *Rhinelander* case moved forward in the New York court system and before a nationwide audience. Racially speaking, an annulment was highly critical for Leonard because a finding of Alice as colored and, more so, of Leonard as aware of her "colored" race before marriage without an annulment would forever mark Leonard as unmarriageable for a more "suitable" wife—meaning a white woman of his class background.

Moreover, for Philip Rhinelander and his family, Leonard's legal filing was about more than just race or the racial purity of the family; money and wealth also figured prominently in the annulment proceedings. As Professors Earl Lewis and Heidi Ardizzone highlighted in their book *Love on Trial: An American Scandal in Black and White,* the wealthy Rhinelander family had already exhibited their strong disapproval of class mixing when Leonard's uncle, William Copeland Rhinelander, the twenty-one-year-old son of William Rhinelander and Matilda Cruger Oakley Rhinelander, fell in love with and married Maggie McGinness, the first of his two working-class wives. McGinness, who claimed to be a direct descendant of an Irish king, was a white immigrant who worked as one of the family's servants.[22] As punishment for his class transgression, William Copeland was essentially cut off from his family's estate, disinherited and disowned. William Copeland even changed the spelling of his name to "Rynlander" so as to keep his family from further embarrassment.[23] Additionally, William Copeland was completely left out of his Aunt Serena Rhinelander's will. Indeed, although Serena left much of her $2,000,000 estate to William Copeland's brothers in her will, she did not even acknowledge William Copeland in the document. Second, William Copeland did not get very much of his part of his mother and father's estate, which was valued at $50,000,000, receiving only $5,000 a year—$100 per week—from his parents.[24] Even years after William had already crossed the unthinkable line of master and servant, his family still tried to reclaim and protect the Rhinelander name by offering William's first wife, Maggie, money to return to Ireland forever. This act made William Copeland angry enough to shoot the family's attorney, John Drake, in the shoulder. Even though William Copeland was never charged for the shooting of Drake (even after Drake died six months later), William Copeland remained separated from the rest of his family, living in Canada and Brooklyn before he finally settled down in Schenectady, New York.[25] The last anyone heard of William Copeland, in 1914, he was blind and paralyzed, living in Schenectady with his second wife.

With Alice, too, the Rhinelander name and the transfer of wealth were at stake for the family. An annulment, as opposed to a divorce, would completely sever all ties between the Rhinelanders and Joneses because it would place Leonard and Alice back into their original positions as unmarried persons. By law, it would entirely erase their marital union. As a result, an annulment could leave Alice with no claim to either alimony or property from Leonard or his family.

Despite the importance of a victory at trial for Leonard and, more so, the Rhinelander family, numerous questions arose as to whether Leonard even wanted to file his Complaint for annulment and thereby end his relationship with Alice. It was rumored throughout the case that a love-stricken Leonard had actually begged Alice to fight the lawsuit so they could remain together as husband and wife. In fact, the Jones family's attorney, Judge Samuel Swinburne, indicated that Leonard had sent Alice the following note: "Honey Bunch, old scout—I hope you will win this case. Get the best lawyer."[26] Additionally, the *Chicago Defender,* a prominent black newspaper, made the following report about Leonard's true desires: "Despite the filing of the annulment the young millionaire has informed his wife to have courage and believe in him. . . . [Leonard Rhinelander] informed [Alice] to fight the case to the end. He advised her to get the best lawyer obtainable."[27] Finally, according to Alice herself, Leonard told her that he was forced to leave her side. She told the *Chicago Defender:* "After Leonard left he wrote to me and told me what was being done. He repeatedly tells me to have faith in him. He says that everything will be all right. He claims there is but one thing that can separate us, and that is—death. He said, 'Dearest, this little separation will but draw us closer to each other. You know I love you, and you only; there is nothing that can happen that would make me change.'"[28]

In fact, many observers suspected that Leonard's father, Philip, had forced the lawsuit upon him. Alice even openly questioned who was behind the case, publicly declaring through her attorney that she believed Leonard was being held against his will. The *New York Times* reported that "Mrs. Rhinelander . . . still has 'the greatest faith' in her husband and believes that the suit was brought and is being prosecuted by his relatives. She refuses to believe that he has had any part in it whatsoever."[29]

Leonard's family, however, denied any involvement in the lawsuit's filing and insisted that Leonard was acting "on his own initiative."[30] Indeed, the day after Leonard filed his lawsuit, the Rhinelander family's spokesman stated that "the family had no foreknowledge of the legal step, but [was] delighted to hear that [Leonard] had 'come to his senses.'"[31] Additionally, the lawyer for Philip Rhinelander, Spotswood D. Bowers, asserted that "the family would not interfere beyond refusing to receive the wife,"[32] a statement which at least partially proved to be very true. The Rhinelander family never gave in to welcome Alice as a family member with open arms. And, ultimately, neither did Leonard.

2

Openings and a Closing: Shutting the Door on Reconciliation

AS SHOWN IN CHAPTER I, EVEN AFTER Leonard filed his lawsuit for annulment, Alice believed that Leonard would return to her one day. Indeed, she described this desire to a *Chicago Defender* journalist, proclaiming: "We [Leonard and I] love each other. I have known him for nearly four years and kept steady with him until we married last October. We were engaged for three years. It did not make any difference to him about my color then, and it doesn't now. We were happy together until his parents had to interfere. He did not care anything about what society said, so why should I? . . . All I am anxious about is when this affair will be over so Leonard and I can join each other and live happily as we had anticipated."[1] It also was rumored that Alice had refused a $250,000 settlement offer—the equivalent of $3.2 million in 2011—prior to the trial, instead choosing to hang on to her love.[2]

For any diehard romantics who wanted the newlywed couple to reconcile despite Leonard's lawsuit, hopes for such reconciliation were dashed within the first few minutes of the *Rhinelander* trial. Leonard's attorney, former judge Isaac N. Mills, made sure of that with his opening statement. Isaac Mills was near his retirement at the time of the *Rhinelander* trial, but he had formerly served as a state senator and New York Supreme Court justice. A graduate of Amherst College and Columbia Law School, he also had served as the district attorney of Westchester County, including during a period when Alice's lead trial attorney, Lee Parsons Davis, was an assistant district attorney.[3] At his table, Mills was joined by Leon Jacobs, the attorney who pulled Leonard away from Alice on November 20, 1924, and who worked for Bowers, Sand, and Gerard, the firm that performed legal work for Philip Rhinelander (see fig. 2.1).

In his opening statement, Mills revealed a strategy that centered around personal attacks, not just on Alice and her reputation, but also on her family and its reputation. Specifically, Mills exposed Alice and Leonard's premarital sexual encounters as well as the private sentiments that the two lovers expressed to each other in hundreds of letters. Mills also revealed Alice's secret of a prior sexual relationship with another man as well as her mother Elizabeth Jones's long-held secret—a secret that even the Jones sisters had been unaware of—about a white child named Ethel who was born to Elizabeth and a white man in England when Elizabeth was eighteen and who was then farmed out for work when George and Elizabeth Jones arrived in the United States.

With those few moves, Mills set off a fire in Lee Parsons Davis, who was then serving as an attorney at Clark, Close, and Davis, a private practice firm in White Plains, New York. Prior to that, Lee Parsons Davis, a white graduate of Columbia Law School, had worked as an attorney in private practice; as the assistant district attorney of Westchester County from 1908 to 1913; as a private practice attorney at Clark, Close, and Davis; and then as the district attorney of Westchester County, having been elected to that office in 1916 and remaining in the office until 1922. Throughout his career, "Davis was recognized as a trial lawyer of exceptional ability with an extraordinary talent for cross-examination."[4] Years after the *Rhinelander* trial in 1936, Davis became a justice of the New York Supreme Court, Ninth Judicial District. At trial, Davis was joined by Counsel Samuel F. Swinburne, a former judge, and Richard Keogh, son of the former New York Supreme Court justice Martin J. Keogh.[5]

In his opening statement, Davis vowed to fight back against Mills's tactics and protect his client. Davis promised to prove how "the Rhinelander millions—not young Rhinelander's but Philip Rhinelander's millions—are [at the] back of this, to crush a concededly humble family, to save what they consider to be an ancient name, trailing back to the original Huguenots of New Rochelle."[6]

Fig. 2.1. Seated from right to left are Leonard Kip Rhinelander and his attorneys, Leon Jacobs and Isaac N. Mills. © Bettmann/Corbis

In this chapter, I explain the strategies of both the plaintiff, Leonard, and the defendant, Alice, as laid out during the parties' opening arguments at trial. I first present the trial strategy and arguments of Leonard and his attorneys and then present the defense strategy of Alice and her legal team.

Leonard's Opening: Enslaved by Love

In his opening statement, Isaac N. Mills laid out what would constitute the three components of his trial arguments for freeing Leonard from his marriage to Alice. Having made the unusual request in an annulment case for a jury trial, instead of a bench trial, Mills knew that he had to demonstrate three separate factors to convince the jury of his client's allegations: (1) that Alice was of colored blood, but could realistically pass as white; (2) that Leonard was simple and easy to manipulate; and (3) that Alice was a master of trickery, someone who used her ability to pass as well as her nature as a mature and sexually advanced, colored woman to take advantage of an unsuspecting, unevenly matched Leonard and enslave him through sex and lust.

Before detailing his strategy, however, Mills spelled out the law for the jury. He first explicated the meaning of the term *material* as applied in annulment cases, noting that a fact is "material to the matrimonial relation, such that if known to the other party it would naturally have prevented the marriage."[7] He then explained that fraud as to race could occur in two separate ways: (1) by an actual false representation "—in this particular instance the statement by the young woman or others . . . that she is entirely of white blood. . . ."; and (2) by concealment of a material fact.[8]

Thereafter, Mills moved on to the issues as presented in the case pleadings. In so doing, he identified the questions that he understood, at that time, would be submitted to the jury upon the trial's close:

The first one. At the time of said marriage of the parties, was the defendant colored and of colored blood?

Second. Did the defendant, prior to said marriage, represent to the plaintiff that she was white and not colored and had no colored blood?

Third. Did she make the said representations with the intent to deceive and defraud the plaintiff and thereby induce him to enter into the said marriage?

Fourth. Was the plaintiff, by said representation made by the defendant to him, induced to enter into the said marriage?

Fifth. Did plaintiff enter into said marriage with the full belief that the said defendant was white and without colored blood?

Sixth. Has the plaintiff cohabited with the defendant after he obtained full knowledge of the facts constituting the said fraud and the falsity of the said representation or with full knowledge by him that the defendant was not entirely of white blood?[9]

Mills then turned his attention to the first question of race. In so doing, he noted his intent to "prove that [Leonard] is of pure white stock, and a descendant of one of the original French Huguenot settlers of New Rochelle," and that Alice "has a substantial strain of black blood . . . that . . . come[s] to her through her father."[10] Mills explained that, despite the best efforts of his team of lawyers and investigators, he could not present direct evidence regarding the ancestry of Alice's father, George Jones, because his investigators could not trace back the father and, in fact, found no trace of him in either the place that the father claimed as his birthplace or the place that he claimed as his childhood home.

After explaining why he would not be presenting some expected evidence about George Jones's racial background, such as direct historical proof of George Jones's racial background, as part of the plaintiff's case, Mills identified the actual evidence that he would use to prove that Alice was not of pure white blood, but instead of colored blood. This evidence included: (1) the naturalization papers of Alice's father, George Jones, papers that were signed by Justice Joseph Morschauser—the trial judge in the *Rhinelander* case—and that identified George Jones as a colored man; (2) the driver's license application of George Jones from September 30, 1924 (just a few months earlier), that identified him as "colored"; (3) the birth certificate of Alice's oldest sister, Emily Jones, born on December 4, 1895, on which she was "recorded as mulatto"; (4) the birth certificate of Alice, born on July 9, 1899, on which Alice was recorded as "Color, black"; and (5) the birth certificate of Alice's younger sister Grace, born on July 11, 1903, on which she was recorded as "black, negro, mixed" (see fig. 2.2).[11]

However, at the same time that Mills spelled out how he would prove Alice's nonwhiteness, he made intimations that seemed to go against his very arguments about her ability to pass by suggesting that Alice's ability to pass was not so great. In particular, Mills hinted at the obviousness of George Jones's race by suggesting that, if Mills had seen him before the trial, he would not have delved as deeply into discovering the Jones father's racial background. Mills asserted, "[M]y eyes never rested upon the father until today. I hadn't seen him then, and I deemed it incumbent upon us to trace him back as far as possible."[12] Such moments during the *Rhinelander* trial revealed exactly how difficult Mills's job of representing Leonard was, because, in order to obtain a victory for his client, Mills had to prove that Alice had an ability to pass and actually did pass within a world where even he himself seemed to believe that race was real, biological, clearly visible, and clearly identifiable.

Fig. 2.2. Alice is flanked by her sisters, Grace Miller, left, and Emily Brooks, right.
© Bettmann/Corbis

Furthermore, as Mills's opening statement shows, he also understood that race was about more than just the physical—that it also was about the performance of race. With this understanding, Mills further argued that the actions of Alice and her family clearly demonstrated her guilt for racial fraud. In her book *What Blood Won't Tell: A History of Race on Trial in America,* Professor Ariela Gross explained that, in southern trials involving determinations of whiteness during the nineteenth century, a person's exercise of the privileges of white citizenship and acceptance by whites in the community often positively affected a court's determination of the party's status as white or black. In other words, Gross explicated that, if a person could show that she "exercised the privileges of whiteness," she was one step closer to legally proving that she was white.[13] At trial, with this notion in mind, Mills intimated that he could show how the actions of Alice and her family proved that they were not white citizens. Specifically, Mills described his plan to offer evidence such as "photographs of [Alice's] sister Grace, the younger sister, consorting with colored people" and Alice's keeping "company with a colored man" during an earlier period in her life.[14]

Mills also stressed Alice's behavior in not investing the litigation funds she received from Leonard (at least $3,000 in counsel fees—the equivalent of $40,000 in 2011) into proving her whiteness. This argument was certain to hold strong weight with the jurors. After all, if Alice were truly white, wouldn't she fight against declarations of colored blood at all costs? In suggesting that Alice had not acted as a true, white person would have in such a situation, Mills stated: "We shall prove also in this connection that although, as the record shows, ample funds were allowed to [Alice], at our expense, by order of the Court, and paid to her, to conduct an investigation abroad as to her ancestry, no money has been expended for that purpose. In short, gentlemen, it will not be in doubt for a second that the allegation in our complaint that she is of substantial colored blood is true, and I challenge any proof to the contrary."[15]

To win, Mills felt the need not only to smear Alice, but also her family, and his revelations about the Jones family history were not limited to just race, or rather proving race: they also aimed to tarnish the Joneses and their reputation as upstanding citizens. In a move that Alice's attorney, Davis, would refer to as "heartless" repeatedly throughout the trial, Mills besmirched the name of Alice's mother, Elizabeth Jones, by revealing that she "had a perfectly white child [Ethel]" when she and George first arrived together in the United States from England on the Steamship *Majestic* in 1891, and that Ethel had been hired off to a man by the name of Carson soon after George, Elizabeth, and Ethel arrived in the country.[16] Indeed, this fact was such a secret before trial that none of Elizabeth's daughters—Emily, Alice, or Grace—even knew about Ethel until Mills mentioned Ethel and his tracking her down at a nearby farm during the trial. Over objections from Davis during the opening, Mills promised to bring Ethel, who was now married to a man by the name of Moore, before the jury to testify about George's race. Mills stated: "[W]e will bring her here tomorrow in court—[now] Mrs. Moore, the wife of the farmer, mother of five children. She will tell you how this man [George Jones] appeared in Huttoft [the town in England where Elizabeth Jones's parents lived]. She will tell you of her mother and she will tell you how this man stood at the door and never stepped his foot across the threshold of this woman's parents. He stood at the door, shielding his black face with his arm."[17]

With this one move, Mills highlighted that he would go to the very ends of the earth to win for his client. He also set the stage for how he would later try to portray Elizabeth Jones to the jury: as a white woman intent on raising her daughters' social status and station by marrying them off to white men.

Yet, Mills knew that simply proving that Alice was of colored blood would not be enough. Mills knew that he also would have to show that Alice could pass as white and did so intentionally—at this point, through actual misrepresentation. During his opening, though, Mills spent very little time on this point, choosing instead to focus on proving Alice's race and her alleged deceitfulness. Mills, however, did point to two specific documents as circumstantial evidence that Alice not only passed as white but also intended to pass as white: (1) the October 14, 1924, marriage license application of Alice and Leonard, where both of them were listed as white; and (2) the March 11, 1915, marriage license application of Emily, who married a black man named Robert Brooks (see fig. 2.3). In the eyes of Mills, Alice and Leonard's marriage license application demonstrated that Alice intentionally asserted in at least one official instance that she was white (see fig. 2.4). It also revealed that Alice actually could pass as white if she wanted; after all, the clerk surely would have identified Alice as colored on the license if her being colored was obvious. The marriage license of Alice's sister, Emily—whom Mills portrayed as a woman who was willing to accept her station as a colored woman, in part because she married a colored man—was spoken of in contrast. Compared to Emily who was recorded as black on her marriage license, Mills hoped that Alice would look more and more like a fraud.

By offering this evidence of the marriage licenses, Mills himself was not only framing the normative ideal of family as monoracial, but also the only logical family as monoracial. As Mills subtly implied through his description of Leonard's evidence, Alice had to be colored if her brother-in-law was colored and if her sister, with the same mother and father, also identified as colored on an official form. There could be no other explanation. After all, what right-minded white woman—assuming Emily looked like Alice, which she did—would identify herself as colored or marry an "out-and-out colored man"?[18]

Fig. 2.3. Alice's sister Emily and her husband Robert Brooks, a butler, stand outside the courtroom. © Bettmann/ Corbis

Additionally, with the promise of this evidence about Alice's ability to pass, Mills gave us just a glimpse of one of many ways in which the body—the black body in particular—would be used as evidence at trial. Referring to Robert Brooks, Alice's black brother-in-law, Mills, proclaimed to the jury, "We have subpoenaed him in court. We shall exhibit him to you."[19]

Having exposed the jurors to his plans on proving Alice's ability to pass, her intent to pass, and her race, Mills moved on to Leonard, working to establish the framework for showing how Leonard—a man from the right family with all the right goods—could be duped by a working-class, colored chambermaid. He began by describing the testimony that would reveal "what [Leonard] was when he first became acquainted with" Alice.[20]

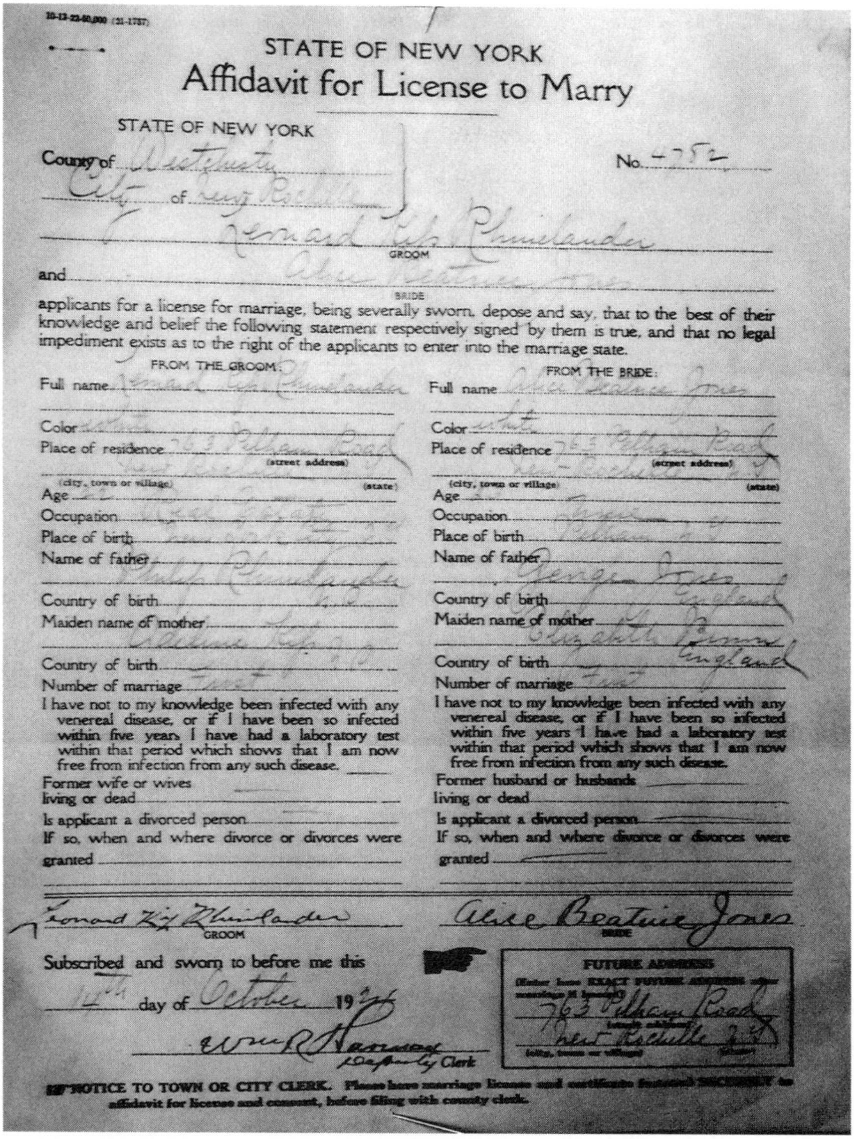

STATE OF NEW YORK
Affidavit for License to Marry

STATE OF NEW YORK

County of _____   No. _____

City of _____

_____ *Leonard ___ Rhinelander*
GROOM

and _____ *Alice _____*
BRIDE

applicants for a license for marriage, being severally sworn, depose and say, that to the best of their knowledge and belief the following statement respectively signed by them is true, and that no legal impediment exists as to the right of the applicants to enter into the marriage state.

FROM THE GROOM:	FROM THE BRIDE:
Full name _____	Full name _____
Color _____	Color _____
Place of residence _____ (street address)	Place of residence _____ (street address)
_____ (city, town or village)	_____ (city, town or village)
Age _____ (state)	Age _____ (state)
Occupation _____	Occupation _____
Place of birth _____	Place of birth _____
Name of father _____	Name of father _____
Country of birth _____	Country of birth _____
Maiden name of mother _____	Maiden name of mother _____
Country of birth _____	Country of birth _____
Number of marriage _____	Number of marriage _____
I have not to my knowledge been infected with any venereal disease, or if I have been so infected within five years I have had a laboratory test within that period which shows that I am now free from infection from any such disease.	I have not to my knowledge been infected with any venereal disease, or if I have been so infected within five years I have had a laboratory test within that period which shows that I am now free from infection from any such disease.
Former wife or wives living or dead _____	Former husband or husbands living or dead _____
Is applicant a divorced person _____	Is applicant a divorced person _____
If so, when and where divorce or divorces were granted _____	If so, when and where divorce or divorces were granted _____

Leonard ___ Rhinelander
GROOM

Alice Beatrice Jones
BRIDE

Subscribed and sworn to before me this

_____ day of *October* 19__

_____ Clerk

FUTURE ADDRESS
_____
_____

NOTICE TO TOWN OR CITY CLERK. Please have marriage license and certificate _____ affidavit for license and consent, before filing with county clerk.

Fig. 2.4. This marriage affidavit listed both Alice's and Leonard's "Color" as white.
© Bettmann/Corbis

To Mills, what Leonard was when he first met Alice was a "boy" four years younger than his lover; a boy whose mother had died in 1915 when he was just twelve years old and whose brother had died across the ocean in the war; a boy who "ha[d] suffered, from a physical infirmity, which affect[ed] his speech, which tongue-tie[d] him"; a boy who received treatment for his infirmity at an institution in Stamford called Orchards, which was for "'[t]he care and treatment of persons afflicted with nervous and mental disorders'"; and a boy who fell into the hands of Carl Kreitler, the older man whose lifestyle brought Leonard together with the Jones sisters.[21]

Thereafter, Mills moved on to present an image of Alice as a scheming woman who had tricked Leonard into marrying her with sexual lures and lustful letters. Mills argued that the younger Leonard, who suffered from "mental backwardness" because of a problem with stammering, had become "an utter slave in [Alice's] hands."[22] As the remainder of Mills's opening statement would reveal, the reference to Leonard as a slave was no coincidence. Mills intended to invoke the image of reversed racial and societal roles between Alice and Leonard in order to emphasize Alice's unnatural control over a defenseless Leonard. For example, during his opening, Mills noted that he would offer into evidence a November 17, 1921, letter from Alice to Leonard to illustrate how the older and more experienced, colored woman began her goal of luring the "tongue-tied, diffident" "boy, upon whom no woman ever smiled before" into marriage.[23] This letter read in part: "Listen, Leonard, I have had some sweethearts but I have not loved them like I have taken to you so. I have never let a fellow love and kiss me the way you do, Leonard, because you make me feel so happy, and lovable towards you dear. But, would it be awful if you had me, myself alone[?] What you would not do to me I can imagine."[24]

Using letters such as this one, Mills made the claim that Alice enticed Leonard to fall for her with hints of future sexual satisfaction and then actual sexual satisfaction, starting on December 22, 1921, the couple's first night together in the Hotel Marie Antoinette. Likewise, Mills emphasized that Alice, unlike Leonard, was sexually experienced, having engaged in sexual intercourse with another man before the couple's relationship began. Mills intimated that Alice had lied to Leonard, quoting from her November 17, 1921, letter: "'I never let a fellow love and kiss me the way you do, Leonard.'"

Four years older than he and we shall show you that before that time she had been the mistress of another man."[25] Finally, Mills contended that Alice's deceit may have run as far as her making a false claim about having an abortion on Leonard's account just two weeks after the couple's first stay at the Hotel Marie Antoinette. With regard to the alleged abortion's effect on Leonard, Mills proclaimed, "I do not say it was not true. He thought it was true. He thought he was bound to her in honor. But it was mighty quick work, we shall argue. And the recovery was quick because before the end of the month they went back there at the hotel again."[26] The gist of Mills's primary argument, then, was that the allegedly awkward and dimwitted Rhinelander boy was no match for the more mature, loose, and deceitful Alice; indeed, Leonard, a white man, was shockingly her slave.

Mills also promised to show at trial how Alice had become more ambitious in her future plans for Leonard. He argued that "there were [several] stages of her fastening upon [Leonard]: The first stage was her effort to become his mistress. There is not a word about marriage in these letters in this first stage, or engagement. . . . The next stage was when she set out to get engaged to him."[27] Overall, Mills painted a picture of Alice as a woman who was initially after only an apartment from Leonard, where Leonard could keep her as his mistress, but then became more ambitious and moved on. to the goal of winning Leonard's affections and ultimately his hand in marriage. Mills argued that Alice sneakily accomplished this task not just through premarital sexual escapades at the Hotel Marie Antoinette, but also through constant reminders of these sexual affairs in her 426 letters to Leonard, threats regarding the interests of other white male seekers as well as the attractiveness of such seekers, and intense written pressures for Leonard to defy his father and marry her secretly before he turned the age of twenty-one and after he received his inheritance of $280,000, an amount "[h]is father could not cut him off from."[28] As Mills declared, Alice made Leonard "her slave, body and soul."[29]

Moreover, Mills asserted that he would offer evidence at trial to show that Alice and her mother deliberately lied to Leonard before the marriage, when Leonard first learned of Robert Brooks, the black husband of Emily (Jones) Brooks, by telling Leonard that Emily had married a Negro despite much protest and shunning from the Jones family. Mills explained: "They

[the Joneses] told him that it [Emily's marriage to Robert] was a great griev-
ance to them, that they had not known it was going to happen, they had
not consented to it, that they had refused the sister the house for two years,
refused her the house, ostracized her, but finally it being accomplished
they recognized it, and that it had disgraced them because they were white,
they were of pure English ancestry upon both sides, they were white."[30]
Mills further declared his intent to show that Alice continued with her lies
after her secret marriage to Leonard was exposed in the newspapers. In
so doing, Mills suggested that Leonard was so far out of his senses by this
point that he could not see beyond the family's lies, sending Alice a message "to hire the best lawyer and fight the case and prove [she is] white."[31]
Indeed, Mills proclaimed to the jury that he would show that Leonard was
Alice's total slave, one who believed Alice up until the very moment that
he was presented with the hard evidence of her birth certificate where "she
was classed as black."[32]

In the end, Mills hoped that the jury's racial prejudices would bring
them to conclude that Alice had simply crossed an inappropriate line by
intentionally passing as white to become Leonard's wife. As Mills asserted
near the end of his opening: "[Leonard] will testify that if he had known she
was black or of black blood, if they had told him the truth when they talked
to him, he would not have married her. He will testify that he was ready to
accept her inferior social position, her less wealth, her poverty, her inferior
social position, he knew those things, he was ready to take them; but this
ancient and proud lineage [that of the French Huguenots], he would not
inflict upon it the undying disgrace of an alliance with colored blood. That
is where he drew the line."[33] In this sense, Mills tested the jury to see if
they, too, would be willing to cross that line. Indeed, Mills likely made the
unusual choice of a jury trial, rather than a bench trial, in this annulment
case, because he believed that jurors were less likely than a judge to overcome their race-based prejudices. Though New York judges, too, were not
free of racial prejudice, their training as lawyers and then judges made it
less likely that they would succumb to racial fears and hatred in reaching
a decision than would lay citizens. What Mills hoped for is that the jurors,
unlike a judge, would vote "according to their hearts."

Fig. 2.5. Lee Parsons Davis defends Alice at trial. © Bettmann/ Corbis

Alice's Opening: Race Only a Blind Man Could Not See

If Mills put the first nail in the coffin of Alice and Leonard's relationship at trial, then Alice's attorney, Lee Parsons Davis (see fig. 2.5), pounded the remaining nails in and then buried the casket. Mills's tactic of making personal attacks on Alice and the Jones family seriously angered Davis, and Davis exhibited his disgust at such tactics during his opening. Indeed, Davis declared the following in response: "[T]here is a bit of a feeling of nervousness that I may not be able to restrain [my] . . . feeling of anger and open this case calmly on behalf of this defendant. . . . [I]t was not my purpose to hurt this man Rhinelander or hurt his father unnecessarily unless it became absolutely necessary in order to protect this girl from injustice. . . . In my twenty years at the trial bar I have never in my life listened to a more vicious opening. I have never listened to one that was more uselessly cruel, and I have never listened to one that was more un-American than that emanated from the lips of eminent counsel."[34]

Davis, then, not only began his opening with a concession that surprised everyone at trial—the concession that Alice was of colored blood and the concession that made it impossible for Alice and Leonard to remain together as husband and wife, even if she won—but Davis also pushed back against the Rhinelanders' tactics. In so doing, he mocked Leonard for his blindness, teasing him for not seeing the obvious race of Alice and calling the Rhinelanders ruthless, hypocritical, and heartless.

First, Davis drew a line right through the question of Alice's ancestry, surprising not only Mills but all of the *Rhinelander* trial's followers when he admitted there was "colored blood in [Alice's] veins."[35] Davis stated: "Before opening, the defendant desires to state for the benefit of the record at the outset of this litigation there was interposed a technical legal denial on advice of counsel as to the blood of this defendant. In the interest of shortening this trial, the defendant's counsel withdraws the denial as to the blood of this defendant and for the purposes of this trial admits that she has some colored blood in her veins."[36]

Up until that point, it looked as though Alice would follow Leonard's purported wishes and comply with his pleas to challenge the lawsuit by proving her whiteness. Just a few days after news of the Rhinelander marriage broke, a newspaper reported that Alice's sister, Grace, publicly denied that the Joneses were colored and blamed the rumors about Alice's race on jealousy. According to the paper, Grace, who married an Italian immigrant, Albert "Footsy" Miller, proclaimed: "This whole thing about our being negroes is just jealousy. . . . My father isn't colored but is of West Indian descent. It was the same way when I got married. Women make me sick, anyway. There are a lot of girls around here who are sore because they didn't cop off a millionaire like my sister. My sister and her husband paid well to keep this out of the newspapers. They were married Oct. 14 and it's a dirty trick for this story to get out now."[37]

Then, a few days after Leonard had filed his Complaint, Judge Samuel Swinburne, the Jones family attorney, proclaimed, "There is only one way to settle this suit now . . . and that is by Mr. Rhinelander dropping the entire action and recognizing his wife. [Alice] does not want a money settlement. She is ill and she wants her husband back."[38] Moreover, Swinburne asserted that "his client's main objective would be to prove that she is white."[39] As one journalist reported, Swinburne had declared his understanding to be that Alice was legally white under New York law "inasmuch as her mother is of pure white origin" (see fig. 2.6).[40]

Furthermore, soon after Leonard's lawsuit was filed, the *New York Times*

Fig. 2.6. Alice watches the trial with her white mother, Elizabeth Jones. © Bettmann/Corbis

reported that Alice's father, George Jones, declared that his naturalization papers, which listed him as colored, were inaccurate. Indeed, Swinburne explained just how George Jones came to be listed as "colored" in his naturalization papers, stating: "Like so many other people in daily routine, [George Jones] failed to read the papers as filled out by the Clerk of the Mount Vernon court. Jones had nothing to do with filling out the papers and he never read them. When finally they were presented to a Supreme Court Justice and Jones learned that he was classed as a 'colored man,' he strenuously objected, but not being of an aggressive nature he did not press the matter. The Clerk did not ask Mr. Jones his race. He probably saw his dusky complexion and put down 'colored man.'"[41]

Furthermore, in her Answer to Leonard's original Complaint, Alice had denied each and every allegation related to Leonard's claim of fraud. Less than two months later, when Leonard filed an Amended Complaint that separated his allegation that Alice was of colored blood into its own paragraph, Alice responded to the allegation by denying "that she [had] any knowledge or information sufficient to form a belief as to" Leonard's statement concerning "colored blood in her veins."[42] Still, Alice did not admit to being of colored descent in her Amended Answer, and from all outward appearances, she maintained a desire to prove that she was white and save her marriage. Less than a month before Alice filed her Answer, rumors surfaced that she planned to "seek an extra allowance from the court for expenses to cover a trip of an investigator to England and to the West Indies to trace the ancestry of [her] father and grandfather."[43] Then, a few days after Alice had filed her Answer, the *New York Times* reported that Alice's attorneys had actually "received sworn affidavits from investigators in England to prove that Mrs. Rhinelander's ancestors were not of West Indian origin."[44]

At the same time that Alice's legal team hinted at a strategy to "litigate her whiteness" or prove her whiteness,[45] they also seemed to signal that such litigation plans could be abandoned in the future. For example, just days after the lawsuit was filed, Swinburne declared that Leonard "knew the entire situation."[46] Specifically, he asserted: "In our defense, we will neither affirm nor deny that Mrs. Rhinelander is of negro blood. They have made that charge and they will have to prove it. That has nothing to do with our end of the case. We are concerned with their charge of fraud and will concentrate on that. Young Rhinelander knew this girl and her family for some time before the marriage. He paid attention to her sister before he courted Alice. He knew the entire situation."[47]

During his opening, Davis not only contended that Leonard knew of or should have known of Alice's race, but that Leonard had embarrassed and humiliated Alice due to no fault of her own. Making it clear to the jurors that Alice's race was no longer at issue, Davis proclaimed, "Did she represent to this man Rhinelander that she had no colored blood in her veins and was pure white? . . . That is really your first issue, because the question of colored blood is not in issue any more on our admission. So, really, your first inquiry is, did Alice Rhinelander—not 'this woman' as Judge Mills referred to her, after referring to this young gentleman—did Alice Rhinelander represent to Leonard Rhinelander before her marriage on October 14, 1924, that she was pure white? Now, that is clear, is it gentlemen?"[48]

From that point on, Davis emphasized to the jury how evident it was that Alice was colored and mocked Leonard and his family during the process. To do so, Davis used the highly effective tactic of selling ideas of clear, biological racial distinctions—namely, racial differences in skin color. This ploy was certain to have some force in light of the resurgence of the eugenics movement during the time period, a movement that used "science" to support notions of genetically tied, physical differences as well as white supremacy. Davis first utilized the notion of clear and visible race in his explanation of the issues of the case. Using an idea of biological race that would become central to Alice's case, Davis argued to the jury that even if Alice had told Leonard that she was pure white, such a statement would not be enough to grant a verdict for Leonard; the jury must find that Leonard actually believed this misrepresentation. Davis joked lightly: "The third and last issue, giving them to you just in a nutshell . . . did he believe such representation and believing them and relying upon them, did he then marry? You see that is an essential thing, because if I make a representation to you—suppose I told you that a clear Chinaman was an American Indian or of pure white American blood, I represented that to you; well, that would be false, but you would not believe it. Of course, you would have to be blind, you see, to believe that."[49]

In fact, Davis harped on this notion of race by phenotype by indicating that he would offer evidence to show that, as early as 1921, Leonard had crossed clear racial lines when he met and interacted kindly and socially with two people who were "concededly and in appearance" colored, Robert and Roberta Brooks, respectively, the brother-in-law and niece of Alice. Deriding Mills on his alleged proof of deception by Alice, Davis stated: "I think the issue that Judge Mills should have presented to you was not mental unsoundness but blindness. Blindness. . . . [Y]ou are here to determine whether Alice Rhinelander before her marriage told this man Rhinelander that she was white and had no colored blood. You are here to determine next whether or not that fooled him. Whether or not he could not see *with his own eyes* that he was marrying into a colored family."[50] In this sense, Davis's suggestion was that the outcome of the case rested on the eyes of the jury alone, who, unless blind, would easily conclude, as Leonard must have done, that the Jones family, including Alice, was of colored blood.

At the same time that Davis discussed the clarity and obviousness of race, Davis tried to invoke sympathy for George Jones, as an English man of dark skin who found himself in the unfortunate position of being regarded as "negro" when he came to the United States. As Davis would describe him, George was a man from England who did not know his father because he died when George was a toddler, who knew only what his mother told him of his father, and who was viewed in England as "mulatto," which held a different status overseas than "negro" did in the United States. Davis explained:

> I have never gone out to Colorado Springs . . . to find out whether I was born there or not. I took my dear mother's word for it. And so he [George] took his mother's word for it. She told him that her father was a West Indian. Now, in those times, in England, negroes, as we regarded them—I mean those that we regarded here in this country as negroes—were not plentiful in England. You know, we are the chaps that brought the negroes over here. They didn't invite themselves over here. . . . It wasn't so in England. He was looked upon as a mulatto in England, and the viewpoint in England and the Continent and France, as you know, is entirely different towards a dark skin than it is here. He is 67 years of age, and he has been here thirty-five. During that other portion of his life he went with white people and was regarded as a mulatto. No disgrace there. He really didn't know what negroes were or the viewpoint towards them that, unfortunately, some of us Americans adopt, until he came to this country. . . . [A]nd here he found himself regarded as a negro.[51]

Additionally, Davis played upon a wide variety of stereotypes during his opening statement by highlighting what he viewed as the heartless tactics of the wealthy and focusing on race and gendered notions of sexual aggression. For example, Davis played upon white female, gendered stereotypes regarding sex and chastity; subtly criticized Leonard's weakness in not standing up to his father; and rejected the claims of seduction by Alice through many taunts such as: "That this little girl here seduced father's boy. I am speaking coldly and frankly. . . . Papa's son was seduced. That is the first time, although I have prosecuted much in the way of crime, that I have ever heard a girl charged with raping a man. [The alleged seduction of Leonard] is tantamount to that. . . . He didn't need to go to the sanitarium. All he needed was this influence [of Alice leading him to the Hotel Marie Antoinette] . . . to cure his braintied proposition. So she leads him to the Antoinette. But he knows enough to sign husband and wife."[52]

Along those same lines, Davis mocked the very idea of Leonard as a tongue-tied and innocent victim. Essentially, Davis painted a picture of Leonard as a man whose impairment was greatly exaggerated; as a man who was far less innocent than he was depicted to be by Mills; as a man fearful of the powerful and stubborn father who was behind the lawsuit; as a man eager to obey a father who had allegedly made his employees suggest threats from the Ku Klux Klan to the Jones family; and as a man willing to take advantage of a woman of humble origins like Alice, who had been nothing but honest and loving toward him. First, rejecting Mills's argument about Leonard's impairment as ridiculous, Davis told the jurors: "So you see, gentlemen, that is one ground for annulling this marriage. This descendant of a long and ancient line stuttered and went to stammering school and was so braintied that he didn't know what that letter meant. . . . In other words, no matter what it cost this little girl, she got in contact with a stammering nut. And I don't say that humorously, gentlemen. Everything about this case is serious."[53] Indeed, Davis wondered why if Leonard was so braintied, he was able to serve both as editor of the school paper and editor of the final yearbook at his school.

Thereafter, noting Mills's claim of evidence regarding Alice's previous sexual intimacy with another man, Davis mocked the idea of Alice then deceiving Leonard about her race. He stated: "Why, she admitted to him that she had been the mistress of another man. That is another reason, gentlemen, assigned for you to break bonds of this marriage. . . . She admitted to him, Rhinelander, that she wanted to marry him. Admitted frankly to him that she had had the most intimate relations with another man—that thing which is most precious to a woman, Judge Mills says that she admitted. Although she admits that, they claim that she deceived him as to her color. Imagine it!"[54] Most of all, Davis intimated that Leonard knew what he was doing when he was pursuing Alice sexually, even within her own home and, more so, when he was writing her letters requesting that she remain true to him. For example, at one point during his opening, Davis stated: "From [the time Leonard met Alice] Leonard Rhinelander began to make love to his now wife Alice, and there was hardly a night passed, gentlemen, we will show you, that this brain-stormed Rhinelander was not accepting the hospitality of the humble home of Mr. and Mrs. Jones and there carrying on his courtship. . . . He was just as sane, and I will show it to you by his letters, just as sane and knew what he was doing as any man who is in love."[55]

Davis also lambasted the Rhinelanders for dishonoring the name of the Jones family in a way that only the very powerful rich could do to a decent and hard-working family, who lived "in the humblest kind of home . . . as clean as the finest mansion in Fifth Avenue."[56] He especially criticized the Rhinelanders for their work in uncovering the secret of what happened to Elizabeth Jones's white daughter, Ethel (borne to a white man), after the Jones family arrived in the United States. Davis asserted:

> In other words, it is not enough that this son of wealth comes into this humble home and takes this girl, but because Papa gets cross about it afterwards, he has to drag her into the slime to get rid of her. That is what they want you to do. But they don't stop at that, and as proof that no effort will be left unused to crush not only Alice Rhinelander but the entire family, look at this. . . .
>
> What insinuation did he [Mills] want you to draw from the fact that a white child came over there with this lady? What has it got to do with this case? Nothing. This woman, Mrs. Jones, this lady, humble as she is, thirty-five years, we will show you, living in Westchester County—they are not content with dragging this child [Alice] into the dirt, but they want to take her, too. That is the kind of a case, gentlemen, that they want you to try. . . .
>
> That is why I asked you if you could give this girl a square deal in the face of the assault, backed by the millions of the Rhinelanders.[57]

In this sense, Davis began to play upon the two parties' social disparities, both in gender and in class, to set up the case as one of David versus Goliath. In sum, Davis argued that it was not Alice who had misbehaved, but instead Leonard and his family who had acted improperly. Davis's opening rested on two notions: (1) on biological race as so obvious that only those who were blind could not see it in a person and be deceived; and (2) on social race and class as so defined that only those who intended to cross it did so, and then punished others for their very own actions.

Furthermore, like Mills had done with Alice, Davis argued that Leonard's behavior proved his case—proved that Leonard knew that Alice was of colored blood and did not care. To Davis, if Leonard's claims were true he would have left Alice the very minute that the stories of his marriage to a "negress" broke. Davis asserted: "And they stayed inside that house, besieged, with the press coming out daily with these glaring stories, with glaring headlines 'Rhinelander's son marries into a negro family.' They slept in the same room. . . . They continued their married life . . . he [Leonard] having the newspapers brought up to him mornings as he lay in bed, he read these glaring headlines that he had married into a negro family. No remonstrance. He was happy. He would go around the house in his pajamas and a fine pair of moccasins he had brought from the West and a bathrobe. He did not care, and continued in the face of this, this is evidence that he was not fooled, in the face of all these newspapers that he read branding this family as negroes, and he had his own eyesight before."[58]

In the end, Davis fought back hard with his own description of Alice's evidence and with his sense of who the Rhinelanders truly were. Angered by what he viewed as the unnecessary and cruel exposure of Alice's premarital sexual experiences and the secrets of her family, Davis declared: "But I will say that if they want to start throwing slime—they will be the first ones to do it—at this young girl, I will lick this boy on his own letters. If he starts calling her black, I mean in morals, and he makes it necessary, he will find that the kettle is just as black. . . . Judge Mills has taken the lid off and now, if it is to be a real fight, let the fight go on and you be square from now on."[59]

With that, the two parties moved forward with their cases. Leonard would soon tell his story in both direct questioning and cross-examination, while Alice would remain silent, speaking only with her body in what would come to be known as a heart-wrenching moment in history.

3

Testimonies

AFTER BOTH LEONARD'S LEAD ATTORNEY, Isaac N. Mills, and Alice's chief attorney, Lee Parsons Davis, finished explaining their strategies to the jury, the two men and their legal teams began a month-long trial in which they worked to fulfill the evidentiary promises they made during their opening statements. In this chapter, I describe the evidence that Leonard set forth in proving his case to the jury as well as the evidence that Alice presented in her defense. Specifically, I describe the evidence that Leonard's attorneys used to try to demonstrate their claim that Alice used sexual conduct to gain control over a mentally backward Leonard and make him her "love slave," and that Alice's alleged deceit was the product of her and her family's desire to gain access to Leonard's wealth, class, and race status. I then lay out the evidence that Alice's attorneys used to make these three arguments in her defense: (1) that Alice's race was so obvious that only those who were literally blind could not see it; (2) that Leonard's knowledge of Alice's race could easily be inferred from his willingness to cross clear boundaries of race, not just with Alice but also with others, such as Alice's black brother-in-law, Robert, and niece, Roberta; and (3) that given Leonard's wealth and status, he, as "a normal man with [a] normal sense of perception,"[1] should be punished for his acts of racial betrayal.

Leonard's Case

Because of Alice's concession of "colored blood" during her opening, Mills began Leonard's case with less of a blow to Alice's case than he expected. His original plan was to embarrass Alice with evidence that disproved any claims to whiteness; however, Alice's earlier admission of colored blood obviated that presentation. Nevertheless, Mills still offered evidence during Leonard's case to demonstrate and confirm that Alice was not of pure white blood—possibly, to fan the prejudice of the jurors. Had Davis not conceded that Alice was of colored blood at the trial's beginning, this evidence certainly would have been damning to Alice's defense.

After presenting evidence to establish the racial background of Alice, Mills then called witnesses to support his theory of why Leonard was so susceptible to Alice's charms: his alleged mental backwardness. These witnesses included Dr. L. Pierce Clark, who treated Leonard at an institution called "Orchards." Dr. Clark identified Leonard's "primary, main difficulty . . . [as] a speech one—a stammering—chronic stammering speech disorder; stuttering," but he also confessed, on cross, that Leonard had gotten better and, by August 1921, had taken the lead in speaking to some girls in one instance.[2]

In addition to Dr. Clark, Julie Despres, the former governess of Leonard's sister, testified about Leonard's mental infirmities. She described how Leonard's stuttering affected her ability to teach him French. Similarly, Sidney Ussher, a former pastor of the Rhinelander family, detailed how Leonard's stammering negatively affected him as a child in Sunday school. Finally, J. Provoust Stout, a former math teacher, described Leonard in high school as "slow and diffident and easily influenced."[3]

Each of these witnesses, however, was cleverly cross-examined by Davis. At the end of each of their testimonies, Davis left the jury with an understanding that Leonard's stammering did not, as Stout conceded, make him "deficient," or as Stout admitted to Davis, that Leonard's stuttering did not mean that he, "a boy that was a little slow in spelling [could not] work[] fast when he made love."[4]

Thereafter, Mills moved to the heart of his case, the testimony of Leonard Rhinelander. However, relying so heavily on Leonard as the primary

Fig. 3.1. Leonard Kip Rhinelander is seated on the witness stand. He was the primary witness and focus during the trial. © Bettmann/Corbis

witness, and for many days in a row, was not easy. Despite his class background, Leonard was not an impressive witness (see fig. 3.1). The newspapers often described him as expressionless. The *New York Times* once reported, "If [Leonard Rhinelander] cared what was going on around him in the occasional sprightly encounters of counsel which drew laughter from the audience he gave no sign of it."[5] Later, the *New York Times* would describe Leonard's efforts as a witness in the following manner: "Rhinelander was not a prepossessing figure on the stand. There was an expression of bewilderment in his eyes, which peered through heavy glasses, and an intense effort at concentration. When he attempted to speak it was usually with a violent physical effort, which showed in his tense muscles. His hands clasped and unclasped over his knees, and then the words would shoot forth spasmodically, brokenly, sometimes only in a rapid mumble in which his meaning was indistinguishable."[6]

Mills, however, had to press on with what he had. His most difficult and vital task was in proving to the jury that Alice had misrepresented her race through direct expression and, more so, that Leonard believed those misrepresentations. First, Mills had to establish why the misrepresentation was important. To that end, Leonard testified at trial that he would not have married Alice had he known she was of colored blood. The trial testimony revealed this colloquy:

> *Mills:* If you had known, what is now conceded to be true before you married Alice, that she is of colored blood, would you have married her?
> *Leonard:* Absolutely not; no.
> *Mills:* When you married her did you believe her statement that she was white?
> *Leonard:* I did. I always believed her.[7]

With that foundation laid, Mills then worked to prove not only that Alice had tried to deceive Leonard but that she could have so deceived him. As part of this argument, Mills had to demonstrate that Alice was a colored person who could easily pass as white because of her light skin and Caucasian features. Indeed, in his closing statement, Mills declared to the jury that the trace of colored blood in Alice was almost imperceptible. Unlike Davis, Mills had the difficult task of arguing that race was more fluid, and not rooted solely in biology, an idea that was generally less comforting to whites during that era.

Next, in addition to convincing the jury that Alice possibly could have deceived Leonard, Mills needed to demonstrate that Alice acted with the intent to induce Leonard to marry her. To accomplish this task, Mills offered as evidence many of Alice's private letters to Leonard, which were filled with misspellings and other grammatical mistakes—and all of which just reinforced the class differences between Leonard and Alice. These letters included one letter from Alice on January 2, 1922, which revealed the ways in which Alice routinely played on Leonard's jealousies. Alice wrote the following in this letter: "Now Lenard, on the level, I will say dear, you have been lovely to me, But when it comes to give Edward back his ring, I think dear, that I should not. Because he is very fond of me, which I no, and I also no that you hold the same of me. You want me, as you say, and you do not want me to go about with others. But Lenard, if you want me to keep steady company with you, I love you enough to be true to you dear, But you will after give me a ring, a right one like, what Ed gave me, And if you do, you will never hear any more about any man."[8] Other letters used as evidence included statements that Alice made about other men, such as the following two assertions:

1. You will after to try and come home or I will after fall back on Ed, which I do not want to do, but darling its terrible for me.
2. And all of the boys seems to like me. I could have a date every night of the week. But I do not wait, because I have dear Leonard. I love him best.[9]

Mills also worked to discredit Alice by exposing the misleading nature behind one of her ploys to make Leonard jealous. In a letter to Leonard dated August 4, 1922, Alice insinuated that she had spoken to and flirted with Al Jolson, the famous 1920s blackface performer, at the club resort Paul Smith's that day, even though she had never interacted with the actor. Alice wrote: "He [Jolson] was in swimming, but he is some flirt with the girls. There is four fellows with him. His cottage is next to ours, and they have instruments, and we had some orchestra here today."[10] At trial, Jolson engaged in the following colloquy on both direct examination with Mills and cross-examination with Alice's chief attorney, Lee Parsons Davis, in each case proving to be witty and humorous. Jolson's exchanges with the attorneys went as follows:

Mills: Now, Mr. Jolson, where do you reside? . . .
Jolson: Hartsdale, New York.
Mills: Then you are a Westchester County man?
Jolson: Yes.
Mills: Now, do you see the defendant? She is the woman sitting at the very foot of the table there. You can see her well, can you?
Jolson: Perfectly. . . .
Mills: Did you ever have any conversation with her before today?
Jolson: Never in my life.
Mills: Did you ever see her before today in your life?
Jolson: No, sir.
Mills: . . . Now, is there any truth in [what Alice wrote about speaking to you at Paul Smith's on August 4, 1922], Mr. Jolson?
Jolson: Where was this at? . . .

Mills: Paul Smith's, yes.

Jolson: May I speak in my own way?

Mills: Certainly.

Jolson: I have never in my life seen the plaintiff or the defendant. I wasn't in Paul Smith's at any time, any moment, any day or any month of the year of 1922.

Mr. Davis: You needn't get excited, because we don't claim you were.

Jolson: Thank God for that. I have had enough trouble out of this. My wife don't talk to me. But any way—I just want to show you. Here is the hotel bill in Atlantic City from July 27 to August 7 in the year 1922. I was in bathing, but not at Paul Smith's.

Mills: Your proof is complete.

Jolson: I thank you.

Mills: I just want to ask you something—

Jolson: I hope I will be able to eat breakfast at home tomorrow.

Mills: What do you say about this allegation that you were some flirt with the girls?

Jolson: Oh, I have got to be a flirt in the show business.

Mills: Is there any cross examination? . . .

Davis: I am awfully glad to meet you, Mr. Jolson.

Jolson: I am a deputy sheriff of Westchester County. I don't want a smirch on my name in this fair county. That is the main thing.

Davis: Let me relieve your mind. You are a prominent chap, aren't you? Don't be modest about it, now. This is a good headline for you?

Jolson: I know, but the other wasn't. Make this different, will you?

Davis: You are prominent, aren't you, just waiving the modesty?

Jolson: Yes.

Davis: And prominent people often have people nickname them by their name? That is so, isn't it?

Jolson: Sometime.

Davis: Now, let me relieve your mind. Up at Paul Smith's there was a chap that was nicknamed after you because he was witty and funny.

Mills: Are you testifying, Brother Davis?

Davis: Yes.

Davis: Do you know that to be so? I will put it in a legal question, so that the Judge won't object. Did you know that there was a chap up there that was nicknamed after you, "Al Jolson"?

Jolson: No, I did not.

Davis: Are you relieved?

Jolson: Yes—a lot.

Davis: Go home and make up with your wife.

Jolson: Well, I want to tell you this: every time I go in my dressing room the orchestra starts to play, "Alice, where art thou going?"[11]

On top of introducing evidence that exposed Alice's "jealousy games" with Leonard, Mills introduced a letter from May 19, 1922, that he claimed revealed the ways in which Alice repeatedly played upon sexual enticements to win Leonard's marital affections. In this letter, Alice wrote the following: "I got undressed and got in bed which you can see me in bed like the Antoinette, and snuggled in bed. And read all of your letters, but you made me feel very passionate for the want of you, telling me how happy my little hand as often made you feel, and several other things, but can't help to tell you. . . . Just now writing this letter to Edward just call me up. Wanted to go out to movies but I went to Phone said Hello, I said yes he said Alice I said Yes. Would you go out to-night or can I come down[?] I said no so ran off then Phone rang again so I told operator not to call the number, so he was cut off."[12] Mills admitted into evidence yet another letter from Alice, in which she wrote, "Gee, please come to me [Len], because I want to feel you again like that. . . . You can always have it, and be at your service."[13] Additionally, Mills introduced numerous other letters from Alice, in which she spoke longingly about her and Leonard's sexual escapades at the Hotel Marie Antoinette.

As a final step in his strategic use of letters, Mills offered into evidence letters from Alice that demonstrated how she continually pushed for marriage from Leonard. For example, using a letter that was written on May 31, 1922, Mills worked to show how Alice allegedly worked her magic to obtain control over Leonard. In this letter, Alice wrote the following about her desire to marry Leonard: "And I do hope you are going to reward me for it in making you happy. . . . I pray and hope every night I wished Len, you was my husband, what things I would tell you, and make you happy, but I do not want to tell you yet because, I do not own you yet. . . . I often wish you and I was down at Antoinette again, but I am afraid, we will never see it any more. I do not want to go to a hotel any more what we should have Len, our own little house and we could go up whenever we wanted."[14] As another example of the games that Alice played to lure Leonard into marriage, Mills pointed to this letter from September 22, 1922:

Len, I want you, to forget me try and think you never new me, it was only a dream, as I am not, going to write no more, as you after do the right thing, for your father. . . . But you will after forget me completely, until you get at age, That's if I am not taken, before that, you can have me. . . . As all of this, is going to be a waste of time, which I can see now. You could of married just as easily not before you went away, but your money came first before me, or we could of kepted it a died secrt, which no body would ever, had known. And I could be living home, And not working, like I am, And you away having a gret time, what you spend in going around, it would keep me, nicely. . . . If I cant have you now Len you will never get me, in the future, as I will fall back on the one I love second best, from you. . . . I never want you to bother me, again, dear until you are at age, Probly then you will be to late, entirely, I am afraid you will. . . . I hope you read over severl times, And understand it right, And get the right idea.[15]

In the end, Mills used well over one hundred letters to establish what he viewed as Alice's three primary threats to Leonard: loss of Alice to another man; loss of the sex that the "experienced" Alice introduced to Leonard, "a boy upon whom no woman ever smiled before"; and loss of Alice in general if he abided by his father's wishes and failed to marry her.

Yet, Mills knew that proof of a plan to obtain marriage by Alice was not enough, so he also worked to present evidence of the most important representation, or rather in this case misrepresentation, that Alice allegedly made to Leonard: that of her race. To support Leonard's allegations of racial fraud, Mills offered a broad range of evidence. Primarily, he offered the testimony of Leonard himself, who asserted: "Between the months of May and September, 1924, in the presence of Alice and Mr. and Mrs. Jones, Mrs. Jones told me that they had done everything in their power to prevent Emily from marrying Brooks, but, seeing that it was of no avail, they had denied Emily and Brooks the house for two years, telling me they were not colored—they were English—they were born in England. 'The first time we ever saw a colored person was on our arrival in America, while walking on Sixth Avenue. We were surprised and didn't know what they were.' Then Alice entered the conversation and said, 'Of course, we are not colored. We never associate with colored people and never will.'"[16]

Unfortunately for Mills (and for Leonard), such testimony was refuted later by Leonard's own words during cross-examination. Despite Leonard's claim that Alice specifically denied inquiries as to her parentage when he allegedly learned in 1924 that her sister Emily had married a Negro, Leonard admitted on cross-examination to meeting Robert Brooks as Alice's brother-in-law three years earlier, in 1921, and to socially interacting with him before leaving again for travels and school in 1922. Likewise, Leonard's claims about the Jones family's statements regarding the marriage of Emily and Robert Brooks were directly contradicted by the testimonies of Robert and Emily Brooks themselves, who asserted that they both met Leonard at the Jones family home in 1921, not 1924, and denied any protest to their marriage by the Joneses because of Robert's race (as opposed to Emily's young age), and by Alice's mother, Elizabeth Jones, who gave the same testimony.

Mills, however, did not end his evidence of Alice's alleged misrepresentations with Leonard alone. He offered both a letter and testimonies from other witnesses who claimed to have been deceived by Alice about her race. For example, through Leonard's direct examination, Mills offered as evidence a letter from Alice, in which she wrote about meeting a man from Harvard, who referred to her as Spanish, and about how she replied that she was of "Spanish extraction." Alice wrote in this letter: "He calls me Spanish kid. [H]e doesn't believe that my people is English born. I said, I was very glad, I was a little Spainard."[17]

Additionally, Mills put on the stand persons who asserted that Alice told them she was of pure white blood. Two witnesses of this kind were Joseph Rich, a furniture store owner who had sold items to Leonard for his and Alice's place at Pintard Apartments, and his wife, Miriam Rich. Joseph and Miriam eagerly began a social relationship with the newlywed Rhinelanders. Both Joseph and Miriam were well aware of the prominence of the Rhinelander family and, given their ambitions, they desperately wanted to befriend Alice and Leonard. In fact, the newlywed Rhinelanders and Riches had become such close friends after their business transaction that, when Leonard reluctantly left the Jones family home with attorney Leon Jacobs on November 20, 1924, he asked the Riches to keep Alice for a few days in their house until he could return to her. The Riches, according to Miriam's testimony, happily kept Alice for several days after November 20, 1924, because Alice repeatedly insisted that she was white. Miriam contended that she and her husband believed Alice because they found her to be charming. Miriam also indicated that she and Joseph thought that Alice would sue the newspapers for their alleged lies about her racial background. At trial, Miriam testified that Alice never told her that she was of colored blood. Instead, Miriam noted that during dinner at a Chinese restaurant before the two couples saw the Marx Brothers' play *I'll Say She Is*, Alice had claimed to be of Spanish descent. Miriam testified: "I happened to mention that I was in an evening gown, and I felt that, being invited at the time by Mrs. Rhinelander, that I had the evening gown and she didn't, and I mentioned to her the long sleeve dress, and Mrs. Rhinelander said, 'Why, don't bother about that,' she said, 'I generally wear short dresses or long sleeves, but my complexion is dark. As you know, Mrs. Rich, we are Spanish descent, and I have long sleeves on tonight.'"[18] Additionally, a very excited and agitated Miriam gave Alice a look of scorn from the witness stand and claimed that Alice had further represented herself as being of pure white blood during her stay at the Riches' house after she and Leonard were separated on November 20, 1924. According to Miriam, she had become the laughing stock of her community for defending Alice as a white woman. Miriam's trial exchange with Mills on this point was as follows:

Mills: What did she say in [regard to her color]?

Miriam: Well, Mrs. Rhinelander was very, very unhappy, and I was very, very unhappy, also, and she told me all of this story [that announced that Leonard had married a "negress"]. She said to me that if it takes every penny her father has in this world that she is going to sue the newspapers for daring to call her colored. . . .

Mills: I want to know did she say anything as to whether or not she had told Mr. Rhinelander anything about her being white?

Miriam: She said that Mr. Rhinelander had forbidden her to read any more newspapers, and he said, "Alice, I am thoroughly convinced that you are not colored, so I want you to destroy all the papers, and I don't want you to read any more papers." And furthermore, she said that her husband practically had cried—and these, if I remember, were her very words: she said, "My poor Leonard. He would rather have married an Indian than he had married a negress."

Mills: Did she say anything as to whether she had told Mr. Rhinelander that she was white and that he believed her?

Miriam: Yes. She said, "Leonard will stick to me." She said, "You heard Leonard's conversation with me at the other end of the phone tonight." That was the same night they went away, and on the strength of Mr. Rhinelander's telephone call, she was at the house, shielded, I presume, from the world, just because she was a dark girl and not a millionaire or a wealthy girl, and I protected her, which she knew.[19]

Miriam's husband, Joseph, testified to similar alleged statements by Alice in November 1924 during his own examination at trial. One particular exchange went as follows:

> *Mills:* Did she say anything about her descent then?
> *Joseph:* She said her father was English and she was English, of Spanish descent.
> *Mills:* Did she say anything as to spending every dollar?
> *Joseph:* Every dollar that her father had he would spend to sue the newspapers and prove that they were white.[20]

Finally, on the same issue of Alice's alleged misrepresentations of her racial status to others, Mills offered the testimony of William Lawby, a reporter for the *New York American,* who testified that Alice had insisted to him that she was of pure white blood. He testified: "I explained to Mrs. Rhinelander the purpose of our being there and told her that the report that she was colored was widespread, and that possibly one of the best ways that she could have of disproving that would be to make a statement and to sit for a photograph. . . . At first she was disinclined to submit to either a picture or an interview. . . . She said, 'I don't see how any paper would have the nerve to print a story of that kind, and they will have to pay for it, and pay for it dearly.' . . . Mr. Rhinelander . . . told her, 'For your sake and for my sake, Honey, I think you had better give this gentleman a frank statement.' She said, 'Well, we are not colored. There is no colored blood in us.'"[21]

Davis, however, considerably weakened Lawby's testimony when he made Lawby confess that Leonard had privately told him that Mr. Jones was from the West Indies. Davis also exposed on cross-examination that Lawby had altered quotes from Alice to make them grammatically correct, which at least indicated the potential for other alterations in his stories. Moreover, in revealing this action by Lawby, Davis implicitly highlighted Alice's language and grammar during her interview, both of which could be viewed

as characteristic of a poorly educated colored woman and another strong
signal that Leonard knew or should have known of Alice's race.

In the end, Mills presented testimony from four witnesses, including
Leonard, who claimed that Alice represented herself as white. However,
given the anger of Joseph and Miriam Rich and Lawby's confession and
alterations, a question remained whether the jury would buy their claims
about Alice's alleged deception upon them.

In fact, Mills hoped for more than just a belief in deception by Alice. He
wanted to brand her entire family as deceivers. As part of the trial story he
offered about fraud on Leonard, Mills insisted that not just Alice but much
of the Jones family had been in on the racial fraud. For example, Mills attempted to suggest broad deceit by the Jones family when he asked Elizabeth Jones whether she "design[ed] to have [her] daughters marry white
men" and later asked her to identify other white men whom her daughters
had entertained in the house.[22] Mills also questioned Elizabeth Jones about
how she cared for her daughters, noting how she went for days and even
two weeks without knowing of Alice's whereabouts when Alice and Leonard stayed at the Hotel Marie Antoinette.[23] Later, in his summation, Mills
would say the following about Elizabeth Jones: "I recognize the terrible
temptation which was upon her when she found in this country the black
skin of her husband isolated them. . . . I recognize the temptation she was
under. I appreciate how she was tempted beyond endurance to make for
her younger daughters access to what she believed was a higher walk of
life. I throw no rocks at her."[24] Mills also highlighted during Leonard's case
how the marriage licenses of Grace and Alice, both of whom married white
men, identified the women as white, and compared them with that of their
sister Emily, who had married a colored man and was identified as colored
on her marriage license. Indeed, Mills questioned Grace about why she did
not correct her marriage license when she saw that she had been incor-
rectly identified as white on the document, insinuating that it was Grace's
intention all along to pass as white. Mills's questioning of Grace proceeded
in this manner.

Mills: . . . Now, Madam, you recognize you are of colored blood, don't you?
Grace: Yes, sir.

Mills: You haven't ever disputed that, have you?

Grace: No; never.

Mills: Now, you married a white man, did you not?

Grace: Yes.

Mills: Mr. Albert Joseph Miller?

Grace: Yes, sir.

Mills: And you married him on April 25, 1922?

Grace: Yes, sir. . . .

Mills: In obtaining your marriage certificate or license for marriage, you had to state your color, did you not?

Grace: No, sir. He didn't ask me my color.

Mills: Well, it is entered, it is in evidence here, as "white." Do you mean to say that he only, from his observation of you, wrote you down as "white"?

Grace: Yes, sir. He never—

Mills: He had never seen you before, had he?

Grace: No, never.

Mills: You didn't correct him?

Grace: No, sir, because I didn't know what he was putting down.

Mills: You didn't know what you were put down as?

Grace: No.

Mills: Didn't you receive the license?

Grace: Yes.

Mills: Didn't you look at it?

Grace: After we went out.

Mills: When you saw that you were put down as "white" and you knew you were of colored blood, did you go back to have a correction made?

Grace: No, sir.[25]

Even with Emily, who had married a colored man, Mills implied that she was trying to have her daughter, Roberta—who, as Mills revealed, had auburn hair and attended a white Sunday school—cross the line into a socially white world. In essence, Mills worked to prove that racial deceit extended beyond Alice and into the entire Jones family—that the fraud was, in a sense, a family affair.

As a general matter, Mills strove to have the jury interpret all of this proffered evidence as proof of Alice's successful domination over an easily influenced and mentally backward Leonard. He expected the jury to view this domination as occurring through Alice's successes in obtaining a promise of engagement from Leonard in July 1922, a ring from him in March 1923, and ultimately marriage to him in October 1924, right after he had become of age, twenty-one, and received approximately $280,000—nearly $4,000,000 in today's terms—under the will of a grandparent.

Alice's Case: A Normal Man with a Normal Sense of Perception

Throughout the trial, Davis turned the tables on Leonard, using cross-examination to expose Leonard as less innocent than he had been portrayed. First, Davis got Leonard to agree that the only mental problem he had was his stuttering and that he was editor of his school paper, played on the tennis team, and graduated at the head of his class. Then, Davis exposed Leonard's knowledge of questionable activities before he even met Alice, such as playing poker, knowing how to kiss a girl and "play with her" with his hands, and knowing about "rubbers" and how to get them. Also, Davis managed to pull from Leonard a confession that he fell in love with Alice after just a couple of weeks of knowing her. In so doing, Davis was able to suggest that it was not Alice, but instead Leonard who was the aggressor. Additionally, Davis offered the following part of an October 7, 1921, letter from Leonard to Alice, in which Leonard revealed his intent to put the thought of sexual intercourse into Alice's mind just two weeks into their relationship: "Well, my car, I hope, will be ready by the middle of next week or perhaps sooner and then, dear, you and I can take some long rides and maybe if you are real nice to me once in a while, I will let you drive. I bet I know you are wondering what I mean by being real nice. Well, I leave that to your imagination."[26] Finally, Davis exposed Leonard to be deceitful in numerous ways. For example, during cross-examination, Davis unveiled Leonard's deceit to his father of his marriage to Alice and his deceit to hotel clerks as he and Alice went to the Hotel Marie Antoinette and Leonard registered them as husband and wife. Additionally, Davis revealed during his cross-examination of Leonard that Leonard had taken Alice on a trip throughout New England and had gained her parents' permission to do so by promising the presence of a chaperoning, married couple, which did not exist, and that he had continued the fraud on the trip by lying to her parents about how much the chaperones, supposedly Mr. and Mrs. Matthews of Rye, New York, were enjoying themselves.

As noted earlier, Davis also exposed Leonard's lies in his bill of particulars regarding his alleged inquiries about Alice's "color" and her allegedly resulting lies in response. In so doing, Davis also revealed how the work of Philip Rhinelander's attorney Leon Jacobs was a major cog behind the wheel that began the *Rhinelander* lawsuit. This important exchange between Leonard and Davis went as follows:

> *Davis:* When did you first meet Mrs. Brooks [Alice's sister Emily, who had married Robert Brooks, a black man]?
>
> *Leonard:* 1921.
>
> *Davis:* Who introduced you to Mr. Brooks in 1921?
>
> *Leonard:* I believe Alice did.
>
> *Davis:* You know she did, don't you?
>
> *Leonard:* I do not. I am under the assumption she did; yes.
>
> *Davis:* Then you met him and knew him as Alice's brother-in-law, the husband of Emily, her oldest sister?
>
> *Leonard:* Yes.
>
> *Davis:* Yes. So in 1921 you knew that Emily had married a colored man?
>
> *Leonard:* I did.
>
> *Davis:* Now, did you swear to this in the bill of particulars: "First of all, that the statements were made by Alice as to her color between May, 1924, and October of 1924"?
>
> *Leonard:* Around there, yes.
>
> *Davis:* You swore in your bill of particulars that the false statements were made between those times, didn't you?
>
> *Leonard:* Yes.
>
> *Davis:* Now, didn't you give as a reason for making the inquiry [about her race] this: "Plaintiff had become informed of the fact that Emily, a sister of the defendant, had married a colored man and was residing with him as his wife in said city of New Rochelle or its immediate neighborhood, and this fact led him in some way to introduce the question of color"? You swore to that, didn't you?
>
> *Leonard:* Yes. . . .
>
> *Davis:* You swore that you learned that she had married a colored man, and that is the reason you made the inquiry as to her blood. You say that, don't you?

Leonard: I did not make the inquiry.

Davis: No, but you say there that the reason for your making the inquiry was that you learned that Emily had married a colored man.

Leonard: Yes.

Davis: Now, that isn't true, is it? You learned that away back in 1921, didn't you?

Leonard: Yes.

Davis: So that that statement there is untrue?

Leonard: Yes, it is.

Davis: That is four untruths that you swore to in that bill of particulars, is it not? We have pointed them out to you?

Leonard: Yes.

Davis: On vital matters?

(There was no answer.)

Davis: On vital matters, Mr. Rhinelander. That is so.

Leonard: Yes.

Davis: And you followed the advice of Mr. Jacobs [your father's attorney] in swearing to those falsehoods?

Leonard: I did, yes.[27]

Leonard also admitted that he had repeatedly engaged in sexual intercourse with Alice in her parents' house. In the end, Leonard's many lies to Alice's parents—lies that had been exposed by Davis on cross-examination—helped to make it even more difficult for the jury to accept his claims of fraud by Alice, especially in light of consistent, contradicting testimony by the members of the Jones family.

Davis's biggest ploy at trial was his use of Alice, herself, as an exhibit at trial. In support of his claim that Leonard knew of Alice's race because he saw her naked body during previous sexual relations with her, Davis offered what he viewed as the strongest evidence of Leonard's knowledge of her race: her bare body. Before doing so, he questioned Leonard as to his eyesight:

Davis: How is your eyesight? Are you colorblind?

Leonard: I am not, no. . . .

Davis: You can distinguish black from white?

Leonard: Yes.

Davis: Brown from white?

Leonard: Yes.[28]

He also questioned Leonard endlessly about previous times at which he had been able to see Alice in the nude. For example, in one instance, Davis engaged in the following exchange with Leonard:

> *Davis:* Well, were [all of her clothes] taken off?
> *Leonard:* Yes.
> *Davis:* And you saw her in the daylight—her entire body?
> *Leonard:* Not in the daylight.
> *Davis:* In the electric light, then?
> *Leonard:* Yes. . . .
> *Davis:* Well, under the electric light you could see her entire body clearly?
> *Leonard:* Yes.
> *Davis:* And you saw its color?
> *Leonard:* Yes.
> *Davis:* You bathed her?
> *Leonard:* Yes.
> *Davis:* In the bathtub?
> *Leonard:* Yes.
> *Davis:* Without any clothes on?
> *Leonard:* Yes.
> *Davis:* And you did the bathing?
> *Leonard:* Yes.
> *Davis:* Bathed her entire body?
> *Leonard:* Yes.
> *Davis:* And you came in close proximity to it and its color?
> *Leonard:* Yes.
> *Davis:* No suspicions crept in your mind then?
> *Leonard:* No.[29]

In the end, Davis brought Alice in to allow Leonard to identify the color of her skin. Davis put Alice on display for Leonard and the jury in the justice's chambers outside of the courtroom. One can only wonder what thoughts were in the two lovers' heads at that moment. Did Alice despise Leonard at the moment? Did Leonard even try to look Alice in the eye? Did Leonard himself shed one tear or exhibit any emotion? Little is known of this key moment during the trial.

The *New York Times* reported that Alice "was crying as she was led to the room and crying as she left it."[30] The court record described the spectacle in the following manner:

The Court, Mr. Mills, Mr. Davis, Mr. Swinburne, the jury, the plaintiff, the defendant, her mother, Mrs. George Jones, and the stenographer left the courtroom and entered the jury room. The defendant and Mrs. Jones then withdrew to the lavatory adjoining the jury room and, after a short time, again entered the jury room. The defendant, who was weeping, had on her underwear and a long coat. At Mr. Davis' direction she let down the coat, so that the upper portion of her body, as far down as her breast, was exposed. She then, again at Mr. Davis['] direction, covered the upper part of her body and showed to the jury her bare legs, up as far as the knees. The Court, counsel, the jury and the plaintiff then re-entered the court room.[31]

Once back in the courtroom, Davis asked Leonard if he had seen all of the parts of Alice's body during this "exhibit" in chambers. Leonard replied that he had seen everything but her "legs" because his view was somewhat obstructed. Davis then asked only one more question: "Your wife's body is the same shade as it was when you saw her in the Marie Antoinette with all of her clothing removed?" Leonard responded, "Yes." And, as though Alice's body spoke for itself on the issue of race, Davis then ended, "That is all."[32]

This scene of Alice, presented as evidence to the jurors, would shock the public that read newspaper stories about it. Even without seeing it, the image of such an event stands out in the midst of this already sensational trial. Davis himself would be affected by the incident, having to change his plan to call Alice as a witness the next day. After having to reveal parts of her body to the jury at trial, Alice, the public was told, suffered a breakdown that rendered her unable to testify as scheduled.

Nearly twenty-five years later, Alice's humiliating feature at trial would be brought to life by movie producers in the 1959 film *Night of the Quarter Moon*, which "depicted a light-skinned black woman removing her clothes in a courtroom scene in order to prove that her white husband knew that she was 'dark' all over and not just tan on her face before their marriage" (see fig. 3.2).[33] Even today, the mere thought of Alice revealing her body before the jury leaves readers speechless.

In addition to selling a notion of race as clear and visible to all but the blind, Davis displayed his complex understanding of race as being defined by not just what one looks like but also by what one does. In other words, Davis revealed at trial his understanding that race was as much about non-

Fig. 3.2. This poster for *Night of the Quarter Moon* includes a quote from the leading man, modeled after Leonard, who proclaims, "I don't care *what* she is . . . she's mine!" MGM/Albert Zugsmith Productions

physical markers of racial identity, such as performance, language, grammar, tone, and the use of colored doctors, as it was about skin color. In so doing, Davis offered other evidence that he viewed as belonging to colored people. For example, Davis questioned Leonard about Alice's use of a purported "negro expression." The exchange went:

> *Davis:* Did you ever hear anybody say "I am going on a strutting party"?
> *Leonard:* Yes.
> *Davis:* Hear Alice say it?
> *Leonard:* I believe so, yes. . . .
> *Davis:* You never suspected that she had any colored blood when you heard her use that expression?
> *Leonard:* I did not. . . .
> *Davis:* Combined with her appearance?
> *Leonard:* No. . . .
> *Davis:* Did you recognize that as being a typically negro expression, strutting party?
> *Leonard:* No. I can't say that. . . .
> *Davis:* A person with clear white skin might use this term "strutting party" without exciting any suspicion as to her color. That is so?
> *Leonard:* Yes.[34]

Along the same lines, Davis often highlighted Alice's poor spelling and grammar in her letters, in part to emphasize her race and in part to stress her social class. For example, at one instance, Davis pointed out Alice's frequent misspellings of the phrase "have to," which Alice spelled as "after." On another occasion, he identified the way in which she misspelled "here," meaning "at this place," as "hear" and the word "know," meaning "to be acquainted with" as "no." At yet another time, Davis highlighted Alice's misuse of the word "worst" as "waste."

Additionally, Davis presented, through the testimony of Dr. Caesar McClendon, a colored doctor, evidence that Alice saw him when she was sick. Such an act was critical for signaling her race because, in 1920s New York, seeing a colored doctor was an act reserved only for colored people. No "respectable" white person received treatment from a colored doctor.

Finally, countering Mills's presentation of witnesses who claimed to have heard Alice misrepresent her racial background, Davis offered testimony from witnesses who asserted that Leonard had informed them that he knew that Alice was not of pure white blood and that he loved her in spite of her racial ancestry. For example, Davis brought Barbara Reynolds, a reporter for the *Standard News Association of New York City* and the *Standard Star* of New Rochelle, to the witness stand. Reynolds testified to interviewing Leonard on November 13, 1924, the very day the story of Alice and Leonard's marriage became public. Reynolds claimed that Leonard admitted to her that he was married to a colored woman and that he had not informed his father of the marriage because he knew that his father would be displeased. The colloquy between Reynolds and Davis at trial—a colloquy that would later prove to be very useful to the jurors—proceeded in relevant part as follows:

> *Davis:* I will not ask you your age. Women do not like to be asked that question. In 1924, Mrs. Reynolds, what was your occupation?
> *Reynolds:* Reporter.
> *Davis:* Reporter for what paper?
> *Reynolds:* The Standard News Association of New York City and the Standard Star of New Rochelle.
> *Davis:* Now, do you know the plaintiff in this action, Leonard Rhinelander?
> *Reynolds:* I know him to see him.
> *Davis:* Do you recall when you first saw him, Mrs. Reynolds?
> *Reynolds:* November 13, 1924. . . .
> *Davis:* Where did you see him?
> *Reynolds:* I saw him in the Jones residence.
> *Davis:* At the Jones residence. Outside or inside?
> *Reynolds:* Outside.
> *Davis:* And under what circumstances did you see him?
> *Reynolds:* I went there to get an interview from him. . . .
> *Davis:* I think the jury will be glad to have you just tell in your own way what you said to him and what he said to you.
> *Reynolds:* Why, I waited for Mr. Rhinelander. He was not at the Jones residence and of course, not knowing the man, I hung around on Pelham Road waiting for a car. It came along and I rushed up behind him, not knowing whether it was he or not, and I said, "Mr. Rhinelander" and he turned around and said, "Yes." I knew he was my man and so I immediately went to interview him. The first question I fired at him was "Is it

true, Mr. Rhinelander, that you are married to the daughter of a colored man"? He said after great effort, "Yes, I am."

Davis: What next was said[?]

Reynolds: . . . I asked him if his people knew that he was married. He said his mother was not alive. I said, your father? He said, yes. I said, "Does your father know that you are married"? And he said "No." I said, "Would it make any difference if he did know?" He said, "Oh, yes, it would mean my wife's happiness and mine." Then I asked him "Are you going to tell your father"? He said, "No." Then he asked me who I was and I told him. I said, "Didn't you realize when you married Miss Jones that the outcome would be quite a bit of publicity"? He said, "No" he would like to avoid that, if possible, and asked me if there was any way that he could do so. I then said it was too late and presented him the afternoon edition with the story of his marriage in the paper.[35]

Likewise, Ross Chidester, a chauffeur for Philip Rhinelander, testified to the following exchange with Leonard in which Chidester claimed to have specifically questioned Leonard about Alice's race:

Mills: And what, if anything, did [Leonard] say about that clock to you?

Chidester: He said, "Ross, here I want to show you a Christmas present I bought for Alice." . . .

Mills: Now, what did you say to Leonard Rhinelander when he told you he was going to give that Christmas present to Alice?

Chidester: I said, "Do you mean to tell me you bought her a Christmas present? . . . Don't you know her father is a colored man?"

Mills: What did he reply?

Chidester: He said, "I don't give a damn if she is."[36]

Alice's relatives also offered confirming testimony about Leonard's alleged lack of concern over Alice's race. For example, Alice's mother, Elizabeth Jones, testified that, after the story of the marriage broke, Leonard told Alice not to worry, as "he had married the girl he wanted and he did not care for anybody."[37] Furthermore, contrary to Leonard's claims, several relatives of Alice declared that Leonard had never discussed Alice's race in their presence.

In addition to offering evidence of alleged explicit admissions of knowledge about Alice's racial background, Davis highlighted what he regarded

Fig. 3.3. Robert Brooks, the husband of Alice's sister, Emily, stands as evidence of Leonard's knowledge about Alice's true racial background. © Bettmann/Corbis

as implicit admissions of such knowledge. Specifically, Davis emphasized, through his examination of Leonard and Robert and Emily Brooks, Leonard's willingness to cross racial boundaries by socially interacting on friendly terms with Alice's clearly colored brother-in-law and niece, Robert and Roberta Brooks, respectively (see fig. 3.3). For example, with respect to his relationship with Robert Brooks, Davis first had the following exchange with Leonard:

> *Davis:* You didn't want to marry into a colored family?
> *Leonard:* I did not; no.
> *Davis:* You didn't want to associate with those of colored blood?
> *Leonard:* No. . . .
> *Davis:* You did not want to be on terms of intimacy with colored people?
> *Leonard:* No.[38]

Then Davis questioned Leonard about two postcards that he had sent to Robert and Emily Brooks. The first one read: "Dear Emily and Robert, Motored around Cape Cod today and am now spending the night in Plymouth. . . . Love to Roberta. As ever, Leonard."[39] In the second postcard, Leonard began with an even less formal greeting, leading with "Dear Em and Bob" (see fig.

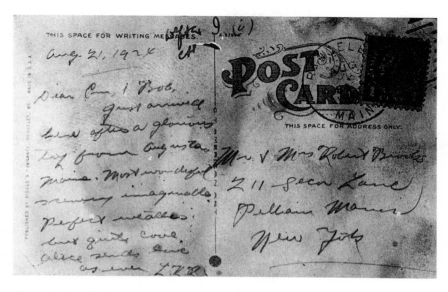

Fig. 3.4. Leonard refers to Robert and Emily Brooks as "Em" and "Bob" in a postcard, which were nicknames considered to be too affectionate for a white man, especially one of Leonard's stature, to use toward a black man and a black woman during the 1920s. © Bettmann/Corbis

3.4).[40] Davis used this postcard to continue to highlight how Leonard had crossed clearly drawn racial lines. The exchange went as follows:

Davis: And you addressed the colored man, Mr. Brooks, as Bob. Is that right?
Leonard: Yes.
Davis: That is terms of intimacy, isn't it?
Leonard: Yes.[41]

The testimony of Robert Brooks confirmed Leonard's cross-examination testimony. Brooks, who came across as an honest and sincere witness— even by Mills's own admission—testified that Alice had introduced him to Leonard as her brother-in-law in 1921, that Leonard never objected to his race but instead sat and ate dinner and drank tea with him at the same table on a number of occasions, that he and his wife Emily regularly drove Leonard down to the train station after visits with Alice at the Jones family home, that Leonard played with his daughter Roberta, and that he and Leonard referred to each other as "Leonard" or "Bob."

In all, through Leonard's cross-examination and the presentation of defense witnesses such as Robert Brooks, Davis hoped to demonstrate that
Leonard's willingness to cross readily established social boundaries of race,
even if it did not directly show that Leonard knew Alice's race before the
marriage, surely hinted that he did not care about her race and would have
married her in any event. Indeed, the expectation for a white man to distance himself from colored people was so high in 1920s New York that
Davis even grilled Leonard about his relationship with the daughter of the
Brookses, Roberta.

> *Davis:* Now, in one of those postals, being Exhibit H, you sent "Love to
>   Roberta"?
> *Leonard:* Yes.
> *Davis:* Roberta is a sweet little colored girl, isn't she?
> *Leonard:* Yes. . . .
> *Davis:* Weren't you very nice to little Roberta in 1921 when you saw her about
>   in the house [of the Jones family]? She was about three years old then,
>   wasn't she?
> *Leonard:* I believe I was; yes.[42]

These questions by Davis imply that, in 1920s New York, friendliness by
a white man even to a colored child was seen as crossing an established
social boundary of race. Ultimately, the desired conclusion was that if Leonard would cross these clear racial lines he must have knowingly done so
when he married Alice.

Furthermore, underlying all of Davis's arguments was the suggestion
that Leonard was not acting like the gentleman he was raised to be with all
of his wealth and privilege. For example, Davis stunned the courtroom with
several readings of letters from Leonard to Alice. In fact, the letters were so
racy that Justice Joseph Morschauser had all young people removed from
the room. The Justice also suggested to adult women that they should leave
the room, stating, "I want to give every woman a chance to leave this courtroom. If I were a woman I would not want to stay in this room and hear
these letters."[43] While some women left, others remained behind, taking
the seats of the women who departed the standing-room only court venue.

Among the letters from Leonard that Davis read was one particularly graphic letter that Leonard claimed to have written at a time when he had no intentions of marrying Alice, a woman he purportedly believed to be white: "Oh, Sweetheart, many, many nights, when I lay in bed and think about my darling girl, it [his private organ] acts the very same way and longs for your warm body to crawl upon me, take it in your soft, smooth hands, and then work it up very slowly between your open legs."[44] A similarly explicit letter read as follows:

> Do you ever long for my lips? Yes, love, my warm lips and tongue, which have often made you very, very happy. You said you liked my ways, didn't you dear? Well, sweetheart, I just love your little ways, too. They are all so gentle and have a manner all their own. Do you remember, honeybunch, · how I used to put my head between your legs and how I used to caress you with my lips and tongue? You loved to have me do that, didn't you, old scout? Can't you feel me, darling, as I am talking to you, trying to recall past days when we were in bed together? Oh! I often think when I used to lift up your nightgown and crawl down to the foot of the bed, so as I could be right under you. "Please, dear, *come.*" Do you recall how I asked you to do that[?] Oh! blessed child, when my lips and tongue were making you so happy you used to say to me, "Oh, Len, Oh! Len." You were in heaven, dear, because your old faithful, true boy was with you.[45]

With each letter, Davis chastised Leonard for writing such smut to excite a woman, a woman whom the young Rhinelander did not intend to honor with marriage. Such behavior was not fitting for a man with the Rhinelander name, and more so, not befitting him if he truly believed his then-girlfriend to be white.

Finally, Davis worked to convince the jury that Leonard continued to cohabit freely with Alice after learning of her race. During his cross-examination, Leonard replied that he had continued to sleep in the same bed and engage in sexual intercourse with Alice from November 13 to November 20, 1924, when his suspicions about her "color" finally arose. As Davis would highlight, this meant that, for a full week after the allegations of Alice's being colored appeared in the news, Leonard remained in the home with Alice, never once trying to leave or even investigate the newspaper stories.

At the end of the trial, two voices were missing from the event. The first was Alice's, and the second was that of her father, George Jones. Davis explained their absence as witnesses as a desire not to drag Alice through any more filth after her private letters and her body had been exposed and as his having no need for the testimony of the father. But, these two excluded witnesses at the trial left room for the jury, and even us many years later, to wonder why Alice never testified on her own behalf. Or more so, it left us wondering to what extent Alice had a voice at all in the strategy employed in her defense and ultimately the course of her life after the trial.

4

A Verdict against the Heart

TOWARD THE END OF THE TRIAL, LEONARD successfully fought to add to his Complaint an allegation that Alice had defrauded him by remaining silent about her racial background when she had a duty to inform him of it before the marriage. This amendment by Leonard marked the second time that he had modified his Complaint since filing his lawsuit. Prior to this amendment, Leonard had alleged only that Alice explicitly had misrepresented her race to him.

On December 2, 1925, Leonard served this Second Amended Complaint on Alice, and on December 3, 1925, Alice responded with an Amended Answer that admitted that she was of colored blood. Alice also asserted that Leonard cohabited with her despite knowledge of her racial background. Both parties then prepared for closing arguments and the jury's verdict.

In this chapter, I complete my description of the *Rhinelander* trial by detailing the parties' closing arguments. In so doing, I begin to connect the bridge between Part I and Part II of *According to Our Hearts* by engaging in an analysis of the surprising verdict in favor of Alice as well as the public's reaction to the verdict. Specifically, I highlight how the jury's verdict for Alice was paradoxically both a racial victory and a loss for racial equality.

The outcome of the trial raises two major questions. First, was Alice limited from the very beginning in the strategic choices that were available to her to defend herself against Leonard's claims? Although Alice's strategy of conceding race ultimately proved successful at trial, we know now that she spent the rest of her life pining for Leonard, her one true love, because she identified herself as "Alice J. Rhinelander" on her gravestone in 1989. If Alice's true desire was to be with Leonard as his wife and proving her whiteness was the only way to fulfill this desire, why, then, did her legal team decide not to litigate her whiteness? Second, why did the jury vote in Alice's favor? Or, rather, what, apart from strong evidence at trial, made it possible for the jurors to decide in her favor during 1920s New York?

Given commonly held racial prejudices against blacks in 1920s New York, one would have expected Leonard to win, regardless of what the evidence indicated. As Professors Lewis and Ardizzone explained, "Few had believed a white jury capable of such an unbiased finding."[1] As Lewis and Ardizzone noted, there was a "reported 5 to 1 betting odds among townsmen and spectators that Rhinelander would win an annulment."[2] In fact, even after the jury announced its verdict for Alice, people expressed disappointment with the decision. For example, the wife of a juror named Fred Sanford expressed her disapproval of the verdict, asserting, "Leonard Rhinelander should have been granted annulment. . . . It isn't right for a man of his standing to be tied to a girl with colored blood."[3] Moreover, as we know from the title of this book, one juror admitted that the verdict in Alice's favor was not "according to their hearts." As this juror Henry Weil explained to the public after the trial, "If we had voted according to our hearts the verdict might have been different."[4] In other words, if they had followed their hearts, Leonard would have won instead. Considering such widely held sentiments, what were the social and legal forces that enabled the jury to reach its difficult decision to deny Leonard's request for an annulment?

Alice Rhinelander's Closing Statement

Lee Parsons Davis, Alice's attorney, delivered his summation to the jury first. He began by reminding the jurors about the importance of their work and pleading with them to put aside their "race hatred."[5] He asserted: "Do you realize as you sit there that you, and each one of you, constitute the foundation, literally speaking, the foundation upon which our present form of government rests[?] By your verdict in one case you could tear out

Fig. 4.1. Philip Rhinelander poses with his military medals. © Bettmann/Corbis

a portion of that foundation and set a precedent for others to follow. . . . [I]n this case you are the only tribunal that can say to this young girl 'You are a fraud.' . . . And speaking frankly, if there is any man in this jury box . . . that has any feeling of race hatred in his veins, applicable to this case, you cannot be fair unless you cast it aside. . . . Let us try this case on evidence and not on sympathy or feelings of passion."[6] Davis then reiterated his arguments from trial. He first pointed, again, to Philip Rhinelander and attorney Leon Jacobs as the brains behind the operation, blaming them for the annulment lawsuit (see figs. 4.1 and 4.2). Davis also repeated his arguments about how members of the Jones family clearly did not deceive or intend to deceive Leonard about their respective races. After all, George and Elizabeth Jones did not try to hide the truth about their races when they entered the country or when each of their daughters was born.

Thereafter, Davis restated his assertion that, contrary to what Leonard's attorney, Isaac Mills, claimed, Leonard was not "mentally backward" because of a childhood stuttering problem. Davis argued that the way in which Leonard repeatedly corrected Davis's misquotations from the witness stand, "which, [Davis] confess[ed] . . . [he] made deliberately," demonstrated that Leonard was in fact mentally sound and sharp.[7] Indeed, Davis contended that, despite Alice's older age, Leonard was not outmatched by her maturity, as all of the privileges afforded to the young Rhinelander through education and travel counteracted any age disparities. As Davis explained, it was Leonard who deceived both Alice and her parents during

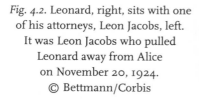

Fig. 4.2. Leonard, right, sits with one of his attorneys, Leon Jacobs, left. It was Leon Jacobs who pulled Leonard away from Alice on November 20, 1924. © Bettmann/Corbis

their courtship. It was Leonard who knew about immoral matters such as drinking prior to meeting Alice. It was Leonard who was running around with a cheating married man like Carl Kreitler. It was Leonard who was tempting Alice with naughty suggestions in his correspondence with her. It was Leonard who took Alice, a woman he supposedly believed to be white, to the Hotel Marie Antoinette with no intention of marriage. And, it was Leonard who then allowed Alice's private letters to be read aloud at trial.

After establishing Leonard as the more calculating of the two lovers, Davis began to slowly chip away at the arguments and evidence presented by Mills through his witnesses on direct examination. First, Davis explained away Alice's many pleas to Leonard for marriage in her letters by asserting that Alice made such requests because "she, a household maid, not having had the benefits of education such as [Leonard] had, was being held up to scorn and ridicule" by her friends, friends who questioned Leonard's motives and believed that he was just taking advantage of her.[8] Likewise, Davis reasoned that Alice's references to her many other suitors were just part of the "funny way [that girls have] . . . of trying to make the chap they love jealous."[9] In other words, it was only natural that Alice would respond that way to Leonard and that she would not fully trust a man who had slept with her over extended periods on two occasions, but then left her alone for two years.

More important than his establishment of Alice as a regular girl with no ulterior motive, Davis repeatedly made references to the notion of morphological race in his summation. For example, Davis told the jury that it should not conclude that Alice misrepresented or concealed her ancestry "[b]ecause [Leonard] is not colorblind and he had unlimited opportunities to look [referring to their sexual encounters]; unlimited."[10] Likewise, Davis pointed out that Leonard had seen Alice's entire body at the Hotel Marie Antoinette, and Davis proclaimed the obviousness of Alice's race based on skin tone. Referring to his use of Alice's breasts, shoulders, and legs as physical exhibits, Davis said to the jury: "I let you gentleman look at a portion of what he saw. You saw Alice's back above the bust. You saw her breast. You saw a portion of her upper leg. He [Leonard] saw all of her body. And you are going to tell me that he never suspected that she had colored blood! That is what he testifies to. You saw [her body] with your own eyes. A boy of twelve would have known that colored blood was coursing through her veins."[11] If that was not enough, Davis contended that Leonard saw her family, many of whom were even more clearly colored than Alice.

Finally, to establish Alice as a sympathetic figure and, more so, to paint Leonard as a man unworthy of any sympathy, Davis highlighted Leonard's consistent failures to meet the expected roles of a wealthy, white gentleman. Davis exposed, over and over again, Leonard's pattern of resisting social norms around race. For instance, Davis stated these words during his closing: "One who has come down through a long family and has been surrounded by everything that is refined, has been surrounded by everything that is in comfort, has been surrounded by wealth, has less excuse than a boy who is born in a hovel and has not a long family name behind him. So much for the Huguenots."[12] It was the Rhinelanders, Davis insisted, who were acting poorly—who would "tear everything to pieces that confronts them."[13] With his final words, Davis pleaded to the jury not to impose any more wrongs upon Alice than the Rhinelanders had already done. He asked the jury to not further damage Alice's name and reputation by labeling her a fraud when she had been nothing but honest and good to Leonard. Davis proclaimed: "The Rhinelanders have torn the Jones home down over their heads. They have wrecked everybody in sight. They have thrown this girl into the sewer and the slime, and she has only one thing left—one—to be saved from the charge of being a defrauder. . . . Please bring in a verdict that is based on the evidence, uninterfered with by prejudice, and give this girl—and I don't care what her color is—give her clearance of this charge of fraud."[14]

Most of all, Davis asked the jury not to bend to any racial prejudices.

In so doing, he stressed that a verdict for Alice did not mean a continued marriage or relationship for the Rhinelanders. By all means, Davis wanted to avoid a situation where the jury would find for Leonard out of pure sympathy or out of fear that a ruling in Alice's favor would mean that the two lovers would have to continue to be together as husband and wife. Davis explained to the jury: "Don't go out into your jury room and say 'Here. We won't tie this young man up with one with colored blood.' You are not being asked that question. Remember it. And remember, when you retire to your jury room, that what has happened in this courtroom has destroyed any possibility of their ever living again together."[15]

Leonard Rhinelander's Closing Statement

Mills followed Davis in delivering his closing statement. At the beginning of his summation, Mills noted that he joined Davis in the "American sentiment" that "there should be no race prejudice."[16] Nevertheless, Mills repeatedly tried to invoke the racial fears of the jury throughout his closing statement. Mills stressed that he viewed the trial "as a case of life and death," declaring, "You might as well, gentlemen of this jury, bury that young man six feet deep in the soil of the old churchyard . . . as to consign him to be forever chained to that woman."[17] Afterward, Mills made a racial plea to the jurors, declaring: "There isn't a father among you—and you remember I sought to get fathers—there isn't a father among you who would rather not see his son in his casket than to see him wedded to a mulatto woman. This feeling of race does not belong to the whites alone. Decent blacks have the same feeling. . . . There is not a mother among your wives who would not rather see her daughter with her white hands crossed above her shroud than to see her locked in the embraces of a mulatto husband. And everyone [sic] of you gentlemen knows that in this respect I speak unto you the words of truth and soberness."[18]

Then, Mills continued with his trial argument that the older and more sexually mature Alice had simply outwitted and tricked Leonard into marriage. Mills proclaimed, "Women of that race are mothers at fifteen. Women of that race mature earlier, gain such beauty as they may have, earlier."[19] Mills also reiterated his arguments about Alice's plan to capture Leonard by comparing their letters with one another and arguing that Alice's letters were more sexually aggressive. Mills wanted to show that Alice, not Leonard, was the seducer. In so doing, Mills highlighted how Alice frequently referred to the couple's stays at the Hotel Marie Antoinette in her letters and how she often mentioned other suitors in her papers to trick Leonard into her plan. Explaining away Leonard's admission at trial of pursuing Alice, Mills stated, "Mr. Davis says he was the aggressor, and the poor fellow thought he was. Of course, that was her high art, the man following the woman."[20] Overall, Mills argued that Alice "had him [Leonard] so . . . that he did not know black from white, that he did not have control of himself. . . . The woman had made her conquest. He lay at her feet, her captive. Her will was his law. He was her slave. . . . She owned him body and soul."[21] As Mills explained to the jury, Leonard was so enslaved by her that he forgot their stations in life. Mills noted with horror: "The descendant of the Rhinelanders was so stricken down, so hurt by the news she had written [about not being with him], that he thought she might think he was not good enough for her!"[22]

Furthermore, Mills contended that this action was not the plan of Alice alone, but also her mother. According to Mills, Elizabeth Jones instilled in Alice and Grace a "vaulting ambition" to move into the white world for a better life, as demonstrated by the white church and Sunday school that the Joneses attended, the white friends of the family, and the decision by Grace and Alice to marry white men.[23]

Lastly, Mills harped on Alice's ability to pass as white as well as the performances she needed to engage in to pass as white, highlighting all of those whom Alice had allegedly fooled. This list included the clerk at the Hotel Marie Antoinette, because Alice "could not have been at the [respectable] hotel if she had not appeared to be white."[24] The list included the clerk at the City Court who listed Alice as white on her marriage license. The list also included Miriam and Joseph Rich, the ambitious couple who worked to befriend the newlywed Rhinelanders. And, it included the clerks at the numerous hotels that Alice and Leonard stayed in during a trip throughout New England. Mills asked the jury: "Now are you going to blame Leonard Kip Rhinelander, who was befuddled with her, in love with her, who wrote that letter from the very depths of his soul, are you going to blame him for taking her as white when all these unbefuddled, independent witnesses, took her for white?"[25] In fact, pointing to the original Answer in which Alice denied that she was of colored blood, Mills also claimed that both Davis and another one of Alice's attorneys, Judge Samuel Swinburne, had been fooled by Alice.

Thereafter, to emphasize how easily Alice could be mistaken for a white woman, Mills referred to the physical features of Alice and her father, noting their white features—a somewhat odd tactic given that Alice's mother, Elizabeth Jones, was, to all spectators, unquestionably white. He first began with George Jones by stating: "Consider his [George Jones's] face. What I say in regard to his face is that every feature of his face is distinctly caucasian except the color. I say if by some miracle you could change the color of his skin as he sits there he would pass anywhere for a white man. Let us see. He has got the nose of a white man. His nose is far more aquiline than mine. He has got the same nostrils as a white man; thinner than mine. He has got the high cheek bones which do not belong to the African race. He has got a narrow face. He has got the long face, not the round face of colored blood."[26] Mills then moved on to Alice, noting what he identified as Caucasian features and stressing her color. He said: "To look at her she inherits from her father. She has got the same features largely that the father has. Long face. Aquiline nose. The other features of the Caucasian. Her lips are not different from the father's lips. The father's lips are as thin as my lips. That is her facial appearance. You have seen her color. You see it now. You see her face. You see her neck; her hands. . . . [H]er appearance by herself would not condemn her anywhere as being of colored blood."[27] In this sense, Mills, too, played on biological notions of race, but instead of confirming them, he demonstrated the fluidity of race, a much more difficult notion for white jurors to swallow during the 1920s. In the end, Mills worked to invoke white people's fears of racial passers, stating: "Your verdict, gentlemen, shall answer once more that ancient question put in Holy Writ: 'Can the Ethiopian change his skin?' This mother, in her love for her girls, from her ambition . . . entered upon that problem. It cannot be done. Your answer, gentlemen, to that ancient question, by your verdict, must be in the negative—'No, it cannot be done.'"[28] For Mills, there was only one person who needed to be punished for her deceptive actions and that person was Alice, the racial trespasser.

From the Charge to the Jury to Life after the Verdict

At the end of the trial, Justice Morschauser charged the jury to consider seven issues. The charge came on the heels of excitement and commotion from the day before. Although George Jones had remained calm throughout the month-long trial, even upon hearing Leonard's letters to Alice, he broke out in an angry outburst when Mills referred to him as "this negro hack driver" during Mills's closing statement. At that moment, the pressures of the trial had finally built up inside of George Jones. He "jumped at the amiable Judge Mills, who gazed blandly at him with astonishment," and as the *New York Times* reported, "[u]nintelligible words sputtered from" George. Eventually, Alice's attorney, Davis, was able to quiet George, who said, "I won't have that. . . . He shouldn't say that—I had a license."[29] In the end, Justice Morschauser identified these seven questions for the jury to consider.

1. At the time of the marriage of the parties, was the defendant colored and of colored blood?
2. Did the defendant before the marriage by silence conceal from the plaintiff the fact that she was of colored blood?
3. Did the defendant before the marriage represent to the plaintiff that she was not of colored blood?
4. Did the defendant practice said concealment or make said representation with the intent thereby to induce the plaintiff to marry her?
5. Was the plaintiff by said concealment or by said representation, or by both, induced to marry the defendant?
6. If the plaintiff had known that the defendant was of colored blood, would he have married her?
7. Did the plaintiff cohabit with defendant after he obtained full knowledge that the defendant was of colored blood?[30]

With respect to question 1, Justice Morschauser directed the jury to answer it in the affirmative because it was conceded: Alice was of colored blood. During the requests to the charge of the court, Justice Morschauser also provided his definition of "colored," stating, "'Colored blood' really means, when you get to it, that her skin is colored."[31] In so doing, Justice

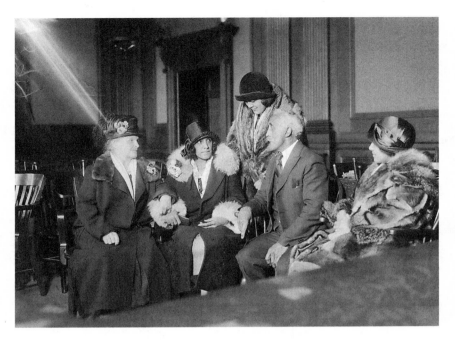

Fig. 4.3. Alice, seated center, is flanked by her parents, George and Elizabeth Jones, and surrounded by her sister Grace, standing behind her, and her sister Emily, seated to the right of George Jones. The family awaits the jury's verdict.
© Bettmann/Corbis

Morschauser implicitly validated the view of biological, visible, and obvious race that Davis had developed during the trial.

The jury deliberated only on the remaining six questions (see fig. 4.3). The jury consisted of the following men: (1) Clarence R. Pietsch, merchant, Greenburgh, foreman; (2) Michael Plunkett, clerk, White Plains; (3) Henry V. Weil, art dealer, Greenburgh; (4) Frederick Sanford, heating, Yonkers; (5) William J. Demarest, real estate, Rye; (6) Max Mendel, exporter, Mount Vernon; (7) Harry J. Shaw, broker, Greenburgh; (8) Simeon Brady, retired, Somers; (9) John D. Markel, builder, Mount Pleasant; (10) James Horton, superintendent, Cortlandt; (11) William J. Humphrey, architect, Scarsdale; and (12) Joseph M. Doyle, contractor, Rye.[32]

During deliberations, the jury asked for a reading of "the testimony of Mr. Rhinelander in reference to Barbara Reynolds's testimony" that Leonard admitted to being "married to the daughter of a colored man" and asked her if there was any way that he could avoid having his father find out. No such testimony, however, was ever provided to the jury during its deliberations because both Mills and Davis agreed "that while Mrs. Reynolds made the statement [about Leonard's not caring about Alice's race, Leonard] did not deny it."[33] A newspaper report would later reveal the importance of this jury request. During cross-examination, Mills had tried to weaken Reynolds's testimony by making her reveal that no one else heard or witnessed her reported admissions from Leonard and that all other newspapers at the time reported denials by Alice and Leonard of Alice's status as a colored person, but his attempts apparently were unsuccessful. Jury foreman Clarence Pietsch later made the following statement about the importance of Barbara Reynolds's testimony to the verdict: "We very early made up our minds as to how the case should be decided. . . . We took up the questions one at a time, and the number of the questions delayed us somewhat. The only question which gave us trouble, however, was the sixth, as to whether he would have married her if he had known that she was colored. That was the reason we came in and asked for the testimony of Barbara Reynolds and Rhinelander's reply on that point."[34]

On December 5, 1925, after twelve hours of deliberation, the jury returned a verdict in favor of Alice. The jury answered "yes" to questions 1 and 6 and "no" to questions 2 through 5. The jury followed Justice Morschauser's orders to leave question seven blank if they answered in Alice's favor on the first six. "From the very first ballot it was said that the jury had stood 10 to 2 in favor of" Alice.[35] Though the jury verdict turned out to be different from what most expected at the very outset of the case, by the time of the verdict, even the attorneys for both parties expected a win for Alice. As the *New York Times* reported on December 6, 1925, "somehow word of [the verdict] had been flashed around White Plains during the night."[36] In fact, as early as November 27, 1925—more than a full week earlier, "[t]here was said to have been much talk of the certainty of a victory for Mrs. Rhinelander in the trial."[37]

On the day that the verdict was announced, Leonard remained in his room at the Hotel Gramatan in Bronxville, New York, avoiding the loss he knew was coming. However, Leonard did not exhibit a strong reaction to the jury's verdict when he learned of it. The *New York Times* reported that he "took the decision as calmly as he told his unpleasant story on the stand."[38] Although Leonard showed little emotion both during and after trial, the trial was said to have taken a significant toll on him. Even his chief attorney, Mills, declared so. Just a week before the jury's verdict was announced, Mills said: "The strain [of the case] is telling on my client, and he is aging rapidly. Then, too, he is almost broken-hearted over the case and feels most deeply the humiliation he has undergone. If it were not that I know from the official record that my client was only 22 I would take him for a man at least 35."[39]

Unlike Leonard, his attorney, Mills, did not respond as calmly to hearing the news of his trial loss. Though Mills praised Davis for his great skill as a lawyer, he expressed his disappointment with the jury's decision. He declared: "I am not here to give my views as to how the jury was misled . . . but it is obvious that they gave these answers without any intelligent comprehension of the questions. They simply answered them in the manner which they thought would produce the result they desired."[40]

Much like with Leonard, the *New York Times* reported that Alice showed little emotion when the jury announced its verdict. All she did was slightly lower her head. Immediately after the trial, Alice reluctantly granted an interview to journalists. She was described as being "more frightened and nerve-weary than elated over her victory."[41] The *New York Times* noted that Alice's "voice was so low that one had to lean over her to hear what she said, and she often looked out the window, turning her head away, as if about to cry."[42] Speaking about her win at trial, Alice asserted, "Naturally, I am happy over it, but I was not happy over the torture I went through."[43] When one journalist asked Alice if she thought any good would come out of the trial, Davis jumped in for her. He proclaimed that no good could come out of such filth, meaning that no good could come out of the way that Alice and her family had been publicly shamed at trial.

Later, Davis, who told the jury that the verdict was a great personal victory for him, issued the following statement.

> While I still feel that the trial in this case, with the publicity that necessarily followed it, was most unfortunate for the parties involved and the public at large, counsel for the defense are naturally most gratified at the result.

There was but one danger facing the defendant, namely, race prejudice. It is also most gratifying to be reassured that the jurors in Westchester County, at least, can rise above passion and prejudice and decide cases upon the facts and the law.

I have but one single regret and that is that Judge Mills, with his sweetness and graciousness, by force of circumstances, was on the losing end.

Counsel for Mrs. Rhinelander desires to express their keen appreciation of the kindly and courteous treatment accorded them by the Presiding Judge and the able and dignified manner in which he conducted the trial.

Mrs. Rhinelander has of necessity been under a decided strain, and it is her wish and her counsels' desire that she be permitted the opportunity of resting and regaining her strength.[44]

Several of the jurors spoke out after the trial. A number of them echoed Davis's comments about the absence of race prejudice in their determination. For instance, juror William J. Demarest stated: "We want it clearly understood that not for a single instance did race prejudice enter into the consideration of our verdict. That was gratifying to all of us. We considered and discussed the evidence presented in court and the evidence alone. The fact that we had to argue so long was due to discrepancies in our understanding of certain parts of the testimony. Every doubt in our minds was dissolved, however, before we affixed our signatures to the verdict."[45] Such claims against race prejudice were critical, as at least one juror, Fred Sanford, claimed that "several prominent people in Yonkers [including Dr. James Clark Bennett, who was not indicted by a grand jury] had approached him during the trial."[46]

Another juror, Henry V. Weil, demonstrated that there was some sympathy for Leonard, when he declared, "If we had voted according to our hearts the verdict might have been different."[47] In other words, if the jurors had voted according to their hearts, the verdict would have been for Leonard. Such comments raise many questions, including what role the jurors' hearts may have unconsciously played in their verdict. What else was at stake in the case, and how did those factors shape its outcome?

In the end, Leonard made a motion to set aside the verdict for a new trial, but on March 29, 1926, Justice Morschauser denied Leonard's motion to set aside the verdict. On July 19, 1926, the court entered a judgment that dismissed the complaint upon the merits. Thereafter, Leonard filed his appeals. Both the Appellate Division of the State Supreme Court and the New York Courts of Appeals affirmed the trial court judgment.

For both Alice and Leonard, life after trial proved to be very lonely and isolating. The *New York Times* reported that Leonard went into seclusion with his bodyguard Captain Toby Peterson in tow.[48] The young Rhinelander, who still remained cut off from his father's wealth, had spent $50,000 of his own small fortune for both his and Alice's fees in the annulment lawsuit and was predicted to spend $5,000 more on his appeal.[49] Leonard had already lost his standing in elite New York society. For example, before the trial even began, Leonard had been removed from the *New York Social Register*, a marker of membership in one of New York's most elite families. Leonard never quite recaptured the type of existence he had before Alice or, in some ways, even with Alice. He never married again, and he moved away from his family until 1930, when he was finally able to obtain a divorce from Alice. Upon receiving a divorce and thus ensuring that Alice could never access Philip Rhinelander's wealth, Leonard came back to New York where he worked in his father's Manhattan real estate office until he passed away. Leonard died of pneumonia on February 20, 1936, at the young age of 34.[50] He never fell in love again and never remarried. Upon his death, one of Leonard's work colleagues described how he had won over the respect of his associates, proclaiming "'He made one big mistake [by marrying Alice], but he tried to make up for it.'"[51] Alice, too, commented when Leonard died. At that time, Alice was living with her mother, who was widowed, and stated that "news of [Leonard's] death made her 'very, very sad.'"[52] Alice further declared, "'I never loved anybody but Leonard, and I will never love anyone else.'"[53]

Unlike Leonard, Alice lived a very long life—through her eighties. Immediately after the trial, Alice went on a ten-day trip—location unannounced—with her mother Elizabeth Jones. The circus that followed her right after the trial showed such a move to be wise for Alice. On December 7, 1925, just a couple of days after the verdict was announced, a man named Theodore Dorn broke into Alice's sister's house, claiming that he was Leonard Rhinelander, that he was returning to his bride, and that he needed to discuss some letters with Alice. Though Dorn's family committed him to the Hudson River State Hospital for the Insane at Poughkeepsie on December 9, 1925, the post-trial drama did not end for Alice there.[54] On December 14, 1925, men from the local Ku Klux Klan in Florida visited four hotels—the Atlantic, El Paso, Colonial, and Alpena—looking for Alice, who was reported to have arrived in Fort Pierce, Florida, from New York.[55] The Ku Klux Klan members also stood guard at the local railroad station to prevent Alice's entry into the city. Hotel managers in Fort Pierce and West Palm Beach, Florida, announced that they would not allow Alice through their doors. In response, Judge Samuel Swinburne, one of Alice's attorneys, made it clear that Alice "had never contemplated a visit to the South."[56] Finally, in February 1926, New York State Senator J. Griswold Webb announced that he was considering presenting a bill that would not just prevent marriages between blacks and whites but also would make such marriages felonies;[57] Senator Webb's action was said to be inspired, in part, by the Rhinelander marriage.

Still, there were those who seemingly hoped for a happy ending for the Rhinelanders. More than half a year after the trial, rumors spread that suggested continued meetings between Alice and Leonard in Europe. Indeed, Alice had to denounce such rumors before one trip that she took with her mother on the White Star Liner *Majestic* to England. Alice declared, "I'm going to meet my mother's people in England. . . . I am not going to meet my husband, who is in Paris. As far as reconciliation is concerned, you can see my lawyer about that. I have nothing to say except that there's nothing to it."[58]

In the end, Alice survived throughout her life on her $31,500 settlement—the equivalent of $400,000 in 2011—and a payment of $300 a month that she received from the Rhinelander family until 1940 under the divorce settlement—a payment that should have been for life, as the agreement indicated, but was successfully challenged in court by the Rhinelanders after Leonard and Philip died. In 1989, when Alice passed away, she would show us the truth of her words about loving only Leonard. Never having married again, like Leonard, Alice buried herself with a headstone that read "Alice J. Rhinelander" (see fig. 4.4).[59]

Fig. 4.4. Alice leaves us with one last reminder of who her true love was and, what is more, who she was— a Rhinelander. http://www.findagrave .com/cgi-bin/fg.cgi? page=pv&GRid=97536 443&PIpi=67608296

On Not Litigating Whiteness

One question left unanswered after the *Rhinelander* trial ended was why Alice and her legal team pursued the strategy of conceding nonwhiteness. After all, such a strategy meant that Alice and Leonard had absolutely no chance of living together again as husband and wife. If the ultimate goal was to preserve the Rhinelanders' marriage, then the decision to abandon any attempt to prove Alice's whiteness does not make sense. Overall, the decision to concede "colored blood" as a courtroom strategy left a number of questions unanswered about Alice's intentions with Leonard after trial. Had Alice fallen out of love with Leonard? Did she hope for reconciliation, even with a concession of colored blood? Just a few months before, Davis had announced to the press that there could be no settlement of the lawsuit since Alice was "extremely desirous of having her husband return to her because she loves him."[60] Indeed, rumor had it that Alice had previously declined a $250,000 settlement—the equivalent of $3.2 million in 2011—and instead decided to pursue a defense against Leonard's annulment claim at trial. If Alice really just hoped to remain Leonard's wife, then why did she act in a way that was not according to her heart by seeking a strategy that, at best, meant divorce? Why did Alice not try to litigate and prove her whiteness?

The idea that Alice could have tried to litigate her whiteness is not outrageous. After all, as Jamie Wacks has suggested, Alice purportedly identified as white. In fact, Wacks wondered whether Alice was never put on the witness stand because she viewed herself as white and would have stated so if asked about her racial identity on the stand.[61] Additionally, it was possible that Alice, who looked white, could have been identified as white based upon how she exercised the privileges of whiteness in her social and community life. Alice and her family moved in and out of white circles even in racially segregated New York. According to Professor Joanna Grossman, Alice and her family "belonged to a white church, commingled with white neighbors, and did not belong to any obviously black community."[62]

Furthermore, there was some case law in other states that supported recognition of a concept of race not linked to biology or, in some sense, ancestry. Though these cases were not binding, they could have presented hope of trial success in the event that Alice decided to litigate her whiteness. For example, in *Ferrall v. Ferrall* in 1910, the North Carolina Supreme Court set aside the verdict of a husband who had filed for annulment of his marriage and requested an exemption from support of his wife and their child on the ground that she was "of negro descent to the third generation."[63] The North Carolina Supreme Court entered judgment for the defendant wife, awarding her alimony for herself and the child. In so doing, one of the judges on the court chastised the husband for branding his wife and child "for all time by the judgment of a court as negroes—a fate which their white skin was certain to make doubly humiliating to them."[64]

More notably, in *White v. Tax Collector* in 1846, the Court of Appeals of South Carolina affirmed a jury verdict that found the grandchildren of Elijah Bass, "a dark quadroon" or confessed "mulatto," to in fact "be free white people."[65] In *White*, the children of Elijah Bass sought an exemption from a capitation tax on the ground that they and their children were white people. The Court of Appeals reviewed the jury's finding that the children of Elijah Bass were free mulattoes, and that Elijah Bass's grandchildren were free white people. In so doing, the court, through the presiding judge, began by noting that "if any people tinged with African blood are worthy to be rated as white, the relatrix and relators [Elijah Bass's children] present the very best claim to be so rated."[66] Noting that daughter Martha's baby "was a fair, blue-eyed white child [for whom] no one . . . would say that it had any admixture of African blood," the court held that "[w]here color and features are doubtful," a person's race is not determined "solely by the distinct and visible mixture of negro blood; but by reputation, by reception in society, and by the exercise of the privileges of a white man."[67] Here, the court found no issue with Bass's grandchildren being declared white because Elijah Bass was "always . . . treated by his neighbors as a free white man," was respectable, and never refused any of the privileges of a white man, and because his children were well-educated at white schools and treated as white persons.[68] In other words, in antebellum South Carolina, a court had determined that the descendants of a confessed mulatto were white based on "respectability of the family; the marriage of two of them with white persons; their social equality in the neighbourhood; and the omission of the tax collector to enforce from them, for many years, the capitation tax."[69] The similarity of these facts between the Bass family and the Jones family in *Rhinelander* is astounding, with both involving a mulatto ancestor, a respectable family that was accepted by and treated well by whites, and two family members who had married white people. If anything, the decisions in *White* and *Ferrall*—if known to her attorneys—could have shed a glimmer of hope for Alice in terms of litigating her whiteness. Although not binding, and only persuasive, these cases offered some basis for establishing Alice's whiteness and allowing her to remain with Leonard as his wife. Nevertheless, Alice, through her attorney Davis, chose not to take this riskier route of litigation, even though she, or rather, he, Davis, knew that it would mean the end of her marriage. The natural question is why.

One short answer is that, based on applicable legal precedents, Alice had only one choice for a trial strategy if she wanted to win: to concede "colored blood." Closer examination of even the aforementioned persuasive authority reveals that the tide was simply too much against young Alice if she wanted to be legally and socially identified as white. First, while the *Ferrall* case was promising in the sense that it chastised the husband for branding his wife and children with the label of "Negro" for life, Alice differed from the wife in *Ferrall* in three important respects. To begin, the wife in *Ferrall* was never alleged to have deceived her husband regarding her race. Indeed, the concurring judge declared that the wife, "if she had any strain of negro blood whatever, was so white [the husband] did not suspect it till recently. . . . [And] she herself must have been unaware of the fact, if it existed."[70]

Second, Alice and Leonard had no children together; thus, there was no possibility of the impoverishment and bastardization of innocent children. Third, Alice was the daughter of a man who was "confessedly a mulatto," and the *White* case, while promising, recognized only the "whiteness" of a confessed mulatto's grandchildren, not his children, as Alice was to George Jones.[71]

Moreover, despite cases like *Ferrall* and *White*, United States Supreme Court cases involving other legal matters on definitions of race seemed to close the lid on any claims by Alice to whiteness. For example, in *Ozawa v. United States* in 1922, the United States Supreme Court denied a Japanese man's claim to American citizenship as a "free white person." In making his argument, Takao Ozawa focused on two different points of relevance: (1) that the original framers defined white persons as individuals who were not Negro or Indian; and (2) that many Japanese people have white skin, which is lighter than that of persons already included in the category of white persons. In response, the Court held that the term *white* was a racial distinction, not a distinction based on skin color alone. Reviewing the statute that identified who was entitled to citizenship in the United States, the Court proclaimed that "[t]he intention [of the founding fathers] was to confer the privilege of citizenship upon that *class of persons whom the fathers knew as white,* and to deny it to all who could not be so classified [as white]."[72] Although it was announced in a different context, the *Ozawa* holding about the relationship between whiteness, our founding fathers' expectations about who satisfied whiteness, and citizenship was bad news for Alice if she intended to prove her whiteness. If anything was certain during the age of the one-drop rule, it was that those who were popularly known as white by the founding fathers did not include individuals with a mulatto parent like George Jones. As Ozawa's arguments before the Court revealed, the original framers defined "white persons" as persons who were not Negroes.

Similarly, in *United States v. Bhagat Singh Thind* in 1923, the United States Supreme Court declared that a man who was of "high-caste Hindu stock . . . and [was] classified by certain scientific authorities as of the Caucasian or Aryan race" was not a "free white person" entitled to citizenship in the country.[73] In so holding, the Court reasoned that the ability to trace one's ancestral line to Aryan or Caucasian forefathers was not determinative of the question of whether Thind was a "free white person." As in *Ozawa,* the court made clear that the statute was intended "to include only the type of man whom [the framers] knew as white."[74] Stressing the importance of visibly distinguishing characteristics, the Court explained, "It may be true that the blond Scandinavian and the brown Hindu have a common ancestor in the dim reaches of antiquity, but the average man knows perfectly well that there are unmistakable and profound differences between them today. . . . It is a matter of familiar observation and knowledge that the physical group characteristics of Hindus render them readily distinguishable from the various groups of persons in this country commonly recognized as white."[75] Thus, given the decision in *Thind,* the dark skin of Alice's father, George Jones, and Alice's own skin color as displayed at trial, Alice had little hope of successfully litigating her whiteness (see fig. 4.5).

More so, even if the appearance of Alice's skin and features were sufficiently "white," Alice's birth certificate marked her as "black." This certificate forever stamped Alice as nonwhite. A legal document had already established Alice as "black" from birth. Indeed, as Verna Cassagne would learn just fifteen years later—when her white husband, Cyril Sunseri, would seek an annulment on the ground that she was legally Negro—there was no "freeing" one's self from blackness if one was considered black on her birth certificate, even if that person was phenotypically white, was born in the white maternity ward, exercised privileges of whiteness, and associated only with white people.[76] In sum, even though Alice, like the plaintiff in *Plessy v. Ferguson,* was purportedly only one-eighth black, a combination of factors, such as her darker-than-white skin, the prevalence of the one-drop rule across the country, the legal characterization of her race at birth, and the physical appearance of her family essentially allowed for only one winning strategy at trial.

Furthermore, Alice's behavior, both in public and in private, left her with no ability to truly litigate her whiteness at trial. Alice never separated herself from her family—in particular, those who were black or multiracial—enough to truly be considered white. In order for Alice to truly pass as white, she would have had to have cut all ties with the black world and solely exist in a white world. Yet, she never disclaimed her sister Emily

Fig. 4.5. Alice Rhinelander poses with her parents, George Jones, who was a "confessed mulatto" from England, and Elizabeth Jones. © Bettmann/Corbis

or rejected her brother-in-law and niece Robert and Roberta or her father, George. In the law of litigated whiteness, associations with colored people only heightened the likelihood of an "unfavorable" determination of coloredness. For example, in *Hopkins v. Bowers*, the North Carolina Supreme Court affirmed a judgment for the plaintiffs, who had sought to recover real property from Eliza Bowers, a relative of Ann Boothe. The plaintiffs rested their case on the grounds that Ann Bowers—or Ann Boothe—who had allegedly married Nathan Boothe, was a colored person. The court held that evidence of Ann's associations with colored people was admissible to show that she was a colored woman. As the court explained, "Juries are certainly competent to give the proper weight to such evidence in accordance with the social customs prevailing around them, and which are matters of common observation."[77] In essence, Alice could not have chosen a trial strategy of litigating whiteness (that is, if she wanted to win), because she failed to sufficiently distance herself from colored people and therefore had failed to fully exercise the privilege of white citizens.

"Normal" Perceptions and Performances

Apart from the influence of prior case law on Davis's choice of a trial strategy, other forces had an impact on the Rhinelanders' annulment case and specifically on Alice's trial court victory. In particular, the notion of purely biological race may have pushed the jury to vote in favor of Alice, despite the tug in their "hearts" from what they had internalized all their lives about race. Additionally, the jury may have been influenced by the fact that Alice seemed to act in accordance with socially expected roles of race and gender while Leonard seemed to act in contradiction to those expected of him. In sum, in addition to favorable evidence, Alice may have been able to successfully defend against Leonard's claims for three socially discouraging reasons: (1) because the all-white jury needed to believe in race as a pure biological construct with distinct physical markers; (2) because Alice, unlike Leonard, met the jury's social expectations through her behavior, which fell in line with commonly held stereotypes about hypersexual and aggressive black women; and (3) because Leonard's actions did not conform with the jury's expectations of his racial and gender identities as a white man, much less a wealthy white blueblood. In other words, Alice's courtroom victory may have been enabled by the fact that Alice performed her racial identity as the all-white, all-male, and all-married jurors expected of a colored woman—she was uneducated, sexually experienced, and willing to engage in and talk about sexual encounters with Leonard. Moreover, her win may have been further spurred by the jury's desire to punish Leonard for his racial betrayal. Unlike Alice, whose behavior matched what the jury expected of black women, Leonard failed to perform his racial, gender, and class identities as expected of him as a white, wealthy gentleman. Specifically, he failed to abide by the social norms of not crossing clear racial boundaries of white and nonwhite. And, as married white men, the jurors all had a sense of how a white man who was trying to court a white woman should behave toward her as well as how she should portray herself to him. Moreover, as men who were fathers or who might have become fathers, they had a sense of what they may have wanted for their children, male or female, in the future.

1. The Art of Knowing Race When One Sees It

The first reason why Alice may have been able to defeat Leonard at trial is that a win for Alice worked to assure white people that they would know race when they saw it. Although surprising, Davis's decision to not litigate Alice's whiteness was clever in that it allowed him to play upon general beliefs of biological race within the white population. During the period of the *Rhinelander* trial, blacks who chose to pass were in their greatest numbers.[78] Thus, the idea of purely biological, clear, and visible race helped to allay the fears of many whites who had become increasingly concerned about blacks who were passing as white. In this sense, Davis's reinforcement at trial of the belief that a person would know race when he or she saw it was critically important to Alice's defense. Her jury of all-white men may have needed to believe that race, or rather that any taint of the colored race, was a factor that would be visible and recognizable to the eye. Such assurances to the jurors and the spectators of the trial were needed in order to maintain the value of whiteness to white citizens and give comfort to them that their status as "white" was free from challenge.

Throughout the trial, Davis played upon the notion of race as easily recognizable. Davis understood that he could not win the case by arguing that Alice was white because an all-white jury would value the idea of pure whiteness. As Professor Cheryl Harris has explained, for many whites during this time period (and even now), belonging to the white race had a greater value than just access to better housing, jobs, and opportunities in general. For them, the real value of whiteness was in the widely accepted and socially understood "superiority" of white persons over non-white persons. Professor Harris writes that the right to exclude is "a central principle . . . of whiteness as identity, for mainly whiteness has been characterized, not by an inherent unifying characteristic, but by exclusion of others deemed to be 'not white.'"[79] Understanding this unspoken value of whiteness, Davis indirectly posed this question to the jury: "If Alice, despite all of her connections to the colored world, were white, what did that mean about the jurors' own whiteness and potential challenges to it?" In other words, if whiteness was not a state of being by birthright alone and could be held or obtained by those who dared to mingle so closely with blacks, then there could be no claim to racial purity and, more so, no claim of inherent racial superiority by whites. Indeed, recognizing this threat to the notion of pure whiteness, Davis highlighted the idea of apparent and physical race at several points during the trial. For example, as noted previously, during one of Davis's cross-examinations, he used Alice herself as physical evidence to convey the comforting idea to whites that race could not be hidden. Specifically, Davis "went around behind [Alice], as she sat at the end of the counsel table in front of the jury box,"[80] and engaged in the following interrogation of Leonard:

> *Davis:* Did your wife look the same as she does now when you met her?
> *Leonard:* Yes. . . .
> *Davis:* And you are now looking at her with her hat off?
> *Leonard:* Yes.
> *Davis:* And she looked just the same?
> *Leonard:* Yes.
> *Davis:* No inquiry arose in your mind as to her color?
> *Leonard:* None whatever, no.[81]

On another occasion, Davis, as I explained earlier, required Alice to reveal portions of her body so that the jury could confirm her obvious race based on skin color. Unlike he had done throughout the trial, Davis did not engage in extensive questioning about this "piece" of evidence, Alice Rhinelander. Rather, he left the jury with the legal notion of *res ipsa loquitur*—"the thing speaks for itself." Davis asked only if Leonard could see his wife, and then he stated, "That is all."[82] Indeed, after seeing Alice's bare shoulders, arms, legs, and breasts at trial, no all-white jury in 1920s New York would have determined that Alice was purely white. To find otherwise—especially in the face of George Jones's appearance and admitted colored ancestry—would contradict all that the jury members had known and grown to accept about race during their lifetimes. In fact, after the trial, the jury's foreman, Clarence Pietsch, explained the jury's decision, stating: "Race prejudice didn't enter into the case at all, and neither did the unsavory details in the letters. We decided it merely as a case between a man and a woman, and in reaching our verdict considered Rhinelander as *a normal man with [a] normal sense of perception.* We didn't consider what the future might hold for them, as that was not up to us for decision."[83]

The idea was that Leonard knew, or at least he should have known, race when he saw it—that is, when he saw Alice's naked body before their marriage. For, Leonard was a "normal man with [a] normal sense of perception."

2. A Winning Performance

Alice and Leonard's failures or successes in acting in accordance with racially and socioeconomically expected social roles also provide one more potential explanation for the outcome of the *Rhinelander* trial—that is, apart from the fact that Davis presented strong evidence on behalf of Alice. In fact, Davis's strategy of not litigating whiteness and of highlighting Leonard's failures to appropriately distance himself from blacks indicates that Davis must have understood the importance of expected racial and gender performances. He understood that, while Leonard Rhinelander would be punished by the jurors for failing to perform his racial, class, and gender identities as an upper-class white man, Alice—despite her attempts at challenging hierarchy by stepping over racial and class boundaries—would be "rewarded" by the jury for performing the role of the stereotypical "Black Jezebel" and vamp, an oversexed and sexually aggressive black woman with no morals.

Throughout the trial, Davis highlighted the ways in which Leonard failed to comply with the expectation that he not commingle with those who are clearly black, even young children. For example, Davis engaged in the following exchange with Leonard during his cross-examination about Leonard's relationship with Alice's undeniably black brother-in-law:

Davis: . . . Did you ever have a meal with Mr. Brooks?
Leonard: Yes.
Davis: I would like to have you tell this jury how often you accepted Mr. Brooks' hospitality.
Leonard: About five times.
Davis: Five times. Before you were married?

Leonard: Before and after; yes.

Davis: Before and after. You accepted his invitation to sit down at his table in his home?

Leonard: Yes.

Davis: And you sat there and you ate with him?

Leonard: Yes.

Davis: And you still tell this jury that you didn't want to associate with colored folks? You still say that, do you?

Leonard: Seeing that they were Alice's relations, I did, yes. . . .

Davis: So you were willing, as long as they were Alice's relations, to associate with colored people before you were married to her?

Leonard: Yes.

Davis: And willing to accept a colored man's hospitality?

Leonard: Yes.[84]

By establishing close relationships with Robert and Roberta, and even worse sitting at the same table as them, Leonard had become a race traitor. He had crossed an unforgivable line, and there was no coming back. He would have to be punished by the jury—at least, that is what Davis hoped.

Additionally, Davis understood that Leonard would have to be reprimanded for his failure to live up to his background as a gentleman and wealthy white blueblood. For this reason, Davis tried to show at trial that Leonard had not only acted cowardly by allowing Alice's letters to be read at trial, but that he had failed to act like his own man when he allowed his father to take over his affairs and bring this lawsuit. For instance, at trial, Davis questioned Leonard incessantly about why he let his attorneys, specifically Leon Jacobs, who was an attorney for Leonard's father, admit Alice's letters into evidence despite his promises to her to keep them secret. One exchange proceeded as follows:

Davis: [Jacobs had] [n]o authority from you to go and take your personal letters from your wife before you were married? What? No authority from you?

Leonard: No.

Davis: What authority did you give him?

Leonard: He was my attorney.

Davis: What authority did you give him to go into your trunk or into your bureau drawer and take these exceedingly confidential letters?

Leonard: In that particular case, it was his own initiative. . . .

Davis: So that is twice he acted on his own initiative? Once he took your wife's furniture away from her without your orders, and the next thing he did was to take all of these confidential letters that have been spread on this record for days? That is correct, isn't it?

Leonard: Yes.

Davis: He was still working in your father's office at this time?

Leonard: Yes.

Davis: Did you object to the letters being used in this trial? Just yes or no. Take your time.

Leonard: I did, yes.

Davis: When did you object? When did you object to their being used at trial?

Leonard: In September some time.

Davis: This year?

Leonard: Yes. . . .

Davis: Did you object after that?

Leonard: It was for my own benefit. I had to permit them.

Davis: You were told for your own benefit that you had to submit them to the jury in open court, were you?

Leonard: Yes. . . .

Davis: Then you didn't object any more, did you?

Leonard: No.

Davis: Then you were willing to have them used? You didn't object any more, you say. You were willing to have them used?

Leonard: Yes, after that. . . .

Davis: Willing to have these letters read about somebody crawling over your stomach, as long as it was for your benefit?

Leonard: Yes. . . .

Davis: And you had promised this little girl that you would keep them safely, hadn't you?

Leonard: Yes.

Davis: But as long as it was for your benefit to put this stuff on the record in Court, you were willing to forget that promise to her, were you? You were, weren't you?

Leonard: I was . . . I followed the advice of my counsel. . . .

Davis: You are a man, aren't you?

Leonard: Yes.

Davis: And a gentleman?

Leonard: I try to be one.

> *Davis:* And, as a man and a gentleman, as long as they could be used for your benefit, you were willing to break the promise to this girl that you would keep them safely? That is right, isn't it?
>
> *Leonard:* Yes.
>
> *Davis:* And you still consider yourself a man, do you? Just yes or no. Do you?
>
> *Leonard:* I can't answer that by yes or no.
>
> *Davis:* You can't answer it. Do you still think you are?
>
> *Leonard:* Yes.[85]

Additionally, Davis worked to leave the impression that Leonard also had not acted like a gentlemen when he concededly designed to have sex with Alice, a woman he supposedly believed to be white, without any intent to marry her. As Davis highlighted at trial, even if Alice had tried to deceive Leonard about her race, real men could see that Leonard's deceit was actually worse. To demonstrate, Davis asked the following of Leonard: "Which in your mind is the worst deception—to lead a girl to love you and believe that you are going to marry her, and to take that from her which is most precious to a woman—Is that worse deception than for a girl to say, 'I am white and have no colored blood'? Which is the worst?"[86]

On the flip side, the jury could reward Alice for her behavior with a favorable verdict. After all, she had acted in line with stereotypes of black women. She had already engaged in sexual intercourse with one other man, and had even engaged in sexual intercourse with Leonard within three months of meeting him and without promise of marriage—acts that the jurors likely viewed as being in line with the stereotype of the Jezebel and vamp. More so, Alice had even enjoyed sleeping with Leonard before marriage, asking him repeatedly in her letters for more. Because Alice's alleged behavior did not challenge popular conceptions of social roles for colored women, her offenses were, to some extent, understandable as mere actions of "a stereotypically ignorant negro with laughably grandiose social aspirations."[87] In other words, unlike Leonard, she reinforced rather than challenged racialized and gendered stereotypes and thus served as no threat to white domination, supremacy, and patriarchy. In this sense, it is no surprise that Alice, despite pervasive race prejudice, was able to ultimately win over the "hearts" of the jurors, in spite of what many perceived to be their hearts' leanings toward Leonard at the trial's beginning.

But, what does the *Rhinelander* trial—from its beginning to its end—teach us about our own hearts, about our own families, and our own society today? In Part II of this book, I explore this very question as it relates today to interracial marriage rates, privilege, housing, employment, children, and the law.

PART II

5

Understanding the Black and White of Love

ALTHOUGH OCCURRING ALMOST A CENTURY AGO, the lives of Alice and Leonard Rhinelander remain relevant in today's society. In addition to teaching us about the various struggles that can occur in defining one's own racial identity, especially for multiracial individuals like Alice, the *Rhinelander* narrative forecasts a strong lingering taboo against interracial marriage in general and black-white marriage in particular. More so, the story of the Rhinelanders provides us with many important lessons about how law and society have often functioned together to frame the normative ideal of family as monoracial, both in our history and in our present.

In this chapter, I provide background information for understanding the joint role of law and social norms in framing the ideal of family as monoracial. I do so by exploring *Rhinelander*'s basic lessons about what I call the black and white, or ranking, of love, not just along racial lines, but also across constructions of gender. Although I address how the normative ideal of family is also defined as being rooted in heterosexuality, I focus my analyses primarily on black-white, heterosexual couples. In so doing, I readily acknowledge the widespread exclusion of gay and lesbian couples and their children from normative definitions of family.[1] Because antidiscrimination law generally excludes gay and lesbian individuals from protection from discrimination based on sexual orientation and because there is prevalent, open prejudice against same-sex couples in our society, the lack of legal protection and social acceptance for gay and lesbian couples and their families is widely exposed for all to see. However, it is not so easily exposed for interracial, heterosexual couples; my goal in this book is to make such lack of acceptance and protection under the law for multiracial families more visible for others to see and understand.[2] In this second part of *According to Our Hearts,* I unpack the widely held assumptions about how law adequately protects interracial, heterosexual couples in a post–*Loving v. Virginia* era, showing, instead, how law and society function together to create both a legal and social placelessness for multiracial families and the individuals within them. In essence, I expose the holes in legal and social protections for families and individuals that exist at the intersection of race and family.

With regard to race, I focus only on black-white couples, not just because Alice and Leonard were viewed by their jury as well as the public as a black-white couple, but also because the experiences of black-white couples provide critical insights into the state of race relations and racism within the United States. As Professor Heather Dalmage has explained, *"family* has been the primary means through which a racially divided and racist society has been maintained."[3] Furthermore, as Professor Erica Chito Childs has highlighted in her book *Navigating Interracial Borders: Black-White Couples and Their Social Worlds,* "the experiences of black-white couples are a miner's canary, revealing problems of race that otherwise can remain hidden, especially to whites. The issues surrounding interracial couples . . . should not be looked at as individual problems, but rather as a reflection of the larger racial issues that divide the races."[4] In sum, the unique histories of black enslavement and discrimination against blacks, and thus black-white couples, "enable us to see [just] how racial borders still exist" today, not only in society but also in law.[5] Moreover, much like Professors Kevin Johnson, Randall Kennedy, and Rachel Moran, I believe that the significant disparities between the outmarriage rates of whites with other racial minority groups, including Latinos,[6] and the outmarriage rates of whites with blacks signal a distinctly isolated status for blacks and thus black-white couples in our country.[7] As the *Rhinelander* narrative demonstrates, there is a hierarchy among the various racial combinations of interracial couples within the United States, and that hierarchy places black-white intimacy, both marital and nonmarital, at the bottom of all intimacies.

To set up the foundation for the analyses that I will provide in this part of *According to Our Hearts*, I first briefly detail historical and contemporary perceptions about black-white marriages within the United States and compare such perspectives to contemporary views concerning other types of interracial marriage within the country. Thereafter, I analyze how perceptions about black-white marriage can become even more complicated when one examines the gendered dimensions of black-white intimacy. The most prominent historical image of interracial intimacy in the United States is Mildred and Richard Loving, a black female–white male, married couple who fought for and won national legal recognition for all interracial marriages in a case aptly called *Loving v. Virginia*.[8] However, the racial and gender make-up of the Lovings is rarely reflected among today's interracial couples. Indeed, black women and white men are among the least likely individuals to marry each other in the United States. Such gendered dimensions of interracial intimacy become even more startling when one considers the past treatment of relationships and marriages between black men and white women, relationships that historically have been viewed as more threatening and as more deserving of harsh punishments than other types of interracial unions, including those of black women and white men. These gendered dimensions further signal the unique isolation of black women in our society, or those like Alice who are deemed to be black women, and thus their families. Here, we see that the normative ideal of family is not just raced, but also gendered—apart from sexuality. After providing the empirical data regarding the rates of interracial dating and marriage involving black women as compared to others, both in opposite-sex and same-sex relationships, I finally ask what the *Rhinelander* case and story can teach us about the reasons for the disparities between the rates of interracial dating and mating involving black women and the meaning of such disparities in the normative definition of family.

Marriage in Black and White

If the *Rhinelander* trial teaches us anything, it is that black-white love is the greatest taboo of all interracial intimacies—that black-white marriages are the least normative of all (heterosexual) relationships. Alice's once-dear friend, Miriam Rich, declared as much during her trial testimony against Alice. According to Miriam Rich, after the story of Alice's race and marriage to Leonard became public, a distraught Alice vehemently promised to prove her whiteness, proclaiming that Leonard "would rather have married an Indian than he had married a negress."[9] In other words, as Miriam Rich and even Alice supposedly believed, anything would have been better for Leonard than marrying black. The mere count of statutes in the United States that banned black-white marriages as compared to other types of interracial marriages confirms as much. The number of state statutes that prohibited marriages between blacks and whites far exceeded those that prohibited marriages between whites and any other type of racial or ethnic minorities. As data from Professor Rachel Moran's book *Interracial Intimacy: The Regulation of Race and Romance* reveals, of the thirty-eight states that, at some point, banned interracial marriage and sex, *all of them* prohibited *black-white* relationships, but less than one-half—only fourteen of them—prohibited Asian-white marriage, and less than one-fifth—just seven of them—prohibited Native American–white relationships; none of them prohibited Latino or Hispanic-white marriage, though as Moran notes, that was "presumably because treaty protections formally accorded former Spanish and Mexican citizens the status of white persons."[10] Here, the absence or presence of law or certain legal restrictions on marriage worked to establish and define the ideal of family, an ideal in which interracial marriages just did not fit and specifically in which black-white marriage could rarely fit.

Given this legal history of black-white relationships as compared to other interracial relationships, it should come as no surprise that blacks remain uniquely isolated in terms of interracial marriage with whites when compared to other racial and ethnic minority groups in the United States. Even after legal restrictions against interracial marriage have been erased from the books for decades, social norms continue to perpetuate the race-based marriage hierarchy that was established by law across the nation. Recent statistics show that more than 93 percent of blacks have same-race marriage partners, while only 70 percent of Asian Americans and Latinos and less than 33 percent of American Indians have same-race marital partners.[11] Indeed, the differences in rates of outmarriage between blacks and other ethnic minorities rise as great as 48 percent.[12] With the exception of whites, blacks are the least likely of any racial or ethnic group to marry across racial lines.[13] Such facts are critical to blacks and the improvement of blacks' status within American society, not because whites are a superior group with which blacks should want to mix, but rather because "[i]ntermarriage . . . signals that . . . outsiders [here, blacks] are gaining acceptance in the eyes of those in the dominant population and are perceived by them as persons of value on whom it is worth risking one's future[,] . . . because [intermarriage] breaks down the psychological boundaries that separate and distance people on racial grounds, . . . [and because] [i]ntermarriage encourages the inculcation of transracial empathy that is crucial for enabling people to place themselves in the shoes of others racially different from themselves."[14] As Professor Randall Kennedy has explicated, "[f]ew situations are more likely to mobilize the racially privileged individual to move against racial wrongs than witnessing such wrongs inflicted upon one's mother-in-law, father-in-law, spouse, or child."[15]

Even among new marriages, a disparity remains between the outmarriage rates of blacks and other racial minorities, including Latinos. Although a record 14.6 percent of all new marriages in the United States were interracial in 2008 (much larger than the overall 8 percent for all marriages), black outmarriage and, particularly, black-white outmarriage remain a small part of that growth. Of the 14.6 percent of interracial new marriages in 2008, 41 percent of them consisted of Latino-white couples, 15 percent of them consisted of Asian-white couples, and 11 percent of them consisted of black-white couples. While, at first glance, the 15 percent figure for Asian-white couples may not appear to be significantly different from the 11 percent figure for black-white couples, it is actually quite significant because the black population is nearly four times that of the Asian population in the United States. Overall, of the 3.8 million people who outmarried in 2008, 9 percent of whites, 16 percent of blacks, 26 percent of Latinos, and 31 percent of Asian or Asian Pacific Americans made up that group.[16] Thus, while white individuals remained the least likely of all races to outmarry, outmarrying at just slightly more than half the percentage of blacks, nearly twice the percentages of Latinos and Asians outmarried than that of blacks. More so, individuals' approval of outmarriage to blacks remained much lower than that for other racial groups, with survey participants indicating approval of outmarriage to whites at 81 percent, Asians at 75 percent, Latinos at 73 percent, and blacks at only 66 percent.[17] In fact, studies show that not just whites, but also Latinos and Asian Pacific Americans have consistently marked blacks as the least desirable marital partners for their children.[18]

The Jim and Jane Crow of Love

Within the already comparatively low rates of outmarriage for blacks, another significant disparity exists: the disparity between the outmarriage rates of black men and black women. Although this disparity does not line up evenly with the history of legal regulation on interracial marriage through prison and punishment, it certainly does so with regard to regulation of access to wealth. As Professor Ralph Richard Banks has highlighted in his book *Is Marriage for White People? How the African American Marriage Decline Affects Everyone,* black women are far less likely than black men to marry across racial lines. Indeed, at one point, 73 percent of all black-white marriages involved black men and white women, leaving black female–white male marriages to account for only the remaining 27 percent.[19] In 2000, 9.7 percent of married black men were married to whites while only 4.1 percent of married black women were,[20] and out of new marriages in 2008, 22 percent of all black male newlyweds outmarried as compared to just 9 percent of all black female newlyweds.[21] Overall, "[b]lack men outmarry 2.4 times more frequently than [b]lack women."[22] In sum, even today, modern-day Alices—meaning black or biracial, black-white women[23]—and modern-day Leonards—meaning white men—are unlikely to become intimate partners, and even more so, marital partners.

Historically speaking, black female–white male marriage numbers, much like white female–black male numbers, have always been low. Although *sex* between black women and white men was not viewed as taboo, *marriage* between black women and white men was.[24] During the antebellum period, sex between black women and white men—often in the form of rape—was not only accepted, but in many ways expected. "A northern traveler in South Carolina commented, 'The enjoyment of a negro or mulatto woman is spoken of as quite a common thing: no reluctance, delicacy or shame is made about the matter.'"[25] Although, in certain instances, the relationships between black women and white men developed into true intimacy, rarely did that intimacy ever result in marriage. For example, in *The Hemingses of Monticello*,[26] Professor Annette Gordon-Reed presents substantial evidence that supports a decades-long relationship between Thomas Jefferson and one of his slaves, Sally Hemings, a relationship which resulted in several children but never in marriage. Despite such evidence over the years, even today, many resist the idea of true intimacy between Jefferson and Hemings, and the idea of marriage would offend such resisters even more. As Alexis de Tocqueville once proclaimed, "[T]o debauch a Negro girl hardly injures an American's reputation; to marry her dishonors him."[27]

However, the fact that even true relationships between black women and white men did not frequently result in marriage during the antebellum, postbellum, and even pre–civil rights era is not life-shattering news. Interracial marriage was not just legally forbidden but also socially reviled during both the antebellum and postbellum periods. Black-white marriage challenged widely held beliefs about the inferiority of blacks. Marriage legitimized relationships, and permitting and recognizing legal marriage between whites and blacks not only would have validated such relationships but also the black people within them. With respect to black female–white male marriage in particular, because of the way in which economic benefits and privilege primarily accrued to men, and not women, interracial marriages involving black women threatened the social and legal order because they provided a means through which black women (like Alice) and their children could gain access to white wealth. In fact, many courts refused to acknowledge even nonmarital, black-white relationships by denying the testamentary wishes of slaveholding fathers who wished to pass property on to their nonwhite children and lovers because upholding such wishes would have signaled the legitimacy of black-white intimacy, even if nonmarital.[28]

Up until the 1960s, even though black female–white male marriage numbers were low, they occurred at relatively the same rates as those for white women and black men. "Indeed, according to the 1960 U.S. Census, there were slightly more black women married to white men than there were black men married to white women."[29] By 1970, however, that pattern changed dramatically. By the 1970s, white female–black male marriages had increased by 61 percent while black female–white male marriages went in the reverse, decreasing by 9.1 percent.[30]

Today, black women and white men remain among the least likely pair of individuals to marry each other, and black women remain the least likely of all racial and gendered groups to outmarry at all. To some extent, such low numbers of black female outmarriages with white men are not surprising. In the United States, black women hold a particularly low status of social desirability as partners in marriage, marrying at a lower rate than any other group of women. For example, "[a]mong women [between the] ages 40–44, 10% of White women and nearly 30% of Black women have never married."[31] Empirics further demonstrate that black women are nearly three times as likely as white women to never get married at all. With respect to interracial marriages, which are rare in general, black women also fare the poorest among all women. Only 4 percent of married black women are married to men of another race, while 24 percent of married Asian Pacific American women and 14 percent of married Latinas are.[32] As I noted before, although white men and Latinos outmarry at equal rates to white women and Latinas, respectively, black men outmarry at almost two and a half times the rate of black women. Additionally, although Asian and Asian Pacific American men and women outmarry at different rates—20 percent as compared to 40 percent, respectively—Asian and Asian Pacific American men still outmarry at much higher rates than black women by more than 10 percent.

If one were to look at current dating statistics to determine what the outlook of black female outmarriage may be in the future, that picture, too, would not signal an increase in numbers. Instead, it would signal a continuation of a hierarchy that past laws on interracial marriage constructed to deny black women access to white wealth and to deny all blacks access to full citizenship or belonging. Despite daters', especially white daters', expressed openness to cross-racial intimacy, their actual behaviors indicate that the black female–white male color and gender line is often too much for them to cross. For example, in 2009, Professors Cynthia Feliciano, Belinda Robnett, and Golnaz Komaie of the University of California, Irvine published the results of their study involving the gendered and race-based exclusions of white, heterosexual internet daters who articulated their racial preferences and excluded potential mates based on racial preferences in their website profiles. Among the small group of whites who were willing to express their racial preferences in mates and exclude persons based on race, black women ranked the lowest among women of all races and ethnicities as desirable partners. In that study, the researchers analyzed the stated racial preferences and exclusions of these white internet daters regarding whites, blacks, Latinos, Asians, East Indians, Middle Easterners, and American Indians as a means of comprehending and explaining different racial and gender groups' standings within hierarchies of interracial intimacy. Referring to prior studies that reveal that black men are more likely to marry whites than black women are, the researchers sought to further explore gendered and raced differences with respect to the openness of white men and white women to interracial dating.[33] Overall, they found that white men express a racial preference for dating only white women much less frequently than white women expressed a similar preference for dating only white men, with only 29 percent of white men indicating a whites-only preference and 64 percent of white women doing so.[34] In fact, "white women are 1.8 times as likely to state a racial preference as white men."[35] The Irvine researchers further found that white men who articulated racial preferences (59 percent) by excluding certain racial groups included a greater number of different racial and ethnic groups of women, at an average of 3.42, than did white women who provided such racial preferences (72 percent), who included on average 1.84 different racial and ethnic groups.[36] Specifically, the researchers determined that, while over 90 percent of white women who articulated racial preferences and exclusions preferred not to date men from four groups—East Indians, Middle Easterners, Asians, and blacks—"[w]hite men with stated racial preferences, in contrast, only prefer[red] *not* to date one group at levels above 90%: black women."[37]

Also, in 2009, the dating website OkCupid released statistics about its customers' preferences that revealed blacks, and in particular, black women, to be the least desirable partners, not among just heterosexuals, but also among gays and lesbians. For its study, OkCupid examined the first-contact attempts and response rates for its customers based on race, and found that the sender's race played a huge role in whether he or she ever received a response back from those contacted. Specifically, OkCupid reviewed the actions and behaviors of its Asian, black, Latino, Indian, Middle Eastern, Native American, Pacific Islander, and white customers of both sexes. When OkCupid began its investigation, it preselected its data pool "so that physical attractiveness (as measured by [its] site picture-rating utility) was roughly even across all the race/gender slices."[38] The company ensured the same results with men and height. In the end, the company expected the match percentage and reply rate for various racial groups to look similar. As the company explained, "[i]n general, the correlation between match percentage and reply rate means that whenever we compare the match/reply charts for a given breakdown of the population, they should look about the same."[39]

Yet, OkCupid's expectations of matching percentage and reply rates would not be fulfilled. Instead, the company's data first showed that, while black, heterosexual women were the most likely of any group of heterosexuals to reply when contacted—at 1.5 times the average response rate, they received, by far, the fewest replies. As the website explained, "*Men don't write black women back. Or rather, they write them back far less often than they should. Black women reply the most, yet get by far the fewest replies. Essentially every race—including other blacks—singles them out for the cold shoulder.*"[40] Overall, OkCupid discovered that white men have the best response rate. Falling in line with the Irvine study, OkCupid found that: "*White women prefer white men to the exclusion of everyone else—and Asian and Hispanic women prefer them even more exclusively. These three types of women only respond well to white men. More significantly, these groups' reply rates to nonwhites [are] terrible. Asian women write back nonwhite males at 21.9 percent, Hispanic women at 22.9 percent, and white women at 23.0 percent.*"[41] As OkCupid declared in its first release of their data, "The takeway here is that although race shouldn't matter in messaging, it does. A lot."[42]

In addition to looking at how race affected the first-attempt and response rates for heterosexual customers, OkCupid also analyzed the same data from gay and lesbian customers. Noting that its sample size for certain groups, for example lesbians of Indian descent, was rather small, OkCupid

announced that similar race-based prejudices showed up among the response behaviors of its gay and lesbian clients, though the prejudices were
not as pronounced as they were for the website's heterosexual clients. Overall, blacks received the fewest responses. Gay black men fared the worst,
receiving "20% fewer responses than non-blacks, which is about how
straight black men fared."[43] Black lesbians remained the female group that
other lesbians replied to the least, but "the discrepancy is much smaller in
the lesbian community" than in the heterosexual community.[44] Although
white gays and lesbians were not the most in demand (Asian women were
the most in demand for lesbians, and Middle Eastern men were the most
in demand for gay men), white gays and lesbians responded *"by far the
least to anyone,"* responding 15 percent less often than nonwhites.[45] As
OkCupid explained, "[W]hite gay men show[ed] a marked preference for
other whites. On the other hand, gay white women don't have the segre-
gationist tendencies of their straight counterparts; they just dis everyone.
Whereas [with heterosexuals] we saw that straight white women strongly
preferred whites to the exclusion of other groups, lesbian whites respond
to all 9 racial groups roughly evenly."[46]

The results of the studies by the Irvine scholars and the OkCupid dating website are reflected even within popular culture, where black women
are often socially tagged as the least desirable love interest, even in films
that star black men. More importantly, though there are exceptions, black
female actors are rarely considered for roles in which they may be the love
interest of white men—that is, apart from those movies in which the interracial intimacy itself is the storyline. Even in Hollywood, the stain of the
nation's past legal restrictions remains strong. As Jasmine Guy, a black
actress who starred in the television series *A Different World*, bluntly proclaimed, "I used to fight battles with my agents. . . . 'Why can't I go up for
a part that Meg Ryan and Julia Roberts are going up for? That's what I am.'
They're like, 'They won't make this an interracial couple.'"[47] Why? Interracial couples, especially those like Alice and Leonard, do not fit the normative ideal for intimacy.

More recently, during an interview with *Playboy* magazine superstar
singer John Mayer highlighted the marginality of black female–white male
relationships. Mayer came under fire after he honestly revealed his aver-

sion to dating black women. In response to a question regarding whether black women throw themselves at him in the same way that white women do, Mayer, who ironically sings a black form of music called "the blues," provocatively answered, "I don't think I open myself up to it. My dick is sort of like a white supremacist. I've got a Benetton heart and fuckin' David Duke cock. I'm going to start dating separately from my dick."[48] When asked to be more specific about "dating separately from his dick," Mayer replied, "I always thought Holly Robinson Peete was gorgeous. Every white dude loved Hilary from *The Fresh Prince of Bel-Air*. And Kerry Washington. She's superhot, and she's also white-girl crazy. Kerry Washington would break your heart like a white girl. Just all of a sudden she'd be like, 'Yeah, I sucked his dick. Whatever.' And you'd be like, 'What? We weren't talking about that.' That's what 'Heartbreak Warfare' is all about, when a girl uses jealousy as a tactic."[49]

Although Mayer caught flak for his comments about black women, and rightfully so, he, just like Miriam Rich during the *Rhinelander* trial, also revealed several key insights that are critical to understanding the centrality of race in framing the normative ideal of family and intimacy as well as the particularly low status of black female–white male relationships within the hierarchy of families. First, Mayer exposed the way in which interracial relationships have often been viewed as purely sexual and physical—the result of animal attraction or, as one movie referred to it, "jungle fever." In talking about his decisions not to date black women, Mayer equated interracial sex with interracial love. He explained that, in order to stop being like "David Duke," he had "to start dating separately from [his] dick," which he noted functioned separately from his "Benetton" heart, the very organ that our society widely regards as governing all true intimacy. With his crass and simple words, Mayer demonstrated the way in which black-white relationships are often socially cast as being about sexual gratification or forbidden fruit, rather than by what we commonly view as real love.

For example, consider the initial reaction of the mother of one of my survey participants, Edith, a black woman who is married to a white man, after Edith introduced her then-boyfriend to her family. Edith explained, "Initially, my mom was not okay with our relationship. She thought it was based in part on the stereotype that white men perform oral sex and black men do not. However, she had come around by the time we decided to marry and was very happy for us at the time of the wedding."[50] Similarly, Camille Nelson, the black dean of Suffolk University Law School, has discussed how strangers have completely sexualized her relationship with her white husband. In one instance, Nelson described an occasion in which a man next to them in a bar could make sense of their relationship only by thinking of them as porn stars. She wrote:

> Enjoying digestives in the piano lounge, the query of the man sitting next to us at the bar shocked us: "Are you two porn stars?" he asked. I nearly fell off the barstool. After regaining my composure, I explained to him that we were vacationing in celebration of our tenth wedding anniversary, that we had three children, that I was a law professor, and that my husband worked in film (but not that way). I honestly cannot remember exactly what my husband said, but he did mention, snidely, that we would have a lot more money if we were porn stars and wouldn't be driving a minivan and a Cavalier—I doubt we were very coherent. We were shocked and had no time to summon the full force of our annoyance. . . .
>
> There in the lounge, an external assessor and his lascivious questioning eclipsed our romantic musings. Our critical consciousness demanded that we both simultaneously "claim the normal." We both used the tried-and-true strategy used by many interracial couples—we constructed our lives like everyone else's in order to highlight the banality of it all. No, we are not porn stars; we wanted, in that moment, to blend in and not be seen—nothing unusual here, no racialized spectacle to be observed—just plain, ordinary, and racially average.[51]

Alice and Leonard Rhinelander, too, found themselves defined in sexual terms by others, particularly by Isaac N. Mills, Leonard's chief attorney, during the trial. Indeed, as Mills intimated repeatedly during the annulment trial, the only way that Alice and Leonard's relationship could even be explained was through sex. In the eyes of Mills, nothing else could make a Rhinelander—Leonard Rhinelander—fall so deeply for the working-class, colored girl. As Mills argued, Alice's hold over Leonard was simply the work of a sexually experienced, colored woman—women, he claimed, who are known to be mature beyond their years—over "a boy upon whom no woman ever smiled before."[52] Mills conveyed this message about the sexual nature of interracial intimacy to the jurors in a variety of ways at trial, but particularly through numerous oral readings of Alice's letters to Leonard, many of which referenced sex and sexual activity between the two lovers.

Overall, the desire to define interracial intimacy as linked to sexual gratification alone, rather than to love, stems in large part from white supremacy, the notion, whether consciously or not consciously held, that whites are superior to blacks—a notion that was reinforced for decades in part by antimiscegenation laws. The basic idea is that, in an *unnatural* world, guided solely by physical pleasure, persons of different races may act upon their animal instincts, giving in to their "jungle fever" or impure desires. It is for this reason that "sleeping with someone of a different race" merits a full point on a typical "purity test," designed to discern an individual's sexual purity.[53] But in a natural world, individuals are attracted to those like them, their hearts reaching out to their true soulmates, who are "naturally" expected to be people of the same race.

For instance, each year during the "Race and Family" section of my Critical Race Theory course, students, particularly white students, explain the widespread, monoracial constructions of families across the nation as the consequence of simple human nature. Students, who just previously understood and analyzed how race is socially constructed and how magazine and movie images can shape racial stereotypes or even our attraction to model-thin women or men with six packs, declare, "You can't help nature. You can't help whom you're attracted to." In their eyes, because they believe in racial equality and are liberal, they do not view their mating choices or those of their friends as influenced at all by racial bias. Instead, their choices regarding dating and marriage become marked, not by unconscious or conscious cues about race and intimacy or by constructed images of beauty and attractiveness, but rather by natural, personal preference. As Professor Erica Chito Childs has highlighted in her research regarding the reaction of many whites to interracial relationships, whites tend to explain their reactions to, or rather avoidance of, interracial intimacy as being the result of pure personal preference, not the framing of any normative ideal for couples as monoracial. Chito Childs explains:

> When speaking about their own dating choices, white college students explained their decisions not to date interracially as based on personal prefer-

ence; not being attracted to blacks; a lack of common interests, different cultures, values, and beliefs; or the way they grew up. However, they denied racial preference. . . . In making these statements, they were drawing on norms and rules of race relations into which they were socialized by their family and group, yet they did not see it that way. These white college students did not believe that they *chose* not to interact with blacks but that it occurred naturally or as a result of the black students' actions. . . . These statements reflect a colorblind discourse that is dominant in American society, where it is considered polite to "ignore" color or racial differences, without abandoning various prejudices and racialized ways of thinking.[54]

It is in this sense that Mayer in his *Playboy* interview brings us another important lesson about race and intimacy: that even after *Loving v. Virginia*, our intimate relationships, and thus families, in the United States are not shaped solely by personal preference but also by social and legal cues about the normative ideal for families. Although Mayer reinforced ideas about the purely sexual nature of interracial relationships, he also challenged the view of his own monoraciality in dating and mating as inevitable. Mayer, here, was different from the white participants in Chito Childs's study. Rather than defending his dating practices as his natural personal preferences, Mayer criticized them by articulating and explaining their link to what even he identified as white supremacy—as David Duke in action. In this way, Mayer separated himself from many whites, who explain their dating and mating choices as the simple result of natural, personal preferences. Unlike those participants as well as the internet daters in the Irvine study, Mayer openly and honestly spoke about his preferences as racist, asserting his desire to change them and, most importantly, his willingness to challenge them as wrong and closed off.[55]

At the same time, however, Mayer also exposed the undying salience of race to dating and marriage and the undying strength of the normative framework for families, even for people like him, who have a desire to change and challenge their views and actions. Where Mayer can be criticized in his comments is in his articulation of the specifics about potential black female love interests, which in addition to shedding light on the low status of black woman in the mating market, also reveals much about the role that raced and gendered stereotypes play in influencing perceptions not only about the essence of interracial relationships—here, between black women and white men—but also about the essence of individual beings, black women in particular. Of the black women whom Mayer identified as part of his pathway to change, at least one—Hilary from the *Fresh Prince of Bel-Air*—can be framed as a "white," black female character or at least a character whom writers intended to script as "whitened." As Mayer noted, "[e]very white dude loved Hilary." Mayer even specifically described Kerry Washington, another potential black love interest, as "white-girl crazy," revealing that even in the negative attributes of the women he desires, Mayer, like the all-white and all-male jurors in the *Rhinelander* case, finds race—in particular, whiteness—to be *of the essence* in his intimate relationships. Even in his "going black," Mayer forces himself into the ideal of the monoracial couple norm.

Not only whites but also blacks exhibit an adherence to the ideal of the monoracial family. Unlike whites, however, blacks do not tend to engage in a color-blind discourse when considering interracial relationships and do not tend to see interracial relationships as outside the realm of possibility within their circles. Instead, blacks tend to express what Chito Childs calls "oppositional support" for interracial relationships. Specifically, while blacks offer "many reasons why they distrust and discourage interracial relationships, they also acknowledge loving and accepting many interracial couples among their families and friends."[56] In Chito Childs's study, blacks focused on two aspects regarding interracial relationships: (1) blacks' hope and desire that loved ones will avoid being hurt by racism inside or outside of those relationships; and (2) the view of such relationships as occurring because of the black person's "negative image of oneself" and "a devaluation of blackness."[57] In other words, for blacks, the interracial union gets framed as deviant, and not normal, not because of either social or legal views regarding inherent differences between blacks and whites, but rather because of fears about racism—in some cases, a remnant of our legal past—or the existence of internalized racism. For instance, one story from Professor Catherine Smith's article "Queer as Black Folk?" in the *Wisconsin Law Review* demonstrates how fears of past (and present) racism can influence the opposition of certain black family members to the interracial relationship of their loved one. In this article, Smith explained her father's initial reaction to her coming out to him as a lesbian, a reaction premised primarily on her father's historical and childhood understanding of the dangers presented to black men who fraternized with white women in the South—which, to his mind, also would include black lesbians who dated white women. Smith wrote:

> Born in 1933, my dad grew up in segregated, rural South Carolina. When I came out to him as a lesbian at age twenty-one, he said he would rather I be a whore than be gay. Being gay, he told me, placed me in the shoes of a black man in America and that, as such, I would be stereotyped and targeted as a sexual threat to white women. My dad put me into a box born of his own experience as a black man in apartheid America—a racist box that said if you were black and had sex with women, white society would stigmatize you or worse. In my father's mind, my potential to have sex with a woman made me "the same as" a black man, and accordingly, he gave me the same message he had given my three older brothers when they were young boys.[58]

In addition, comments from one survey participant—Janice, a white woman in a civil union with a black woman—help to confirm Chito Childs's arguments regarding oppositional support of interracial relationships from blacks. In explaining the reactions that she has received from blacks about her relationship with her black partner, Carla, Janice noted that "[g]enerally . . . folks are okay once they realize that I strive to do 'race work' justly and well."[59]

Indeed, take for instance Alice Rhinelander's father, George Jones, who demonstrated a form of oppositional support when he expressed strong reservations about a marital union between Alice and Leonard. Purportedly, George Jones had tried to stop the Rhinelander marriage by calling "on the young man [Leonard Rhinelander] many times before the wedding and plead[ing] with him not to marry his daughter."[60] According to the *Chicago Defender*, "'[George] told [Leonard that] he had his daughter's interests at heart in making his plea, saying that such an alliance must come to a bad end.'"[61] Furthermore, according to one report, George told Leonard that he and "his family were English working people and that there was a social gulf between his daughter and Rhinelander which could not be bridged."[62] Though it is unclear from these statements whether George was concerned more about racism or classism affecting the marriage, it is evident that George's desire was to shield Alice from hurt as a result of outside prejudice—prejudices of "likes" and "unlikes" marrying, regardless of how "like" or "unlike" was defined.

But, even to the extent that the Jones parents can be viewed as embracing the newlywed Rhinelanders and resisting the monoracial ideal by taking the Rhinelander newlyweds into their home after their wedding, the Joneses arguably embodied the other concern that Chito Childs found that blacks commonly expressed in opposition to interracial relationships: self-hatred and the internalization of a belief in white superiority. With the Jones family, there was at least some sign that they generally did not like to be identified with blacks in the United States, which, for some, would be interpreted as a form of self-hate. During her testimony, Alice's mother, Elizabeth Jones, proclaimed that, while her husband accepted being called "colored," he did not like being characterized as a Negro.[63] Indeed, Elizabeth "winced" when "Davis admitted in court that there was negro blood in Alice Rhinelander's veins."[64] Leonard's attorney, Mills, even accused Elizabeth Jones of trying to teach her daughters to improve their station by encouraging them to date and marry white men; if true, such actions by the Joneses can hardly be identified as evidence of resistance to the monoracial ideal of marriage, especially if Elizabeth viewed not only herself but also her daughters, and even her husband, as white or as anything other than "Negro" or "black." If anything, such action could be defined as only blind acceptance of the monoracial norm.

Why Aren't There More "Alices and Leonards"?

In the end, in our post–*Loving v. Virginia* era, one must ask why couples like Alice and Leonard—married black female–white male couples[65]— remain among the least common of all minority outmarriages and commitments with whites (see fig. 5.1). In particular, why do such couples remain so far behind black male–white female marriages, which actually have historically elicited much harsher and more volatile reactions from society? Why do they remain the farthest from the normative ideal for families?

In fact, unlike for white men and black women, interracial sex between black men and white women has always been considered to be taboo as well as punishable by law. Historically speaking, black men and white

Fig. 5.1. Michele Bratcher Goodwin and Gregory Shaffer, a black
female–white male couple, pose
on their wedding day in Chicago.
Photograph courtesy of Michele
Bratcher Goodwin and
Gregory Shaffer

women who entered into intimate relationships with each other received
severe legal and extralegal punishment for their transgressions, black men
often being penalized with death through lynchings or lengthy and harsh
prison sentences and white women receiving punishment through ostra-
cism and imprisonment.[66] As the late scholar Peggy Pascoe explained in
her book *What Comes Naturally: Miscegenation Law and the Making of Race
in America:* "In actual practice, the legislators who enacted miscegenation
laws and the judges who enforced them nearly always had particular race-
and-gender pairs in mind when they did so. When those pairs included
White women, the tendency to enact, enforce, and elaborate miscegenation
laws was sharper, the tendency to resort to criminal law stronger. Images of
White women and Black men often sparked the passage of miscegenation
laws; criminal prosecutions often reflected the desire to protect white womanhood that buttressed white supremacy in many of its forms, including
miscegenation laws as well as lynchings."[67] Indeed, historian Charles Robinson has shown how black men and white women received harsher pun-

ishments than black women and white men, including longer sentences, as a result of their transgressions because their actions tended to threaten the racial and gender order the most.[68] Furthermore, scholars such as Professor Reginald Oh have analyzed how early antimiscegenation laws specifically focused on deterring white women from engaging in interracial sex and marriage with black men.[69] In fact, the earliest laws seeking to regulate interracial sex and marriage often sought to deter white women from having interracial relationships with black men. For example, during slavery, white women who engaged in relationships with black men could lose their very freedom, being forced into indentured servitude.[70] Also, for white women, giving birth to biracial children could result either in their being heavily fined or their being sentenced to indentured servitude for five years.[71] The punishments for interracial intimacy also extended to the children of black male–white female couples. For instance, whereas the fact of having a white mother (as opposed to a black mother) once guaranteed freedom for biracial children during the antebellum era, in 1691, the Virginia Assembly declared that the small population of mixed-race children of white mothers would become indentured servants until age thirty.[72] Even in the postbellum period up to the civil rights era, legal regulation of cross-racial intimacy focused on preventing white women from becoming involved with black men. Indeed, as Professor Renee Romano has explained, segregation laws, including in public schools, were often "justified by the need to protect white women from 'bestial' black men."[73] As one example of more recent regulation of interracial intimacy, Professor Kevin Johnson highlighted the way in which a corrupt, undercover police officer had framed about 20 percent of the African American adults in Tulia, Texas, for drug crimes, specifically targeting black men who either were or had been in interracial relationships with white women.[74]

Though no definitive data shows that black male–white female couples continue to experience more resistance or harsher "punishments" than black female–white male couples, black male–white female couples today still experience strong social resistance to their relationships (see fig. 5.2). Though the imprint of law is no longer explicitly towering over such interracial relationships, studies show that white women continue to report more disapproval from family members than their white male counterparts for

Fig. 5.2. Bertrall Ross and Joy Milligan, a black male–white female married couple, share hugs and laughs. Photograph courtesy of Bertrall Ross and Joy Milligan

entering interracial unions.[75] Additionally, researchers Suzanne Collins, Michael Olson, and Russell Fazio recently found that "White women appear to receive more pressure to date and marry White men than White men receive to date and marry White women."[76]

Outside of the family, most of us can point to anecdotes and events that reveal continued hostility toward black male–white female couples. In a number of those cases, some of "[t]he most vocal opposition [has come] from black women, many of whom continue to be vehement critics of black men's relationships with white women."[77]

Consider, for one moment, the difference in the responses to two separate magazine covers from *Essence* magazine, a popular magazine that focuses on the concerns and issues of black women. The first cover appeared on *Essence* in February 2010 and featured New Orleans Saints running back Reggie Bush, while the second cover appeared in April 2010 and featured *Avatar* actress Zoe Saldana. At the time, both Bush and Saldana were involved in serious romantic relationships with whites; Bush was involved with reality television star Kim Kardashian, who is a white ethnic (half Armenian), and Saldana was involved with her then-long-time boyfriend, actor Keith Britton. Yet, only Bush's cover ignited a firestorm among *Essence* readers, and did so precisely because he was dating a white woman at the time. In the March issue that followed Bush's cover, numerous readers published letters that criticized *Essence*'s selection of Bush for a cover. For example, T. L. Zeno from New Orleans, Louisiana, remarked: "*Essence* was created to embrace and empower African-Americans, particularly our women. Reggie Bush's current girlfriend, Kim Kardashian, is a clear indication that African-American women could not 'live (their) fantasy' with him."[78] Another reader, Ada Giles from Baltimore, Maryland, asserted: "I am saddened that *Essence* chose to highlight Reggie Bush ['What's Your Fantasy?' February 2010]. There are so many other Black men, dating Black women, who would have made a great cover. This issue has left a bad taste in my mouth."[79] One reader, A. E. Johnson from Houston, Texas, simply stated, "Stop promoting Black men who do not support Black women!"[80] Even one male, Aaron Sailor from Pasadena, California, responded with his disapproval, noting: "I am a 30-year-old Black male. Let me start out by saying that I have been an admirer and subscriber to *Essence* for many years. In a society and world that ignores, demeans and maligns Black femininity and womanhood, it is important that *Essence* uplift Black women's self-esteem and self-worth and put Black women first."[81]

In fact, the response to the Reggie Bush cover was so strong that, in the next issue, the magazine featured a full-length-article response to the cover by writer Jamilah Lemieux, entitled "If I Were *Your Woman*." In her impassioned piece, Lemieux articulated the following words:

> I admit it. I was hurt and disappointed when I saw Reggie Bush on the cover of my *Essence*. . . . I'm not okay with Black men choosing to spend their lives with non-Black women. . . . Every day from Brooklyn to the Bay Area, we see the same images of Black men lovingly embracing non-Black women everywhere from the movie theater to the mall. . . . I'd be lying if I said a hurt feeling doesn't overtake me when I see these couples. Black women significantly outnumber our men. Forty-two percent will never marry. . . . Black men are our brothers and our lovers. We share a history, we share everyday struggles, we share blood. Whether a Black man is recognized around the world, or even in his own backyard, he should want to have us there by his side. Black men should want to build families with us.[82]

On the flip side, even though Saldana's article was the only one of the two celebrities to mention a romantic partner, the response from readers to Saldana's cover was entirely positive. In fact, the following May issue of *Essence* contained no letters in response to Saldana at all, although it still included letters regarding the selection of Bush for the February cover. It was not until the next month's issue, in June, that two readers finally published letters praising the very talented actress, with one even noting how Saldana was inspiring because of her attractiveness to black men. The first response came from Ashley Caldwell of Waterloo, Iowa, who wrote, "It was great seeing Zoe Saldana featured on the April 2010 cover. I look forward to seeing more things from her in the future."[83] The other response came from Christina Jackson of Seattle, Washington, who said: "I loved your April 2010 cover with Zoe Saldana. And what I love more is that she is a naturally superskinny girl like me. I do consider myself attractive, but because I don't have that bada-bing-bada-boom body I don't think I'm considered beautiful in our community. But to have Zoe come along and have so much success and even have Black men checking for her is such an inspiration!"[84]

The reasons for such differing reactions to black male–white female and black female–white male relationships in *Essence* magazine could be many. It may simply be a matter of readership, as black women are the target audience for *Essence*. There are, however, other potential explanations for the differing responses to the covers featuring Saldana and Bush. For example, one of my survey participants, Cameron, a black woman who is married to a white man, indicated her belief that what she views as a greater acceptance of black women's relationships with white men stems from the "assumption [within the black community] that [such black women] couldn't find a suitable black man. This acceptance is often based on the 'shortage of black men' presumption of interracial dating."[85] Similarly, Becca, a black woman who is married to a white man, identified the difficulty in finding a black husband as one of the reasons why her parents were not "troubled" by her interracial marriage, stating "my parents knew that it would be harder for me as a black woman to find a black man to date and marry."[86] Moreover, reading closely the above quote from Christina Jackson about Saldana, one could extract another reason why a black woman's relationship with a white man—here, Saldana's—may not be as troubling for some individuals—here, *Essence* readers: that Saldana does not have that "bada-bing-bada-boom body" that black men love. Here again, though, a black woman has received a pass that a black man has not; after all, couldn't the same rationale apply to Bush's former relationship with Kardashian, who does have a "bada-bing-bada-boom body"?

Of course, this is not to say that black male–white female couples experience resistance at every turn. For some couples, the image of the black woman who is angry at white women for "stealing" black men has proven to be just that—an image. For instance, Julie, a white woman who is married to a black man, indicated that, though she anticipated such hostility, there has actually been very little of it in her life. She explained, "I am sensitive to the idea of white women 'taking' black men, especially highly educated ones. That actually worried me a bit about the relationship at first. So I am wary of potential negative reactions from black women and may even imagine some that aren't necessarily there, *but there really aren't that many that I can remember.* For some reason, it seems to soften people to us when they see us with our son, I've noticed."[87] Similarly, Julie's husband, Barry, stated that while he has felt "anxious about [black women's] potential reaction . . . there hasn't really been much of a reaction that [he] discern[s]."[88]

Additionally, my observations about comparative hostilities to black male–white female and black female–white male relationships are not at all meant to suggest that somehow black female–white male couples do not experience disapproval and hostility from others. They definitely do. In fact, of the couples whom I surveyed, many of the black female–white male couples described negative reactions to their relationship from strangers, particularly from black men and white women. For example, Margaret, a black woman who is married to a white man, noted one troubling incident when she and her husband were rushing to the hospital. She said: "Once, while in a taxi to get my husband to the hospital after a finger cut, after the driver (who was a black male) learned that it was my husband whom I was helping, he reduced the speed and drove more slowly to the emergency room. I have been told that black women should not leave 'the race.'"[89] Additionally, a few responses from same-sex couples whom I surveyed suggest that black-white relationships between gay men elicit hostility similar to that of black male–white female relationships. For example, John, a white man who is in a civil union with a black man, explained, "Generally speaking, I think that black women do not like our relationship. I guess that they do not like both that my partner is gay and that he is with a white man. I am not sure what they dislike most. Sometimes, it may be that black women perceived my partner as a good man who could have raised a good family with a black woman."[90] On the flip side, others in black-white gay relationships such as Bryan conveyed the opposite view—relief by black women that they were with white men instead of white women. Bryan, a black man who is married to a white man, explained, "The black women I've discussed this with joke that at least I'm not dating a white woman."[91]

However, the question remains: why do black male–white female marriages consistently and significantly outnumber black female–white male marriages when, historically, there has been greater legal punishment for and social animosity toward black male–white female intimate partnerships? Here, too, the lives of Alice and Leonard Rhinelander may prove to be instructive. The couple's experiences teach us how law and society have worked together to frame the normative ideal of family not only as monoracial but also as heterosexual, and in a way that could define black female–white male intimacy as the least normative of all intimacies. As I explained in Chapter 4, one of the possible reasons why the jury was able to rule for Alice, and against Leonard, at the trial's end is that Alice acted according to the racial stereotype of the Jezebel and vamp by engaging in premarital sex with Leonard and writing about their sexual encounters in her love letters to him, while Leonard purportedly acted against racial, class, and gender stereotypes by interacting with poorer people and also clearly black people like Robert Brooks, and allowing himself to be "controlled" by a woman. Indeed, Leonard's attorney, Isaac Mills, worked hard to portray Alice as the vamp, the controlling and oversexualized, black female aggressor who seduced and lured a dim-witted and weak-willed Leonard with her lasciviousness and who forced him to follow her plan of marriage. Alice's own attorney, Lee Parsons Davis, contributed to the depiction of Alice as vamp when he introduced her body for inspection by the all-white and all-male jurors.

But as much as the image of Alice as the vamp or Jezebel may have worked to help her defeat Leonard's claim for annulment, it also worked to push her and Leonard's relationship further outside of the normative ideal for couples in our society—here, across gender lines. Regardless of whether such a framing is actually desirable, the ideal couple in our society, especially during the 1920s, is framed as being gendered "feminine" and "masculine." Labeled as the sexual aggressor and dominant one in her relationship with Leonard, Alice was, like so many black women, deemed to be the masculine one, subverting not only the roles of race by making Leonard her "love slave" but also the roles of man and woman. In fact, the Jezebel or vamp was not deemed to be a woman at all, but instead an unladylike creature, which made the assault and rape of her by white men acceptable in white society and by law and the exploitation of her work in the fields and elsewhere free from challenge.[92] Such stereotypes of black women continue with similar force today in media images of racialized welfare mothers and family-destroying and domineering matriarchs, images and stereotypes that place black women outside of the normative ideal of family by framing them in traditionally masculine terms and roles.

This stereotype of reversed gender roles applies also to physical perceptions of black women. Research shows that whites are more likely to mistakenly identify black women, than they are white women, as men, and that such miscategorizations are influenced by race. Scholars Phillip Atiba Goff, Margaret Thomas, and Matthew Christian Jackson conducted a study that demonstrates that the "the conflation of 'Black' and 'male' [that formed during the antebellum period]—has cognitive analogs that persist today."[93] In their research, the professors examined 292 white undergraduates from Pennsylvania State University to see how the intersection of race (black versus white) and gender (male versus female) affects a person's perception of the sex of other individuals. The researchers found that their subjects made significantly more errors when categorizing black women by sex than they did for any other raced and gendered group. They also found that such associations of black women with "maleness" resulted in black women being rated as less attractive, which the scholars' mediational analysis showed was reconciled by the two female groups' ratings on masculinity.[94]

In the end, because perceived unattractiveness in women grows proportionally with perceptions of them as masculine, the associations between black women and masculine appearance and behaviors are part of the reason why black women are consistently viewed as the least desirable female partners and thus as outside gendered definitions of the familial ideal. Such factors, combined, work to place black women at the bottom of the marriage market, which in turn contributes to the significant difference between the rate of intermarriage between black women and white men and black men and white women and reinforces notions of such couples as outside the normative ideal for family.

One more reason why Alices and Leonards are so much more unlikely to exist than other married interracial couples is the loss of race and gender privilege that often comes to people, especially white men, after intermarriage. These factors must play a role, whether consciously or unconsciously, in any individual's decisions about marriage. As Professor Renee Romano has explained, historically speaking, it was the white partner in a black-white marriage who assimilated into the black community, which often meant living in black neighborhoods, attending black churches, sending children to black schools, and reinforcing the one-drop rule by raising biracial children with only a black identity.[95] While with some black female–white male couples it was the black women who assimilated into the white community, the white men in those relationships were unable to maintain their full social status and privileges in the white community. Again, consider the case of Leonard Kip Rhinelander. Although Leonard came from one of the most powerful families in New York and possessed $280,000 on his own in 1924—the equivalent of $3.7 million in 2011—even he, with all of his wealth, could not freely live anywhere he wanted to in New York once he married Alice. Instead, he lived in a room in the modest home of George and Elizabeth Jones and then later, for a brief time, with Alice in a modest apartment in New Rochelle, New York. Even after the infamous *Rhinelander* trial had ended, Leonard remained cut off and isolated from most of his family and family connections for several years, only to die just a few years later at the young age of 34. While today, marrying interracially would not necessarily result in a similar loss of status and privilege, as I discuss in Chapter 6, there are many privileges that are automatically lost for all black-white couples in a society where laws and rules presume monoraciality among families.

Race as an Acceptable Basis for Annulment Today?

Overall, one must wonder to what extent a broad cross-section of our nation's citizens today, especially white citizens, view knowledge of racial background—specifically blackness—as a factor that goes to the essence of marriage.[96] Professor Wendy Greene has explained that, during the 1920s, "the discovery of Black ancestry for those who physically appeared white could automatically relegate such persons to Blackness, the most degraded class."[97] During the twenty-first century, one still must ask whether such discoveries and revelations could serve as a basis for finding the central purposes of marriage destroyed. In other words, could a litigant today successfully identify racial fraud as a factor that goes to the essence of marriage in an annulment case?

Courts have held that the concealment of matters such as "'incontinence, temper, idleness, extravagance, coldness or fortune'" cannot serve as the basis for an annulment.[98] Likewise, courts have held that a misrepresentation about financial means or social position does not go to the essence of marriage.[99] Rather, the misrepresentation must be so material and important that it essentially destroys the marital agreement.[100]

But what would the answer to this dilemma be regarding representations of racial background after *Loving v. Virginia?* The fact that *Loving* forever changed family law, and thus families, by striking down all antimiscegenation statutes does not in itself resolve this legal question about race and annulment. After all, even in *Rhinelander*, where New York did not ban interracial marriages between blacks and whites, knowledge of a spouse's race was, without question, viewed as satisfying the lower standard of being material to decisions about marriage. Furthermore, as this chapter shows, online dating data confirm that the vestiges of prejudice enveloped in laws against interracial marriage continue to be potent.

The short answer to my question is that, today, knowledge of a spouse's race is unlikely to provide a sufficient legal basis for an annulment. The longer answer, however, reveals a much more complex response that leans toward yes.

Looking first at the short answer of no, courts are unlikely to find knowledge of race to be a sufficient basis for annulment for reasons ranging from the fact that annulments do not serve the same purpose today as they did during the 1920s to the fact that Supreme Court case law suggests that decisions of family law cannot be made based on such prejudices. First, in our society, annulments are not as key to ending marital relationships as they were prior to the no-fault divorce revolution of the 1970s. During the era of restrictive, fault-based divorces, annulments served a very important purpose, as they provided the primary—in some cases, the only—mechanism for people to dissolve their marriages. Since the no-fault divorce revolution, however, divorces have become relatively easy to obtain, making the need for the remedy of annulment less necessary than it was during the time of the Rhinelanders. In 1924 and 1925, when Leonard was seeking an annulment of his marriage to Alice, New York allowed divorces between couples on the grounds of adultery only.

Moreover, in a no-fault regime, it would be difficult to grant an annulment based on what could be viewed solely as race prejudice. Though involving a completely different set of facts, *Palmore v. Sidoti* suggests that racial prejudice cannot serve as a basis for breaking up aspects of family.[101] In *Palmore*, a white father, Anthony Sidoti, sued to modify a custody order to remove his white daughter from the custody of his ex-wife, a white woman named Linda Palmore, after she had married a black man. The Florida trial court awarded Sidoti custody, reasoning that the impact on the child if she remained in the racially mixed household of Palmore and her new husband would be damaging. The trial court judge asserted: "This Court feels that despite the strides that have been made in bettering relations between the races in this country, it is inevitable that Melanie will, if allowed to remain in her present situation and attains school age and thus more vulnerable to peer pressures, suffer from the social stigmatization that is sure to come."[102] The Florida District Court of Appeals affirmed the trial court decision, but the U.S. Supreme Court reversed it, explaining that the issue is not whether or not the "reality of private biases and the possible injury they might inflict are permissible considerations for removal of an infant child from the custody of its natural mother."[103] The Court proclaimed, "We have little difficulty concluding that they are not. The Constitution cannot control such prejudices but neither can it tolerate them."[104]

On the other hand, a wide variety of factors suggest that, even today, many people view annulments to be important and, more so, consider knowledge of race as central to the purposes of marriage. To begin, although annulments generally serve a different purpose than they did before the no-fault divorce movement, annulments still serve an extremely important purpose for many people. For some people, it "may help alleviate the social stigmas sometimes associated with divorcees."[105] For others, it may enable them to protect their property from or otherwise avoid financial responsibility to a person who defrauded them about a factor that went to the essence of their marriage.[106] While granting an annulment based on racial fraud in a post–*Loving v. Virginia* world does not, at first glance, seem to be likely, it is hard to imagine, given the current state of race relations, that some judges would not be sympathetic to an argument from a man or woman who had been deceived about the race of his or her spouse. In this sense, 1920s New York, where Alice and Leonard were socially, not legally, forbidden from remaining together as husband and wife, is not so different from today's society. Although there is case law indicating that concealment of fanatic racism by a spouse is conduct that goes to the essence of a marriage[107]—an act that suggests not only that awareness about a spouse's racism could be grounds for annulment but provides hope about our ability to move beyond race—our entire practice of regulating intimate relationships reveals that our society fervently protects people's preferences to "discriminate" on the basis of race in terms of the people with whom they form intimate and familial relationships. As Professor Rachel Moran has highlighted, "When 95 percent of all marriages in America take place between people of the same race, race shapes marital choice; but, just as importantly, marriage shapes racial identity. . . . The freedom to select our intimates is also the power to define racial difference."[108]

Furthermore, as Moran explains, because we view private relationship choices as nondiscriminatory in nature, rarely do we pose the question of why 95 percent of all marriages are same-raced or consider whether such statistics are the result of racial bias. For instance, consider what OkCupid uncovered about its customers' views toward interracial dating and marriage. As part of its survey, OkCupid posed the following two questions to its customers: (1) Is interracial marriage a bad idea? (2) Would you strongly prefer to date someone of your own skin color/racial background? In so doing, OkCupid discovered that their customers largely did not view interracial marriage as a bad idea, with "yes" responses (which were against interracial marriage) ranging from 2 percent to 7 percent and with whites having the highest "yes" rate at 7 percent. However, although the customers did not see interracial marriage as problematic, much higher percentages of them "strongly prefer[red]" to date someone of their own race. Minority preferences for same-race dating ranged from 11 percent to 33 percent, with black men at 11 percent and Native American women at 33 percent. Both white male and white female preferences for same-race dating, however, far exceeded both the highest same-race preference rate and average same-race preference rate for minorities, with white men at 40 percent and white women at a whopping 54 percent. On average, only 20 percent of nonwhites preferred to date someone of the same race compared to 45 percent of whites.[109] The responses of gay and lesbian customers indicated similar disparities between whites and racial minorities. First, like with heterosexual customers, gay, lesbian, and bisexual customers did not view interracial marriage as a bad idea, with "yes" responses ranging from 0 percent to 4 percent. However, when asked about same-race preferences for dating, whites, again, exhibited a significantly greater preference for other whites. Minority gay, lesbian, and bisexual preferences for same-race dating ranged from 6 percent to 21 percent, with black gay men at 6 percent and Middle Eastern gay men at 21 percent. White gay, lesbian, and bisexual preferences for same-race dating, however, far exceeded both the highest same-race preference rate and average same-race preference rate for minorities, with white gay men at 43 percent; white, bisexual men at 27 percent; white lesbians at 31 percent; and white, bisexual women at 32 percent. On average, only 15 percent of nonwhite gays, lesbians, and bisexuals preferred to date someone of the same race compared to 35 percent of white gays, lesbians, and bisexuals.[110]

Even in the face of decisions such as *Loving* and *Palmore,* the law continues to facilitate the use of race as a determinative factor in the construction of families by individuals. Indeed, courts have recognized a legal "loss" to persons whose ability to construct families based on monoracial preferences has been marred by third-party interference. For example, in Ireland, even as their multiracial son was ten years old, a white couple remained strong in their efforts to obtain damages from a fertility clinic that fertilized the wife's eggs with "Caucasian cape coloured" sperm (meaning sperm from a particular minority group in South Africa) as opposed to the "white Caucasian" sperm they requested, a mistake that resulted in a darker-skinned child for them.[111] The couple's explanations of the harm to their family reveal just how unbending the framing of the normative ideal for family as monoracial is in society. Among the couple's harms to them and their family included humiliation and emotional damage from suggestions of extramarital affairs and demeaning looks from people who openly stared at them. Their family's lack of monoraciality immediately worked to cast suspicion upon them. As the husband explained, "We can't go out together because people openly stare at us. My wife has been asked if she's had an affair with an Indian man on holiday. In public, she'll shrug it off. But in private, she's often in tears."[112] In the United States, a New York judge recognized a similar claim by a bicultural Dominican and white couple, who sued a clinic that had used sperm from a black donor to conceive their daughter during in vitro fertilization. Like the couple in Ireland, the New York couple proclaimed their love for their child, but mourned the daily and visual reminder of the mistake that had been made. Reportedly, the mistake came to their attention because of the unusually dark color of their newborn as compared to her brown—or at least in U.S. terms, "black-looking"—mother and white father. The couple was reported as saying, "It is simply impossible to ignore,"[113] revealing that, in some instances, the monoracial ideal for families extends beyond race and all the way to even color.

Similarly, as Professor Ralph Richard Banks has explicated, society allowed for years explicit state facilitation of the use of race in parental selection of children for legal adoption, by not discouraging parents' racial preferences for adoptive children.[114] Today, "[e]ven many adopters and adoptees who have together created loving multiracial families nonetheless believe that, all other things equal, same-race adoption is preferable to interracial adoption."[115] Moreover, as Professor Solangel Maldonado has explained, although the law no longer allows race to be used as the reason to deny or delay placement of a child for domestic adoption or foster care, it participates in discrimination by facilitating the decisions of many white adoptive families who may be choosing to adopt European and Asian children from abroad instead of black and brown children in the United States based upon unconscious as well as conscious racial preferences.[116]

In sum, the ways in which we protect potential race discrimination along lines of intimacy and have used law as a tool to regulate race and adoption in the family hint at the continuing prominence of race as an "essential" of marriage, or more broadly speaking, of family today, even if courts will not explicitly recognize knowledge of a spouse's race as "essential" in an annulment case. In a society that views children as central to marriage, it is difficult to imagine that some courts would not sympathize with arguments concerning whether the suing partner willingly chose to have racially mixed children. In fact, for those blacks who passed as white, a common fear among them was that, despite their having married whites, a trace of their colored blood would appear in their children. Such fears are wonderfully displayed in author Kate Chopin's short story "Desiree's Baby," about a "white" couple, Desiree and Armand. In that story, the main character Desiree, who was raised by a white mother who found baby Desiree sleeping near a stone pillar, marries a man named Armand, who comes from one of the "oldest and proudest" families in Louisiana. After Desiree gives birth to their first child, Armand tells Desiree to leave his home forever because the baby appears to be a "quadroon." In the end, the reader learns that it is Armand who is secretly passing as white—his own mother "belong[ing] to the race that is cursed with the brand of slavery."

We know of at least one former judge who has expressed sentiments against interracial couples because of his concerns about biracial children (see fig. 5.3). In 2009, Keith Bardwell, then a judge in Tangipahoa Parish, Louisiana, refused to marry an interracial couple—a thirty-two-year-old black man, Terence McKay, and his thirty-year-old white female partner, Beth Humphrey—because Bardwell feared for their mixed-race children. Bardwell argued that biracial children would not be accepted by either whites or blacks. He further asserted, "I don't do interracial marriages because I don't want to put children in a situation they didn't bring on themselves. . . . In my heart, I feel the children will later suffer."[117] In an effort to explain his actions more, Bardwell stated that, in his experience, interracial marriages do not last long.

Lest one think that Bardwell was just one rogue judge who ignored the law (thus making his actions "meaningless" in terms of the lessons they impart about societal and legal norms on race and family), consider the fact that some of Bardwell's colleagues seemed to know what he was doing in

Fig. 5.3. Dresden McIntosh Farrand and Clint Farrand, a black female–white male married couple, smile at and cuddle with their first child, Owen. Photograph courtesy of Dresden McIntosh Farrand and Clint Farrand, taken by Lindsey Dyer

refusing to marry interracial couples, and not only never reported him but in fact accepted his referrals of interracial couples to marry. It may have been that Bardwell's colleagues saw his views about interracial couples in the way that so many individuals view questions of intimacy among lovers and families—to be mere personal and natural preference, not racism. In fact, Bardwell himself explained his beliefs in this way, asserting: "I'm not a racist. I just don't believe in mixing the races that way. . . . I have piles and piles of black friends. They come to my home, I marry them, they use my bathroom. I treat them just like everyone else."[118] But it is exactly this failure to examine our perception of these intimate matters as private decisions deserving of both social and legal protection that works to perpetuate the framing of the monoracial family as the normative ideal, an ideal that comes with a plethora of social privileges and benefits. Luckily, Bardwell, through his actions and words, made it easier for so many people to see the connections between these "private" decisions and the social and legal cues and norms that work to perpetuate racial hierarchies, both among individuals and families. Bardwell made us all ask ourselves: Who comes to our homes? Whom do we marry or see as marriageable? Or even, shamefully, whom do we allow to use our bathrooms? And finally, how have individual courts worked to regulate race within families, both consciously and unconsciously? Or more so, in our society, do we and our families all receive the same, social and legal privileges and benefits, regardless of race, or more specifically, monoraciality? In the next chapter, "Living in Placelessness," I explore this last question, analyzing the privileges that may appear or disappear depending upon one's position at the intersection of race, sexuality, and family.

6

Living in Placelessness

JUST AS THE *RHINELANDER* TRIAL TEACHES us much about the black and white, or ranking, of love, it also provides us with significant lessons about the social and legal advantages and disadvantages that can exist at the intersection of race and family. Much like privileges may attach to membership in the dominant racial or gender group in the United States, privileges also may attach to the lives of heterosexual, monoracial couples and their families, even as those privileges may vary based upon the shared races and socioeconomic classes of those couples and families. Indeed, the loss of privileges that can result from being part of an interracial family unit also plays a role in the low rate of black-white marital and committed relationships within the United States. For example, consider just the basic facts of the Rhinelander case. Leonard Kip Rhinelander, a wealthy white man, left Alice Beatrice Rhinelander, the love of his life, not because he no longer loved her or loved her less because she was part black, but because he feared the privileges he would lose—not just privileges attached to the enormous wealth of his family line, but the privilege of remaining connected to his family members and all that New York elite society had come to mean to him.

For many individuals, the mere fear of losing the privileges that come with monoracial couple status provides an incentive for deciding against black-white intimate relationships and, ultimately, black-white marriage or commitment. In the end, such decisions work to bolster the framing of the monoracial and heterosexual family as the normative ideal by reinforcing commonly held notions about how "natural" it is for people of the same race and different sexes to form intimate unions and by allowing us as a society to ignore the very social and legal cues and norms that govern our cross-racial and same-sex interactions. Additionally, the actual loss of privilege that certain individuals may experience in black-white relationships can work further to reinforce this normative ideal of family by causing such persons to actually end their relationships when they feel the costs of their transgressions have become too high.

In this chapter, I identify and examine the social and legal privileges that can attach to couples and their families based upon race and sexuality. Although I broadly explore the wide range of privileges that can attach to monoracial couples, I ultimately end by focusing on just one form those privileges take: the privileges that certain couples may experience over others with respect to housing, housing choice, and the application of housing discrimination law.

I first begin by identifying and comparing the social and legal privileges that white and black monoracial, heterosexual couples may experience over each other, over same-sex couples of any race, and over black-white heterosexual couples in particular. In making these comparisons, I not only expose the invisibility of black-white, heterosexual couples and their families in our laws and in society, but also reveal how the monoracial and heterosexual family has been established as the ideal within our culture. Finally, I focus on privileges that can attach to couples with respect to housing, housing choice, and housing discrimination law. In so doing, I analyze how our segregated residential patterns signal what I call the "placelessness"—the absence of any space—for households headed by black-white couples. I briefly explore how law can operate together with social patterns and norms to both define and reinforce the monoracial family as the ultimate standard. Specifically, I examine housing discrimination law to demonstrate the connection between the daily social disadvantages of black-white, heterosexual couples, their families, and other multiracial families, and the lack of legal recognition for black-white couples, their families, and other multiracial families within the housing arena.

Understanding Race, Sex, Sexuality, and Monoracial Couple Privilege

In the late 1980s, Professor Peggy McIntosh became one of the first white scholars to analyze the theoretical concept of white privilege in her paper "White Privilege: Unpacking the Invisible Knapsack."[1] "White privilege," she said, "is like an invisible weightless knapsack of special provisions, assurances, tools, maps, guides, codebooks, passports, visas, clothes, compass, emergency gear, and blank checks,"[2] which includes individual advantages such as, but not limited to, the following:

1. I can if I wish arrange to be in the company of people of my race most of the time.
2. I can avoid spending time with people whom I was trained to mistrust and who have learned to mistrust my kind or me.
3. If I should need to move, I can be pretty sure of renting or purchasing housing in an area which I can afford and in which I would want to live.
4. I can be pretty sure that my neighbors in such a location will be neutral or pleasant to me.
5. I can go shopping alone most of the time, pretty well assured that I will not be followed or harassed.[3]

Today, McIntosh's words about white-skin privilege ring equally true. As a scholar who examines the intersections of race and the law, I have given McIntosh's work serious thought over the years, both voluntarily and involuntarily. In so doing, I have had to acknowledge how all individuals in our society possess one or more invisible knapsacks of unearned privileges, whether they be based on race, color, class, sex, sexual orientation, or any other identity category. At the same time, I have come to understand how individuals also may suffer or endure societal disadvantages that attach to one or more of the same identity categories.

Even more so, as a black woman who is married to a white man and the mother of three biracial, black-white children, I have given much thought to how these identity-based privileges and disadvantages can shape and affect families. For example, in looking at how identity-based privileges can attach to couples, I have examined and studied my own heterosexual privileges and their impact on my family and its relationship to the State. In addition, I have explored how heterosexual-couple privileges can become complicated by other identity categories, such as race, interraciality (defined as one's involvement as part of an interracial family unit),[4] or socioeconomic class. Finally, much like McIntosh described with herself and other white individuals in her essay "White Privilege," I have begun to more fully comprehend, through my work and through my observations of others, how monoracial, heterosexual couples have been conditioned to remain oblivious about their own unearned privileges based on sexual orientation and shared race.[5] It is in this way that I have really come to appreciate how the widespread assumptions about monoraciality among couples can work to make interracial couples and families invisible in law and life, including in our post–*Loving v. Virginia,* and as some would argue, postracial era.

Ironically, one of the clearest ways to highlight and expose the many privileges of monoraciality among couples and families is to consider first the general privileges and disadvantages that single-race, white (and in some cases, single-race, black) heterosexual couples enjoy as compared to single-race, white same-sex couples. After all, one would be hard-pressed to legitimately contest the way in which sexuality—specifically, heterosexuality—has worked to privilege couples and their families.[6] Indeed, our laws generally exclude gays and lesbians from protection against discrimination based on sexual orientation. In our society, the lack of protection for the families of gays and lesbians is simply undeniable.

A brief listing of just some of the advantages that white, heterosexual couples enjoy reveals exactly how law and society often function together to frame the normative ideal of family as heterosexual. Consider just these fifteen examples of heterosexual privilege for white couples, some of which may also apply to similarly situated, black heterosexual couples, but none of which apply to same-sex couples of any racial make-up.[7]

1. In all fifty states, white, heterosexual partners can marry each other as long as they do not violate other marital restrictions, such as age

or number restrictions, and can have their marriage recognized by every other state in the union.

2. White, heterosexual couples generally do not have to engage in endless discussion and questions regarding their identity as a couple from strangers and acquaintances, including questions such as "How did you *ever* meet?" Their relationships are generally considered unremarkable.

3. White, heterosexual couples do not run the risk of being reduced to a single aspect of their lives as a unit, as though their being single-race and heterosexual sums up all of who they are.

4. White, heterosexual couples can assume that their relationship will not be viewed as the result of sexual deviance or that it will not be described in terms that suggest a sickness or disease.

5. White, heterosexual couples are free to reveal and live in their intimate relationships openly by referring to each other by name, going out in public together, and displaying pictures of each other on their desk or on their walls.

6. When out in public, the same-race children of white, heterosexual couples, whether by birth or adoption, are presumed to "belong" to them as parents. Generally, such heterosexual couples are not asked questions about their parental circumstances, such as, "Is that your child?"

7. So long as they are otherwise qualified, white, heterosexual couples can adopt children in all fifty states.

8. If white, heterosexual couples break up or divorce, they can generally assume that people will not attribute their dissolution to the type of relationship they are in.

9. Individuals in white, heterosexual couples can live with the comfort of knowing that other people's assumptions about the race and sex of their partner is correct.

10. White, heterosexual couples can turn on the television or read the newspaper and see reflections of their intimate relationships widely represented.

11. White, heterosexual couples can go shopping together, fairly well assured that people will understand that they are intimate partners

and not just friends. When checking out, they rarely encounter the question: "Is this together?"

12. Individuals in white, heterosexual couples can assume that their and their partner's race and sexuality will not be used to determine whether they fit in at work, whether their co-workers will feel comfortable working with them, or whether they experience an adverse employment action in their workplace. If they encounter mistreatment, they are much less likely to wonder whether their relationship with their partner played a role.

13. The children of white, heterosexual couples are given texts and classes that implicitly support their family unit.

14. White, heterosexual couples generally can go out in public together and can travel together without any expectation of embarrassment in or mistreatment by those who deal with them and without fear of being challenged or attacked by hate groups. If they are victimized, they generally will not be asked what they were doing there in the first place.

15. Should white, heterosexual couples need to move, they can be fairly sure of renting or purchasing housing in an area in which they can afford, in which they would want to live, and in which the neighbors would not disapprove of their household.

Of course, this particular list of privileges for white, heterosexual couples is not an exhaustive one. Yet, even this limited list illustrates McIntosh's point about how privilege can make insiders "feel welcomed and 'normal' in the usual walks of public life, institutional and social," and can make outsiders feel unwelcome and without a home in those same areas.[8]

For instance, in all of the examples listed above, same-sex couples and their families are essentially marked as outsiders. Yes, same-sex couples may find themselves "welcomed and normal" in a few, rare instances, such as in media representations, because gay couples and their families have appeared on popular shows such as *Modern Family* and *Brothers and Sisters*. But these moments are rather infrequent and almost never result in equal representations of intimacy among gay couple–headed families and heterosexual couple-headed families. In the end, we are left with an essentially

Fig. 6.1. Homophobia and racism can make everyday experiences for the Smith-Holladay family difficult. Yet they have hope for change in the near future. Photograph courtesy of Catherine Smith and Jennifer Holladay

uncontested framing of the normative ideal of family as heterosexual—not just socially, but also legally (see fig. 6.1).

Indeed, given the state of the laws in the United States, the fact that same-sex couples and their families lack many privileges in our society is not surprising at all. What is surprising, however, is the frequency with which some heterosexual couples—specifically, interracial heterosexual couples—may also find themselves marked as outsiders and without protection. Because of the interlocking nature of hierarchies in our society, not all opposite-sex couples possess the same privileges and advantages over same-sex couples. As Professor Kimberlé Crenshaw illustrated in her seminal work on intersectionality,[9] different groups of people may encounter varied forms of discriminatory behavior based upon the intersection of two or more identity categories.[10] Intersectionality recognizes that power, privilege, disadvantage, and discrimination are influenced by interlocking spectrums of identity and that individuals may have distinct vulnerabilities and may actually experience discrimination differently from one another based on those interlocking spectrums.[11]

In addition to individuals, Crenshaw's work also applies to couples and their families. For example, when I apply Crenshaw's theoretical framework of intersectionality to the list above for single-race, black heterosexual couples (instead of single-race, white heterosexual couples), I can identify several important differences between the advantages that white, heterosexual couples and black, heterosexual couples may enjoy at the intersection of race, sexuality, and family. Here, the race of the single-race, black heterosexual couples works to deprive them of some of the privileges that are more broadly enjoyed by white, heterosexual couples. Consider, now, the same list as above; only in this instance, it has been reconstructed to fit with the lived experiences of single-race, black heterosexual couples. Roughly speaking, the first thirteen examples apply with similar breadth to single-race, black heterosexual couples, with a few important modifications (in italics). However, the last two examples from that same list reveal very different results for black, heterosexual couples, with the identified privileges attaching in no form or not nearly as frequently for black, heterosexual couples, despite their shared heterosexuality.

1. In all fifty states, black, heterosexual partners can marry each other as long as they do not violate other marital restrictions, such as age or number restrictions, and can have their marriage recognized by every other state in the union.

2. Black, heterosexual couples generally do not have to engage in endless discussion and questions regarding their identity as a couple from strangers and acquaintances, including questions such as, "How did you *ever* meet?" Their relationships are generally considered unremarkable.

3. Black, heterosexual couples do not run the risk of being reduced to a single aspect of their lives as a unit, as though their being single-race and heterosexual sums up all of who they are *(though as individuals, blacks often are reduced to one single aspect of their lives—their race)*.

4. Black, heterosexual couples can assume that their relationship will

not be viewed as the result of sexual deviance or that it will not be described in terms that suggest a sickness or disease *(though as individuals, black women and black men tend to be viewed as sexually deviant, with black women stereotyped as promiscuous vamps and Jezebels and black men stereotyped as sexually crazed and overly virile).*

5. Black, heterosexual couples are free to reveal and live in their intimate relationships openly by referring to each other by name, going out in public together, and displaying pictures of each other on their desk or on their walls.

6. When out in public, the same-race children of black, heterosexual couples, whether by birth or adoption, are presumed to "belong" to them as parents. Generally, such heterosexual couples are not asked questions about their parental circumstances, such as, "Is that your child?"

7. So long as they are otherwise qualified, black, heterosexual couples, much like white, heterosexual couples, can adopt children in all fifty states.

8. If black, heterosexual couples break up or divorce, they can generally assume that people will not attribute their dissolution to the type of relationship they are in.

9. Individuals in black, heterosexual couples can live with the comfort of knowing that other people's assumptions about the race and sexuality of their partner are correct.

10. Black, heterosexual couples can turn on the television or read the newspaper and see reflections of their intimate relationships widely represented *(though the representations are not in line with or proportional to demographic data and often are highly stereotypical and negative).*

11. Black, heterosexual couples can go shopping together, fairly well assured that people will understand that they are intimate partners, and not just friends or strangers. When checking out or dining out, they rarely encounter the question: "Is this together?"

12. Individuals in black, heterosexual couples can assume that their and their partner's race and sexuality will not be used to determine

whether they fit in at work, whether their co-workers will feel comfortable working with them, or whether they experience an adverse employment action in their workplace. If they encounter mistreatment, they are much less likely to wonder whether their relationship with their partner played a role.

13. The children of black, heterosexual couples are given texts and classes that implicitly support their family unit as heterosexual and monoracial *(though such texts and classes rarely support their identities as contributing, black individuals).*

14. *Unlike white, heterosexual couples, black, heterosexual couples generally cannot go out in public together or travel together without any expectation of embarrassment in or mistreatment by those who deal with them and without fear of being challenged or attacked by hate groups. As Professor Jeannine Bell has highlighted in her article "Hate Thy Neighbor: Violent Racial Exclusion and the Persistence of Segregation,"[12] black families that are integrating into white neighborhoods tend to face significant violence and intimidation when doing so. When black, heterosexual couples are so victimized, some will ask, "Why were they moving there in the first place?"*

15. *For reasons similar to those expressed above, should black, heterosexual couples need to move, they cannot be fairly sure of renting or purchasing housing in an area in which they can afford, in which they would want to live, and in which the neighbors would not disapprove of their household.*

In sum, while the experiences of black individuals and white individuals may vary greatly based on upon race privilege and disadvantage, the experience of single-race, black heterosexual couples and single-race, white heterosexual couples *as couples* mirror each other in many ways, even as they may differ from one another in crucial ways based upon context.

In light of the fact that individuals have legally been permitted to marry across racial lines in the United States since the *Loving* decision in 1967, one would expect that a similar list of privileges for black-white, heterosexual couples would resemble the lists above for both black and white, single-race, heterosexual couples. Indeed, in the eyes of many, the disadvantages that were often linked to interracial couples in the pre-*Loving* era have all but disappeared in our now "postracial" society. Such views are not completely unwarranted. The rate of black-white marriage in the United States has grown from less than one in a thousand *new* marriages in 1961 to one in sixty *new* marriages in 2008.[13] Not only has the rate of black-white marriage significantly increased, social attitudes toward black-white marriage have also improved markedly. In 1958, only 4 percent of Americans approved of black-white marriage. Although less than 50 percent of Americans approved of black-white marriage as recently as 1994, polls have shown that 77 percent and 83 percent of Americans approved of black-white marriage in 2007 and 2009, respectively.[14]

A recent episode of the popular ABC television show *What Would You Do?* with John Quiñones, reveals exactly how far we have come since the *Loving* decision in a segment of the show entitled "Interracial Couple Harassed."[15] In that episode, Quiñones sets up an experiment for testing how people will respond to the harassment of an interracial couple in the deep South. In this scene, two actors, Markus and Lisa Lloyd (who are actually married in real life), portray a black male–white female, married couple at a diner in Farmers Branch, Texas, a suburb of Dallas, Texas. As part of the experiment, another actor—an adult, white male—aggressively harasses the couple as they enjoy each other's company in the restaurant. The "What Would You Do?" experiment takes place over the day, and throughout the day, at various intervals, the harasser yells at or mocks the couple with statements such as: (1) "You really married up dude!" (2) "Keep it intact. Keep the race intact!" (3) "I'm just worried about my property values, bro!" (4) "Good thing you don't have kids. That would be polluting our race." (5) "Doves need to stay with doves, and blackbirds need to stay with blackbirds." At one point, when the couple kisses at their table, the harasser tells the couple, "Take it somewhere else!"

As Quiñones does with all his experiments, he shows a variety of responses from real-life customers who have witnessed his project but who did not know that the players in the scene were actors. Though a few customers in the diner are not bothered by the harassment, such as one older, white man who proclaims, "[That's] the establishment's problem, not mine," and an elderly, white woman who asserts that she "couldn't care less" about comforting the targeted, interracial couple, nearly all the other customers shown during the episode respond with great support for the couple. The first two supporters shown are two black women. These two women first ignore the harasser, but ultimately speak up in response to the following comments by the harasser: "I just feel bad for the ladies over here [pointing to the two black women]. You got two attractive single girls over here. They're probably just waiting on a man like you to pick them up, and you got chocolate and vanilla shake going." Immediately, Adriana Thompson, one of the black women, responds, telling the harasser: "Don't even go there. Mixed relationships. . . . That's fine with me. We're all human beings. If you have a problem with that . . . then you need to be somewhere where it's not common to have that type of relationship . . . but I don't know where you're going find it 'cause this is America. . . . Like I said, either you're going to sit there by yourself and have your meal and leave us alone, or you're going to get up and walk out."[16] Eventually, Thompson leaves the restaurant, telling the targeted couple, "Our apology, guys. Don't deal with ignorance." Here, arguably one of the last people we would expect to defend the Lloyds, a black male–white female couple—a black woman—comes to the couple's rescue.

In another run of the same racial experiment, one middle-aged white man leaves the diner in protest, declaring to a white waitress, "I'm not going to sit next to and listen to ignorance like that." In yet a different run, another middle-aged, white man goes to two white waitresses to report the harassment, asserting, "Why don't you throw this man out? He doesn't belong here. . . . I'd call the cops and throw his ass out." The last scene shown involves the rallying together of several customers—all white men—against the bigoted harasser. It begins with one brave, middle-aged white man who passionately tells the harasser: "Why don't you take it somewhere else? Everyone is tired of hearing you talk. . . . Everyone wants you to leave. You're an a-hole." This man is then followed by a younger white man, who declares, "The racist comments, man. . . . That's not cool." When the harasser follows up by telling the interracial couple that they should never have kids, all "heck" breaks loose. The second protester immediately stands up, yelling at the harasser: "Get out! If you don't get out, I'm calling the cops. Get it? I'm dialing 9-1-1. . . . You're offending people in a public place. . . . Get the fuck out! . . . Nobody wants you here." The first speaker joins in with the second protester, announcing to the hired harasser, "You're an asshole. You need to go."

In the end, Quiñones, as always, follows up with those customers who witnessed the scene and responded or did not respond, asking them why they acted as they did. The middle-aged, white man who left the diner earlier in protest appears distraught when approached by Quiñones and declares, "I wish I would have spoke[n] up sooner. That's the only thing I regret." Another middle-aged, white man—the person who first bravely stood up to the harasser in the scene where other customers rallied together against the harasser—leaves us with a message of hope for society. He states, "There's good people and bad people in all races. The situation never goes away when you don't stand up to it."

Yet, despite these and other important changes in both the number of and attitude toward black-white, heterosexual couples, same-race couple privilege remains prevalent in our society. Indeed, the data on changing attitudes toward interracial marriage in general can be misleading. While polls indicate that 83 percent of Americans approved of interracial marriage in 2009, only 63 percent "said it would be fine with them if a family member married 'out' to all three other major racial and ethnic groups tested in the survey."[17] In other words, for at least 20 percent of that 83 percent, interracial marriage was fine so long as it remained outside of their family—so long as their own families remained within the norm. Additionally, many black-white couples, including those in my survey, report experiencing hostility from others based on their relationship. For example, Janet, a black woman who is married to a white man, described one incident when a "black man in Louisiana refused to check [her husband Sam and her] in together on a flight."[18] Indeed, many of the individuals in my survey recalled receiving looks of disagreement, being verbally accosted with comments such as, "Oh no, my sister! A black man isn't good enough for you?" or being served more slowly than other customers at restaurants or stores.

Moreover, returning to the lists of fifteen privileges above, when those same lists are applied to black-white, heterosexual couples, the resulting list for black-white, heterosexual couples looks quite different than those for both single-race, black and white, opposite-sex couples. Rather than resembling the lists of privileges for single-race, heterosexual couples, a reconstructed list for black-white, heterosexual couples looks more like the empty list for all same-sex couples, though not nearly as stark. Although more than forty years have passed since the *Loving* decision was issued, our society does not recognize multiracial couples and families in all aspects of life. For black-white, heterosexual couples in particular, their interraciality as a couple tends to complicate their ability to "enjoy" the full range of heterosexual advantages for individuals and their families. In sum, as Professor Heather Dalmage has explained, "those of us who do not come from or live in single-race families [have to] daily negotiate a racialized and racist system that demands [they] fit [themselves] into prescribed categories."[19] These categories nearly always assume and presume monoraciality for families, a factor which works to eliminate many privileges of heterosexuality from the lives of black-white, heterosexual couples. For instance, out of the fifteen privileges identified above for single-race, white heterosexual couples, only two of those privileges even apply to black-white, heterosexual couples, numbers 1 and 7—a much smaller number than the thirteen (or ten if I am being less generous) that applied to single-race, black, heterosexual couples.

Indeed, the remaining privileges seem to disappear when applied to black-white, heterosexual couples. When reconstructed to generally comport with the realities faced by black-white, heterosexual couples, the full list now reads as follows, *with the shared privileges in italics this time:*

1. *In all fifty states, black-white, heterosexual partners, like single-race, heterosexual partners, can marry each other as long as they do not violate other marital restrictions, such as age or number restrictions, and can have their marriage recognized by every other state in the union.*

2. Unlike single-race, heterosexual couples, black-white, heterosexual couples must often engage in endless discussion and answer numerous questions regarding their identity as a couple from strangers and acquaintances, including questions such as, "How did you *ever* meet?" Their relationships are frequently considered remarkable.

3. Unlike single-race, heterosexual couples, black-white, heterosexual couples are often reduced to a single aspect of their lives as a unit, treated as though their being an interracial couple sums up all of who they are.

4. Unlike the relationships of single-race, heterosexual couples, the relationships of black-white, heterosexual couples are often viewed as the result of sexual deviance or curiosity or described in terms that suggest a sickness or disease. In fact, director Spike Lee created an entire movie centered on this notion, *Jungle Fever.*

5. Unlike single-race, heterosexual couples, black-white, heterosexual couples are not as free to reveal and live in their intimate relationships openly by referring to each other by name, going out in public together, and displaying pictures of each other on their desk or on their walls. A number of employment discrimination cases reveal circumstances under which employees were harassed or taunted at work once other workers discovered that their partner was of another race.

6. When out in public, the children of black-white, heterosexual couples, whether by birth or adoption, are not presumed to "belong" to them as parents. Generally, individuals in such couples are asked questions such as, "Is that your child?" Little children tell them that they do not "match" their children.[20]

7. *So long as they are otherwise qualified, black-white, heterosexual couples, like single-race, heterosexual couples, can adopt children in all fifty states.* But, even now after the Multi-Ethnic Placement Act, they as an interracial couple would encounter difficulty in adopting children, especially children who were not of African descent.[21]

8. Unlike single-race, heterosexual couples, if black-white, heterosexual couples break up or divorce, they can expect that some people will attribute their dissolution to the type of relationship they are in.

9. Unlike individuals in single-race, heterosexual couples, individuals in black-white, heterosexual couples do not live with the comfort of knowing that other people's assumptions about the race and sexuality of their partner are correct.

10. Unlike single-race, white heterosexual couples, black-white, het-

erosexual couples cannot turn on the television or read the newspaper and see reflections of their intimate relationships widely represented. While their intimacy as heterosexuals dominates media accounts, such couples do not often (although increasingly) see reflections of themselves as an interracial couple, especially as a married couple, widely represented in the media. Even when they do, the plot line tends to end in tragedy that is spurred by the mixing of races.[22]

11. Unlike single-race, heterosexual couples, black-white, heterosexual couples cannot go shopping together, fairly well assured that people will understand that they are intimate partners, and not just friends or strangers. When checking out or dining out, they frequently encounter the question: "Is this together?"

12. Individuals in black-white, heterosexual couples cannot assume that their and their partner's race and sexuality will not be used to determine whether they fit in at work, whether their co-workers will feel comfortable working with them, or whether they experience an adverse employment action in their workplace. If they encounter mistreatment, they, especially the white individuals in such relationships, may wonder whether their relationship with their partner played a role.

13. The children of black-white, heterosexual couples are not given texts and classes that implicitly support their family unit. Their children's texts almost never reflect or support the interethnic, interracial diversity of their families.

14. Unlike white, heterosexual couples, but much like black, heterosexual couples, black-white, heterosexual couples generally cannot go out in public together or travel together without any expectation of embarrassment in or mistreatment by those who deal with them and without fear of being challenged or attacked by hate groups. Like monoracial, black families that are integrating white neighborhoods, interracial couples face significant violence and intimidation when moving in. In our incredibly segregated society, there are few neighborhoods that reflect the diversity of their families. Furthermore, when black-white, heterosexual couples are so vic-

timized, many will ask questions such as, "What was he doing there with a white woman in the first place?"

15. Unlike single-race, white heterosexual couples, should black-white, heterosexual couples need to move, they cannot be sure of renting or purchasing housing in an area in which they can afford, in which they would want to live, and in which the neighbors would not disapprove of their household. Unlike white, heterosexual couples, they encounter difficulty, at times, in finding neighborhoods where people approve of their household and, where possible, they often "steer" themselves directly to integrated neighborhoods. In fact, black-white couples are the most likely of any couples to live in integrated neighborhoods.

As the above list demonstrates, even in a post–*Loving v. Virginia* world, black-white, heterosexual couples encounter discrimination at the intersection of race and family. This discrimination works to mark them as being outside the normative family ideal, an ideal, which through social and even legal cues, gets defined as not just heterosexual but also monoracial. For many black-white, heterosexual couples, the interraciality of their family tends to make their very existence as a couple invisible and places many of the privileges that generally attach to same-race, heterosexual couples and families outside of their reach.

Indeed, some of my social experiences with my husband as well as those of other black-white couples, such as those in my survey, confirm this reality. Consider just a few of the examples from all of the lists of privileges above. For instance, as the last list of privileges briefly notes, unlike for single-race, white heterosexual couples, fear of mistreatment plays a role for many black-white, heterosexual couples when choosing public accommodations. In our own experience, my husband, Jacob, and I usually try to carefully plan where we will eat, play, or stay overnight as a means of avoiding discrimination on the road.[23] At times, we even "game" the system, sending Jacob, who is white, in first to scope out the premises or to check us in at a hotel. As Suffolk University Law School Dean Camille Nelson, a black woman who is married to a white man, explained in her article "Lovin' the Man: Examining the Legal Nexus of Irony, Hypocrisy, and Curiosity":

"Navigation of the public space, versus the private sanctuary, is an issue requiring some deliberation on the part of many interracial couples. Like other racialized couples, my partner and I do not have the luxury of simply venturing where we might—we often reflect upon whether certain venues will be welcoming, comfortable, or safe."[24] Indeed, in those instances when black-white couples fail to engage in such deliberate thinking about which spaces are welcome, they may find themselves encountering unwelcome reminders about why they still must engage in such planning. For instance, consider this experience by Jim, a white man who is married to a biracial, black-white woman. On the return drive from his family vacation, Jim found himself surprised by the welcoming and then unwelcoming reaction of a white woman at the Welcome Center in the South. Jim asserted:

> When we went to Disney World as a family in 2008, we chose to drive back to Iowa through Georgia, Alabama, and Mississippi, largely because I had never been there. As we do with all states we haven't been to before, we stopped at the Welcome Center on the highway on the way in to Alabama. There I was warmly greeted by the elderly lady behind the counter, but she grew colder when the rest of my family followed me in. My first thought was that I had spoken back to her, my lack of a drawl making it clear we weren't from around here. But, looking back on it, it is more likely that she was reacting to our family's racial makeup. It was a feeling that never comes up at home; it took some time to process what really took place there.[25]

In other instances, the general placelessness of interracial couples, particularly during travel, can leave one or the other of them feeling "belittled." Julie, a white woman who has been married to Barry, a black man, for five years and has been with him for ten years, described one such instance, asserting that "[s]ometimes traveling abroad presents its challenges, such as a trip to the Dominican Republic, where Barry felt particularly alienated because of felt perception of others that she was not [his] partner."[26] She further noted that he felt "denigrated as a black man."[27]

Additionally, black-white, heterosexual couples, much like all same-sex couples, routinely experience having their relationships and families assumed away. With respect to same-sex relationships, a number of my surveyed black-white, same-sex couples noted that it was difficult to know when people were responding to their interraciality as a couple as opposed to their sexuality because people rarely noticed that they were even together as a couple (because of the strong presumption of heterosexuality). For instance, Carrie Berks, a white woman who is in a committed relationship with a black woman, explained the following general reaction to her and her partner: "With strangers, they generally think we're friends. Once they're clued in, they're confused. Once it sinks in, they seem to give off a vibe like we just haven't met the right guy yet."[28] Similarly, Bryan, a black man who is married to a white man, asserted, "It depends on where we are. I think most strangers of the opposite sex assume we're friends. Especially outside of New York. At restaurants outside of New York, we're often asked if we want separate bills."[29]

A few of the surveyed same-sex couples wondered whether their experiences would be different if they were of the opposite sex of each other. In many ways, the experiences clearly would be different. As all of the varied lists above suggest, the presumption of heterosexuality in our society is stronger than that of even monoraciality. Indeed, Crenshaw's theory of intersectionality teaches us that the two cannot be separated. For instance, John and Vernon, a black-white, gay couple in a civil union, explained the following about the impossibility of separating their life experiences into neat boxes and about their general placelessness as a same-sex, interracial couple within a homophobic and racially segregated nation. The two men wrote:

> It is important to stress that we are a same-sex interracial couple and that our difficulties originate from both race and sexuality issues. Thus, it is complicated to differentiate these two very important vectors of oppression. But, if we have to focus on race, it seems that one major issue surrounds questions about acceptance from the black community. For instance, this means that we have encountered more acceptance with John's immediate family[, a white family in Europe]. This does not mean, however, that the white community has been more welcoming of our relationship, but rather, that we have found more opportunities as a couple within international immigrant communities that are not based on the U.S. black-white binary. It has been difficult, and in truth we have not attempted to, to find inclusion in the U.S. black community be it cultural or religious. Here demographics play a strong role. This weekend in Chicago, we went to a queer people of color disco and felt at home. This gave us hope that there are black and

interracial communities in which we could thrive. In contrast, it has been difficult to even find the possibilities for a community in the area we currently reside.[30]

Yet, with black-white, heterosexual couples, other people often assume that the individuals in these couples are not intimate partners when they go out together, even when all the social cues point to marriage or commitment. Just recently, for example, my husband and I experienced what I call "relationship erasing" when we went to an ice-cream shop at the end of a double date with a monoracial, black heterosexual couple. When the four of us reached the front of the line, our couple friends each individually ordered a cup of ice-cream, ending up with two different flavors in two different cups, each in two different hands. When our friends approached the register together, the same woman who scooped their ice-cream tallied their treats together on one bill and reported what they owed, no questions asked. Jacob and I then ordered our ice-cream from the same woman, only we ordered just one cup of ice cream after reaching a consensus in front of our server on one flavor. Yet, when Jacob and I approached the counter together—one ice-cream cup in my hand and Jacob pulling out his wallet— the cashier asked, "Is this together?" Jacob and I just paused for a moment, staring at her in disbelief. As a couple that has been together for twenty years, we have figured out both subtle and obvious ways to communicate to servers that we are together in such public settings (even though some people never actually pick up on those cues). But here, there seemed to be no need for such communications. There was just one item. There was nothing to not be "together." Finally, Jacob lifted his hand and pointed at the one ice-cream cup while I said matter-of-factly, "There's only one ice-cream." It still took her a few minutes to catch on.

Such experiences, however, are not rare for black-white, heterosexual couples. Strangers often try to fit such couples into comfortable tropes of blackness and whiteness. For instance, on many occasions in department and grocery stores, cashiers and other customers have assumed that Jacob and I are friends (or strangers to each other), even with our rings on our hands and our children with us. In the worst scenarios for cashiers, they speak to me or Jacob—usually me, as though we are random strangers throwing items into another person's basket. In the worst case scenarios for customers, other customers perceive us together in a racialized server-and-served trope—as store clerk and shopper, almost always approaching me, the black person, to ask if I will assist them as well.[31] In this light, the question, "Is this together?" takes on a deeper meaning, revealing the power of the questioner over the couple in that encounter. In that moment, the questioner gets to exercise her privilege in discerning and naming who is family and who is not. In that moment, the questioner gets to communicate to the couple the non-normalcy of their family. The question is not "Will this check be together?" or "Will this bill be together?" but rather "Is this together?" or, more specifically, "Are you together?" Jane and Ted, a black female–white male married couple, described one such telling incident, noting that "once a clerk made a somewhat rude comment [to them]. . . . [S]he asked if [they] were together, and when [they] said yes, said, 'I wouldn't know.'"[32]

Many of my interracial, heterosexual-couple friends describe similar stories, even as their experiences may vary from ours based on context, race, and gender.[33] For example, one couple friend—an Asian American male–white female couple—told my husband and me that when they go shopping together in a grocery store, they are unlikely to be perceived together as the Asian American male store worker who is assisting a white female customer. Neither race nor gender stereotypes, much less those of Asian American men, lend themselves to that type of imagery.[34] However, just changing the store involved alters their experience. For example, when they are in an electronics or computer store, our Asian American male friend is often perceived to be the employee who is helping a white female customer. Our friends are not viewed as a couple, and he is then often approached by other customers who believe that he is a store worker who can help them. In essence, as Professor Rashmi Goel explained in her article "From Tainted to Sainted: The View of Interracial Relations as Cultural Evangelism": "When faced with a mixed-race couple, people seem to ignore or disbelieve activity that—for a same-race couple—would be indicative of a relationship. People often express surprise at the existence of an interracial couple, asking in dumbfounded tones, 'Are you two . . . together?'"[35]

Surprisingly, such experiences can occur even in the very homes of interracial couples. Three of my surveyed couples identified times when others had presumed that the minority spouse was not an owner of the relevant couple's house. For instance, Fred and Deanne, a black male–white female couple, recalled a time when "a realtor assumed Fred was a renter when she came to see the house."[36] Similarly, Jim, a white man who is married to a biracial, black-white woman, asserted, "My wife has had people assume (because they think she's Puerto Rican) that she works in our house, not owns it."[37] Finally, Margaret, a black woman who is married to a white man, Geoffrey, recalled two different instances where her relationship with her husband was challenged by workers in her own house. She said, "I was called a nigger by the carpenter working in the home we currently live in. Another contractor—a plumber—told me that he did not have to give me his name (he was in my kitchen), because I could be an 'impostor' and not the owner of the house. He was fired, but his boss called my husband to try to have him rehired."[38] Margaret encountered a similarly horrifying experience at her father-in-law's funeral, a time when both she and her husband were emotionally vulnerable. She described: "At my father-in-law's funeral, one of the guests (an older white woman) insisted that I was the secretary to my father-in-law, despite the fact that my husband was holding my hand, and had been crying on my shoulder. In the receiving line, she informed me, and the crowd, 'You were such a good secretary to Y.' It was a telling moment."[39]

Perhaps the most telling story of what I refer to as "relationship erasing" came during an interview with Janice, a white woman who is in a civil union with a black woman. With both chuckles and sighs of frustration laced throughout her storytelling, Janice described one experience that exposed not only how strong the heterosexual and monoracial norm is, but also the many layers of lessons to learn about the experiences of multiracial families at the intersection of race, sexuality, gender, and family. Janice explained:

> One year, we went on vacation in Hilton Head, South Carolina with our friends, Adam and Janet . . . a straight couple, a black woman and a white man . . . and their children. Our daughter, who is black, was with us, too. After days of fun, we—the adults—finally decided that we just needed a nice dinner outing. Alone. So we hired a babysitter, and off we went. Imagine what we looked like walking in!

Let me just say. The food was delicious. Overall, the service was fine, too. But, you know, it took our waitress four tries before she got the bill right. Four! To me, it just wasn't that hard. Adam was sitting right next to Janet. They both were sitting across from us, me and Carla, and Carla and I were sitting right next to each other. We were each sharing food from our partners' plates. Adam was not sitting across from me. And, we each discussed our choices with our partners right in front of the waitress.

But when we we're done, guess what the bills looked like? We made sure to ask for two bills, but we did not think to explain anything. It all seemed obvious to us. . . . Our waitress came back with three bills. One for Adam and me. One for Carla, and one for Janet.

So, we then clearly and carefully asked for two bills—one for Adam and Janet, and one for me and Carla. We even pointed to ourselves—all very polite and kind. But it was like she never heard us. She brought two bills the next time—one again for Adam and me and the other for Carla and Janet. And, the bills mattered because Adam and Janet do not drink, and Carla and I do. . . . Don't worry. We weren't driving. So, we explained how the bills should come out again.

The third time, our waitress regressed, coming back again with three bills. Now, she understood that Adam and Janet were together, so they had one bill. But she brought separate checks for me and Carla. I guess we could have taken pity on her at that point and just paid the bill separately, but now, it was personal. It hurt. With her actions, she refused to see our family. We wanted to set it right.

Anyway, she finally ended up coming back with the right bills. One for Adam and Janet, and the other for me and Carla.

But do you know how that feels? . . . Nearly forty years of love between the two couples, scratched out just like that.[40]

At other times, those posing the question of togetherness are not acting out of ignorance but rather out of hostility. For instance, as described earlier, once a store clerk asked Jane and Ted, a black female–white male, married couple, if they were together. When they said yes, she replied, "I wouldn't know."[41] Cameron, a black woman who is married to a white man, noted that such hostility has been shown to her and her husband in a variety of ways, highlighting that those who are "uncomfortable" with her and her husband will "ask a lot of questions, such as, are you two together, are you married, do you have kids, where are you from. On occasion, men have called us zebras, glared at us or asked us inappropriate questions about our sex lives."[42]

On the flip side of having their relationships and families erased and assumed away, black-white, heterosexual couples also may find themselves bound by their status as an interracial couple. In these instances, after others have recognized and acknowledged the couple as an actual collective, questions abound—with the inquiries generally focused on the couple's interraciality and often presuming that such interraciality or that race itself sums up the relationship. Black-white couples are frequently asked, "How did you ever meet?" or as Ted, one white survey participant, put it "[H]ow in the world did you meet?"[43] as though there must be some exotic or exciting story behind the relationship. Yet, as the black-white couples in my survey show, the stories of how the two partners met are rarely exciting. They occur in the same bland ways as they do for monoracial couples. In fact, the black-white couples in my survey all met in fairly standard ways: in a bar; in high school, college, or graduate school; through a brother or sister; on the job or at a job-related social function; at a mutual friend's party; at church; at a nonprofit event; at a café; or through an online dating service. Other questions for black-white couples focus on race relations, seeking the couple's opinions about racism. While black-white couples themselves often discuss race and racism on a regular basis with each other, they can, at times, find such inquiries by others to be burdensome. For example, Susan and Ethan Capers, a black, Latina female–white male, married couple, articulated their own frustrations with these types of interactions, asserting: "People outside our families, continually want to talk about racial issues because we are a mixed couple. Discussing racial issues over and over quickly becomes boring and a bit irritating to us. As far as discussions of racism, we choose not get into it with other people. There is no point in aggravating ourselves over issues and situations we have no control over."[44]

The types of slights, assumptions, and intrusions described so far in this chapter often reach beyond the lives of the interracial couple itself and into the lives of their children, if there are any (see fig. 6.2). Parents of black-white, biracial children frequently find that their position as parents gets contested and questioned by those outside of the family. They may get questions like: "Are you playing Big Brother/Sister today?" or "Where did you get him/her from (as though their children were commodities easily purchased in a mall)?"[45] Writer Veronica Chambers, a black woman who is married to a white man, wrote about such challenges in her *Essence* maga-zine article "I'm Her Mother, Not Her Nanny." Describing her frustration with being mistaken for the nanny of her biracial, black-white daughter in public, Chambers writes: "On several occasions I've heard, 'What a beauti-ful baby!' from women approaching me in the grocery store or on the street in Philadelphia, Brooklyn and even now in the New Jersey suburb where we currently live. 'How long have you been taking care of her?' At first, the question stunned me, but eventually I became accustomed enough to for-mulate a snappy response: 'I've been taking care of her ever since I almost died giving birth to her.'"[46] One of my survey participants, Caleb, a white man who is married to a black woman, described a similar, though more subtle, experience he had when he was out with his biracial, baby daughter: "Once, in the YMCA, an older black man saw me with the baby; [my wife] Amber was nowhere around. He asked me, 'Is that your baby?' When I said yes, he added, 'She looks just like her mama.'"[47] Along those same lines, Shondra, a light-skinned black woman who is much lighter than her brown-skinned mother, recalled one time during her childhood where a stranger assumed her mother was not her mother. Shondra said: "My mom took me to Marshall Fields and she always made me dress nicely and a woman asked her to find out where my charge's mother bought my dress. My mom is darker and she assumed I was white and my mom was the nanny. My mom was surprised and told her she was my mom and where [she could] find the dress."[48] Years later, Shondra, now a mother, finds that she encounters similar questions that try to place a connection between her and her red-headed, blue-eyed, and even lighter-skinned daughter. She noted: "White women are subtle. When I am out with Britney, they ask, 'Where did she get that red hair?' or 'Where did she get those blue eyes?' When I said from both sides of the family or her dad's side, they would keep asking questions. Then it dawned on me; this is a subtle way to ask about race, and now when I say from her German-Irish father, they say, 'Oh she's beautiful' and that's it. [Y]ou can see the light bulb go off, mys-tery solved. Black women will tell me she is cute, then state, 'Your husband must be white,' which is funny."[49]

On a far more serious note, the parents of biracial, black-white children, especially the white ones, may find themselves in awkward situations

Fig. 6.2. My husband, Jacob, sits with our two youngest children. Photograph by the author

where people view them as criminals rather than loving parents. For these parents, the absence of monoraciality within their family does not just place them outside of the normative ideal, it makes them criminally suspicious. Here, not just social issues but also legal ones come into play. One episode from the popular television series *What Would You Do?* revealed as much, in a segment entitled "White Father with Black Daughter." In this scene, Quiñones makes arrangements for a white male actor to play a coffee shop employee who openly questions the motives of a white father, another actor, while he is sitting at a table with his young, biracial, black-white daughter, a child actor. In this scene, the employee first asks the daughter whether she is "okay." When the father asks why he is making such inquiries, the employee responds, "I see a black child with an older white man," and then demands to see the white father's identification so that he can "know what [the father's] name is." What is more striking than the employee-actor's reaction, however, are the responses from other customers, who also begin to view the father-actor as a criminal. One woman calls 9-1-1 at her table, proclaiming "[It] doesn't seem right" to the operator. Even when the black female actor playing the child's mother walks in and hugs the father-actor, the same woman still mouths to another woman,

"I bet that's not her mother." In yet another run of the same experiment, where the biracial daughter clearly yells out to the white father-actor, "I love you, Daddy," the father-actor is still viewed with suspicion. This time, it is an off-duty police officer who calls 9-1-1 with his concerns about the girl's safety.

Of course, challenges to suspicious-looking adults are very understandable, particularly where the children look uncomfortable and out of place with an adult. Indeed, such challenges to suspicious persons are highly desirable and needed. As one customer-witness said to a black actor who was playing the father of a white-looking child during a similar experiment, "Maybe it [the challenge to status as a parent is] not coming from a racist place. . . . It [could be] a . . . could my daughter be helped in this situation if it were somebody else?" However, when the suspicion is rooted solely in the fact that parent and child do not seemingly "match" by race and is not based on any other social cues—cries, glances around the room, or looks of discomfort or fear—the challenging individual and all those around him are working only to reinforce the normative ideal of family as monoracial. The message sent? Multiracial families do not either look or feel right.[50]

Perhaps one of the funniest but also most depressing stories concerning such parental experiences of black-white couples comes from the book *Mixed: My Life in Black and White,* in which black-white, biracial writer Angela Nissel describes her father's response to such an encounter when he was once in the video store with his children.

> Video Tape Library was a small store in our local strip mall. . . . I had just picked out my *Heckle and Jeckle* tape when Dad called out that it was time to go. I grabbed [my brother] J.R.'s hand and followed him to the counter, where we stood by my father and waited for him to pay. The cashier suddenly stopped ringing up the videos and glanced down quizzically at my brother and me, then up to my father. "Do you know whose kids these are?" the cashier asked.
>
> "Never seen them in my life," my father said, his eyes scanning our bodies, like if he concentrated hard enough he might figure out how these two kids got by his side. . . .
>
> The cashier leaned over the counter so he could be at my eye level.
>
> "Where are your parents?" he asked.
>
> Hello, I'm a kid; probably the guy I'm standing next to and the guy my

brother looks like a tan version of—that would be a parent. Of course, I didn't say that. . . .

With an expression that in my advanced age I now recognize as the *I don't get paid enough for this shit look,* the cashier stood back up and addressed the entire shopping audience.

"Whose kids are these?" he yelled. Everyone in the small video store glanced pitifully at the two lost black kids, shrugged their shoulders and went back to perusing the tape selections. . . .

My father laughed. "These are my kids, man." The cashier looked at him for a moment, to ascertain if he was joking, and then lowered his head.

"I'm sorry. I thought, because they were . . ." The cashier's voice trailed off. . . . He gave the bar codes the same rapt attention I've seen anthropology professors give to rare caveman skulls, and handed our rentals over to us without a further word.

That was my last trip to Video Tape Library. I never wanted to go back after that.[51]

Here, children, too, learn the lesson of their family's placement outside of the normative ideal. For little Angela Nissel, what started as a fun family evening ended with a painful event that signaled that neither she nor her family was right. Sadly, in the end, she discovered that even some place as harmless as a video store could become another space that was not for her family.

When faced with learning about these experiences of black-white, interracial couples and their families, strangers, other outsiders, and even friends will often remark, "But the law cannot change attitudes. You have to admit that things have gotten a lot better. Time is all that is needed. Everything changes with time." This reaction is true—at least partially. As noted above, the attitudes toward, experiences of, and lives of those who are in multiracial families have all greatly improved and continue to improve as time goes on.

Still, such responses by others are problematic for two reasons. First, these responses fail to acknowledge what these social slights or intrusions, whether taken alone or together, tell us about belonging—about the "citizenship"[52]—of those who cross racial boundaries of intimacy. Such responses also fail to recognize the great, emotional toll that these slights or microaggressions can have on people and in some instances, how certain reactions to interracial couples can come and have come in the form of physical harm. Even in the spring of 2011, four white men in Arkansas set a married, black male–white female couple's trailer home on fire with Molotov cocktails.[53] Although no one was injured, the couple's home was destroyed, and the couple certainly would have been injured had they not been able to put the fire out.

Second, and more important, such responses are based upon the mistaken assumption that all the slights, mistreatments, and intrusions toward multiracial families are purely social. These responses ignore the way that law can work and has worked to perpetuate and reify norms and practices that continue to place interracial families on the margins of our society or rather in a zone of placelessness. Indeed, the very last identified privilege from the various lists above—the privilege of being able to freely select housing "in an area in which [one] can afford, in which [one] would want to live, and in which the neighbors would not disapprove of [one's] household"—provides a strong example of just how law has functioned together with society to frame the normative ideal of family as monoracial and heterosexual. Here, in the housing discrimination arena, the law is clearly not intended to exclude or marginalize multiracial families, but rather to protect them and all individuals. But because the law is designed around socially constructed categories and framings that essentially assume monoraciality and heterosexuality, certain instances arise in which the experiences of interracial, heterosexual couples—couples presumed to be protected under the law—are made to be invisible.

Uncovering Placelessness: A House Is Not a Home

In fact, the lives of Alice and Leonard teach us much about the pattern of housing experiences and decisions that can make the lives of interracial couples invisible in law and life. Their experiences instruct us on the many ways in which social norms function together with law to define and reinforce the idea of the normative family as monoracial. During the 1920s, although New York became infused with the Harlem Renaissance, and the advent of this renaissance created social spaces in which blacks and whites could and did interact with each other, inside New York's residential neighborhoods racially integrated spaces were few and far between. Rather, New York, like many other northern states affected by migration, was becoming increasingly segregated by race.

Alice's family, however, owned and lived in a home in one of New York's rare integrated spaces: New Rochelle. Alice grew up within this area, in a house where she and Leonard would ultimately live together as husband and wife for a few short weeks. As a consequence of her growing up within racially integrated spaces, Alice became accustomed to interacting with people of differing races, not only within her own family but also within her residential neighborhood. Indeed, for years, the Jones family, a "colored" family in part, had established close ties to many whites in New Rochelle, including Judge Samuel Swinburne, who represented Alice at the beginning of her case and who assisted with the case until its end. Such relationships with whites, along with Leonard's money, enabled Alice to eventually secure a highly accomplished and skilled attorney such as Lee Parsons Davis to be her primary advocate.

The marriages of Alice's two sisters, Emily and Grace, also reflected the rich racial diversity and interaction within the Joneses' private lives. For example, Grace married a working-class, Italian immigrant named Albert Miller. Emily married a monoracial, black man named Robert Brooks, who, too, would become close friends with Leonard. Only, unlike Emily and Robert, whose family for all outward appearances functioned as monoracial, Alice and Leonard did not live on their own after their marriage—despite Leonard's wealth and ability to purchase a place for the newlyweds. Instead, Alice and Leonard first lived in the home of Alice's parents, George and Elizabeth Jones (see fig. 6.3); after all, the area's segregated topography left the young couple with few other spaces in which they could remain together, anonymous and unbothered. To have lived anywhere other than places like New Rochelle would have exposed Alice and Leonard in a race- and class-segregated New York, which like many places was supported by a legal structure that did not readily punish or regulate housing discrimination based on race. In a society that Alice and Leonard clearly understood to be hostile to their kind of cross-racial, cross-class love, the couple instead

Defendant's Exhibit O-1.

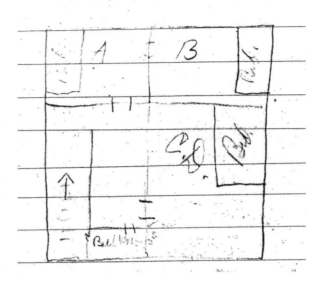

Fig. 6.3. Here is a diagram of the very modest home of the Jones family, which was used an exhibit at trial. It was used at trial to show how impossible it would have been for Leonard not to come across George Jones within the modest home. Reproduced from trial exhibits

chose to live within the only space they knew for a fact would embrace their family: the already tested home of George and Elizabeth Jones and, later, for a very brief time, an apartment in the already tested New Rochelle.

In sum, like many multiracial families, Alice and Leonard existed within an American landscape that had no real, recognized spaces for them and their lives. Indeed, in our residentially segregated culture, multiracial, black-white families often find themselves with no "comfortable" spaces in which to reside. Often, much like Alice and other biracial, black-white individuals who have been made to choose one identity over the other—"black" over "white" or "biracial"—black-white families are frequently faced with difficult choices about which spaces to live in. In fact, research shows that, where available and affordable, black-white families will seek and choose integrated neighborhoods over segregated ones. For instance, one black female–white male, married couple, Shondra and Michael noted, "When we got married, we looked for a racially diverse area where we would both feel comfortable."[54] Similarly, Julie and Barry, a black male–white female married couple said, "We chose [our] neighborhood because we thought it was more diverse than others. What impressed Barry the most was visiting a coffee shop a few blocks away prior to deciding to purchase the house and seeing how many people of color were in it."[55] They further noted, "Our street has two other mixed-race couples (black/white), but much of the neighborhood is mostly white and Asian."[56]

But in cities such as Detroit, where integrated areas are very limited in number, multiracial, black-white families must instead accept choices that do not reflect the integrated nature of their families, picking black neighborhoods over white ones or vice versa.[57] There are simply few places in which multiracial families "fit," in part because of the lack of regulation on housing discrimination in the past and in part because of failed enforcement of antidiscrimination laws; continued steering, redlining, and racial discrimination by realtors and landlords; and a general view of residential "choices" as personal decisions free from legal regulation. For instance, Edith and Stephen, one black female–white male married couple in my survey, proclaimed that "[f]inding quality, diverse neighborhoods in which to live" was one of the biggest difficulties they faced as a multiracial family.[58] Another couple, Darcy and Charlie, a black female–white male couple, described their feelings of not belonging within their current city home. They asserted, "[It is difficult] living in a city that does not appreciate multiracial couples or children. [Our state] was a slave state, and it's very segregated today. There are areas that we just don't go into, white or black, because we don't feel comfortable. We have put off having children until we move because the schools are so badly segregated—we know that it would not be a healthy situation for a child."[59] Finally, Stephanie, a black woman who is married to a white man, detailed how she "would often have [her husband] Kirk be the primary contact with potential buyers of [their] home" in "order to avoid [the] very real possibility [of race discrimination in their house search]."[60]

In very rare cases, a family's interraciality may prove a benefit in housing. For example, in her book *Mixed: My Life in Black and White*, writer Angela Nissel describes her family's sole experience with what she calls "interracial affirmative action." In that instance, Nissel's family benefited from its interraciality when the white girlfriend of a black, African landlord was moved by their multiraciality to convince her boyfriend to cut Nissel's black mother (and her biracial children) a deal on the rent for a house in a middle-class black neighborhood. Nissel explained: "[N]o one in our family had actually met the [landlord]. All I knew was he was African and the transaction was done entirely through his white girlfriend, who worked at the hospital with my mother. From what I'd gathered through eavesdropping, the white girlfriend and my mother were kinda 'interracial couples' buddies and the white lady convinced her African boyfriend to rent us the house at the lowest rate he could afford."[61] But even this "interracial affirmative action" opportunity occurred within a segregated context, allowing Nissel and her family a great opportunity to live in a middle-class black neighborhood, but not a neighborhood that necessarily reflected their own diverse, multiracial backgrounds. The segregated landscape of the United States, which in itself discourages the formation of interracial families, makes for few opportunities in which racially blended families may find a home.

More than forty years after the enactment of the Fair Housing Act, Title VIII of the Civil Rights Act,[62] we, as a society, continue to live in very segregated residential spaces. Blacks, especially, remain highly segregated compared with other racial minority groups. In fact, almost a third of all blacks live in neighborhoods identified as "hyper-segregated," which means "reflecting extreme isolation."[63] As a general matter, Latinos follow in second and are increasingly becoming more segregated by place, even as residential segregation itself is slowly declining.[64] In metropolitan areas, whites are more likely to be racially isolated than either blacks, Latinos, or Asian Americans.[65]

Such residential housing patterns send dangerous messages about where each race may find a space for its home. For instance, John and Vernon, a black-white same-sex couple in a civil union, described how they had been steered away from certain neighborhoods because of race, ethnicity, and sexuality. They state: "In our town, we were explicitly warned that certain streets or areas would be less welcoming for a bi-national, biracial, same-sex couple. We chose a neighborhood [in an area known for being more open]. . . . [We] think that some of our neighbors may dislike as much that we are two men as that we are an interracial couple, or just that they have a black man living next to them."[66] Julie and Barry, a black male–white female, married couple, described how they were discriminated against (though

not explicitly with words) when they were searching for housing in Alabama. Julie explained, "[W]hile in Alabama we didn't get express negative
reactions, but one white landlady, for example, never called us back after we
came together to see her apartment, even though she had been extremely
eager and persistent in contacting me about it beforehand."[67] In the end,
these messages about race, place, and space work to promote and encourage monoraciality among families and even have an impact on our society in areas that are generally considered to be unrelated to housing and
the law. For example, in his article "Policing, Race, and Space," Professor
Bennett Capers explains how law enforcement practices, such as the ability
to consider "racial incongruity in assessing whether reasonable suspicion
exists to justify a *Terry* stop [a police stop based on reasonable suspicion],"
can work to discourage racial integration and maintain racial segregation
in residential areas by "reinforc[ing] the notion that certain neighborhoods
are white, certain neighborhoods are black (or brown or yellow)," and by
providing significant incentives for the black middle class—the group best
positioned among blacks to integrate neighborhoods—to remain segregated in black neighborhoods.[68] Along those same lines, our segregated
residential patterns provide incentives for individuals to avoid cross-racial
intimacies that could form the basis of these more policed families. They
further provide discouragement for multiracial families who are struggling
to find a place for themselves in a society that likes to create and man-
age clear-cut racial lines. In this way, our living patterns have the effect of
both reinforcing segregated lines that were put in place by past legal practices and decisions and defining and fortifying the ideal image of family as
monoracial.

Furthermore, our segregated neighborhoods serve as obstacles to the
initial meetings between two potential partners that can blossom into long-
term, committed interracial relationships. After all, if we are segregated
in spaces by race, how do we ever meet each other to develop intimacies
across racial lines? In fact, there is a rich history by segregationists to ensure residential and educational segregation for the very purposes of discouraging interracial intimacy. Much of the opposition to desegregation,
both in schools and in neighborhoods, was linked to the desire to prevent
amalgamation. As Professor Herbert Hovenkamp explains in his article

"Social Science and Segregation before *Brown*," segregationists "believed that social integration of any kind was bad because race mixing would eventually lead to miscegenation."[69] Professor Reginald Oh further expounds upon this point in his article "Regulating White Desire":[70] "Even though they believed that it was a universal truth that blacks did not deserve social equality, segregationists feared that some white persons could and would act to grant 'equality for unequals' by relating to blacks with respect and affection. Specifically, they feared the possibility of whites granting blacks social equality by marrying them. The threat posed by interracial marriages was considered so dangerous that segregationists sought to prevent their formation through legal prohibition and through the racial segregation of social spaces. . . . Thus, during Jim Crow, because whites justified their superior position in the racial hierarchy solely on their whiteness, they strictly enforced endogamy."[71]

More so, our segregated residential patterns serve as a constant, social reminder to multiracial families—in particular, black-white families—of their placelessness. Where do such families fit in with these jagged pieces of geography based on race? And specifically, what do we know about how multiracial families see themselves fitting into these spaces? As several of the black-white couples in my survey conveyed, we know that finding a diverse community to live in is of critical importance to many multiracial families. One couple explained that racial diversity "played a big role [in their decision about housing] because [they did] not want to live in suburbs that are all white. [They wanted] to live in a place that has a range of diversity in not only race but religion, culture," and other factors.[72] Other couples described diversity in neighborhood as a playing a "huge role" in or being a "significant" factor, "major factor," or "big" part of their decisions. One couple even avoided taking jobs in southern cities, where they worried about race relations, and another couple "decided not to move to a particular neighborhood because it was predominantly white. [They instead] decided to build a home in a more diverse neighborhood in" the same city.[73]

Additional investigations into the residential decisions of black-white couples reveal that such households are more likely to be found in racially diverse neighborhoods than households headed by both black and white couples. Controlling for socioeconomic status, Professors Richard Wright, Mark Ellis, and Steve Holloway found that black-white couples are drawn to and prioritize diversity no matter which racial group constitutes the majority of residents in the neighborhood.[74] On the other hand, neither households headed by black couples nor those headed by white couples were drawn to diversity except in limited circumstances. Specifically, households headed by black couples cared about diversity only when considering neighborhoods with substantial white and Asian populations. Households headed by whites stressed the importance of diversity only when considering neighborhoods with a large number of blacks or Latinos. In fact, the data suggest that "diversity is a 'turnoff' within White-dominated spaces for same-race White households."[75] Moreover, one study in Seattle revealed that racial diversity was one of the strongest factors in terms of negatively predicting the degree to which whites viewed neighbor relations as harmonious.[76] Overall, in conducting their research Professors Wright, Ellis, and Holloway confirmed their initial hypothesis that "households headed by Black-White couples will avoid the most segregated neighborhoods and congregate instead in places where there is already willingness to traverse racial boundaries"—much like Alice and Leonard did in New Rochelle.[77]

The reason for this pattern in housing decisions is simple. In our segregated country, where strong messages are sent about racial place in neighborhoods, multiracial families are simply trying to find a space for themselves among these rigid demarcations. As Professor Heather Dalmage has explained, in diverse neighborhoods, "multiracial family members find places where they do not have to contend with intense, daily border patrolling," or what she calls "borderism."[78] Indeed, in my interviews, one black-white married, heterosexual couple in Atlanta (Susan and Ethan Capers), who are realtors themselves, described their housing choices as being on either side of a rigid racial divide. They said, "We both feel comfortable being surrounded by either predominantly black or white groups. So, excluding the Georgia counties known for their racist views, race was not a factor for where to purchase our house."[79] While Susan and Ethan ultimately described race as not playing a role in their decision, that conclusion seemed largely based on the fact that most of their neighborhood choices did not reflect the diversity within their own family. In fact, Susan and Ethan identified their choices as "either predominantly black or white" neighborhoods, not integrated neighborhoods.

For some people, though, these choices and complexities about housing are simply too daunting. Some people choose altogether not to engage in interracial intimacies because of race and space concerns, an act that again socially furthers the ideal of family as monoracial. For example, in his *Interracial Intimacies: Sex, Marriage, Identity, and Adoption*, Professor Randall Kennedy highlights one New York City police officer's explanation for submitting a personal dating ad for white women only. Providing an explanation that explicitly referenced race and space difficulties, the officer asserted that he could not also seek black women in his advertisements because his dating a black woman would have "'upset his "Archie Bunker" neighbors. . . . [He] was looking to make life easier.'"[80]

But, the disadvantages that black-white, heterosexual couples can experience in housing are not limited to the social context alone. The law, too, plays its own role in reifying and reinforcing the normative ideal of coupling, marriage, and family as monoracial (and heterosexual). But, how exactly does law work together with our social norms and patterns to reinforce this image of the ideal family?

Historically speaking, law played a very active role in reinforcing these images. For instance, in her book *Race-Mixing: Black-White Marriage in Postwar America*, Professor Renee Romano describes how law facilitated the discriminatory acts of realtors, landlords, and neighbors who worked hard against allowing black-white couples to live in white neighborhoods during the 1950s. In one instance, Romano relates how one white husband of a black female–white male couple tried to avoid discrimination in housing by signing a lease before the landlord met his black wife, only to be later evicted for "racial reasons."[81]

The law, however, also plays a contemporary role in facilitating the placelessness of multiracial families and thus reinforcing the normative ideal of family as monoracial. This tends to come in two forms: (1) through explicit laws, rules, and policies that define multiracial families in a way that reifies clear-cut racial categories; and (2) through implicit assumptions about monoraciality among families in statutes such as Title VIII.

In a society in which formal equality has prevailed as the dominant theory of equality, explicit ways in which law has functioned with social norms to reinforce the image of the monoracial family as the normative ideal are not widespread. However, one personal story of mine provides an excellent example of such explicit work at hand. Approximately a year after I graduated from law school, my husband and I began to look for, found, and bought our first home. At the time, we were expecting our first child, and like many interracial couples, racial diversity was key in our search for a neighborhood and house. We were incredibly lucky with regard to our ability to achieve this goal of residential diversity because we lived in a city (primarily black-white) that had two racially diverse and integrated suburbs. The two suburbs were both centrally located—in fact, more so than even some parts of the city itself—and the suburbs' schools were themselves racially diverse as well as highly ranked. For decades, both of the two suburbs had worked hard to maintain the racial diversity within their limits. They did so through passing ordinances and policies that, for example, prohibited For Sale signs to discourage white flight. The two suburbs also each had a very low-interest loan program for first-time home buyers that was designed, in part, to encourage people to maintain proportional, racial, black-white diversity. After a long search, my husband and I finally found the house we wanted to sign our lives away for. We made a bid, which was accepted, and, based on the suggestion from the group that we worked with in finding our home, we went to the city office to see if we could get one of its low-interest, homebuyer loans. When we got there, we learned that we did not actually qualify for the loan because 60 percent of the families on our desired street were black, and a city policy did not allow for these special low-interest loans to be given to a new family where they would take the street outside of a 60 percent–40 percent, black-white balance (either way).

We certainly understood and supported the city's goal of diversity. In fact, the racial diversity of the city was one of the reasons why we wanted to live there. But we did not see how we changed the balance of our desired street. After all, we were an interracial family, *not* a white family or a black family. We literally added balance to any street, and in fact, with our soon-to-be-born baby, we would add racial diversity to any street by adding a biracial person to our household. After making these arguments to the city's employees, we were told that we were a black family because one person in our household was black. We then asked, "Well, would the same rule apply to a white family of four or five people that adopted one black child?" We were told yes. "Really?" we asked, "One black person makes a family of four or five white people black?" We were shocked. The one-drop rule was being applied to a family. Here were law and policy reinforcing society's ideas about racial purity, or rather, racial taint by one drop of black blood. They also were, in some ways, discouraging people from even considering a break with any monoracial norms. More importantly, they were dictating to those who had broken those norms—like my husband and me—that their families could not maintain their own individual unit identities.

In the end, we accepted the decision, not raising any further questions or arguments. After all, we supported the program and, more so, loved being in a city that worked to maintain its racial diversity. But that moment has always stuck with us. Although certainly not with malicious intent, here were city officials highlighting for us the placelessness of our family. Our family did not fit within their normative image of family—a monoracial image—and thus we had to be squeezed into a particular category. They made a space for us, but only on their identity terms, not on our own, and not in a way that would have allowed each of us to claim our own childhood racial identities. Here were law and policy playing an explicit role in framing and reifying the ideal of family as monoracial.

In our post–civil rights society, however, there will be very few ways in which the law's work in reifying a monoracial family ideal will be as explicit. In almost all instances, they will be less obvious. One of these ways is through implicit assumptions about monoraciality among families in antidiscrimination housing statutes like Title VIII. Because such statutes differ from other antidiscrimination statutes in that they focus on the collective—here, families—in addition to individuals, they provide a good means by which to illustrate and explicate the continuities between social discrimination against interracial, heterosexual couples, and the failure to recognize interracial, heterosexual family units within the law.

Under Title VIII, only certain classes of citizens are protected from discrimination in housing. As enacted, Title VIII provided that "it shall be unlawful":

(a) To refuse to sell or rent after the making of a bona fide offer, or to refuse to negotiate for the sale or rental of, or otherwise make unavailable or deny, a dwelling to any person because of race, color, religion, or national origin.

(b) To discriminate against any person in the terms, conditions, or privileges of sale or rental of a dwelling, or in the provision of services or facilities in connection therewith, because of race, color, religion, or national origin. . . .

(d) To represent to any person because of race, color, religion, or national origin that any dwelling is not available for inspection, sale, or rental when such dwelling is in fact so available.[82]

Under Title VIII, plaintiffs can prove discrimination with direct evidence or through circumstantial evidence by using the burden-shifting framework that the Supreme Court specifically developed for evaluating employment discrimination in *McDonnell Douglas Corp. v. Green*.[83] Applying this burden-shifting model to housing discrimination cases, courts have held that a plaintiff has to prove housing discrimination through three different steps. First, the plaintiff must establish a *prima facie* case of discrimination by proving the following four factors: (1) that she is a member of a racial minority; (2) that she applied for and was qualified to rent or purchase certain property or housing; (3) that she was rejected; and (4) that the housing or rental property remained available thereafter. Once the plaintiff proves each of these factors, the court draws an inference of discrimination and moves to the second step, where the owner or landlord must articulate a legitimate explanation for rejecting the plaintiff's application. If the defendant satisfies this burden, then, in the third step, the plaintiff must prove that the defendant's stated reason was a mere pretext for discrimination. The plaintiff can show pretext by demonstrating that the proffered reason had no basis in fact, did not actually motivate the challenged conduct, or was insufficient to warrant the challenged conduct. However, even upon proof of pretext, a jury may still rule in favor of the defendant if it believes that a nondiscriminatory factor was at play. The ultimate burden of persuasion rests with the plaintiff at all times.[84]

Additionally, a person discriminated against because of her association with an individual in a protected class can use the *McDonnell Douglas* framework to prove discrimination against herself. For example, a white individual who believes that she was denied a rental because of her black friends may file a discrimination claim based on race under Title VIII. To do so, she would have to argue that she suffered discrimination because of her own race or protected class, not because of her relationship to someone of another race or protected class.[85] In other words, she would have to contend that, but for the fact that she is white and her friends are black, she would not have been the target of discrimination.

Such statutory tools for filing housing discrimination lawsuits are arguably ineffective for combating the full range of discrimination harms that black-white, heterosexual couples may face as a familial unit. Specifically, the question is: what can an interracial couple or family do in those cases where the couple is being discriminated against, not because of the race of a specific member or specific members of the family—that is, the black person in the family—but rather because of the family's status as a multiracial family, as a unit that was formed through race mixing? After all, an owner could be discriminating against an interracial couple based upon animus toward them as an interracial couple, not because of an individual black or a white person or even as a married couple or an unmarried couple. In other words, it is possible for an alleged discriminator not to treat individuals differently based on race, but instead to treat couples differently based upon racial mixing. For example, a landlord could choose to treat individuals and even monoracial families equally across many races, renting to them freely, but then could, if he finds interracial couples and multiracial families repugnant, treat those couples and families unequally, refusing to rent to them at all. Yet, housing discrimination law fails to fully account for such a possibility for multiracial families. No protected category under the law applies to them in this particular situation.

First, under current housing discrimination statutes, the couple could not pursue an interracial discrimination claim based upon their "familial status," because housing discrimination statutes define "familial status" in relation to one's dependents. For example, Title VIII defines "familial status" to mean "[o]ne or more individuals (who have not attained the age of 18 years) being domiciled with—(1) a parent or another person having legal custody of such individual or individuals; or (2) the designee of such parent or other person having custody, with the written permission of such parent or person."[86] Because the discrimination experienced by black-white, heterosexual couples based on their interraciality would not be based on simply having children in the family, such couples would not fit within the category of persons or families included in the term *familial status*. Additionally, assuming that a black-white, heterosexual couple was in a state that provided protection for discrimination based upon "marital status," the black-white, heterosexual couple here, too, could not prove its claim based on "marital status" because that term generally refers only to the status of individuals as either married or single. For example, in *County of Dane v. Norman,* the Wisconsin Supreme Court made it clear that, under Wisconsin's housing discrimination statute, "marital status" was defined as "being married, divorced, widowed, separated, single or a cohabitant."[87]

In other words, a black-white couple would have to engage in wordplay to explain and prove the factual basis for their claim of discrimination against them as an interracial couple. Specifically, they would each have to assert discrimination based on the law of discrimination by association, claiming separately and individually that, but for the race of their spouse, they each would have been treated differently. In so doing, unlike individuals in a monoracial couple who could plead their discrimination claims together, the individuals in the black-white, heterosexual couple would have to divide up their family unit in their Complaint to assert their discrimination claims.

Importantly, this type of discrimination by association analysis fails to acknowledge the true nature of discrimination against the mixed-race, heterosexual couple due to their interracial status. Such discrimination concerns more than pure race discrimination as it is based on the collective, not just the individual. Specifically, it is based on interraciality and the particular stereotypes targeted at people who *together* intimately cross racial boundaries. As the Michigan Court of Appeals once noted in one of its housing cases: "Discrimination against interracial couples is certainly based on racial stereotypes and is derived from notions that the blood of the races should not mix. We believe that both the broad language of the civil rights act and the policies behind the act should be read to provide protection from discrimination for interracial couples."[88]

Although courts certainly could find discrimination "because of" race for couples under this discrimination by association analysis, such a method does not fully address the problem of housing discrimination against black-white couples based on their race-mixing itself. Rather, it perversely maintains and reinforces discrimination. Specifically, while the discrimination by association analysis technically offers such black-white couples redress through damages and other forms of relief under Title VIII, it fails to address the "expressive harms" or lack of dignity in the continued assumption of monoraciality among families in housing discrimination statutes.[89] Such an effect is critical, because unlike in the employment context, where the law of discrimination by association has been applied to individuals, housing discrimination law is intended to recognize the family unit. Housing discrimination law is intended to protect the principle that not all couples or families are the same. Yet, in this particular context, the law implicitly presents all families and couples as monolithic—specifically, as monoracial and heterosexual. It mandates that claimants in an interracial family split their individual races and family unit in order to factually assert a claim based on race mixing. In other words, it requires that the multiracial family unit be broken up, at least legally, in order to receive protection, and, in so doing, it fails to fully recognize the unit's very existence. Most importantly, it places the interracial family on the margins and operates to reinforce the normative ideal of family as monoracial, not just at home, but more generally in society and in law.

7

Collective Discrimination

AS SEEN IN CHAPTER 6, INDIVIDUALS IN intimate, interracial couples often experience daily disadvantages and microaggressions as well as blatant and subtle forms of actionable discrimination in their private lives as a result of their union. Punishments for crossing racially defined boundaries of intimacy through family and familial-like relationships can extend beyond the more private realms of discrimination and harassment in residential neighborhoods and into more public and social areas. One such location in which these punishments can and do occur is in the workplace, the very space in which people earn money to financially support themselves and their families. Such punishments come in many forms, including but not limited to harassment, the denial of promotions and other advancements, and even the loss or the denial of a job. Whether experienced individually or together, these types of punishments have the effect of reinforcing the normative ideal of family as monoracial because they strongly discourage their victims from crossing racial boundaries of intimacy at all in some cases and ever again in other cases.

The enactment and enforcement of Title VII and parallel state workplace discrimination statutes that prohibit discrimination on the basis of race have been critical in combating the mistreatment of persons who become known to and defined by their co-workers and supervisors as transgressors of racial spaces. However, much like I detailed in Chapter 6 about the gaps in Title VIII and similar state housing discrimination statutes, Title VII and its state-based contemporaries have offered incomplete remedies for addressing the full range of harms that members of multiracial families, and, in particular, individuals in interracial couples, may encounter at work. Such a result, while disappointing, is not surprising. After all, even for traditional race discrimination lawsuits (those not based on interraciality, which I defined earlier as one's involvement as part of an interracial family unit),[1] the legal structures for analyzing workplace discrimination have proven to be ineffective at eliminating race discrimination in the various ways that it is practiced in our society.[2]

Punishment in the workplace based on interraciality can present even greater complications for courts in their legal analysis of discrimination claims, in part because the lines between the social and the legal blur easily and in subtle ways when interracial intimacy is involved. More importantly, this type of workplace punishment can present more complexities for courts in their determinations because antidiscrimination law, and our society in general, is not designed to see the ways in which coupling, and specifically monoracial, heterosexual coupling and family building, is implicitly written into job descriptions and duties.

In this chapter, I examine and interrogate the current legal standards for analyzing workplace discrimination and, in the process, highlight one gap in the law that leaves individuals vulnerable to employment discrimination based on interraciality. In so doing, I acknowledge the rather obvious biases against people in intimate, same-sex relationships. Hostility and discrimination against gays and lesbians abound such that Congress has never enacted a federal workplace statute that protects against sexual orientation discrimination. Such a reality means that multiracial families that are founded at their core by an interracial, same-sex relationship may confront decidedly more complex forms of discrimination based on interraciality, with interraciality, in some cases, taking a secondary or tertiary role to sexual orientation. In fact, several of the black-white couples whom I questioned indicated as much in their responses. For example, Bryan and Sam, a married, black male–white male couple who were able to marry only two years ago but who have been together for a total of twenty years, noted that their experiences as a couple would likely differ if they were heterosexual. In answering one question, they responded, "[I]t was striking how sexuality complicates everything. . . . [We] couldn't help but wonder how different our answers would be were we heterosexual. For example, one 'advantage' we have is that we often aren't 'visible' in the way interracial heterosexual couples often are. At other times, our sexuality 'trumps' race, rendering race secondary or even irrelevant."[3]

That said, because in this chapter, like the rest of this book, I wish to challenge the commonly accepted notion that legal discouragement of and punishment for intimate, cross-racial heterosexual intimacy no longer exists, I focus largely on individuals in interracial, heterosexual couples, and specifically black-white couples, as a means of unpacking and discrediting these legal myths. I begin with a general discussion about the many types of punishments that individuals can suffer because of their involvement in intimate and familial, interracial relationships. Thereafter, I provide a brief history of employment discrimination law as it concerns workplace mistreatment based on interraciality, and in so doing, I examine a few cases to highlight the law's very real effectiveness at addressing particular forms of discrimination and harassment based on interraciality. Finally, I expose and explicate one major hole in the law's protection of heterosexual individuals who are part of multiracial family units in the workplace; to the extent that I address similar gaps in the protections for same-sex, interracial couples, I acknowledge that sexuality further complicates the analysis because there is essentially no or very little protection against discrimination based on sexual orientation.

General Punishments

Although interracial marriage is legal in every state and the number of black-white interracial marriages in the United States has increased from approximately 50,000 in 1920 to 403,000 in 2010, individuals who enter into such relationships still endure social punishments from others for their cross-racial intimacies. Similarly, although the number of multiracial families is increasingly growing as a result of transracial and international adoptions; the use of alternative reproductive technologies; or procreation by interracial, heterosexual couples, members of such families, whether they be parents, children, or siblings, often experience significant mistreatment because of their violations of the monoracial family norm. Indeed, if there is any factor that stands out as the most powerful in defining, reinforcing, and enforcing the normative ideal of family as monoracial, it is this punishment, both social and legal, of those who cross and exist outside of established, societal boundaries against interracial intimacy.

For example, as Professors Randall Kennedy and Reginald Oh have detailed, during the Reconstruction era, interracial intimates, especially black men and white women, were punished severely for challenging racial divisions of love.[4] Racial transgressors suffered incredible harm, which included not only lengthy prison sentences, whipping, and maiming, but even death.[5] Such punishments, to say the least, served as extremely effective deterrents to cross-racial love for many individuals.

Yet, punishments of interraciality need not be as severe as prison or death to encourage citizens to remain within the norms of monoraciality in love and family. Consider the posttrial lives of Alice Beatrice Jones and Leonard Kip Rhinelander. Both before and after their trial, neither Alice nor Leonard suffered literal imprisonment, beatings, or murder as a result of their cross-racial romance, but they figuratively did. More importantly, after their divorce and public shaming through their trial, neither one of them ever again in their lifetimes overstepped their community's socially constructed racial boundaries of love.

Upon their divorce, the two lovers suffered very similar, but completely separate endings. First, they endured what seemed to be the imprisonment and, later, the death of their love. Second, they encountered what were more certain imprisonments, beatings, and deaths of their souls.

First, the ultimate death of the Rhinelanders' love—or at least of their public love together—came at the end of their annulment trial. In a rare moment after the trial, Alice discussed her lost love with newspaper journalists. The *New York Times* reported the following colloquy between Alice and journalists:

> "Do you still love your husband?" she [Alice] was asked.
> She hesitated a long time, looking down at her hands in her lap, and finally said slowly:
> "I do and I don't." . . .
> "Would you go back to your husband?" she was asked.

She hesitated a moment and then said: "I can't answer that," and then quickly added, "No."

"You two were very much in love, weren't you?"

"We was, yes," she said, making her first grammatical slip.

"It was a beautiful love affair," somebody said, and she answered quickly: "It certainly was."[6]

As Alice confirmed in this exchange with reporters, her "beautiful affair" with Leonard had simply died.[7] It ended with nothing more for either her or Leonard personally, and in so doing, it destroyed the potential of their family and what could have continued to be a beautiful affair or, to some, a beautiful lie.

The deaths of Alice and Leonard's souls would proceed slowly for years to come, up until it seemed, their last breaths. Upon divorce, Leonard departed from his life as a prominent, wealthy white socialite by becoming a recluse, separated not just from the public but also his family for the next few years. He never recaptured the life he had before Alice and certainly not the type of life he had with Alice. He died at the young age of thirty-four in February 1936 without ever falling in love again and without remarrying (see fig. 7.1).[8]

Alice, on the other hand, lived until her late eighties, but to use the word "lived" may be an exaggeration. To assist with her living expenses, Alice used the $31,500 settlement she received after the trial plus a $3,600 annuity for life (which actually ended in 1940) from the Rhinelander family. Though surrounded by her family members, Alice remained alone. She never partnered with another man. Marked now as a colored woman, Alice could not marry another white man, unless he was willing to absorb the loss of privilege that would come with such a union. Given what seemed to be Alice's own identification as white, Alice herself may have shunned marrying a black man like her sister Emily had done. Chances are, however, that racial identification played little, if any, role in Alice's decision to never remarry. The facts point instead to Alice's undying commitment to her "beautiful affair" with Leonard, her lost love. In 1989, when Alice passed away, she left us with one last reminder of just how she really "died" more than sixty years earlier in 1925 at her infamous trial's end: she buried herself with a headstone that read "Alice J. Rhinelander."[9]

Fig. 7.1. Pallbearers take Leonard Rhinelander's body from the Episcopal Church of St. James at Long Beach after funeral rites. Alice did not attend the funeral.
© Bettmann/Corbis

But, the detriments to Alice and Leonard encompassed much more than figurative deaths and imprisonments. For Leonard especially, it meant the loss of not only his racial identity as a white person but also the privileges that come with that identity. As a man who was raised white and wealthy, Leonard, in particular, suffered a significant loss of privileges after the annulment trial's end. Unlike Alice, the trial and its outcome did not determine Leonard's racial identity but instead identified him as a racial transgressor. Leonard's choices in marrying Alice and socializing, even eating at the same table, with at least one of Alice's obviously black family members—her brother-in-law Robert Brooks—meant that he had crossed an unthinkable, racial line and had placed himself outside of respectable white society. As Alice's attorney, Davis, repeatedly suggested throughout the trial, Leonard, who had every privilege that money could buy, had failed to perform his identity as a white, upper-class male, not only by rejecting white norms and privileges in his social interactions with some of Alice's family members but also by actually enjoying and cherishing the company and intimate love of Alice, a colored woman. Plain and simple, in 1920s New York, whites did not sit together with blacks at the dinner table, much less fall in love with those who are part black. If whites did, they were "defying the mores of their upbringing" and thus betraying their own people. In fact, the response to Leonard's loss at trial demonstrated as much. White society closed ranks by punishing him, in an effort to protect the lines between the colored and white worlds that Leonard had crossed (see fig. 7.2).[10] Even before the trial began, Leonard was shunned and excluded him from all "clubs" to which he previously belonged. Critically, he was removed from the *New York Social Register,* a marker of membership in one of New York's most elite families. As the *Detroit Free Press* highlighted in 1925, previous editions of the *New York Social Register* had always included the following entry: "Rhinelander, Mr. Philip—Junior, Mr. Leonard Kip Rhinelander, 18 West Forty-eight Street. New York City."[11] Once the Rhinelander trial began, however, Leonard lost his standing within the community. The *Detroit Free Press* reported: "Kip stands outside the fold the symbol of a proud family's shame. Kip now stands on a social register par with his Negro bride, who last spring sailed into the March supplement of the register for one fleeting cruise under her husband's colors, but was dropped overboard in the next edition."[12]

Leonard's removal from the *New York Social Register* did more than signal that his racial transgressions involved openly living with a woman he knew to be part black. His removal made it clear that his transgression involved a deeper betrayal. He had made Alice his wife and allowed her to pass in white society on no more than the strength of his name and recommendation. Indeed, as noted above, Alice had been previously been listed in the *New York Social Register,* though, later, the publishers of the *Social Register* would explain "that Mrs. Rhinelander's name was included in the supplement merely as a notice that Rhinelander had married, and that it would be omitted in future issues."[13]

In addition to social exclusion, Leonard was essentially disinherited by his family until he divorced Alice. He was not allowed to join in the family business or participate in carrying on the family name and traditions through his employment until he was able to "cast off his wife" follow-

Fig. 7.2. After the trial, Leonard lived much of his life isolated from New York society. The Rhinelanders ultimately received a divorce in Las Vegas, Nevada. Here is Leonard at his Mount Charleston Lodge, forty miles from Las Vegas. He is repairing the roof on one of his mountain hideouts. © Bettmann/Corbis

ing a multiyear court struggle. As one colleague said about Leonard in his obituary, he spent the rest of his life trying to overcome "his mistake"—the mistake of marrying a colored woman.

Similar types of consequences for crossing racial lines of intimacy still occur today, and the fear of such consequences causes many individuals in interracial relationships to hide their relationship from loved ones and family members, just as Leonard and Alice did at the beginning of their marriage. For example, as Professor Renee Romano reported in her book *Race Mixing: Black-White Marriage in Postwar America,* one white woman who had married a black man during the 1970s had pretended to be single and childless to her family and home community for nearly twenty years.[14] More recently, in Heather Dalmage's book *Tripping on the Color Line: Black-White Multiracial Families in a Racially Divided World,* one white man in his fifties described the hostility that endured from other workers in his job as a teacher once they learned that his wife is black. He said: "My wife and I walked into a meeting with the white teachers and the people from the neighborhood, and it sent those people into conniptions. I won't forget that. It was my first year teaching there, and from then on it was like, 'God have mercy on my soul,' I was a dead person in that school and that stayed with me for seventeen years—the whole time I was there."[15]

Workplace discrimination because of interraciality is not unique to this teacher, however. For many individuals in interracial relationships, loss of jobs and other workplace opportunities simply becomes part of the territory. In addition to lost jobs and work opportunities, blatant social mistreatment in the workplace may take the form of harassment, or a worker in an interracial marriage or relationship may be ostracized, made fun of, called names, and, in some cases, attacked all because of his choice of partner. Over time, as individuals have brought claims of discrimination based on interraciality in the workplace, courts have been forced to develop legal responses for addressing such harms.

Encountering Interracial Discrimination

In many of the first cases involving allegations of discrimination because of interraciality, and specifically because of involvement in an intimate, interracial relationship, courts did not recognize these types of discrimination claims as valid. In such cases, courts argued that that the plaintiffs lacked standing to sue because they were challenging discrimination based solely on the race of their spouse, not based on their own race.[16]

The early 1980s produced one of the first cases to address employment discrimination based on interraciality. In *Adams v. Governor's Committee on Postsecondary Education*, a federal district court in Georgia dismissed the claim of a white male employee who alleged discrimination because of his black wife, finding that the plaintiff had failed to state a claim upon which relief could be granted under Title VII.[17] The court reasoned: "Plaintiff does not contend that he has been discriminated against because of 'his' race or because of his color, religion, sex or national origin. He contends that he has been discriminated against because of the race of his wife. The words 'such individual's' as used in the statute make it clear that an employer cannot lawfully discriminate against an employee because of *that employee's* race. Neither the language of the statute nor its legislative history supports a cause of action for discrimination against a person because of his relationship to persons of another race."[18] In so holding, the district court in Georgia relied on the decision of another federal district court in *Ripp v. Dobbs Houses, Inc.,* though that case, unlike *Adams,* involved allegations of discrimination based solely upon social attitudes toward platonic friendships with black employees. In *Ripp,* a federal district court in Alabama rejected the plaintiff's lawsuit, asserting that his challenged actions did not constitute discrimination "because of" the plaintiff's own race, but rather involved practices that affected only members of a different race.[19] The court explained, "The Court believes that there can be no better insurance of vigorous enforcement of Title VII than the litigant who is genuinely aggrieved by the practices under attack. Paul Ripp is not that plaintiff."[20]

Since both *Adams* and *Ripp,* however, the vast majority of courts to address cases concerning discrimination based on interracial associations have rejected such restrictive readings of Title VII. Courts now interpret "because of such individual's race" broadly, reasoning that an exclusion of discrimination by association lawsuits runs contrary to the purposes of general discrimination law.[21] According to these courts, a plaintiff in these types of cases—discrimination by association cases—suffers discrimination because of his *own* race or protected class;[22] they reason that, but for the fact that the plaintiff's race differs from the race of his partner, he would not be subject to mistreatment from co-workers.

Courts also have extended this discrimination by association analysis to harassment cases, where plaintiffs have the burden of proving by a preponderance of the evidence that the employer created an environment that was so severe and pervasive in its hostility toward their interraciality that it altered the terms and conditions of their employment. In these cases, too, courts acknowledge that plaintiffs are enduring discriminatory treatment on the basis of their own race as opposed to their partners' race.

The effects of courts' application of the association analysis to interraciality cases has been tremendous, offering protections to claims by plaintiffs who have suffered serious harm as a result of perceived racial transgressions around intimacy. For example, in the 1996 case *Rosenblatt v. Bivona*

& Cohen, P.C., a district court in New York denied an employer's motion for summary judgment against a white male attorney who claimed that his law firm fired him because he was married to a black woman.[23] In evaluating the plaintiff's claim, the district court identified decisions such as *Adams* and *Ripp* that had rejected discrimination by association claims due to standing concerns, but the court ultimately decided to reject those other courts' restrictive holdings.[24] The judge in *Rosenblatt* explained: "Plaintiff has alleged discrimination as a result of his marriage to a black woman. Had he been black, his marriage would not have been interracial. Therefore, inherent in his complaint is the assertion that he has suffered racial discrimination based on his own race."[25]

In even later cases involving discrimination claims based on interraciality, plaintiffs have continued to experience success before courts, either by surviving a defendant's motion for summary judgment or winning at trial. For example, Sheri Sawyer Madison, the plaintiff in *Madison v. IBP, Inc.* who brought a discrimination lawsuit based on interraciality under Title VII, § 1981, and the Iowa Civil Rights Act, won her case before a jury, obtaining an award of $1,638,417. Madison received $266,750 in emotional distress damages, $76,667 in backpay and benefits under the Iowa Civil Rights Act, and $1,295,000 in punitive damages combined under Title VII and § 1981.[26]

In her workplace, Madison encountered repeated acts of harassment from co-workers and supervisors based on her identity as part of an interracial family unit. The co-worker harassment included the type of acts that can often place strains on intimate relationships and, more importantly, can discourage individuals from continuing to challenge the racial norms of intimacy through their relationships.[27] Madison, the white wife of a black man and the mother of biracial children, worked at IBP in Iowa along with her husband. During Madison's employment at IBP, co-workers made inflammatory and derogatory racist comments about her, her husband, and her children.[28] One co-worker told Madison that she had "ruined herself" by marrying a black man and having children with her husband.[29] In so doing, that co-worker revealed a belief still held by some that whites who marry blacks are lowering or demeaning themselves. Another co-worker demonstrated the hostility often directed toward the multiracial children of individuals in cross-racial relationships, children who, for some, serve as undesirable, visible reminders of what can be perceived as severe racial transgressions. This same co-worker referred to Madison's children as "fucking niggers" and proclaimed that all Madison had to do to take care of her kids was to "let them jump on the bed and put Velcro on the ceiling" or have them "lick their lips and stick them on the wall."[30] Still another co-worker read Madison's involvement in an interracial relationship as a sign of sexual impurity or as the basis of removing her from the pedestal of womanhood that has traditionally been reserved for white women. This co-worker offensively fondled and touched Madison while he simulated sodomy on her and forced her to bend over a vat.[31]

What is worse is that the workplace structures that would normally serve to regulate and correct misconduct on the job failed for Madison. Although the harassment of Madison often occurred within the presence of her superiors at work, none of her supervisors ever disciplined the perpetrators, nor was any note regarding their offending behaviors ever placed in their files. Instead, those who complained about harassment, such as Madison, were forced to sign a form that resulted in a "counseling for sexual harassment" notation being placed in their own files.[32] Ultimately, Madison took a demotion to escape the harassment, a forced decision that came with personal financial consequences for Madison and her family and that, speaking broadly, would not only work to further strain relationships in many cases but also could work to discourage the very beginnings of families that challenge the monoracial norm.

For instance, consider the objections often raised against interracial marriage when announced to families: "It's not that I have a problem with it. I'm just concerned about others. Are you ready for that kind of mistreatment?" "Marriage/commitment is already difficult. Do you want to add problems of race to that?" "Your worlds and lives are so different. How will your marriage survive?"[33] In fact, one of my interviewees, Edith, a black woman who is married to a white man, described her father's very intense objection to her marriage, one that was rooted both in the history of sexual assault against black women by white men and the reactions of people both within her family and outside of it. Edith said: "At first, my dad was okay with it. Then he started having nightmares about white men killing black women. He called me on the phone several times and strongly expressed his disagreement with our decision to marry. . . . He was so opposed to our marrying that he did not come to the wedding. He said his feelings stemmed in part from the days of slavery when white masters raped black slaves. His feelings were also influenced by distant relatives' thoughts and comments made to him about his daughter marrying a white man."[34]

Such general reactions to interracial marriage, as well as Edith's father's specific reaction to her black-white marriage, reveal the importance of legal victories by plaintiffs such as Madison, who, as described above, received the opportunity to go to trial and actually won at trial before a jury of her "peers." The availability of remedies to address the harms inflicted upon people like Madison and ultimately their families is critical. Such remedies provide further legal force against the kinds of prejudice and bias that the Supreme Court rejected in *Loving v. Virginia* over forty years ago when it struck down Virginia's antimiscegenation statutes that prohibited marriages between "whites" and "nonwhites."[35]

Like Madison, in *Mackey v. Children's Medical Ctr. of Dallas,* Frances Mackey, a white woman married to a black man and the mother of biracial children, experienced a victory in the legal system when she survived her employer's motion for summary judgment against her claims, a rare occurrence for plaintiffs in employment discrimination cases. Mackey, too, had endured harassment based on her relationship with her husband and the existence of her biracial children while on the job at the Children's Medical Center of Dallas.[36] For instance, one of Mackey's co-workers revealed the continued hostility toward biracial children and the ways in which their very existence challenges social constructions of race when he referred to Mackey's biracial children as "Oreos" and "half-breeds."[37] That same co-worker also exposed the ways in which sexual deviancy can be imposed upon interracial intimacies, as well as the perception by some that interracial relationships are all about sex, when he told Mackey that she must like "big black dick."[38] Finally, like with Madison, the normal workplace hierarchies and structures for correcting and protecting against misconduct failed for Mackey; after all, Mackey's supervisor was one of the culprits. According to Mackey, in response to her protest over an order prohibiting her husband from coming to the workplace, her supervisor, whose face was red and had an "evil" expression on it, yelled, "YES HE WAS [TOLD THAT,] AND THEY [MACKEY'S HUSBAND AND CHILDREN] DON'T NEED TO BE UP HERE ANYWAY BECAUSE YOUR INTERRACIAL MARRIAGE IS AN EMBARR[A]SSMENT TO THIS HOSPITAL!!!!"[39]

Again, as in Madison's case, the law's intervention in cutting off and punishing the discriminators in Mackey's situation proved to be a key tool in combating the remnants of past and current prejudices against interracial relationships and thus challenging the normative ideal of family as monoracial. Indeed, in denying the defendant's motion for summary judgment on Mackey's racial harassment claim, the district court used especially strong language to explain the bases for Mackey's claims by acknowledging that the supervisor's statement to Mackey about her marriage served as a "direct attack on the most intimate matters of her life."[40] The court explicated: "To make matters worse, Mackey had to work in an environment knowing that her superior had such strong negative feelings about her merely because she was, as a white woman, married to an African-American man and had children by him. . . . [R]egarding the history of such viewpoints, laws banning miscegenation played a role in the history of racism in this country, and [Mackey's supervisor's] statement is reminiscent of the environment when these laws were in effect."[41]

What's Missing

Although courts' application of the discrimination by association analysis in interracial harassment and discrimination cases has proven to be very useful in combating certain forms of discrimination based on interraciality, they have not always addressed, acknowledged, and explained the full range of harms that can occur in interraciality cases. As a result, they have left gaps in the protections that the law can provide to individuals who are negatively affected by biases on their jobs against interracial intimacy. For example, courts have failed to acknowledge and remedy the less obvious harm that can occur in jobs where the collective—meaning a partnered couple itself—unofficially plays a role in the hiring or the evaluation of job performance of workers. In such cases, the harm is not just that any individual worker may become the target of harassment and mistreatment as a result of a co-worker's learning about the person's interracial family through a photograph on the desk, and it is not just that any individual worker may choose to remain silent and not "come out" as part of an interracial couple in order to avoid discrimination at work. The damage actually extends much further, because in these particular jobs, although an individual's spouse or partner is not written in as a formal requirement, the expectation by the employer is often that the spouse or partner, if there is one, will serve a vital role in publicly supporting the employee in his work duties. The very existence of such unwritten rules for many high-powered jobs, along with the prejudices and biases against interracial couples and same-sex couples, not only works to frame the normative ideal of the family as both as monoracial and heterosexual but also works to discourage any who aspire to such successes to refrain from cross-racial (and same-sex) intimacies.

Consider, for example, the most prestigious and powerful job on the planet—the job of president of the United States. Having a partner is not an official requirement for the job. The U.S. Constitution provides the official qualifications for the job of president of the United States, noting: "No person except a natural born citizen, or a citizen of the United States, at the time of the adoption of this Constitution, shall be eligible to the office of President; neither shall any person be eligible to that office who shall not have attained to the age of thirty-five years, and been fourteen years a resident within the United States."[42] Nowhere in this clause is there a requirement for an intimate partner, and specifically one of the opposite sex, but it is hard to imagine having a male president today without a wife or with a husband (or, one day, a female president without a husband or with a wife). Indeed, the entire storyline in the fictional movie *The American President,* starring Michael Douglas, revolved around the oddity of a single and dating president.[43] Only one president in this nation's history has been a bachelor, James Buchanan—a man who many have speculated was our nation's first gay president. Furthermore, in the case *Association of American Physicians and Surgeons, Inc. v. Hillary Clinton,* the D.C. Circuit essentially gave legal recognition to the embedded assumptions about unpaid labor by the first lady and, more so, the cultural expectation of such labor when it held that "the President's spouse acts as the functional equivalent of an assistant to the President."[44] By so doing, the D.C. Circuit also rejected the idea that the post of the first lady, a job for which she receives no pay, is purely ceremonial.

In many ways, one could argue that a presidential hopeful's most crucial running mate is not the vice-presidential candidate, but rather the potential first lady. She is one of the most important factors to his success. Yet, just as the potential first lady (or first gentleman) can be a key to success, she also can be a candidate's downfall.

To understand the potentially harmful impact of prejudices against inter-raciality as well as the harm that can stem from antidiscrimination law's failure to acknowledge such prejudices, ask yourself whether our current president, Barack Obama, the first self-identified black president of our nation, would be president today if Michelle Obama were white instead of black. Professor Ali Mazrui has already offered his insights on this question, declaring: "If Obama had chosen a white woman as his wife, that would have decisively destroyed his presidential hopes . . . [because] the Americans are not comfortable with the prospect of a white First Lady married to a black president. They are not able to accept horizontal inter-raciality."[45]

Chances are that Mazrui's predictions about Obama's likelihood of gaining support for the presidency with a white wife, both from whites and blacks, are correct. After all, just the potential of racialized resistance to a fictional, interracial love relationship in the movie *Hitch,* starring megastar Will Smith, was enough to cause casting directors and producers to balk at the idea of making a white woman Smith's love interest in the movie.[46] On a much smaller scale, the mere mention of a possible tryst between former U.S. Congressman Harold Ford, Jr., and a white woman at the Playboy mansion seemed to diminish his prospects for election to the U.S. Senate. During Ford's tight race for the U.S. Senate in Tennessee, the Republican National Committee drew heat for featuring a commercial where a young white woman claimed to have met Ford at the Playboy mansion and whispered, "Call me." As one journalist explained, "The ad smacked of racism—implying that he [Ford] was somehow unfit for office because he was a womanizer who liked white girls."[47] In light of Ford's experience in Tennessee, it is difficult to imagine that Obama would have fared any better with, for example, white voters on a national level had his wife Michelle been a white woman.

But, the prejudices against interraciality through "coupled" jobs do not stop just with white resistance. Consider President Obama's situation again. Black voters, too, would have been unlikely to grant Obama 96 percent of their vote in 2008 had Michelle been white instead of black, though this resistance from blacks, as Professor Erica Chito Childs has explained, probably stems not from perceived inferiority as it does with whites, but instead from what she calls "oppositional support" or fears of racism by whites and the existence of internalized racism among blacks.[48]

In his book *Member of the Club: Reflections on Life in a Racially Polarized World,* Lawrence Otis Graham identifies in-race marriage as the most central element in diagnosing racial loyalty among blacks. He asserts that, in assessing the authenticity of other blacks, blacks "look for what we consider the final determinant of [a] person's black identity—that thing that will allow us to bestow our unqualified appreciation. We look for the litmus test of loyalty to the race: the photo of the person's spouse or significant other."[49] Simple, everyday occurrences and comments confirm this reality as articulated by Graham. Many blacks who attend or have attended predominantly white schools or who work or have worked in predominantly white environments can describe countless times when white friends, colleagues, or acquaintances—while intending to be complimentary—remarked, "I don't think of you as being black." Translation: "You are not like those other blacks. I think of you as being like me—normal. The negative associations that I attach to blackness do not apply to you."[50] Among blacks in interracial couples, the equivalent "compliment" from other blacks is "Really? Your spouse is white?! I would have never guessed that you married someone who's white." Translation: "I usually think of those who outmarry as sellouts. You seemed to be a race man or woman." The black mother of biracial, black-white writer Angela Nissel reminisced about similar reactions she received from friends and acquaintances when she, a former Black Panther, married a white man, Nissel's father. She explained: "You have to understand, I worked for the Black Panthers in their free clinic as a nurse and I worked for the Medical Committee for Human Rights. I probably have an FBI file. I was deep into Power to the People. Some folks didn't understand how I could be with your dad. . . . They didn't understand that I could fall in love with a white man and still work for social justice."[51] According to Nissel's mother, "[b]lack men would shout right at [her], 'You trying to look black with your big Afro, but you're not black!'"

It is against this backdrop that we can see how a white Michelle Obama would have dampened Obama's chances for the job of president, despite his accomplishments, intelligence, charm, and ability to inspire. In fact, one could argue that an interracial marriage would be more damaging for a black man on the job market or on the job than a black woman because the sellout label attaches even more strongly to black men who marry white women as a result of the stereotype that black men outmarry as they move up the professional ladder or because, as I noted in Chapter 5, black male–white female intimacy has historically been viewed as more threatening than intimacy between black women and white men. Take, for example, the experience of one of my black, male professor friends—I'll call him "Bob." Early in his career as a professor and before the 1990s sexual harassment revolution that made professors reluctant to meet with students behind closed doors, my friend Bob, like many of his colleagues, met with students who came to his office behind closed doors—male, female, white, black, and so on. Bob later came to learn, however, that several of his white male colleagues had complained about him—the only black male on the faculty—because he held meetings with white, female students behind closed doors. Bob's colleagues expressed their belief that such meetings were inappropriate, even though they themselves met with white women behind closed doors and did not complain at all about Bob's closed-door meetings with black women (or white men), or even their own closed door meetings with black women.

And also, it is against the broader backdrop that encompasses prejudices, not just from whites but also from blacks, against interracial relationships that a black, and in particular, a brown-skinned, Michelle Obama was able to give her husband, Barack, a racial credibility with black voters that he otherwise would have lacked because of his own interraciality as an individual and his Kenyan background. After all, there was no shortage of blacks in the public eye who questioned Obama's authenticity as a black man. For example, writer Debra Dickerson proclaimed, "Barack Obama would be the great black hope in the next presidential race—if he were actually black."[52] Yet, as Mazrui has explained, "Obama was compensated by his wife Michelle who is a quintessential African-American"—the descendant of slaves in the United States and a dark-skinned (not a light-skinned) woman who grew up on the South Side of Chicago.[53]

Here again, the experience of Harold Ford, Jr., proves illustrative of the harms that may attach to interraciality in jobs that implicitly require a heterosexual collective. After his Senate loss in Tennessee, Ford married Emily Threlkeld, a white woman, and moved to New York. When asked about his move to New York, Ford responded that it was easier to be in an interracial marriage in New York than Tennessee. He announced, "There was so much bad racial stuff out of Tennessee on Obama. I'm in an interracial marriage. I don't want to subject my wife to this."[54] But by outmarrying, some speculated that Ford had doomed his political prospects. Although Ford, at the time, had recently begun a seven-figure job at Merrill Lynch and was only thinking about running for Secretary of State Hillary Clinton's former Senate seat, the public reaction from blacks suggested that he had engaged in political suicide by marrying a white woman. For instance, Pat, a black citizen from Harold's former home state Tennessee, asserted, "I think he has not given his political career any thought. If he runs for any office again, surely he won't win. You don't carry the black vote and marry white."[55] Similarly, Danielle Belton wrote a piece on BlackSnob.com, in which she stated the following: "It is PRETTY DAMN HARD to get elected if you're a black politician with a white wife. Not only do you have to deal with crap like the racist TV ad campaign that torpedoed Harold Ford Jr.'s Senate dreams in Tennessee, but there's that little problem with that usual Democratic lock—*the black vote.*"[56]

Such prejudice against interraciality on the job market and on the job, however, extends beyond politics. The jobs of president, senator, and congressman are not the only ones to which a "couple requirement" attaches. Various jobs exist in which a spouse—in many cases, a wife—is viewed as a key asset to job performance and, in some cases, of simply being hired onto the job. Many of these jobs, especially those for which people serve as formal or informal representatives of their companies or institutions, come with an implicit requirement for spousal help or at least spousal existence. Take college presidents, for example. The Association of American Universities (AAU) recognized the implicit requirement for work by the spouses of college presidents when it "adopted guidelines urging members to recognize the spouses' role and consider offering a titled position with a job description, salary and/or benefits" in 2001.[57] In fact, recent decisions at the University of Iowa present a good example of this invisible-spouse requirement for college presidents and the implicit expectations of unpaid work—work that spouses should be compensated for—but particularly those expectations for the spouses in couples that satisfy the traditional gender norm. In 2012, local news sources reported that the Iowa Board of Regents had refused to pay the wife of the Iowa State University President Steven Leath for her fundraising duties when, just five years earlier in 2007, it had agreed to pay the University of Iowa's President Sally Mason's husband, Ken Mason, a yearly salary of $54,000 for his fundraising duties (even though it had not paid the previous two male presidents' spouses for similar work).[58] Although the Board of Regents indicated that Janet Leath, the wife of Iowa State University President Steven Leath, would have "many official duties on behalf of the university" and gave her the title of President's Associate to use on official stationery and business cards, it also indicated that she would receive "no formal salary compensation for her position."[59] This seemingly different treatment between the husband of President Mason and the wife of President Leath (and also the wife of the current male president at the University of Northern Iowa), which are all led and overseen by the Iowa Board of Regents, prompted one local reporter to pose the following question: "The sentiment was that wives of university presidents have long been expected to support the careers of their more prominent husbands, attending events and playing the supportive spouse. But, they didn't get paid for it. Now that women are assuming more leadership roles, why is it that a man is getting paid for similar duties[?]"[60]

On the other hand, in jobs where a spouse is not viewed as a "necessary," or even helpful, asset to job performance, then prejudices against interraciality, whether conscious or not, are not as likely to have a big impact on employees. Take, for instance, the job of being a U.S. Supreme Court justice, which does not appear to come with an implicit requirement to be part of an intimate, cross-sex relationship. Being a U.S. Supreme Court justice is not a job for which workers are expected to maintain a particular public face, at least not in the same manner as politicians or other institutional representatives. Rather, it is considered a job of isolation, a job of the mind, and a job that arguably may be performed better without the distraction of a spouse; more importantly, it is a job guaranteed for life. Candidates for and appointees to the job are unlikely to be hindered by either not having a spouse (unless the person is openly gay and cannot marry) or by having a spouse of a different race. To confirm this reality, all one has to do is look at a few recent and current members of the U.S. Supreme Court: Former Justice David Souter never had a publicly known partner while on the Court; Justices Sonia Sotomayor and Elena Kagan do not have publicly known partners (though both were certainly subject to gender-biased charges about their temperament in part because they were unmarried); and Justice Clarence Thomas, the sole black man on the Court, is married to a white woman (though certainly some of the public criticism of him relates to his having a white wife). This, of course, is not to say that judicial candidates or nominees do not face unfair speculation about their sexuality or, worse, verbal disparagement if they are perceived as being gay; however, such actions do not disprove these points, but instead bolster them, specifically as they relate to the implicit requirement to be coupled with someone of the opposite sex, if coupled at all.

Nevertheless, even in jobs with a couple requirement, damage or harm does not *always* attach to employees based on interraciality. In fact, one could argue that interraciality can work to the "advantage" of some employees in their workplaces or on the job market. For example, in my own job as a law professor (for which being heterosexual and coupled is certainly not a requirement, but can help with social events), I, as a black, female race scholar, have experienced positive reactions from other law professors as a result of having a white husband. In light of the stereotypes that can attach to smart, assertive black women within the workplace—specifically the stereotypes of the racial nag (consider how many white professionals generally do not have to think about race and do not like being forced to think about race) or the angry black female (think of Michelle Obama on the cover of the *New Yorker* with an Afro and a sash of bullets on her body), my husband's whiteness can provide comfort to those who might otherwise find me threatening or off-putting because of my race, my gender, and any accompanying stereotypes. In some ways, my marriage to a white man counteracts stereotypes that I "may be hung up on race" and signals to whites that "I do not dislike white people."[61]

Indeed, several black individuals in my surveys indicated similar reactions from co-workers to their having a white partner; in fact, this theme was fairly consistent among blacks in the black-white couples I surveyed. For instance, Bryan,[62] a married, black, male professor in a same-sex relationship, noted that he incites the same reaction as I do as a result of his white spouse. He explains, "If anything, I think it works to my . . . benefit. As I've written about, my white partner helps to make me racially 'palatable.'"[63] Susan, a black, Latina real estate worker, noted the same: "In business, white people that really do not have many or any black associates seem to feel more at ease once they find out that my husband is white."[64] Similarly, Darcy, a black, female public-policy worker who is married to a white man, Charlie, described how she senses more comfort from her white co-workers after they meet Charlie. She stated, "I felt like as soon as people met [Charlie] for the first time at a potluck, people were much more open to me and talked to me more."[65] Even Darcy's husband, Charlie, has noticed the favorable reactions toward Darcy once other whites meet the two together, noting that "[w]hite women are less intimidated by my wife once they meet me because I am white."[66]

However, the experiences of Bryan, Susan, Darcy, and me do not represent the experiences of all individuals in black-white, intimate relationships. For one thing, our experiences are largely one-sided, demonstrating how such "benefits" may accrue primarily to blacks because of the way in which racial privilege, advantage, and disadvantage operate in our society. More so, to label such reactions as a "benefit" is, in many ways, a misnomer. After all, the positive reactions that blacks may experience from whites as a result of their interracial marriage are only benefits because of the ways in which blacks are generally disadvantaged by being viewed and treated as outsiders—those who are more difficult to get to know, approach, and thus work with and fit in with—in predominantly white work spaces.

This is not to say, however, that feelings of comfort and ease do not come in the reverse for whites who are part of committed black-white couples. Take, for instance, the comments of Ted, a white male educator who is married to a black woman. Ted noted that his black secretary "was pleased that [his] wife was black," and he "thinks this has happened with other black co-workers" as well.[67] Likewise, Susan's husband, Ethan, also a real estate agent, described how racial minority co-workers would warm up to him once they learned about his wife. He pointed out, "[A]t my jobs, it has seemed to work to my advantage. Once black and minority co-workers find out that my wife is black, they tend to act as if I am one of the 'brothas.'"[68] Again, such experiences by Ted and Ethan are not the norm.

More so, the "beneficial" experiences of all the black and white individuals above are, to some extent, unusual because of their work environments, particularly for those in higher education, where workplaces are generally reputed to be more open. On top of that, closer examination reveals that the described "benefits" may be limited by more than just environment or race; gender, too, may play a role. For example, each person who claimed a workplace "benefit" from his or her interracial relationship in my study was part of a black female–white male relationship, excepting one couple, a black male–white male couple. Indeed, it is important to note that the circumstances under which a person may "benefit" from interraciality in the workplace may be highly contextualized. Returning back to our examples from politics (and also considering analyses from Chapter 5), imagine now that Condoleezza Rice is married to a white man and has decided to run for president. Unlike for Obama, who most would agree could not have succeeded with a white wife, a white husband could actually serve to help Rice in her campaign for office, especially given the racial make-up of the Republican Party and the historically less threatening view of black female–white male relationships in the United States. Indeed, unlike Obama, for whom it arguably would be better to be single than married to a white woman, for my imaginary potential Rice candidate, career-related, gender prejudices could make it such that it would be better for the imaginary Rice as a politician to be married to a white man than not married at all.

Still, despite the fact that there can be some "benefits" to interraciality in the workplace, there are also disadvantages, even in the most unlikely of environments. For instance, in his law school—a place where one would expect a good number of students to be committed to equality—Fred, a black, male law professor who is married to a white woman, has received negative feedback from his students about his spouse. As Fred explained, "[b]lack students seem to note that [he has] a white wife, not necessarily with approval," and Fred has to work hard each day—harder than other monoracially married, black professors—to maintain his relationship with the Black Law Students Association.[69] Moreover, in many jobs where there is an unwritten requirement or suggestion for an opposite-sex spouse, having a different-raced spouse can be damaging. In fact, having a spouse of a different race can be fatal—particularly, if the applicant or employee is white, and the "assisting" spouse is black (as the loss of or change in privilege is more noticeable for the white person). Indeed, all but one of the interraciality employment cases I found involved just that—a white plaintiff married to a black person.

Consider, for example, the case of Craig Holcomb, a white man who in *Holcomb v. Iona College* asserted that he lost his job as a college-level assistant basketball coach because he was married to a black woman.[70] Holcomb worked as an assistant coach for the men's basketball team at Iona College. When he began working for the team in 1995, Holcomb was single. In 1998, Jeff Ruland, who was an alumnus of the Iona College as well as a two-time NBA all-star, became head coach. Ruland promoted Holcomb to associate head coach, which made Holcomb the top assistant coach. Ruland, too, was single at the time. Although Ruland was not the head coach at the time that Holcomb was hired and thus did not hire Holcomb, Ruland and Holcomb became fast friends. Ruland also worked with two other assistant coaches: Tony Chiles, a black man, and Rob O'Driscoll, a white man who was the most junior coach of the three assistants and was not partnered with a black woman. During the first four years of Ruland's leadership as head coach, Ruland and his assistant coaches enjoyed considerable success, as their team won the Metro Atlantic Athletic Conference in 1998, 2000, and 2001, and earned a spot in the National Collegiate Athletic Association (NCAA) Men's Division I Championship Tournament in each one of those years as a result.[71]

In 2000, Holcomb began to date a black woman, Pamela Gauthier, whom he eventually married.[72] According to Holcomb and a third-party witness, Richard Petriccione, a vice-president of the college, made especially offensive comments when he received Holcomb and Gauthier's wedding invitation. Petriccione allegedly asserted to Holcomb, "[Y]ou're really going to marry that Aunt Jemina? You really are a nigger lover."[73] In 2001, Ruland started a relationship with Iris Hansen, another black woman who was Gauthier's friend.[74] Together, Hansen and Gauthier supported their partners by attending the men's basketball games and postgame functions. Holcomb's wife, Gauthier, also attended events of the Goal Club, whose members gave or donated money to the college and received invitations to pre- and postgame receptions along with other special events.[75]

According to Holcomb, from 1997 until 2003 his wife regularly accompanied him to Goal Club events; also, local high school basketball players, most of whom were black, were allowed regularly to attend Goal Club postgame parties. In late 2003, Shawn Brennan, the director of athletics, barred all local high school players from future events. According to Jamie Fogarty, the assistant athletic director for compliance at the time, the college decided to ban students from Goal Club functions because of concerns about potential violations of NCAA rules against having highly prized student recruits at such events. Fogarty said that he was particularly concerned about one highly sought-after recruit, whom Fogarty noticed at one event.[76] But Holcomb disagreed, noting that such attendance was at worst "a gray area."[77]

In response to the decision to bar all local high school students, Holcomb told Brennan that such a new policy would harm recruiting efforts. Because Holcomb was suspicious that Brennan wanted to reduce the number of blacks at Goal Club functions, he inquired whether Brennan was "looking for a reason not to allow student athletes to come."[78] According to Holcomb, Brennan, at that time, also told him that his wife as well as Ruland's girlfriend Hansen, both of whom were black, were no longer welcome at Goal Club events because they were neither alumni nor donors.[79]

Beginning in 2002, the Iona College men's basketball team began to perform more poorly than in previous years, failing to make it to the NCAA tournament in 2002, 2003, and 2004. Off the court, the men's basketball team also ran into trouble. In late 2001, several team members were caught engaging in a fraudulent scheme where they were purchasing books with book vouchers and then selling them for cash. Two starting players on the team were dismissed for poor academic performance in both the 2002–3 and 2003–4 seasons.[80] In late 2003, the NCAA informed Iona College that it would be investigating the team's players and coaches for possible rule infractions. In completing its investigation, the NCAA interviewed only Coaches Ruland and O'Driscoll; it did not interview either Coaches Holcomb or Chiles. Later, when the NCAA issued its report identifying several secondary violations by the team, it did not attribute any of the violations to either Holcomb or Chiles. Only O'Driscoll, the white assistant coach who was not partnered with a black woman, was mentioned in the report. O'Driscoll was listed for a secondary violation as a result of his moving one player's personal belongings from the dorms to his garage.[81]

In March 2004, Brennan prepared an evaluation of the men's basketball program for Brother James Liguori, the Iona College president, and the Board of Trustees. In it, Brennan recommended against firing the head coach, Ruland, because Ruland, who was the highest-paid person at the college, had a high-paying contract for several more years; thus, firing him would cost the college a tremendous amount of money.[82] He also recommended against firing all three assistant coaches, stating that such action would result in "only . . . cutting off appendages to the issue while the core remains."[83] Although Brennan did not explicitly criticize Holcomb in the report, he did critique the coaching staff, asserting that they could not get along and did not work hard. Brennan described only one coach with praise, writing that "Rob O'Driscoll works very well with others across campus."[84]

President Liguori and his three vice-presidents, one of which was Petriccione, made the ultimate decision about whom to terminate and when to do so. They decided to fire two of the assistant coaches. In the end, both Holcomb and Chiles were asked to resign. Though Chiles eventually resigned, Holcomb refused to do so and was ultimately terminated. O'Driscoll, the most junior of all the assistant coaches and the only of the assistant three coaches mentioned in the NCAA's investigation report, was not fired, but instead retained. According to Brennan, after President Liguori informed him of the plan to let go of two of the three assistant coaches (without any identification as to which two would be fired), he and the president discussed which person should be retained on staff for continuity reasons;

Brennan told Liguori that "in [his] opinion, the best person to carry that out was Rob O'Driscoll."[85]

After Holcomb was terminated, he filed a lawsuit, alleging discrimination based on his interracial marriage. Specifically, he claimed that Brennan and Petriccione fired him because of his marriage to a black woman and that Brennan and Petriccione were motivated in their decision by a perceived need to appeal to Iona's mostly white alumni, alumni from whom the college was seeking donations. In response to Holcomb's suit, Iona College argued that Holcomb was not terminated because of his interracial marriage, but rather because he was part of the necessary overhaul of a poorly performing team.

The Second Circuit Court of Appeals reversed the district court's decision to grant the defendant Iona College's motion for summary judgment, and, in 2008, held for the first time that there can be a Title VII violation where an employer takes action against an employee because of the employee's association with a person of another race.[86]

Judge Guido Calabresi authored the opinion and was brilliant in identifying the reasons why summary judgment for the defendant was not warranted in the case. First, Judge Calabresi wisely explained why the college's retention of Ruland, who was dating a black woman, did not negate Holcomb's legal claims. Judge Calabresi explained that all agreed "that Ruland was simply too expensive to fire, with over five years left on his contract, whether or not he was in a relationship with a black woman."[87] Judge Calabresi then acknowledged that the college's justifications for its decision to retain O'Driscoll (who was not black or married to a black woman), rather than Holcomb—that O'Driscoll "worked well with others across campus" and "was doing an adequate job"—were not compelling, especially given that O'Driscoll was the only assistant coach investigated by the NCAA.[88]

Acknowledging Brennan's role in the final employment decision to terminate Holcomb, Judge Calabresi then highlighted potential racial motives that may have influenced Petriccione and Brennan. First among them were Petriccione's racist remarks in the workplace, especially his comments concerning Holcomb's interracial relationship: "[Y]ou're really going to marry that Aunt Jemina? You really are a nigger lover."[89] As Judge Calabresi stressed, Petriccione was known for his racial insensitivity. For example, colleagues testified that he referred to a Nigerian employee at Iona as "jungle bunny" and "African princess."[90] When the employee applied for a particular job in Alumni Giving, Petriccione is said to have asked, "[W]hat does she think she is coming from a hut in Africa and thinking she could apply for this job?"[91]

Second, there was Brennan's desire to appeal to the primarily white alumni base of Iona College and to do so in a way that limited the presence of blacks. As Judge Calabresi determined, "[A] rational finder of fact could conclude that Brennan had an incentive, for the purposes of alumni relations, to minimize the number of African Americans involved with the basketball team. Such motive could be inferred from Brennan's decree that high school students could no longer come to Goal Club events, a decision taken after a group of black high school students had attended. Though a jury might credit Brennan's [and Fogarty's] stated rationale, that he feared an NCAA investigation on the issue, a jury might instead determine that this explanation was pretextual, taking into account Brennan's contemporaneous order that neither Holcomb's wife nor Ruland's girlfriend should come to events."[92] Finally, Judge Calabresi was astute in addressing the complexities of racial discrimination, discounting the defendant's argument that it was not liable because one of the new coaches hired to replace the old assistant coaches was black. Specifically, while accepting that pure and simple traditional race discrimination could be at play, Judge Calabresi noted that a more complicated form of prejudice and bias could be at play. He highlighted not only how the decision makers at Iona College could have hired a black man as one of the new coaches in order to conceal prior discrimination, but also how they may not have been motivated "by racism per se, but instead solely . . . disapproval of interracial relationships."[93] Or, as Judge Calabresi explained, "a jury might accept that the college did not act with the motive of eliminating all African-Americans from the program's staff, but find that the college wanted nevertheless to have at least one coach who was neither black nor in an interracial relationship."[94]

In all, Judge Calabresi demonstrated a complex understanding of race and racism in his opinion, acknowledging that racism may involve more than a desire to exclude all members of a targeted group. He explicated that racism may also involve prejudice at the tipping points of inclusion through efforts to limit the number of persons from targeted groups and, more importantly for the purposes of this book, that racial discrimination may not focus solely on the individual and his race, but rather the individual as part of a collective or race mixing.[95]

Still, because of the way antidiscrimination law narrowly considers posted definitions and descriptions of job duties and performance, what Judge Calabresi's opinion, and ultimately other opinions, do not recognize are the harms that stem from prejudice against workers in interracial couples where unwritten job requirements and functions extend beyond the official job description and into the family. For example, even though Judge Calabresi's opinion captured several complexities of race discrimination well, it failed to capture or even acknowledge how Holcomb was discriminated against in part because of implicit job requirements about who his spouse should be, if she existed: someone of the opposite sex and the same race. For instance, there is no discussion about the many inferences that could be drawn from the unquestioned past assistance from previous coaches' same-raced wives. Even an identification of Holcomb's experience as one resulting from racial stereotyping—for example, not fitting the stereotype of a white man by having a black wife—would not fully capture the full range of harms he suffered without an acknowledgment of the expectations underlying his bosses' actions, job expectations about who his partner should be. The failure to give name to and identify the norms that undergird employer expectations about spousal requirements only works to reinforce the assumption of monoraciality (and heterosexuality) as the familial ideal by leaving such norms invisible and free from interrogation. As Professor Holning Lau noted in his article "Transcending the Individualist Paradigm in Sexual Orientation Antidiscrimination Law," courts often fail to recognize the rights of same-sex couples because antidiscrimination law has a paradigm that hinders efforts to properly analyze claims made by same-sex individuals against couple-oriented business establishments.[96] This individualist paradigm, Lau argues, fails to acknowledge how individual's identities are "inextricably linked to [their] memberships in certain social collectives," and thus fails to protect each individual's "right to associate with those collective entities" but also "those entities' aggregate rights to develop."[97] Just as the failure to recognize the aggregate rights of couples—and specifically, same-sex couples—creates a gap in legal protections in public accommodations based on sexual orientation, the failure of courts to acknowledge how individuals in multiracial families are influenced by and defined by their families at work leaves such individuals without the means for remedying the specific harms that they may experience in employment due to discrimination based on interraciality.

In sum, although numerous scholars (and some courts) have acknowledged the notion of the "ideal worker" in the workplace, what these scholars, and antidiscrimination law more generally, fail to note about the characteristics of the ideal worker is that he is not just male, he is not just heterosexual, he is not just white, and he is not just coupled with a wife who takes care of him and enables him to perform job tasks in a firmly committed way; he is coupled with a wife of the same race. What this means is that courts have not unpacked or analyzed the full range of harms that can come from invisible norms about not only who should be at work but also about who behind the scenes must be supporting the worker. In this way, courts have simply reinforced the false conception of work and home as being mutually exclusive of other, with legal doctrines that do not necessarily overlap or inform each other. For example, consider the military's former "Don't ask, don't tell" policy. Nowhere has collective discrimination proven to be more harmful in the workplace than in the implementation and enforcement of this former military policy, in which the requirement to be heterosexual, if coupled at all, was demanded. There, because the government failed to legally recognize that people's individual identities were tied to being part of an intimate collective, numerous soldiers lost their jobs and their means for economic survival simply because of their partner.[98] Although there was no requirement to be coupled when in the military, there was an explicit requirement to be coupled "straight." A similar requirement exists for many jobs with regard to race; only the requirement there is implicit, and that requirement is to be not just heterosexual but also of the same race as one's partner. In sum, courts have failed to acknowledge and examine the individual identity-based collective discriminations that can arise at work. Altogether, this general avoidance by courts suggests that the norm of the supportive spouse as a job assistant is too deeply ingrained to be extricated without specific identification of the problem.

Again, consider the range of occupations where partners of an employee, if they exist at all, are expected to be part of the public face presented at events. Many of these jobs revolve around fundraising and speaking to particular audiences—jobs like college presidencies, military commissions, or, as in the *Holcomb* case, college sports coaching positions. Other jobs include implicit, but less onerous tasks for partners through the attendance of office parties and events. Now imagine our stereotypical ideal worker: white, male, heterosexual, and coupled with a supportive wife. Then imagine that this worker hosts an event at his home or he shows up to a workplace event—an unofficial task in many jobs—with a black wife. Pause. Visualize. Imagine the initial silence and discomfort, and imagine the responses the day after at work. Imagine the racial jokes that may be told both behind his back and to his face. Think back to the experiences of plaintiffs like Madison and Mackey.

Given the experiences of plaintiffs like Madison, Mackey, Holcomb, and even my black, male professor friend in their workplaces, it is easy to see how an unwritten couple requirement at work—a requirement that essentially demands both heterosexuality and monoraciality within couples—provides an incentive or an additional reason for individuals, particularly ambitious types, to decide against being part of an interracial couple or multiracial family. It is in this way that what seems to be worlds apart in employment law has a direct impact on family and on the assumptions that we make about families and the disadvantages that flow and will continue to flow from those assumptions until they are routinely challenged.

Remember that Holcomb was single when Iona College first hired him as an assistant coach. Had he known before he met his wife, Gauthier, of the lifelong repercussions of his marital decision, would he have made the same effort to meet, date, and court her again? Or if she had pursued him, would he have responded to her overtures? More so, even if Holcomb would have decided to still pursue and marry his wife or accept her advances (clearly decisions that a number of people make), would Iona College have hired him to begin with had he applied for the job already having a black wife? From what we can tell from the facts of his case, the answer is a no. Or, more so, what burdens would have been placed on Holcomb in navigating his job search in order to obtain the job without subjecting himself to interraciality discrimination? Would he have had to have kept his relationship a secret? Perhaps. In fact, individuals in interracial couples are often strategic about when they first introduce their spouse to co-workers and supervisors and, in some cases, whether they introduce them at all.

I, too, have found myself "passing" as "black," meaning briefly remaining silent about my own marriage. In my essay "Undercover Other," I described a form of inactive passing that may have been similar to Alice's behavior. I wrote: "At times, I find myself sitting quietly when discussions about interracial couples ensue in black circles, passing as a member of what others assume to be a monoracial couple until I know that I am in a safe enough space to 'break the news' of my destabilized blackness—of my identity as a 'seemingly black' woman married to a white man. . . . To them, my liberal politics and appearance initially identify me as one who is authentically black, but my choice in a life partner, which indicates my willingness to be placed in deliberate proximity to whiteness, somehow destabilizes my racial identity."[99]

One very funny experience of mine illustrates the psychological burdens that can come from relationship passing as well as the precautions that individuals may take based upon their past experiences with prejudice against interraciality, even when there is no risk of harm at all to them. During my second year of law school, I interviewed with a number of judges for clerkships, including the first judge whom I actually worked for, an African American man. When I received his offer, I was ecstatic. In law school, though I had had a few female law professors, I had not had one black or minority law professor, and I was eager to add a black mentor among my other mentors—someone who could advise me on navigating issues of race and work throughout my career. I also was excited because my judge had formerly held two jobs that were of great interest to me: law professor and assistant U.S. attorney. After accepting the clerkship, I called one of his current clerks, who I knew also wanted to become a law professor (and who later became a good friend and incidentally also entered into an interracial marriage). During our conversation, I expressed my pleasure at meeting the judge, my excitement about his modesty and down-to-earth nature, as well as my appreciation for his lifelong commitment to mentoring young attorneys, in particular young black attorneys. I then asked this clerk—the one black clerk in chambers—when I should tell the judge about my re-lationship. Of course, I knew the judge was not prejudiced at all because we had discussed not just race and racism during the interview, but also what had motivated him to become a lawyer. But like I described above in "Undercover Other," I naively worried about destabilizing my racial cred-ibility, my credibility as someone committed to uplifting other minorities and women. What followed on the other end of the phone was incredibly loud laughter. When the clerk—now my friend—finally regained his com-posure, he simply said, "The judge's wife is white." I quickly joined in his laughter.

But not all stories of "passing" are so humorous, and not all passers en-gage in only brief passing. For example, in her book *Tripping on the Color Line: Black-White Multiracial Families in a Racially Divided World,* Profes-sor Heather Dalmage detailed the constant struggle of Parsia, a successful black businesswoman, who still preferred not to bring her white husband to certain areas or events.[100] In describing why she would not, at times, bring her husband to some black-centered events, Parsia explained, "I believe that once blacks see me as part of an interracial couple, it changes their perception of me right away. . . and suddenly I become the outsider."[101] Moreover, as we see in many cases like those of Madison and Mackey, the actual act of "coming out" as part of an interracial family can often result in not-so-funny—in some instances scary—consequences in the workplace.

Finally, even if a married Holcomb could have navigated the terrain of keeping his relationship secret until he actually received the job, would the end result at Iona College—his ultimate firing—have been any different (that is, apart from what may have been an earlier termination)? Certainly, general prejudices against interracial couples in our society have signifi-cantly lessened, but individuals in such couples do still encounter mistreat-ment in the workplace, and even in environments that are generally viewed as progressive. For example, Margaret, a black, female professor who is married to a white, male professor, described a situation in which her hus-band's superior at work mistreated him after learning of his new marriage to a black woman. She explained, "Early in our marriage, I noticed that one of [Geoffrey's] colleagues, Associate Dean X, in particular, was quite upset. In fact, [Geoffrey] was slated to receive a sabbatical the year we were married, and Associate Dean X yanked the sabbatical. [Associate Dean X] was aware that we lived in two different states, and the importance for the sabbatical."[102]

In the end, one puzzle remains: how often do questions about the failure to hire or other mistreatment in the workplace because of interraciality not even get raised because the norms that underlie them, particularly the expectation of a spouse of the same race and different sex, are invisible or remain unspoken to many? Current antidiscrimination law's inability to address such questions about interraciality works only to reinforce the job framing of the ideal family as monoracial, not just by discouraging people from crossing racial boundaries of intimacy because of potential consequences at work and in society, but also by essentially codifying such assumptions in law through silence. We need to think of more ways in which we can bring these issues to light, both legally and socially, a task I undertake at the end of the next chapter.

8

Reflections in Black and White, and Where We Go from Here

SO FAR IN THIS BOOK, I HAVE utilized the lives of Alice and Leonard Rhinelander as a window into understanding how law and society have functioned together to frame the normative ideal of family as monoracial (and heterosexual), both historically and presently. Through their tragic love story, Alice and Leonard have provided us with a critical vantage point for seeing how far we have come with regard to race, intimacy, and family. They also have provided us with important lessons about law's invisible role in reifying race and racial hierarchies among individuals and families at home, in the workplace, through children, and even in our courtrooms. Questions remain, however, about what we should do with those lessons in working to expand our framings of the normative familial ideal or, really, in even imagining ourselves without an ideal.

In this chapter, I analyze data from surveys to reflect upon key questions from the *Rhinelander* case and to understand their meaning for today's black-white married and committed couples and their families. I also consider and examine how being part of a multiracial collective may shape the individual racial identities of persons in such families, as well as how such "new" understandings of race may affect or should affect the legal analysis in certain antidiscrimination cases. Thereafter, in light of all of the questions, problems, and concerns that I raised previously in Chapters 5, 6, and 7, I conclude with one proposal for potential change in the law—a proposal that is modest in its form, but could have far-reaching social, environmental, and legal implications; that would work to better capture the identities of multiracial people and their families; and that could more easily reach the harms to multiracial families that are currently disregarded and unacknowledged by the law. Specifically, I consider the potential benefits that could arise from adding the term *interraciality* as a protected category in current antidiscrimination law statutes.

What It Means to Be Alice and Leonard Today

At the beginning of his lawsuit for annulment, Leonard reportedly told Alice, "Our separation cannot last forever; nothing does."[1] Unfortunately, Leonard was wrong about what many believe to be his forced separation from his wife, Alice. Leonard and Alice were never reunited as a couple and instead remained apart even in death. They were buried in different cemeteries, with the only glue between them being Alice's last act of having her marital name "Alice J. Rhinelander" engraved on her tombstone. In simple terms, Alice and Leonard's separation ended up lasting forever-plus.

In many other ways, though, Leonard was correct in declaring that nothing lasts forever. For instance, the very social barriers that worked to force Alice and Leonard apart back in 1924 are far weaker in our society today. Time, alone, might have changed the course of the newlywed Rhinelanders' lives. In 1958, just thirty-four years after the *Rhinelander* case was first filed, Josephine Premice, a black female singer who performed in the Broadway musical *Jamaica,* with Lena Horne and Ossie Davis, married Timothy Fales, the white son of a Wall Street investment banker whose family descended from *Mayflower* settlers and whose family, like the Rhinelander family, regularly appeared on the *New York Social Register.* Though the senior Fales, much like the senior Rhinelander, was initially resistant to the marriage of Fales and Premice, he ultimately warmed to the union, and the Fales couple later had two children and remained together until 1984.

Today, not only have social attitudes and laws changed such that no state can ban interracial marriage in the United States, but the number of interracial marriages, including black-white marriages, is increasing each decade. Additionally, across our nation, many people would publicly criticize Leonard for his actions if he, or rather his father's attorneys, were to try to pull the same legal stunts against Alice today. As a small sample of contemporary attitudes, I polled twenty-seven students who were enrolled in the undergraduate college at the University of Iowa. The polled students ranged in ages from eighteen to twenty-two, with the exception of one person. Two-thirds of them—eighteen total—were either eighteen or nineteen years old, and all but four of them were twenty-one or younger. Although the sample was random and small and not appropriate for making generalized claims, the students' responses provided one snapshot of their contemporary attitudes toward the central purposes of marriage today. Specifically, they provided a sense of just how distant in history Leonard's asserted basis for annulment seems to young people today. Students in the survey responded most strongly against the idea of an annulment brought on the grounds of racial fraud. In fact, they responded more strongly to the hypothetical case involving racial fraud than they did to hypothetical cases involving fraud based on transsexual identity, infertility, immigration, laziness, wealth, and impotency.

In the poll, I asked students "to judge several hypothetical situations and indicate whether the type of fraud described in each scenario 'goes to the essence of marriage' and thus should be a sufficient basis for annulment of marriage."[2] I explained that "[a] factor goes to the essence of marriage if it is an issue that is so material and central to marriage that it justifies court declaration that the marriage never existed." I also asked them to take a few seconds to explain their reasoning for their response to each hypothetical, if they could. I made it clear to the students that they "should not answer the survey questions based on whether [they] would personally seek an annulment based on any of the types of fraud described," but instead that they "should answer each question based on whether [they] think that the type of fraud described in the hypothetical scenario should be a legally sufficient basis for an annulment."[3] As I explained in the instructions, the survey was "intended only to get [their] opinion about what types of fraud [they] think should be able to serve as a basis for an annulment of marriage."[4] Then, I provided the students with definitions for the terms *annulment* and *divorce*, explaining the distinctions between the two.[5] Finally, I asked the students a series of questions based on seven scenarios. The following facts never varied from scenario to scenario: (1) each hypothetical couple dated for a year before they married; (2) the individuals in each hypothetical couple never met each other's families before they married; and (3) by at least the third month of the marriage, one of the individuals in each hypothetical couple discovered a fact about his or her partner that caused him or her to file for an annulment. The only fact that changed in each scenario was the asserted factual basis for the annulment, and in all, I asked the students about seven different, asserted bases for annulment. They included (1) a wife's discovery that her husband lied about being a multimillionaire and was instead flat broke and jobless; (2) a husband's discovery after the marriage that his wife was a male-to-female transsexual; (3) a husband's discovery that his wife kept her infertility secret from him until after they were married; (4) a wife's disappointment when her once sixty-hour-per-week-working fiancée quit his job almost immediately after they got married to sit on the couch every day, drink beer, and watch sports; (5) a husband's discovery that his "white-looking" wife kept the fact that she was half-black a secret from him until after they got married; (6) a husband's discovery that his wife was not an American citizen after she stopped having sex with him and hanging out with him upon marriage; and (7) a wife's discovery that her husband kept his impotency from her until after they got married.

The twenty-seven polled students were most likely to believe that fraud to obtain citizenship status should be a legally sufficient basis for annulment (which it is), with twenty-four of the twenty-seven students (88.9 percent) agreeing that such fraud should be a legally sufficient ground for annulment. Stated rationales for their decisions included comments like, "If she just married him to stay in the country and preyed upon him I think that is a valid reason"; and, "For legal reasons, it should be clear to the citizen partner what her or his mate's status is."[6] Receiving the second highest number of votes as a legally sufficient basis for annulment was fraud as to one's being a transsexual, with seventeen of the twenty-seven students (63 percent) agreeing that such fraud should suffice. For this question, however, the rationales expressed by the students were much more varied. For instance, some students felt that an annulment clearly should be granted to the plaintiff, making comments such as a "sex-changing operation is not natural and it never will be."[7] Other students felt that an annulment clearly should not be granted, arguing that "a male-to-female transsexual has made a concrete commitment to hi[m]/herself to be another sex, and, as such, is not deceiving her/his partner," or that "he [the husband] should have realized it before or sought out to learn more about her."[8] Finally, some students expressed more conflicted sentiments, making declarations like, "I think that she may ha[ve] her own reason for not telling her secret, he should listen to her first, and then make a decision"; or, "That's something Bill [the husband] could have found out before hand [sic], but it's Mary's [the (transsexual) wife's] responsibility to tell him."[9]

The most evenly supported and challenged bases for annulment in the survey were fraud based on wealth, impotency, and infertility. Only fifteen out of the twenty-seven students (55.5 percent) agreed that fraud related to wealth should be a legally sufficient ground for annulment. The fifteen students who supported the basis for annulment in this case made arguments such as, "I feel like Louise [the wife] could have found all that out before they married, but George [the husband] misled Louise with the intention to get her to like him," while those who did not support it argued that Louise should not be granted an annulment because "she never investigated for herself" or simply stated that they "don't believe financial status is grounds for annulment."[10] With respect to impotency, again, only fifteen out of twenty-seven students (55.5 percent) agreed that fraud related to impotency should be a legally sufficient ground for annulment. The fifteen students who supported annulment on this ground made arguments such as, "This is your classic Trey-Charlotte [from *Sex in the City*] relationship. The right to procreate may be one of the highest marriage values and they should be fought for"; while those who opposed it simply made arguments like, "[S]he should have been told, but it's not a big enough deal."[11] Finally, with respect to infertility, only twelve out of twenty-six students (46.2 percent) agreed that fraud related to infertility should be a legally sufficient basis for annulment. For this question, although fewer students expressed support for annulment on this basis, they made strong statements in order to back up their votes when they did. For instance, students made statements such as the following: "This is the strongest case of the ones I've seen so far." "Children mean[] a lot to marriage, she should tell the truth before." "Honesty is always the best policy, and if you are not honest, how can you possibl[y] be a spouse? It is unfortunate that Ruth [the wife] cannot have children, but Steven also has his rights in this situation, the right to procreate."[12]

But, overall, the twenty-seven polled students reacted most strongly *against* accepting knowledge of race as a legally sufficient basis for annulment, with only two students—less than 8 percent—agreeing that such knowledge should suffice. This means a whopping 92 percent of the students felt that racial fraud should not be a legally sufficient ground for annulment.

Only one other tested ground—fraud about laziness—came close in terms of the students rejecting it as a basis for annulment. With respect to deceit about laziness, only five of the twenty-seven students—approximately 18.5 percent—agreed that it should meet the legal standard for annulment. Only one student offered a strong argument for why fraud about laziness should be legally sufficient. That student argued, "Luke [the husband] looks like a liar and a bum, and no one should have to be married to someone who is jobless. It's not even the fact that he is jobless, that is unfortunate. But he lied, and cannot provide for Katie [the wife]."[13] One student, perhaps jokingly, implied that any man would be lazy when the student rejected fraud as a basis for annulment. This student wrote, "Again, this isn't a big enough deal. Katie should also realize that any guy she marries is going to be lazy."[14]

But even when compared to reactions to fraud claims based on laziness and infertility, the reactions to the hypothetical claim based on racial fraud were strong. Bob, the husband who was seeking an annulment based on racial fraud, was called a "racist" by several students. For example, one student wrote, "[I]f you love someone it shouldn't matter what half of their gene code says, Bob should be less racist."[15] Another student declared, "[R]ace should never be a reason to get a marriage annulled and the guy is ridiculous for thinking that is a good reason."[16] One student even questioned my inclusion of this hypothetical in the survey when he or she simply wrote, "This is a stupid question."[17] Even those who had sympathy for Bob made sure to express their personal rejection of his asserted basis for the lawsuit. For instance, one student wrote, "It might have been a good idea to find that out before, but I don't think he should even have a problem with that."[18] Additionally, there was at least one comment by a student that reified problematic notions of race, but still criticized Bob for being stupid. In that one response, a student reinforced the idea of race as clear and obvious—much like Davis did when he argued that Alice's race was so obvious that only a blind man could not see it. In fact, this student voted in favor of allowing racial fraud to be a legally sufficient basis for annulment. The student, however, made sure not to align himself or herself with Bob, explaining, "Clearly Bob sounds like a dumbass to not be able to tell if his girlfriend was white or black. But some people are racist in varying degrees, and it is his right to marry someone he wants, a white person."[19]

If these students' responses tell us much about the potential for shifts in how our society may see and address issues concerning race and family—even when they fail to contest notions about clear and visible race—then there is hope for future change in how we frame and define the normative ideal of family. In fact, the black-white couples who participated in my couples survey responded to questions about race and family much in the same way as the polled students in my annulment study, even though the couples were speaking about Alice and Leonard during the 1920s, a time in which race and racism held a different meaning in our society. When I asked my interracial-couple survey participants about their reactions to the trial involving Alice and Leonard Rhinelander, none of them expressed a view that embraced knowledge of a person's racial background as being material to the decision to marry during the 1920s. One couple simply provided their analysis for why they thought Leonard filed a lawsuit for annulment. They explained, "We feel Leonard's attempt to annul the marriage was to avoid embarrassment or being shunned by his peers. The annulment versus the divorce seems as though he was trying to deny her any rights to marital assets."[20] A few individuals highlighted the sadness of the Rhinelander story without making any judgments about Alice or Leonard, hinting at sorrow for Alice as well as Leonard. For example, Fiona and Peter, a black female–white male, married couple, pointed out the sadness of the separation that lasted forever; they exclaimed, "Wow! How tragic. It's unfortunate that Leonard succumbed to his father's tyranny and that he and Alice were not reunited."[21] Similarly, Bryan, a black man married to a white man, commented on "how sad [the case] was, that their love was thwarted."[22] Edith, a black woman married to a white man, expressed her anger at how Alice was treated as well as her sadness about the thwarted Rhinelander love. Edith proclaimed, "I'm appalled that she had to show her nude body in court and that she would have to prove that she was 'colored.' The fact that neither party remarried and that her tombstone included her married name seems to suggest that they remained each other's true love."[23]

However, such sympathies by Bryan, Edith, Fiona, and Peter were rare among my survey participants. Very few of the participants who spoke about the Rhinelanders expressed any support for Leonard. Only a minimal number seemed to hold sympathy for Leonard at all, despite the time period in which his actions took place. In fact, many of them were highly critical of Leonard precisely because of Alice's own suffering. For example, one couple, Amber and Caleb, simply noted in reaction, "Leonard was a wimp who should have stood up to his father."[24] Another couple, Jane and Ted stated, "We both felt that the lawsuit sounded fishy and that Leonard sounded weak and dim,"[25] while even another couple, Janet and Sam, expressed their sadness for Alice, noting "[i]t's a shame and sad from Leonard having no backbone to Alice being paraded nude during trial. Certainly not one of America's better moments in legal history."[26]

Other individuals expressed sadness for Alice, ripping Leonard, in turn, for his actions. For instance, Raven, a biracial, black-white woman who is married to a white man, asserted, "I have sympathy for Alice because her husband turned on her as a result of her race."[27] Like Raven, Darcy, a black woman who is married to a white man, expressed her extreme disappointment with Leonard's actions. She said, "I am not sure why they didn't get to stay together. If Leonard told Alice to fight the case, then why could they not be together? I would say good for Alice for embracing her heritage and making this such a shocking case, essentially making history. Leonard was a coward and his love for Alice was not strong enough to overcome the pressure of society."[28] Similarly, Geoffrey, a white man married to Margaret, a black woman, declared matter-of-factly, "She [Alice] was courageous and admirable; he [Leonard] was a jerk."[29] Finally, one couple, Stephanie and Kirk, stated that they "both felt sad for Alice and angered by Leonard for being gutless."[30]

Perhaps naively, when I first posed questions about Alice and Leonard to my survey participants, I halfway expected that a few of them would speak about Leonard's failure to stand up to his father within the context of the time period involved, but only two of them ever did. When I thought more deeply about the couples themselves, I realized that their largely unsympathetic responses to Leonard, even when taking the time period into account, were not surprising in light of their own experiences. For one thing, very few of the participants in my survey had encountered much opposition from their families to their marriage or commitment *based on race*. In fact, unlike Leonard during the 1920s, most of them came from families that were supportive and happy that they had finally found true love in their lives. For instance, Raven, a black-white, biracial woman, described the following reaction from her already multiracial family when she began to date Jim, her white husband: "My family instantly loved my husband when we were dating. They've always thought he was hilarious and I think they like him more than me."[31] Similarly, Karen, a black woman who is married to a white man, asserted, "My parents, who are in an intercultural marriage that was opposed by their parents, were neutral on the issue of interracial or intercultural dating. That said, they quickly fell for my husband and still love him very much."[32] For Julie and Barry, a black male–white female couple whose respective families both fell for their partners quickly, they "feel like [they] have had a fortunate life as an interracial couple, perhaps because of where [they] have lived together," which have been places like Brooklyn and Oakland, "the capitals of interracial coupledom."[33]

Even in situations where family members may have more openly desired a same-race partner for their relative, in many of those cases, survey participants eventually received support in their relationship from once semiresistant relatives. For example, Amber, a black woman married to a white man, asserted, "[We received] [n]othing but support [from my family when we married]. I say my dad would have preferred I married someone of the same race, but I mean that abstractly. He once said that he never imagined having kids who would bring so many white people into his house. But once he wrapped his head around it, he was fine."[34]

For a number of the same-sex couples in my survey, although sexuality often posed a barrier for them in terms of family acceptance of their relationships, race never did. Sexuality eclipsed any possible issue of race in resistance, making race the easier part of the relationship to accept. As one survey participant, Bryan, explained about his family's response to his cross-racial, same-sex relationship—now more than twenty years strong, "Well, considering that my family officially learned I was gay shortly after I introduced them to my partner, it's a little complicated. Oddly enough, my father seemed relieved I was dating a white guy."[35] Janice, a white woman who is partnered with a black woman, asserted, "My family did not attend our civil union in Vermont, but I would say that was more about their issues with 'gay marriage' than interracial marriage."[36] Similarly, John, a white man in a civil union with a black man, explained the following about his family's reaction to his commitment: "Race was not an issue, but [my parents] were less happy about my 'marrying' my partner before they had met him. . . . We did [a civil union] for ourselves and did not have a ceremony or guests. . . . My parents and siblings had no problem with the situation. Yet, I must say that some aunts and cousins showed less enthusiasm about the whole thing. I think, however, that their reaction was more due to homophobia than racism."[37] Finally, for Carrie, who is in a committed relationship with a black woman, her family expressed no concerns about race at all, but instead about sexuality. Carrie notes, "Race was not the issue, same sex was. [My partner Amy] is the first woman [whom] I've dated that I've told my family about, so their reaction was centered on that. . . . [My] [f]ather was just relieved that I am not alone . . . [but my] younger born again sister . . . declared that she loves/supports me but that non-hetero partnering is not in God's plan."[38]

The ease with which these couples formed their unions without race-based opposition from family (at least when compared to Alice and Leonard) provides one reason why these couples tended to be less empathetic toward Leonard. But while the individuals in these couples did not experience the outright disapproval from family that Leonard did or that many black-whites couples did in the decades preceding the turn of the new millennium,[39] they did have to overcome social resistance to their decisions to cross the color line in love. As this book has shown, many of these individuals had to ignore and push back all of the social cues that they had learned or had been told, either directly or indirectly, about the monoracial

family ideal. Indeed, all of the individuals in my surveyed couples had received these cues in a variety of ways. For instance, a few of the black-
white, heterosexual couples experienced subtle opposition from their family
members, ranging from passive aggressive resistance to comments about
their relationship that they found to be personally offensive. For instance,
Charlie, a white man who is married to a black woman, described his wife's
first encounter with her sister after his wife told her family about him, an
encounter she found to be personally demeaning. He said: "Before my wife
and I were married, she told me about how she told her family about me
on a recent trip to visit them. She told me that her sister said, 'Oh god. You
are going to have some high yellow babies.' I was very offended because
the man she was dating was basically biracial and it was like this double
standard. I was dumb-founded."[40]

Other people experienced reactions from families that signaled resistance in subtler forms, even as family members expressed their approval
outwardly. For instance, Ted, a white man who is married to a black woman,
described an awkwardness that remained even though his family was outwardly accepting of his relationship. In describing his family's response to
his marriage, Ted declared, "My immediate family seemed fine, although
my mother acted awkward around Jane [my wife], and I think projected
hostility onto Jane. My extended family seemed a bit too curious, as if they
thought Jane was something to look at."[41] Similarly, Fred and Deanne, a
black male–white female, married couple, noted how the embrace that
Fred received from one of Deanne's relatives was discomforting at times.
Deanne wrote, "One relative made a big deal of accepting Fred[, my husband,] and Thomas[, our biracial son,] and generally seemed stuck on the
fact that [they're] black."[42] Finally, Charlie, in addition to experiencing slight
resistance on his black wife's side of the family, described one inelegant,
verbal embrace of his plans for marriage by his grandfather. Charlie explained the way in which his grandfather ultimately came to accept his
relationship as follows: "When I married my wife . . . my grandfather sat
us down and talked to us about race. He said that because Moses married a
black woman . . . it was ok 'what we were doing.'"[43]

Other interviewees had experienced moments in their lifetime when the
social cues about monoraciality, or rather the supposed deviance of inter-

raciality, in love, had been communicated to them at younger ages. For example, Bryan, a black man who is married to a white man, described one incident during his childhood from which he first learned about the supposed shame behind interracial relationships. In fact, this story by Bryan reveals not only the social cues that he received about couple monoraciality as a young man, but also the personal impact of the social cues that he received about couple heterosexuality within the same period. In describing one of his most memorable experiences with race or racism, Bryan said: "My final year in high school, I transferred from my all black high school to a mixed school in the suburbs, where we had recently moved to. The suburban school was about 60 percent white / 40 percent black. One white girl was known for dating black boys, and ostracized by whites. She and I dated for a moment, but the incident that really stands out is when I started talking to a beautiful black girl after a football game. A white tough came over and starting shouting racist insults at me. I was confused until it became apparent that he and the black girl were secretly an item."[44] Bryan's experience exposes the way in which people receive cues about the perceived deviancy of interracial intimacy, a perception so strong that the intimacy should remain hidden if it occurs at all. Indeed, Margaret, a black woman who is married to a white man, revealed in her own response just how this perception still affected her and her views on interracial love. She said: "The socio-cultural history of enslavement in the United States [makes the lives of black-white couples very different from those of other interracial couples]. As well, I was very sensitive to the 'outness' of our relationship. I grew up knowing of black women who loved white men, but those white men were afraid to be seen with the black women they dated. So, as an intellectual, but also deeply spiritual matter I am concerned about love being out of the closet in relation to black women / white male relationships."[45] Additionally, during his teen years, Fred, a black man who is now married to a white woman, experienced one event that reinforced how interracial relationships are viewed as nonnormative and, particularly so because of the idea that they revolve solely around sex and fantasy. Fred recalled "being in undergrad and having a white girl [he] was fooling around with respond to a question from other white friends about whether [he] had a big dick."[46]

Deanne, the white wife of Fred, also remembered an incident during her teenage years that reinforced the notion of interracial intimacy as inherently deviant, so much so that the relationship could only mean trouble, including from law enforcement. Deanne recounted one experience in which a police officer stopped her and a young black man she dated as a teenager. She explained, "When I was seventeen, I worked at a summer camp in upstate New York and had a black boyfriend who was from England. We spent the weekend away in a small town, and a police officer asked him some questions out of my earshot. When I inquired [to my boyfriend] what it was all about, he explained to me that it was simply because he was black and I was white."[47] Similarly, Barry, a black man who is married to a white woman, described one instance where a stranger in a club essentially warned him and a purely platonic, white, female friend against interracial intimacy. Barry explained, "One memorable experience was when I went country line dancing with a white friend during college. I had absolutely no interest in country dancing, but she persuaded me to go. The first comment we get as we are walking into the dance hall was from a white man in a cowboy hat informing my friend that once you go black you can never go back. It was a comment intended to make crystal clear to me where I stood in that establishment."[48] Finally, Liz, a white woman in a committed relationship with a black woman, highlighted the many implicit messages she must have received during her childhood about the deviancy of cross-racial intimacy. Liz noted that one memorable childhood experience with race was when her "cousin [was] marrying someone Puerto Rican." Liz explained, "[T]his was a big deal and it was strange to me, since she seemed just 'like us' in every way."[49]

Other survey participants received social cues about the ideal of mono-raciality for couples from witnessing experiences in the lives of their friends. For instance, Peter, a fifty-something white man who is married to a black woman, described one such experience as a teen: "A black teammate of mine in high school planned to go out on a double date with me and my girlfriend, but he called me up and was almost in tears, saying that the girl he was going to ask out wouldn't go out with him because he was black. [It's] [m]emorable because I was confused that something like that could happen and . . . [that] someone could not want to go out with someone because they were black and not because she didn't want to go out with him."[50]

For some survey participants and interviewees, they received broader messages regarding why blacks and whites should remain separate altogether. At times, these lessons were deeply rooted within the nation's history of racism. For instance, Fiona described the first time that she learned and understood what it meant to be black and white in our society and, along with that, the clear lines of separation between blackness and whiteness. She declared: "We were visiting my grandmother in Jackson, Mississippi. I was about three or four years old. I went to drink from a White water fountain that looked like the ones I drank from in Chicago. My mother snatched me and exclaimed, 'That's the White water fountain! Are you trying to get us killed?'" Another participant, a black woman named Amber, received a strong message not only about her own placelessness as a black person in white spaces, but also about how racial lines should not be crossed even among friends, much less intimate partners. Amber, a woman in her thirties, described an interaction she had as a child with one of her white neighbors after her family moved to a predominantly white area. Amber stated: "I told the boy two houses up that I was sure we would play together because he was my neighbor. He responded, 'Oh, well the colored people are all over on Crayon Road right over there.' I had never heard someone say 'colored' out loud and without a trace of self-consciousness, nor had it ever crossed my mind that race was how we determined playmates."[51]

Finally, some individuals received very explicit messages from friends, family, and even strangers that identified the monoracial family as the normative ideal. For example, some survey participants like Darcy described getting questions from friends, such as, "Does he treat you better than black men you have dated in the past?"[52] Questions such as these imply that there must be a special reason why a black woman would ever forgo dating a black man to date a white one. Amy, a black lesbian in a committed relationship with a white woman, detailed how some people would tell her outright that she should be with a black woman, instead of a white woman.

Amy explained, "Black women, other women of color, and those I don't know have expressed that they would prefer that I was with a black woman. Those who are friends have told me so or I have experienced outright hostility from strangers. This is true whether the women are straight or gay. Those in interracial black/white relationships are the exception. It has been expressed as the notion of a losing a 'black Butch' to a 'white Femme.'"[53] Additionally, Fiona, a black woman who is married to a white man, remembered seeing her mother be "rude to and treat[] the one white girl one of [her] brothers brought home on one occasion very poorly," and recalled that her mother once told her that she "had 'better not bring a white man home unless he was a Rockefeller.'"[54] The most violent cue received by a survey participant was that of Stephanie, a biracial woman who identifies as black and is married to a white man. Stephanie recalled one night when she and her white college boyfriend—who is not her husband—were attacked precisely because of their relationship. She explained: "I attended a party with my then white boyfriend. We didn't realize that it was a black fraternity party. At some point, one of the men at the party started beating my boyfriend because he was white. I decided it would be a great idea for me to get involved. The guy punched me in the face a couple times, knocking me to the floor. We were finally able to leave the party, but it wasn't pleasant."[55]

Reading and hearing survey participants' stories about the negative social cues that they had received about interracial intimacy in their lives prompted me to recall some of my own memories of such cues, including those I had experienced together with my husband, Jacob. The event I remember the most occurred, many years ago, when Jacob and I were walking down the street in a large southern city. Before we knew it, four young African American men—at a local college—jumped out of the car and quickly separated us. Though it did not take long for me to realize that we were not in danger of any physical harm, for a split second, I wondered what was going to happen to us, especially as Jacob and I had been pulled into separate directions and could not immediately see other. The two young men who had pulled me away kept shouting at me, "Don't you know better?" The other two were asking Jacob, "What are you doing here?" Looking back now, and seeing and hearing the stories of others, I view this one experience of mine as a representation of what each and every negative social cue to my survey participants, above, was designed and intended to achieve: the reinforcement of separate and raced lines of intimacy within our society.

But in the end, despite all the cues that my survey participants had received about strict boundaries against interracial intimacy during their lives, when they were faced with the same tug-of-war decision about love and race that Leonard encountered, they still resisted the forces against them to follow their hearts in deciding to whom they would commit themselves. In some instances, they had very touching memories to call upon. For example, Julie, a white woman who is married to a black man with whom she has one biracial child, described one of her early memories about a black-white interracial couple she knew in high school. She recalled:

> My high school was fairly internally segregated by a tracking system as I said, so one of the main settings for cross-racial interaction was in sports. The athletes were the most likely to have cross-racial friendships as a result. When I was a sophomore, a white male senior on the basketball team died suddenly in his sleep of some sort of heart defect. His serious girlfriend was an African American student who was on the women's basketball team. I remember the white and black parts of the high school, especially the senior class, really came together and mourned him. Later, it became known that she was pregnant, and with the support of both families she decided to have the baby. I remember this strongly in part because it was so sad, and also probably because it was an early, rare example of an interracial relationship that was supported with love by the families.[56]

As I looked back at my survey participants' responses about Alice and Leonard, I realized that they, too, were moved by the Rhinelander narrative. They were caught up in the story, just like I was when I first discovered it, and like the nation was during the trial's run in 1925. The real-life drama of the Rhinelanders filled the New York courtroom in which the parties and their witnesses told their stories. It also filled pages of newspapers, where reporters followed the trial with great interest (see fig. 8.1).

I wondered whether and to what extent my survey participants and interviewees had also followed the story of Alice and Leonard, as I relayed it to them, with interest. Did they see themselves in Alice and Leonard? Although none of the couples explicitly spoke about Alice and Leonard in re-

Fig. 8.1. Alice Jones Rhinelander's sisters, Emily and Grace, and brother-in-law, Robert, sit behind her, her mother, and her father (bottom right) during the annulment trial. The courtroom was packed each day of the trial. © Bettmann/Corbis

lation to their own lives, a personal connection seemed to ring through the words of some survey participants. For example, Cameron and Don, one of only two survey couples to acknowledge the time period of the *Rhinelander* case in their responses, spoke with a passion about the case that seemed to reach beyond just Alice and Leonard. They made the following remarks in response to a question about the Rhinelander story: "Tragic. Scandalous. Pathetic. We are not surprised. It was easy to take a lover of color in secret, removed from whatever racial normalcy, but having the fortitude to stand up to one's family and society is another matter. Also, given the timing, 1924, the outcome is not surprising."[57] Shondra and Michael, too, spoke of the *Rhinelander* case in more far-reaching terms, and each did so with a direct reference to their own lives. Indeed, Shondra linked the case not only to her and Michael's lives but also to the experiences of a friend. She stated: "They had it a lot harder than we did. In 1924 I am not surprised at racial attitudes. There were two of my grandmother's sisters who passed for white and cut off all family contact. So I know for people back then it must have been difficult to navigate race when it determined every aspect of your life. It would have taken a strong person to stand up to that and live openly. It also reminds me of a biracial friend's parents who were torn apart by the racism of the mother's wealthy white family and never remarried."[58] Michael, Shondra's husband, also spoke of the case in relation to his own experience, hopeful that times had changed drastically since the *Rhinelander* trial. He said in response to a question about the case: "Pretty shocking and disappointing. Shocking that she had to stand naked in a courtroom and disappointing that he responded the way he did. It's probably naive to think we're so far removed from that type of thing, but that's certainly my hope."[59] Not surprisingly, Cameron and Don and Shondra and Michael were among the few survey couples that experienced initial resistance from at least one family member to their union.

Although times have clearly changed for multiracial couples and families since the 1920s and even the 1970s, 1980s, and 1990s, the couples in my survey understand that much also remains the same. Discrimination and microaggressions just manifest themselves differently. While black-white couples who married during the 1950s and 1960s often experienced rejection and disapproval from their families, particularly from the families of the whites in the marriages, today, as the experiences of my surveyed couples bear out, outright rejection and disapproval from families is less likely to occur.[60] The resistance, if any, is likely to be subtle or even unconscious. The same applies for the types of reactions that can be expected from strangers, neighbors, and employers.

Race remains relevant, just in different ways. For instance, whereas black-white marriage or commitment once meant that such couples and their families had to live in black communities, they do not mean that today. Still, as Chapter 6 demonstrated, considerations of race in deciding where to live are critical to multiracial families as they decide which communities to reside in. In essence, race continues to pervade the lives of multiracial families—here, black-white families. As one surveyed black female–white male couple, Cameron and Don, expressed: "We discuss race all of the time. We cannot escape it. The issue spans everything—race permeates our lives. Anything and everything. . . . We have different ways of seeing the same people, and experiencing the same events. We end up talking about race a lot more then monoracial families likely. This is work. . . . We don't take race for granted and we think about race in intentional ways."[61] Similarly, Julie and Barry, a black male–white female, married couple, asserted that they speak about race "daily," that "many of the issues surround race and [their] child," and that they are "very much interested in civil rights law and racial inequality and discuss these issues frequently with each other."[62] Overall, they said, "[W]e talk about race perhaps more than we would if we were in a monoracial relationship."[63]

This centrality of race to the daily existence of many multiracial families is largely a reflection of the impact of race, and racism, within our society in the United States. It is not that race has any inherent meaning in society or that interracial couples are inherently different. Instead, it is about how race, intimacy, and family have been constructed within U.S. society. As one surveyed, same-sex couple, John and Vernon, explained, when they lived outside of the United States for many years, they rarely discussed race or racism. As they further stated, though, when they moved to the United States, it became a topic of frequent conversation. They wrote:

> [A]fter moving to the U.S. we became quite preoccupied by the subject [of race] due to daily life, studies, encounters with family, and the particular race politics of the United States. We discuss race and racism very frequently, we could say daily. We discuss Latina/o immigration issues; systemic economic inequalities; education and race; queer of color issues; white privilege (in particular regarding education and social status); racism and the academia; religion; cultural phenomena like music, literature, film, and cuisine; race and family, for instance what would it mean to adopt a child of color or a child of color with special needs; histories of race relations (also personal or familial histories); we talk about what it means being a minority in the different countries we know well; we use race almost as a lens to analyze non-U.S. discourses; we experience racism and homophobia often in our daily lives and discuss what these instances mean to us.[64]

Other couples echoed sentiments about the centrality of race and racism to their discussions and family life. In fact, most of the surveyed couples indicated that they discussed issues of race and racism every day or nearly every day. Even for those who indicated only occasional discussion, they described how discussions of race affected many aspects of their lives. For example, Edith and Stephen, a black female–white male, married couple, proclaimed, "Discussions run the gamut from politics, education, sports, religion, race relations, child rearing, racial identity of our daughter, where to live, where to go to church. Pretty much every aspect of our lives."[65] Other couples commented that the frequency of discussions about race depended upon the point in time of their relationship or whether they were raising children in the house. For instance, Susan and Ethan noted that they discussed issues of race more often when they first started seeing each other. They explained: "When we first started dating, race issues were discussed often. We believed it was our time to discover each other's views on the matter. Issues discussed included: raising biracial children, inquiring about any possible objections from family members, possible perceptions of people who saw us together, sociological issues surrounding black women's hair, advantages/disadvantages of being white/black and doing business, fear of entering certain counties in Georgia due to well known racism in that area."[66] Fiona and Peter noted that, while race is still a frequent topic of conversation for them, it was more regularly addressed when they were raising Fiona's monoracial, black children from a previous marriage. They noted: "[We discussed race] [m]ore frequently when Fiona's black children lived at home and had race-related situations arise. Continuously though, as race can be an omnipresent issue and stressor where we live. We also discuss Peter's background and our families' perspectives on race occasionally. We discuss politics, social issues, and other race-related issues and experiences often."[67]

Some individuals even wondered about the impact that their interracial marriage was having on members of the families into which they were born or adopted. They wondered if the views and actions of siblings, for example, had been affected by having an in-law of a different race. For instance, Geoffrey, a white man who is married to a black woman, wondered if his marriage had influenced his sister's decision to adopt a child of a different race. He stated, "[M]y sister[, who is also white,] has adopted recently an Ethiopian boy; I am not close to her and there is much awkwardness there, but I wonder if she chose a black child in part because of us."[68]

Comments from other participants supported this idea about the influence of black-white marriages on other individuals within the two partners' birth or adopted families (see figs. 8.2 and 8.3). For instance, Amber, a

Fig. 8.2. My in-laws, Susan and David Willig, embraced our marriage from the start.
David Willig has fun in a park with our oldest son when he was a toddler.
Photograph courtesy of Susan and David Willig

black woman married to a white man, spoke about how "middle-aged white women often want to tell [her] about their biracial grandchildren, which [she] find[s] odd and slightly endearing."[69] Historically speaking, biracial grandchildren often served as a bridge between interracial couples and grandparents. As Carol Shepherd McClain explained about reactions to interracial couples during the 1950s and 1960s, "the resistance of the White grandparents more or less evaporated at the birth of a grandchild."[70] In his book *Dreams from My Father: A Story of Race and Inheritance,* President Barack Obama described such a reaction from his grandparents when he was born:

> Whether Gramps realized it or not, the sight of his daughter with a black man offered at some deep unexplored level a window into his own heart. . . . There's no record of a real wedding cake, a ring, a giving away of the bride. No families were in attendance; it's not even clear that people back in Kansas were fully informed. . . . And perhaps that's how my grandparents intended it to be, a trial that would pass. . . . If so, they miscalculated not only my mother's quiet determination but also the sway of their emotions. First, the baby arrived, eight pounds, two ounces, with ten toes and ten fingers and hungry for food. What in the heck were they supposed to do? . . . [Gramps] would begin to read newspapers more carefully, finding early re-

Fig. 8.3. Susan coos over and smiles at our oldest son, now a teenager, when he was a newborn. Photograph courtesy of Susan and David Willig

ports of America's newfound integrationist creed, and decided in his mind that the world was shrinking, sympathies changing; that the family from Wichita had in fact moved to the forefront of Kennedy's New Frontier and Dr. King's magnificent dream.[71]

Most of all, individuals in my surveyed couples, especially those who are white, described how their marriage or commitment had changed their own individual identity and perspectives on race. For instance, in addition to wondering about how his interracial marriage had influenced his white sister and her decision regarding adoption, Geoffrey asserted that, because of his relationship, he has to "be aware of race—and responsive to race in a way which is new for him."[72] Similarly, John, a white man in a civil union with a black man, discussed how his own racial identity had changed since meeting his partner. He said: "Even though I knew I had a race, it never was a fundamental part of my identity. I have been more perceptive of my race since I've known my partner. Yet, I have experienced being 'raced' mostly in the U.S.A. Interestingly, here I have been made aware of the fluidity of race. In particular, and even though I 'look' white, I have been perceived as white or as Latino depending on the place I am or with whom I am."[73] Finally, Michael, a white man married to a black woman, spoke about a number of ways in which his marriage had begun to shape his identity and perceptions of race. For example, Michael described how his being married to a black woman had opened his eyes to the ways in which he had previously been privileged not to think about race. He explained:

"On several occasions after we were married, [I was] in situations where I was the only (or one of the only) white people and [I had to] feel[] a little bit of what my wife had experienced many times before throughout her life. In my case, I didn't feel threatened, just that feeling of standing out and wondering what people were thinking and feeling about me more than I may have before."[74] Michael also joked about the way in which his changed perspective had made him an "honorary" black in the eyes of other blacks. Specifically, he noted how his knowledge of black women's hair, especially about black women's fears of getting relaxed hair wet,[75] motivated one of his wife's friends to anoint him as an honorary member of the race. He said, "One of my proudest moments was when we were watching a commercial where a woman was waiting in the rain and I commented that her boyfriend shouldn't do that. My wife's friend declared me honorary for recognizing the danger of that situation."[76]

The way in which being part of a multiracial family unit has shaped the identities of Geoffrey, John, and Michael is not unique to them as individuals. Many people who are in interracial marriages or who are parents of different-raced children express a similar influence on their identities as a result of their families. In fact, Professor Heather Dalmage has written convincingly and eloquently about exactly this kind of effect on the racial identity of whites in her book *Tripping on the Color Line: Black-White Families in a Racially Divided World*. As Dalmage explains, crossing boundaries of racial intimacy affects not just how other people "race" an individual, much like Leonard's marriage to Alice transformed him from white to nonwhite in the eyes of many. Recall again that Leonard was described as having to make up for his "one big mistake" for the rest of his short life.[77]

Being in a multiracial family also influences how individuals, especially whites, imagine their own racial identities. Numerous scholars, such as Professor Barbara Flagg, have analyzed the transparency phenomenon of whiteness, which allows whites to see themselves as raceless in our society. As Flagg, who coined the phrase *transparency phenomenon,* contends, "to be white is not to think about it."[78] Flagg explains: "White people externalize race. For most whites, most of the time, to think or speak about race is to think or speak about people of color, or perhaps, at times, to reflect on oneself (or other whites) in relation to people of color. But we tend not to think of ourselves or our racial cohort as racially distinctive. Whites' 'consciousness' of whiteness is predominantly *unconsciousness* of whiteness. We perceive and interact with other whites as individuals who have no significant racial characteristics."[79] As a result, for whites, being part of a multiracial family and having white privilege stripped away from them as a consequence of their having resisted the monoracial ideal (as I described with respect to housing and employment in previous chapters) opens their eyes such that they begin to understand and see race differently. Dalmage writes: "As whites, they had learned to expect certain privileges—what they considered fair and just practices in society. But once they joined an interracial family, many discovered that the world is neither fair, just, nor equal. The privileges most whites take for granted become glaringly visible."[80]

In fact, Dalmage, a white woman who is married to a black man, has detailed how such revelations about white privilege led her to shift her personal understanding of her own racial identity. What she has found, however, is that, in our society which is built and framed around clear-cut racial categories and which often leaves multiracial individuals and families suspended in placelessness, there is no way for her to describe her "new" racial identity. Describing a situation in which audience members at a conference were confused by her declaration that she no longer claims a white identity, Dalmage detailed the following exchange between her and the moderator of her conference panel:

> Knowing that the audience of a hundred or so people was likewise baffled by my response I said, "Well, racial identities are formed in part through our experiences. As an interracially married woman, my experiences are vastly different from other white women. Things like being seated in the back of restaurants, being denied loans, being steered out of white neighborhoods when we search for housing, being pulled over for no reason, and facing hostility from racist whites are experiences most white people never contend with. Because of my experiences, I no longer take white privilege for granted, and in some cases I am no longer seen as white by other whites.
>
> She [the moderator] pressed, "So what identity do you claim?"
>
> I began struggling for words and found only what seemed to be a confused cop-out: "Well, that's the problem; there is no language to describe it. There is no other racial identity for me to claim. I am still working on that."[81]

The question is: is there a way in which law can integrate these complex notions of race and racial identity as described by Dalmage in her work?

Where Can the Law Take Us?

Much like with social spaces, the law also provides limited space for the inclusion of the more fluid racial identities for individuals in multiracial families. In addition to failing to acknowledge the unique harms that can flow to persons in interracial couples who are in jobs or applying for jobs where there is an expectation of spousal presence and assistance (as detailed in Chapter 7), or to couples that find themselves discriminated against because of their interraciality in housing (as detailed in Chapter 6), courts also fail, for example, to acknowledge the damages that can arise in discrimination cases for an individual whose racial identity has been changed by virtue of her lived experiences as part of an interracial collective. In particular, current antidiscrimination law does not allow for a claim alleging direct, discriminatory harm to a plaintiff where the racial group targeted by the offensive and discriminatory comments is not the racial group to which the plaintiff-employee belongs, but rather the racial group to which the employee's spouse or partner belongs. In these cases, courts' understanding of how people—in particular, whites in interracial relationships—define themselves racially is too narrow. Under Title VII, a "plaintiff may assert only his own right to be free from discrimination that has an effect upon him and may not assert the rights of others to be free from discrimination."[82] Courts have read this legal rule very narrowly, and as a result, plaintiffs who allege direct harm based upon being subjected to and negatively affected by comments regarding the racial group to which their spouse belongs are held to have no standing to sue.[83] Only members of the racial group to which the comments and actions are targeted, whether or not they individually are the direct target of the conduct, can bring a viable claim on this basis.[84] In other words, under current case analysis, a black plaintiff has standing to pursue a lawsuit for harm suffered as a result of witnessing and hearing derogatory racial comments against blacks other than herself. Such conduct is viewed, and rightfully so, as having the ability to directly affect and harm that plaintiff's environment even where she is not identified as the target. But a plaintiff who is not part of the racial group, even if she is married to a person of that racial group, is seen as asserting harm only to a third party. In other words, unless the plaintiff describes her harm from the harassment as her being deprived of a diverse work environment—meaning racial minority co-workers in the workplace—because of the harassment, she has no claim.[85] This limited framing for a claim, however, anticipates only temporary connections and effects from cross-racial work interactions, rather than the long-term or lifelong connections and impacts that occur within families. In other words, the invisible assumptions about whom we may be connected to or should be connected to in friendships as opposed to familial or intimate relationships works to further reinforce the normative ideal of family as monoracial.

In fact, my research assistants and I searched for opinions where courts had acknowledged and analyzed these particular complexities of interracial collectives, and we found practically none. We found only one case where a court truly analyzed a harassment claim in a way that considered how a person's perspective could be influenced by being part of a long-term or interracial collective or family. In that case, *Gibbons v. Demore*,[86] Molly Gibbons, a white woman who had a biracial child from a prior relationship with a black man, and Denise Hooshmand, a white woman who was previously married to a man of Middle Eastern descent, filed claims of discrimination against their employer Sunrise Hospital and Medical Center and their former supervisor Amy Allin, a white woman. According to Gibbons and Hooshmand, Allin had subjected them to a steady barrage of racial insults and comments about racial minorities, including comments that concerned persons who were the races of their loved ones. Hooshmand and Gibbons contended that Allin's behavior created a racially hostile environment for them in the workplace. In addition to making racially derogatory comments about a broad range of groups that excluded whites, Allin's behavior involved calling Hooshmand's ex-husband a "towel head, sand nigger, Arab rat, whatever";[87] telling Hooshmand that she needed to become "Denise 'black' and stop being Denise 'white,'" meaning that Hooshmand was too nice and needed to be mean;[88] and telling Hooshmand that Verna, a black employee, was white, meaning that Verna was "high skill" and "shops at the best shops."[89] Additionally, in response to a statement by Gibbons that she ate a lot of white meat, Allin stated, "No you don't. You only eat dark meat. Just look at your son."[90] Allin also made a whole host of other racially offensive comments about other racial groups. The defendants Sunrise Hospital and Allin argued that Gibbons and Hooshmand could not maintain a claim for a racially hostile environment because both they and Allin were white.

Generally, to prove hostile environment racial harassment, a plaintiff has to prove that she was subjected to harassment that is so severe or pervasive as to alter the conditions and terms of her employment and create an abusive environment.[91] Specifically, a plaintiff must first establish that (1) she belongs to a protected group; (2) she was subjected to unwelcome harassment; (3) the harassment complained of was based on race; and (4) the harassment affected a term, condition, or privilege of employment.[92] In cases involving harassment by a co-worker, the plaintiff must prove one additional factor: that the employer knew or should have known of the harassment in question and failed to take prompt action to correct it.[93] But in cases involving harassment by a supervisor with authority over the plaintiff, a plaintiff need not prove the additional factor needed for co-worker harassment; instead, once the plaintiff establishes the four factors listed above, the employer must show that (1) it exercised reasonable care to prevent and promptly correct any harassing behavior, and that (2) the plaintiff unreasonably failed to take advantage of such corrective measures or did not have good reason for failing to take advantage of the identified corrective measures.[94] In determining whether harassment has occurred, the court considers and reviews all of the relevant circumstances, including but not limited to the frequency of the conduct, the severity of the conduct, the threatening and humiliating nature of the conduct, and the conduct's effect on the employee's work performance.[95]

The court in Demore granted summary judgment for the defendants on the two plaintiffs' hostile environment claims, but it did so only after considering Gibbons's harassment claim "from the perspective of a reasonable Caucasian with a bi-racial son," and Hooshmand's harassment claim "from the perspective of a Caucasian formerly married to a man of Middle Eastern ancestry."[96] In so doing, the court first noted a distinction between claims grounded in comments against nonwhites and those grounded in comments against the plaintiffs based upon their race. The court noted, "Whether Allin's non-Caucasian slurs created a hostile work environment for these plaintiffs is a distinct question from whether the animus for Allin's utterances was the plaintiffs' race."[97] The court then indicated that it would limit its analysis of the plaintiffs' claims to whether Allin's misconduct was due to animus toward the plaintiffs' race or animus toward their interracial relationships. Although the court determined that both Gibbons and Hooshmand had raised a triable issue of fact regarding whether Allin's animus was toward interracial relationships, the court ultimately concluded that Allin's conduct was not sufficiently severe or pervasive to constitute a hostile work environment. Yet, the court did so in a way that accounted for, at least somewhat, a more fluid racial identity for people in multiracial families.

Yet, still, what about those cases where even a willingness to examine harassment claims based on racial animus toward interracial relationships or even from the perspective of the individual who is in an interracial marriage or who has a biracial child is not enough? What about those cases where the harassing conduct is solely focused on the racial group of the plaintiff's spouse, not at all on their relationship, and where any understanding of the plaintiff's harassment claim would have to be predicated upon an acceptance of an actual shift in racial identity for him, for example, a shift in the plaintiff's identity from white to nonwhite, much like Dalmage has explained about her own racial identity? Shouldn't these discrimination claims also be viable? Wouldn't they also advance the purposes of Title VII and other antidiscrimination laws, especially in situations where there was no employee of the targeted race in the workplace to bring the claim? Recognizing such claims would not only allow the "nonwhite, white" person to have the harm to them acknowledged by law, it also would protect those whites who do not want to be unwilling participants in such prejudiced environments.

To fully understand the import of my questions, consider one experience that my husband, Jacob, had within the workplace. Many years ago, when I was working at a law firm during one of my law school summers, Jacob, then a graduate student, accepted a position as a temporary construction worker and mover in the city where my summer firm was located. All of Jacob's co-workers at this company were white and male. Unlike Jacob, though, his co-workers had a penchant for using racial slurs and making racial jokes about black people. Within a day of his start date, Jacob had discovered his white co-workers' fondness for racism. These co-workers did not know that I was black and actually would not find out about me until weeks later when Jacob finally confronted them.

On the first day that Jacob began his job as a summer worker for his assigned company, he was hit with a barrage of racial slurs and offensive comments from his co-workers, including from his supervisor. Being only a temporary worker, Jacob felt vulnerable in his employment and simply worked the rest of the day quietly, speaking only when spoken to by others. When he came home that night, Jacob looked exhausted, and he told me about his day and the difficulty of enduring his new co-workers' comments.

That night, Jacob and I considered his, or rather our, options. Jacob could complain, but to whom could he complain? Jacob had found his job through an agency, and his one supervisor was among the worst of the bunch with his offensive comments. We then considered the option of telling the agency. Jacob could tell the agency about the offensive conduct, but the agency would likely just work to place him elsewhere, and given that it had taken the agency a long time to place him in this job, we decided against this option. After all, we needed the money to meet our separate finances for the school year and could not afford the wait. Ultimately, we decided that it was best for Jacob to simply try to endure his co-workers and their comments. We told ourselves that it was just one summer. Additionally, we simply hoped that Jacob's first day at work was just an anomaly— that his co-workers and supervisor would not utter racially offensive slurs and comments thereafter. The following days proved otherwise. The comments continued, until one day Jacob erupted and confronted his co-workers, telling them that his fiancée was black. They were surprised by his impassioned reaction. Although they never apologized, they eventually stopped with their comments and did not fully exclude Jacob from their workplace interactions.

Although the scenario above reveals how Jacob experienced harm as a result of his racial identity—his identity as part of an interracial marriage or, rather, his identity as a nonwhite, white person—such circumstances would not have provided Jacob with a viable claim for racial harassment under Title VII. Jacob certainly could have demonstrated, on one level or another, four of the five prongs required for proof of harassment: (1) that he belonged to a protected class; (2) that he was subject to unwelcome harassment; (3) that the harassment affected a term, condition, or privilege of his employment; and (4) even that his employer knew or should have known of the harassment in question and failed to take prompt action to correct it. However, under the law then as well as under current antidiscrimination law, Jacob could not have shown that the conduct or comments about blacks were because of his race or even because of his interracial relationship.

A plaintiff would not even have a viable, racial harassment claim in a situation unlike Jacob's, where his all-white co-workers and supervisor reacted less sensitively to his concerns and continued with their racial epithets, jokes, and slurs after confrontation. After all, even though Jacob's co-workers and supervisors could not claim ignorance about my racial background after the confrontation, they could legitimately and convincingly argue to a court that their conduct was not because of Jacob's race, but rather because of their animus toward the protected class that I belong to, blacks, who were the subject of their comments. The fact is that Jacob's co-workers were making racially offensive comments about blacks even before they knew about me or Jacob's interracial association. The animus was not toward interracial relationships, but rather toward blacks in general.

Furthermore, even if a court analyzed such a claim as the court in *Demore* did by considering it from the perspective of a person with a family connection to the targeted racial group, that route, too, would not work for a plaintiff like Jacob. Keep in mind that the court in *Demore* made sure to note a distinction between harassment claims based on comments against nonwhites and those based on comments against the plaintiffs due to their race. The *Demore* court noted, "Whether Allin's non-Caucasian slurs created a hostile work environment for these plaintiffs is a distinct question from whether the animus for Allin's utterances was the plaintiffs' race."[98] The *Demore* court then announced its plan to limit any analysis to whether Allin's misconduct was due to the plaintiffs' race or to the plaintiffs' interracial family ties. With such a framework, the court failed to complicate its understanding of race, relying on the fact that Allin directed her comments at nonwhites, not "whites" like Gibbons and Hooshmand, and excluding from its analysis of severity and pervasiveness any comments not tied to the interracial relationships. In this way, the court failed to see the harm to Gibbons and Hooshmand in a way that incorporated complex understandings of racial identity such as those explicated by Dalmage. Importantly, with respect to Gibbons's claim, the court stated that "Allin directed a single comment to Gibbons *expressly concerning this [interracial] relationship*."[99] The court further explained its decision as it relates to Hooshmand as follows: "[T]hough the remarks concerned Hooshmand's former husband, the severity was significantly diminished relative to the relationship itself. That is, Hooshmand presented little evidence that the remarks were directed to the relationship. Rather, the evidence indicated the remarks were directed at the ex-husband because of his race. . . . Hooshmand has not shown that the workplace was hostile because she was Caucasian. . . . While the offensiveness of these statements would be more severe to a reasonable Caucasian formerly married to a Middle Eastern man than to a Caucasian, the severity is not as great as judged from the perspective of the Middle Eastern man."[100]

Indeed, the only other time that a nonmember of a targeted protected class in a harassment case would have standing to sue under current antidiscrimination law is when he or she alleged harm and damages as a result of losing the benefits of interracial interaction in the workplace because of discrimination against persons in that targeted class. For example, in *EEOC v. Mississippi College,* the Fifth Circuit held that a white plaintiff had standing to sue based on the employer's discrimination against blacks in hiring and recruitment because the plaintiff "could claim that the discrimination deprived her of the benefits arising from association with racial minorities in a working environment unaffected by discrimination."[101] But again, while such claims are important and necessary, they do not cover all potential harms from harassing behavior. In fact, they are, in many ways, premised on more short-term benefits of interracial interaction—the benefits of cross-racial workplace relationships, rather than the longer-term, life-altering relationships of family. In other words, they presume and assume—in fact, encourage—interraciality in workplace friendships, but not beyond the workplace and particularly within families. In this way, they also work to frame and reinforce the normative ideal of family as monoracial. More so, they reinforce inflexible categories of race that fail to account for the way in which interracial relationships can work to shift racial identity for individuals and that end up leaving multiracial families, at times, in placelessness.

One must ask, though: is there any way that law can work to help undo these normative framings of family in our society? More so, is law a tool that can be effective in reframing these norms? After all, the most effective ways for ensuring change in our society is often through cultural shifts in how we as individuals think about and encounter issues and problems. Law, however, has always played a critical role in helping to spark and influence these cultural shifts. For example, prior to *Loving v. Virginia*, multiracial families were not just considered outside of the normative ideal, but rather the result of pure lunacy or sickness. Although interracial families still face social and legal obstacles in their lives, most Americans approve of their existence and reject the very notion of laws that would prohibit them.

One legal change that could help to challenge our framing of the normative ideal for family as monoracial is the addition of the term *interraciality* as a protected category within various antidiscrimination statutes. Although one could argue (to my mind, convincingly and easily) that the phrase *because of* such individual's *race* already encompasses a broad range of harms, including those based on interraciality, there are many practical and policy reasons for adding *interraciality* to the text of antidiscrimination statutes.

First, such an addition to statutes would carry great symbolic and expressive meaning in our society. The power and import of language should not be underestimated. The addition of the term *interraciality* would send a message to lawyers that they should consider and raise in their case arguments the full range of discrimination harms that can occur based on interraciality. It also would send a message that we, as a society, want all the harms of racism to be delved into when examining claims of racial discrimination. In fact, in some instances, the addition of the term *interraciality* is the only means by which the law can address the "expressive harms,"[102] or lack of dignity,[103] that result from the current framing of family in antidiscrimination statutes as monoracial. And, for areas like housing discrimination law, which work to protect not just individuals, but also people as parts of a collective family unit, such inclusion is especially needed.

Furthermore, the need for such changes in discrimination statutes is growing every year. As the Equal Employment Opportunity Commission recently recognized in its initiative known as E-RACE, an acronym for Eradicating Racism and Colorism from Employment, "[n]ew forms of discrimination are emerging. With a growing number of interracial marriages and families . . . racial demographics . . . have changed and the issue of race discrimination in America is multi-dimensional." If multidimensional discrimination against multiracial individuals and their families is to be fully addressed in the discrimination context, legislators must offer the possibility of a more nuanced interpretation of the experiences of such families and the individuals within them. Broad interpretations of the words *because of* such individual's *race* cannot resolve the existing holes in antidiscrimination law because the phrase *because of* such individual's *race*, without the explicit inclusion of *interraciality*, can be construed and interpreted in ways that do not fully encapsulate how multiracial couples and their families are uniquely affected by discriminatory harms that take place at the intersection of race, sexuality, and family. Indeed, the narrow readings that some courts have undertaken fail to address the problem of how the assumption of monoraciality in antidiscrimination statutes can pit the individual against his or her interracial family or collective and, in other instances, how it disregards the manner in which being part of an interracial collective can work to redefine another's identity.

Second, the addition of the term *interraciality* to the text of antidiscrimination statutes will make it clear to courts that they will be following the clear intent of Congress when they incorporate considerations and arguments based on interracial status and being part of an interracial collective into their opinions and orders. In fact, adding the word *interraciality* to these statutes may be the best and clearest response to the trend of strict textualism among a growing number of courts.

Most of all, the addition of the term *interraciality* would work to destabilize our notions of clear-cut, fixed categories of race. In so doing, it would help to erase the placelessness of multiracial families and the individuals within them as well as to strengthen the claims of multiracial individuals in traditional cases, where they are too often forced into particular racial boxes for the purpose of legal analysis.[104] In essence, adding the term *interraciality* to antidiscrimination statutes would make visible the ways in which narrowly framing the ideal for families has stifled us in our growth as individuals and communities, and it would help to expose all the differences in the lives and lived experiences of families, even when they appear to be the "same." As Cameron and Don, a black female–white male couple, have explained: "There is a black-white legacy in this country that is real. History is meaningful and is implicated along both raced and gendered lines. But you cannot say that black and white relationships are the same—add layers of culture, religion, language, and nationality that further complicates things. So not all black-white relationships are the same."

In the end, as the assumptions that have undergirded our social norms and laws slowly begin to catch up to our nation's aspirations for equality, the text within our antidiscrimination laws should also begin to reflect those very goals. Since *Loving v. Virginia* in 1967, there has been a demonstrated change in attitudes of acceptance toward black-white couples and their families. Even though that acceptance may not always come in the prettiest form, such as when middle-aged white women will blurt out to multiracial couples how much they love Barack Obama,[105] the desire for overall change is there, even for those who personally see their own failings with race and racism. One fitting quote comes from Jim, a white man who is married to a biracial, black-white woman and who described how his mother, who is also white, worked at overcoming her own internalized racism from childhood through him. Jim detailed the following lesson that he learned from his mother about racism and the need to overcome it through deliberate action:

My mother grew up in Arizona in the '60s, and there was a fair amount of racism against what we now know as Native Americans. Once we moved to Iowa, that group wasn't really prevalent in our experience, although we did have one Meskwaki [student] in our elementary school. My mom sat me down one day and described her experience growing up and dealing with Navajos. She "came out" as having negative feelings toward them, but told me two things: (1) She recognized this and made sure to quell those impulses, and (2) she wanted to make sure I had no such feelings toward any groups. . . . [S]he wanted me to be better than she was. It taught me that only in admitting and discussing racism can we attempt to counteract it.[106]

In the end, that is what Alice and Leonard needed from our society, and even from our courts, to be able to live their lives as well as their love freely during 1920s New York. They needed to have those around them admit and discuss their own racism in order to counteract it. They needed for their families as well as those in power to look beyond their own narrow conceptions of family and embrace new definitions. One can only wonder what could have been if Philip Rhinelander, Isaac Mills, Lee Parsons Davis, the jurors, and even George and Elizabeth Jones had stopped for one moment to truly engage in these courageous acts, acts that even today many of us are too afraid to perform.

But if the desire for such change in the future is there on our parts, we as a society must seek it, facing our own isms, both conscious and unconscious, along the way. In some cases, that will mean walking away from the things we have internalized as being "according to our hearts," so that we can embrace those things that we actually desire to be a part of our hearts.

Afterword

A CRITICAL COMPONENT OF THE DESIRE TO have a home and employment is the need simply to have a place in society as well as the means and capability to find a safe place for housing family and, in particular, children. Alice and Leonard Rhinelander not only never really had a home of their own; they also never had children. Often when I tell the story of the Rhinelanders to others, people ask, "Did they have children?" When I respond "No," I usually hear a sigh of relief. That reaction invokes mixed emotions in me.

On the one hand, I understand that many people—often the children of divorce like me—feel relieved to learn that no children became victims in the Rhinelander war of love and race. They are happy to hear that there were no little Alices or Leonards who also suffered the newlyweds' fall from grace and that no children were used, or rather misused, in litigation over child custody or, worse, disowned by the elite Rhinelander family. In fact, in other annulment cases involving racial fraud, courts were reluctant to allow children to become casualties of marital separation, both financially and emotionally. According to Professor Daniel Sharfstein, the idea that white men could impoverish their white (at least according to appearance) wives and bastardize their innocent white children was a key factor in many court decisions that denied annulment on the grounds of racial fraud.[1] For example, remember the outcome in *Ferrall v. Ferrall*. In that case, the North Carolina Supreme Court set aside the verdict of a white husband who had not only filed for annulment of his marriage but also had requested an exemption from support of his wife and their child on the ground that she was "of negro descent to the third generation."[2] The court entered judgment for the wife, awarded her alimony for herself and the child, and in so doing, chastised the husband for branding his wife and child "for all time by the judgment of a court as negroes—a fate which their white skin will make doubly humiliating to them."[3]

On the other hand, after hearing other people's sighs of relief about the children that Alice and Leonard never had, there is a small part of me that questions whether those sighs also signify a type of hesitancy, at least unconsciously, toward multiracial families, specifically multiracial children. I immediately think of when Leonard's lead attorney, Isaac N. Mills, announced during his summation that all should be happy that Alice and Leonard Rhinelander never had children. He said: "I thank God for it— there is no child of this union. The law is that in such a case, where a child has been born, although the marriage be annulled for fraud or any allied cause, the child is in law the legitimate child of both parties. But we have no trouble there. Sufficient time has passed so that in the course of nature there can be no child. That is a happy situation."[4]

Popular images and stereotypes of biracial children cast them as confused from birth—the innocent victims of parents whose racial transgressions left them caught in between two naturally separate worlds. Alice herself was portrayed as someone who was trapped in the middle of two different worlds. In the eyes of many, she could never be fully accepted by whites or blacks. Reports of the jury's deliberations in the *Rhinelander* trial suggest that the white men who composed the jury did not view Alice as being fully Negro. For many of those men, Alice was neither white nor black, but rather colored—the same distinction that her father purportedly made with his own racial identity (see fig. A.1). Indeed, it may have been this picture of Alice as one trapped by racial circumstance that helped to provide a sympathetic enough lens for the jury so that it would decide in her favor on the annulment claim. Alice's attorney, Lee Parsons Davis, harped on this notion during his opening statement, asserting: "So gentlemen. . . . Alice Rhinelander must go through this prejudiced world, unfortunate as it is, branded openly now—if it is a disgrace in your eyes, it is in the eyes

Fig. A.1. Alice Rhine-
lander poses for the
camera during trial.
© Bettmann/Corbis

of some white people—with the admission that there is colored blood, to
what extent we really do not know, coursing through her veins."[5] Moreover,
even in speaking about Alice's father, George Jones, Davis spoke of George
as a man unfairly caught in racial limbo. Davis proclaimed: "Mr. Jones, a
mulatto! That is no disgrace, and it is not his fault. We white men are to
blame for that. I don't say that in a personal way, gentlemen. There is many
a white heart that is covered with a dark skin."[6]

Such sentiments about multiracial individuals reveal a placelessness
for those who themselves or through their families break the color line.
Other black-white families, such as those involving transracial adoptions

or second marriages, also are pushed into this placelessness. As Professor Elizabeth Bartholet has highlighted, we as a society so often "assume that it is natural, and appropriate, to think in racial terms in the intimate family context."[7] For example, consider this one joke about white actors Brad Pitt and Angelina Jolie, who have six children, including three biologically related white children; two adopted, Asian children; and one adopted, black child.

Q: What did Brad Pitt say when Angelina brought her mixed race kids and family to Brad's Malibu mansion?
A: What will the neighbors say?

The message? There is not a clear space for Angelina's "mixed race" kids— note that none of the Pitt-Jolie kids are "mixed race"—in Brad's predominantly white Malibu neighborhood, nor is there a space for her "mixed race" family. Indeed, it seems that just having a multiracial family confuses others about the racial identities of the individuals within the family.

Multiracial families formed by both marriage and adoption often face the question: "But what about the children? What would marriage or adoption mean for the children? Where will they fit in?" As one of my surveyed couples, Darcy and Charlie, explained about people's frequent inquiries to them, "We sometimes get questions about our relationship that we are not prepared to answer such as how are you going to raise your kids—black or white."[8] Similarly, Don, a white man married to a black woman, Cameron, recalled that his "aunt was concerned about whether [he] knew what [he] was doing, as [his] children would not be white."[9] Again, here, multiracial families get suspended in placelessness—an either-or choice, with nothing in between. The message that multiracial families receive is that they simply do not belong. In other words, they are left with the question: "Where does the family fit in?"[10]

Recall the story of former Louisiana judge Keith Bardwell, who in 2009 refused to marry an interracial couple—a black man and a white woman— because he feared for their children. According to Bardwell, he had discussed the topic of interracial marriages with both blacks and whites and had come to the conclusion that most blacks and whites do not readily accept biracial children—as a result, he worried about the children's futures.[11] Ironically, Bardwell made these arguments less than a year after our nation had elected Barack Obama, the son of a black Kenyan father and white Kansan mother, to be the president of the United States. As Bill Quigley, director of the Center for Constitutional Rights and Justice stated, "Perhaps [Bardwell is] worried the kids will grow up and be president."[12]

Although news of Bardwell's actions and views were widely disapproved of in the media, the very fact that Bardwell remained committed to his position on refusing to marry interracial couples even after he had been publicly exposed and labeled a racist suggests that at least some people accepted his views on interraciality in marriage. Given the power of peer influence in persuading persons of their wrongs or at least silencing unpopular views, one would have expected Bardwell to more quickly see just how improper his views were and, more so, how illegal his actions were. There must have been people who, even if only secretly, whispered their support for his stance about "the children." Although the approval rates of black-white marriage have increased from 4 percent in 1958 to 83 percent in 2009, there still remains that 17 percent of people who do not approve of such marriages. Moreover, greater than double that number, 37 percent, do not want such black-white marriages within their own families.

Viewed through this lens, those sighs of relief about the fact that Alice and Leonard never had children often make me wonder, not how far we have come since 1925—we have come very far since then—but rather just how much the story of race, family, and intimacy has not changed. As the saying goes, our future is in the hands of our children. If this is true, then what does a continued resistance to multiracial children mean for our future in terms of race, family, and intimacy?

Without further probing, one may think that the very fact that a biracial, black-white man has become president of the United States indicates a full acceptance of interraciality—at least through parentage. In discussing whether Obama would have been elected if he had engaged in "horizontal interraciality" or interracial marriage, Professor Ali Mazrui suggested that Americans were not comfortable with such multiraciality.[13] Mazrui contended, however: "The U.S. is used to vertical interraciality. Nobody is outraged when you are born to parents of mixed race. Sixty percent of black people in the U.S. have mixed parentage [when one considers the number of multiracial blacks born during slavery]. There was greater acceptance of Obama's mixed parentage because he did not choose his parents. But he chose his wife."[14]

But even if Mazrui is right (and I am not stating that he is), what this surface acceptance of Obama and other multiracial individuals hides is the choice that Obama and other biracial individuals "cannot" make in our society, where race is viewed as a fixed and inflexible category. That choice is one of racial identification. Mazrui is correct (to some extent) that the United States is comfortable with vertical interraciality, but that is largely because those who have been "vertically interracial" have, for the most part, just been considered to be monoracial. In the United States, the rule of hypodescent or the one-drop rule, which was established by the U.S. Census Bureau, has prevailed for decades. Although the Census Bureau's count categorized people of African descent as "black," "mulatto," "quadroon," or "octoroon" before the twentieth century, in 1920, people of African descent were identified as either "black/Negro" or "mulatto."[15] Between the 1920s and 1960s, the previous categories were dropped and replaced with "black," as defined by the "one-drop rule," which defined any person with one drop of "black blood" as black. The enduring strength of the "one-drop" rule in our society means that the mere existence of biracial people destabilizes our notion of neat, clean, clear, and fixed categories of race. Consequently, multiracial individuals are still frequently pushed to ground this destabilization through a single racial identification. They encounter pressures from others to pick a racial identity.[16] For instance, as Stephanie, a biracial woman who identifies as black and is now married to a white man, asserted, "In college was the first time people began interrogating me constantly to figure out 'what I was.' This was the first time I really realized that I had a race."[17] Likewise, Raven, a biracial, black-white woman who is married to a white man, described one incident in which her white mother identified her as white instead of as biracial on a school form: "When I was going into first grade, I read the form that my mom was filling out and I asked her why she had checked the 'Caucasian' box. She told me that it meant that I was 'pink.'"[18] Raven later described a similar experience with her mother when she was in high school. At that time, Raven, who by then knew that she was biracial, was applying for high school. Again, her mother "put down only Caucasian because she didn't want [Raven's] elementary school to be 'confused' when they saw it."[19]

In reality, the choice of racial identity for multiracial children has been limited. As Academy Award–winning actress Halle Berry explained, a biracial person's racial identity is often "based on how the world identifies her."[20] Berry asserts, "That's how I identified myself." The fact is that, much like Alice, biracial, black-white individuals today rarely have the option of identifying as white, not if they also want to acknowledge their black half. For example, while there was a debate among the jurors as to whether Alice was a Negro or a colored person, there was absolutely no debate as to whether Alice was white. In other words, while the *Rhinelander* jurors were willing to acknowledge a spectrum of race, the two ends of that spectrum had to be solidly clear: pure white and pure black. And, the most important line of all was made even clearer: white and nonwhite. While biracial, black-white individuals have the ability to claim a black identity, much like our president, and much like Alice or her father could have (if they so desired), that ability is not premised on any real choice, but rather the damaging notion that their "black blood" is so inferior and tainting that it trumps the "white blood" altogether.

Moreover, despite changes in the U.S. Census procedures that now allow people to identify as multiracial, socially claiming a biracial identity for many multiracial individuals is difficult. Professor Matthew Taylor, a biracial, black-white scholar, described the difficulty he has felt in his own life. He asserted: "How do I as a biracial individual construct this notion of 'me' and in so doing reconcile seemingly contradictory aspects of myself that are communicated by the cultural nuances of the day? The imposed template does not fit with my reality."[21] Although scholars Kerry Ann Rockquemore and David Brunsma found among one of their study samples that 61.3 percent of multiracial individuals choose a "border identity" or an exclusively biracial identity, multiracial families, including those with biracial or multiracial persons within them, still must grapple with the intensity of the one-drop rule. A number of the black-white couples in my survey discussed how their own decisions about childrearing have been affected, in part, by the rigid boxes into which society tries to force multiracial families and the individuals within them. For example, Evan, a white man who is married to Karen, a black woman, noted that, before they had children, his "wife made it clear that they [the children] should identify as black because that is how they would be seen."[22] In fact, Evan remarked that "[u]nderstanding that [his] potential children with [his] future wife would be viewed as black and not biracial [was a memorable, racial experience for him]; this took a while to sink in [for him] as a white person."[23] Furthermore, even those couples who personally identified their children as biracial still found themselves affected by the rule of hypodescent. For instance, Amber and Caleb, another black female–white male couple, discussed the potential impact of the one-drop rule on their children's racial identities before they had kids. They stated that they "talked about the one-drop rule and the idea that at some point, kids who are in part black tend to experience the world as black people."[24] Don and Cameron described how they personally identify their children as "mixed-race—black/white"—but decided to *raise* their children as "black out of necessity." They explained, "We felt they would need to appreciate how they were going to be perceived."[25] Even children, at times, feel the tug of identifying with one racial group more than the other. For instance, Raven and Jim stated the following about their own children's racial identification: "The children know they are multiracial, but they identify most closely with Caucasian, probably because they are largely surrounded by Caucasians."[26] More importantly, Liz and Mandy, a black-white lesbian couple, highlighted what can be the difficulty of raising biracial children in a society that automatically marks them as confused. Among the difficulties they described were "[b]alancing the need to validate [their] daughter's correct observations about racism/attitudes toward race in the world," "protect[ing] her from negative attitudes that will affect her self-esteem," and "ensuring positive self-esteem, given that [their] daughter already understands that there is a racial hierarchy in the world."[27]

Overall, the image of the confused biracial or multiracial individual remains remarkably vivid in contemporary times, despite the prevalence of prominent figures such as President Barack Obama and Halle Berry. Here, much like Leonard's attorneys tried to do with comments about Alice and her parents during the trial, the supposed shame of the parents—the racial transgressors—gets mapped onto the children. For instance, Cameron and Don described how "[o]n one jarring occasion in an airport a stranger yelled something at [their] son when he was very young—calling him a zebra."[28] President Obama himself once joked about the way in which biracial individuals get labeled as doomed and confused. In October 2008, Obama engaged in the following exchange with Jon Stewart on the *Daily Show*:

> "The Polls have you up," said Stewart, "but then they keep talking about the Bradley Effect, this idea that white voters when they go to the polls they will tell pollsters they will vote for an African American but they won't actually do it?"
>
> "Yeah, they've been saying that for a while but we're still here," Obama said. "So I don't know. I don't think white voters have gotten this memo about the Bradley Effect."
>
> "Are you concerned in some respects," Stewart joked, "I don't know how to bring this up, your mother is from Kansas, father African, are you concerned that you may go into the voting booth and—"
>
> "I won't know what to do," Obama joked, finishing the comedian's thought.
>
> "—your white half will all of a sudden decide, 'I can't do this!'" Stewart said.
>
> "Yeah," Obama said. "It's a problem. . . . I've been going through therapy to make sure that I vote properly on the 4th."[29]

Furthermore, academic studies of multiracial children reinforce this perception of the impossibility of living within two or more racial worlds. Numerous examinations of multiracial children and their social problems abound. For example, one study involving ninety thousand students revealed that multiracial students are more likely to suffer from depression, substance abuse, sleep problems, and various aches and pains. Another recent study found that black-white children engage in riskier behavior than black or white children and are slightly worse off psychologically. The rationale is that "[m]ixed-race adolescents—not having a *natural* peer group—need to engage in more risky behaviors to be accepted."[30] Finally, in their stories, media pundits and commentators speak of being multiracial as though being multiracial itself were the problem, not the daily task of surviving in a world that demands a limited self-identity—one that requires a partial denial of background. At least with regard to individual racial identity, the story of Alice remains much the same today as it was in 1925.

The narrative also remains the same, in many ways, for multiracial families today—in all their forms. Like multiracial individuals, multiracial families destabilize rigid categories of race in our society, a society which, as I have argued, continues to promote the monoracial family as the normative ideal. For this reason, people also try to squeeze "nontraditional" families into what are viewed as comfortable boxes of race, sex, and sexuality for families. For example, Carla and Janice, a black-white lesbian couple in a civil union, stated the following about how others try to neatly box them up: "The categories people put us in [are one of the most difficult challenges we face]; we're not readily identifiable as a family because we're two women, and people often do not assume the white mom as a mother to our African American child. . . . Our child is not multiracial, but her schoolmates sometimes ask how she has two moms, and why one of us is white."[31] Even in those cases where people accept the multiraciality of families like Carla and Janice's, they still try to force the families into neat boxes, again revealing the complexity of experience at the intersection for identity categories. For instance, Carla described some of the gendered and raced responses to her and Janice's decision to use a black donor as opposed to a white donor when they had their daughter. She said: "I think we see [a raced and gendered response to our family] in relation to our child who is black, when we tell people that we used a black donor. They often ask why we did not use a white donor so the kids would be biracial to reflect both of our races. I think this is based on gender and race because they are treating us as if we can produce a child that is biologically related to both of us and the importance of that to be reflected in the child. It is also raced because our child would still be viewed as black by many even if we had used a white donor because I [a black woman] am her biological mom."[32] In all, the story of Alice and Leonard—in particular, the social enforcement of racial boxes—remains strong, even today, and even as multiracial individuals and families increase in number. Much like with the verdict in favor of Alice at the end of trial in 1925, every racial victory also comes with a loss.

In the end, however, I am hopeful for a time, even for moments of time, when our racial victories in society come to mean only that—racial victory without a loss. Although many signs point to continued stories of winning and losing, or even losing by winning, I have to admit that, as I was writing this book and presenting developing parts of it at different schools, I encountered many people whose stories suggested significant possibilities for true racial victories. The stories came from people whose identities and lives themselves had been altered by the richness of their families. They came from people who resisted against the boxes that others wanted to force upon them. For instance, Raven, a biracial, black-white woman married to a white man, recalled this one promising interaction between her white husband and his mother: "When my husband told me that his mother asked what our baby would 'be,' I was so proud of him when he said that he told her it would be a baby."[33] Or they came from stories of acceptance of children by other members of black-white couples' families that went so deep that all family members proudly claimed their offspring. For instance, Amber and Caleb noted how many members of their family worked hard to tie the beauty of their daughter to their own selves. They wrote, "Everyone thinks she's beautiful. Each grandmother claims she looks just like her mom or dad (their respective children). Paternal grandmother often talks about how beautiful her hair is. Maternal grandmother gives Caleb lectures on how he needs to learn to comb black hair. Maternal grandfather just claims she gets her good looks from him."[34] They came in conversations that monoracial siblings in multiracial families formed by adoption had with other individuals who presumed the monoraciality of their lives. For instance, I recall one wonderful story from a white, male professor with a black, adopted brother who talked about an experience he described as occurring far too often—his confronting whites who made disparaging comments about blacks in his presence—and who felt encouraged by the simple fact that these many interactions had at least uprooted the assumptions of those white individuals about the monoraciality of families.

It is because of these stories from members of multiracial families today, including those like the family that Alice and Leonard were denied in both 1924 and 1925, that I can hold onto hope about a reframing of the normative ideal for family, or better yet, of a release of any need for an ideal at all. Often, in good moments, when I am in the midst of remembering these stories and someone asks whether Alice and Leonard Rhinelander ever had children, I pause before reflexively saying, "No," and instead say, "Yes, they did, but not like you're thinking . . ."

NOTES

Introduction

1. A Bronx Tale, dir. Robert De Niro (Price Entertainment 1993).
2. *Id.*
3. Association of the Bar of the City of New York, New York Supreme Court: Appellate Division—Second Department, Leonard Kip Rhinelander *against* Alice Jones Rhinelander, Transcript of Record at 7, Rhinelander v. Rhinelander, 219 N.Y.S. 548 (N.Y. App. Div. 1927) [hereinafter Court Record] (Complaint).
4. *Colored* is a term that was commonly used to refer to black people in the United States during the 1920s. Throughout this book, I generally use the terms *colored* or *Negro* (in addition to the terms *black* and *African American*) to refer to black people in the United States. I specifically use *colored* when I refer to Alice, and several members of her family to maintain consistency with terms used in the documents in the *Rhinelander* court record.
5. *See* Roth v. Roth, 161 N.Y.S. 99, 103 (Sup. Ct. 1916) (declaring "that a marriage will not be annulled for fraud, unless the facts misrepresented or concealed go to the very essence of the marriage contract"); *see also* Rubman v. Rubman, 251 N.Y.S. 474, 482 (Sup. Ct. 1931): "It has been held that before consummation any fraud which, if known to the innocent party, would result in no marriage is in general sufficient ground for annulment, but after consummation and the creation of a public status the marriage will be annulled only when the fraud goes to the essence of the contract."
6. *Rhinelander Loses; No Fraud Is Found; Wife Will Sue Now,* N.Y. Times, Dec. 6, 1925, at 1, 27 [hereinafter *Rhinelander Loses*].
7. *Nevada Divorce Aim of L.K. Rhinelander,* N.Y. Times, June 13, 1929, at 31; *Rhinelander Divorces His Octoroon Wife,* N.Y. Times, Dec. 28, 1929, at 3.
8. Ariela J. Gross, What Blood Won't Tell: A History of Race on Trial in America 3 (2008).

9. *Id.* at 2.

10. Jennifer Gordon and R. A. Lenhardt, Rethinking Work and Citizenship, 55 UCLA L. Rev. 1161, 1186–87 (2008).

11. *Rhinelander Loses, supra* note 6, at 1.

12. *See Poor Girl to Fight Hubby's Parents,* Chi. Defender, Dec. 6, 1924, at 1 [hereinafter *Poor Girl*] ("It is alleged he was kidnapped by his father and forcibly kept from his wife"); *Rhinelander Trouble May Soon Cease,* Chi. Defender, Dec. 13, 1924, at 1.

13. *Poor Girl, supra* note 12, at 3: "It has been pointed out that the affair will soon blow over. The young couple will go West or to Europe; remarry if necessary and carry out their future plans as anticipated."

14. Court Record, *supra* note 3, at 696 (Trial Transcript, Cross-Examination of Leonard Kip Rhinelander).

15. *Rhinelander's Wife Denies She Is Negro,* N.Y. Times, Nov. 29, 1924, at 15.

16. Loving v. Virginia, 388 U.S. 1, 2 (1967).

17. Cynthia Feliciano et al., *Gendered Racial Exclusion among White Internet Daters,* 38 Social Sci. Research 39, 41 (2009); *see also* M. J. Rosenfeld and B. S. Kim, *The Independence of Young Adults and the Rise of Interracial and Same-Sex Unions,* 70 Am. Soc. Rev. 541–62 (2005).

18. Derald Wing Sue, Microaggressions in Everyday Life: Race, Gender, and Sexual Orientation 5 (2010).

19. *See* Heather M. Dalmage, Tripping on the Color Line: Black-White Multiracial Families in a Racially Divided World (2000).

20. The name Cara is a pseudonym. I use pseudonyms throughout this book, including for the members of the black-white couples whom I surveyed and interviewed.

21. Seminar paper, *She Don't Belong: A Decade of Analysis, a Lifetime of Passing in a Straight White World* (manuscript at 18, on file with author).

22. *Id.* at 4 (footnotes omitted).

23. Survey 21 (Julie and Barry).

24. *Rhinelanders Flee Glare of Publicity,* N.Y. Times, Nov. 15, 1924, at 6.

25. Earl Lewis and Heidi Ardizzone, Love on Trial: An American Scandal in Black and White 36 (2001) (quoting from an article in the *N.Y. Evening Journal*).

26. *See* Randall Kennedy, Interracial Intimacies: Sex, Marriage, Identity, and Adoption 297 (2003); Jamie L. Wacks, *Reading Race, Rhetoric, and the Female Body in the* Rhinelander *Case, in* Interracialism: Black-White Intermarriage in American History, Literature, and Law 162, 163–64 (Werner Sollors ed. 2000).

27. Wacks, *supra* note 26, at 164 n. 6 (quotations omitted).

28. Jane Doe v. Louisiana, 479 So.2d 369, 371 (La. Ct. App. 1985).

29. Amos N. Jones, *Black Like Obama: What the Junior Illinois Senator's Appearance on the National Scene Reveals about Race in America, and Where We Should Go from Here,* 31 T. Marshall L. Rev. 79, 82 (2005).

30. Susan Donaldson James, *Halle Berry Cites "One-Drop" Rule in Battle over Whether Her Daughter Is Black or White,* ABCNews.com, Feb. 9, 2011, http://abcnews.go

.com/Health/halle-berry-cites-drop-rule-daughter-black-white/story?id=12869789 (last visited Aug. 21, 2012).

31. Court Record, *supra* note 3, at 693 (Trial Transcript, Cross-Examination of Leonard Kip Rhinelander).

32. *Id.* at 696 (Trial Transcript, Cross-Examination of Leonard Kip Rhinelander).

33. *Id.* at 697 (Trial Transcript, Cross-Examination of Leonard Kip Rhinelander).

34. *Id.* (Trial Transcript, Cross-Examination of Leonard Kip Rhinelander).

35. *Id.* (Trial Transcript, Cross-Examination of Leonard Kip Rhinelander).

36. We Are Your Sisters: Black Women in the Nineteenth Century 151 (Dorothy Sterling ed. 1984).

37. *Id.*

38. *Id.* at 152.

39. David Marcum and Steven Smith, Egonomics: What Makes Egos Our Greatest Asset (or Most Expensive Liability) 113 (2007).

40. Robyn Dixon, *Runner Caster Semenya Has Heard the Gender Comments All Her Life*, L.A. Times, Dec. 21, 2009, http://articles.latimes.com/2009/aug/21/world/fg-south-africa-runner21 (last visited Aug. 21, 2012).

41. *Id.*

42. Karlie Pouliot, *Report: Champion Runner Has Both Female, Male Sexual Characteristics*, FoxNews.com, Sept. 11, 2009, http://www.foxnews.com/story/0,2933,549021,00.html (last visited Aug. 21, 2012).

43. Maya Rock, *"What Are You?" For Multiracial Students, Declaring an Identity Can Be Complicated*, Princeton Alumni Wkly., Jan. 13, 2010, *available at* http://paw.princeton.edu/issues/2010/01/13/pages/4093/index.xml (last visited Aug. 21, 2012).

44. Angela Nissel, *What Are You? Life as a Bi-Racial American*, NPR.org (May 10, 2006), http://www.npr.org/templates/story/story.php?storyId=5395390 (last visited Aug. 21, 2012).

45. Survey 10 (Edith and Stephen).

46. Osagie Obasogie, *Do Blind People See Race? Social, Legal, and Theoretical Considerations*, 44 Law & Soc'y Rev. 585, 587, 606–7 (2010).

47. *Id.* at 606–7.

48. *Id.* at 607.

49. Follow-up Interview with Janice.

50. Angela Onwuachi-Willig, *A Beautiful Lie: Exploring* Rhinelander. v. Rhinelander *as a Formative Lesson on Race, Identity, Marriage, and Family*, 95 Calif. L. Rev. 2393, 2402, 2455 (2007) (acknowledging "the 'punishments,' both legal and social, that can be imposed upon those who dare to transgress racial boundaries of familial intimacy" and noting that "[w]hites who choose to cross racial boundaries of intimacy may be punished for such social infractions"); *see also* Elizabeth M. Smith-Pryor, Property Rites, The Rhinelander Trial, Passing, and the Protection of Whiteness 252 (2009): "Understanding *Rhinelander v. Rhinelander* in all its complexities may help us grasp why Americans still make race matter."

51. Court Record, *supra* note 3, at 1099–1100 (Trial Transcript, Opening for Plain-

tiff): "She got that boy, we shall prove to you, so that he was an utter slave in her hands."

52. *Rhinelander Loses, supra* note 6, at 27.

53. *Id.*

54. My use of the phrase "because of interraciality" concerns more than just mistreatment based on one's involvement in an intimate, interracial relationship—marriage or a committed, nonmarital relationship. Generally speaking, the phrase encompasses mistreatment based on one's being part of an interracial family unit, which includes sibling relationships and parent-child relationships. It does not extend to mistreatment based on platonic friendships, however.

Chapter 1. A Beautiful Affair

1. Randall Kennedy, Interracial Intimacies: Sex, Marriage, Identity, and Adoption 298 (2003): "The most thoroughgoing effort in American history to prevent and punish passing began in Virginia in the 1920s."

2. Michael J. Klarman, *Race and the Court in the Progressive Era*, 51 Vand. L. Rev. 881, 942 (1998).

3. *See* Earl Lewis and Heidi Ardizzone, Love on Trial: An American Scandal in Black and White 57 (2001) (asserting that Victorian morality prevailed but that the old Victorian image of women was being challenged by the presence of flappers in the 1920s, who were women "who exposed their shoulders and knees in shockingly skimpy dresses; cut their hair short; and drank, smoked, and danced to fast, jazz-influenced rhythms"); *see also* Amii Larkin Barnard, *The Application of Critical Race Feminism to the Anti-Lynching Movement: Black Women's Fight against Race and Gender Ideology, 1892–1920*, 3 UCLA Women's L.J. 1, 2 (1993): "The ideal of True Womanhood demanded purity, piety, and deference to men. In return, a woman who behaved 'like a lady' was sheltered from the harshness of the public sphere. True Womanhood commanded the protection of white ladies by white gentlemen." *But see* Estelle B. Freedman, *The New Woman: Changing Views of Women in the 1920s*, 61 J. Am. Hist. 372 (1974) (describing changing images of women after women's suffrage in 1920).

4. *See* Howard Dodson et al., The Black New Yorkers: The Schomburg Illustrated Chronology 155–73 (2000).

5. John Henrik Clarke, *Introduction* to Harlem: A Community in Transition 7 (Clarke ed. 1964) [hereinafter Harlem]; Glenn Carrington, *The Harlem Renaissance: A Personal Memoir, in* Harlem, at 58 (noting that during the 1920s, Harlem "was considered as one of New York's playgrounds, and attracted many whites who wanted to go slumming or merely wished to see how the 'other half' of the old town lived").

6. Association of the Bar of the City of New York, New York Supreme Court: Appellate Division—Second Department, Leonard Kip Rhinelander *against* Alice Jones Rhinelander, Transcript of Record at 879, Rhinelander v. Rhinelander, 219 N.Y.S.

548 (N.Y. App. Div. 1927) [hereinafter Court Record] (Direct Examination of Grace Marie Miller).

7. Points for Appellant on Appeal from Order Denying Motions for New Trial and From Judgment, Sept. 10, 1926, at 7–8.

8. *Loved Rhinelander, Wife's Letters Say,* N.Y. Times, Nov. 13, 1925, at 1.

9. Court Record, *supra* note 6, at 535 (Trial Transcript, Cross-Examination of Leonard Kip Rhinelander) (emphasis added).

10. *Id.* at 370 (Trial Transcript, Direct Examination of Leonard Kip Rhinelander). In her letters, Alice spelled "have to" as "after."

11. *Poor Girl to Fight Hubby's Parents,* Chi. Defender, Dec. 6, 1924, at 1 [hereinafter *Poor Girl*].

12. *Rhinelander Bride Flays N.Y. Society,* Chi. Defender, Mar. 21, 1925, at 1 [hereinafter *Rhinelander Bride Flays*].

13. *Poor Girl, supra* note 11, at 3.

14. *Rhinelander's Wife Denies She Is Negro,* N.Y. Times, Nov. 29, 1924, at 15.

15. *Rhinelander's Bride Said to Be Grieving, Her Counsel Announces That He Is Preparing Answer to Annulment Suit,* N.Y. Times, Nov. 28, 1924, at 13.

16. Court Record, *supra* note 6, at 9–11 (Amended Complaint).

17. *Id.* at 14–15 (Bill of Particulars).

18. *Id.* at 11 (Answer to Amended Complaint).

19. Di Lorenzo v. Di Lorenzo, 174 N.Y. 467, 472 (N.Y. 1903): "It is obvious that no one would obligate himself by a contract, if he knew that a material representation, entering into the reason for his consent, was untrue. There is no valid reason for excepting the marriage contract from the general rule." Section 1139 of the Civil Practice Act also provided: "[A]n action to annul a marriage on the ground that the consent of one of the parties thereto was obtained by force, duress, or fraud may be maintained at any time by the party whose consent was so obtained."

20. Court Record, *supra* note 6, at 7 (Leonard Kip Rhinelander *against* Alice Jones Rhinelander, Points for Appellant on Appeal from Order Denying Motions for New Trial and from Judgment).

21. *Id.* at 1182 (Trial Transcript, Summation for Defendant).

22. Lewis and Ardizzone, *supra* note 3, at 14; *Rhinelander's Case Suffers Telling Blow,* Detroit Free Press, Nov. 26, 1925, at 1, 19; *Rhinelander Aware Wife Was Part Negro Chauffeur Testifies,* St. Louis Globe Democrat, Nov. 26, 1925, at 4 [hereinafter *Rhinelander Aware Wife*].

23. Elizabeth M. Smith-Pryor, Property Rites: The Rhinelander Trial, Passing, and the Protection of Whiteness 113 (2009).

24. *Rhinelander's Case Suffers Telling Blow,* Detroit Free Press, Nov. 26, 1925, at 1, 19.

25. Lewis and Ardizzone, *supra* note 3, at 14; *Rhinelander Aware Wife, supra* note 22, at 4.

26. *Rhinelander Bride Fears He Is Captive,* N.Y. Times, Nov. 30, 1924, at 14.

27. *Poor Girl, supra* note 11, at 1.

28. *Rhinelander Bride Flays, supra* note 12, at 1.

29. *Rhinelander's Bride Replies to His Suit with Complete Denial of Deceit Charges*, N.Y. Times, Dec. 9, 1924, at 1.
30. *Rhinelander Sues to Annul Marriage; Alleges Race Deceit*, N.Y. Times, Nov. 27, 1924, at 1.
31. *Id.*
32. *Id.*

Chapter 2. Openings and a Closing

1. *Rhinelander Bride Flays N.Y. Society*, Chi. Defender, Mar. 21, 1925, at 1.
2. *Rhinelander Bride Offered $250,000 for Settlement*, Chi. Defender, Dec. 27, 1924, at 1.
3. *See* Association of the Bar of the City of New York, New York Supreme Court: Appellate Division—Second Department, Leonard Kip Rhinelander *against* Alice Jones Rhinelander, Transcript of Record at 1147, Rhinelander v. Rhinelander, 219 N.Y.S. 548 (N.Y. App. Div. 1927, at 1082) [hereinafter Court Record] (Trial Transcript, Summation for Defendant); *see also* Earl Lewis and Heidi Ardizzone, Love on Trial: An American Scandal in Black and White 49 (2001).
4. 50 The National Cyclopedia of American Biography 439 (1971).
5. *See* Lewis and Ardizzone, *supra* note 3, at 63.
6. Court Record, *supra* note 3, at 1111 (Trial Transcript, Opening for Plaintiff).
7. *Id.* at 1082 (Trial Transcript, Opening for Plaintiff).
8. *Id.* at 1082 (Trial Transcript, Opening for Plaintiff).
9. *Id.* at 1084–85 (Trial Transcript, Opening for Plaintiff).
10. *Id.* at 1085–86 (Trial Transcript, Opening for Plaintiff).
11. *Id.* at 1085–88 (Trial Transcript, Opening for Plaintiff).
12. *Id.* at 1088 (Trial Transcript, Opening for Plaintiff).
13. Ariela J. Gross, What Blood Won't Tell: A History of Race on Trial in America 52–57 (2008); *see also* Ariela J. Gross, *Litigating Whiteness: Trials of Racial Determination in the Nineteenth-Century South*, 108 Yale L.J. 109, 157–58 (1998).
14. Court Record, *supra* note 3, at 1091 (Trial Transcript, Opening for Plaintiff).
15. *Id.* at 1091–92 (Trial Transcript, Opening for Plaintiff).
16. *Id.* at 1086, 1089 (Trial Transcript, Opening for Plaintiff).
17. *Id.* at 1090 (Trial Transcript, Opening for Plaintiff).
18. *Id.* at 1087 (Trial Transcript, Opening for Plaintiff).
19. *Id.* at 1087 (Trial Transcript, Opening for Plaintiff).
20. *Id.* at 1092 (Trial Transcript, Opening for Plaintiff).
21. *Id.* at 1092–95 (Trial Transcript, Opening for Plaintiff).
22. *Id.* at 1094, 1100 (Trial Transcript, Opening for Plaintiff).
23. *Id.* at 1096 (Trial Transcript, Opening for Plaintiff).
24. *Id.* at 1096 (Trial Transcript, Opening for Plaintiff).
25. *Id.* at 1096 (Trial Transcript, Opening for Plaintiff).
26. *Id.* at 1098 (Trial Transcript, Opening for Plaintiff).
27. *Id.* at 1100 (Trial Transcript, Opening for Plaintiff).

28. *Id.* at 1102 (Trial Transcript, Opening for Plaintiff).
29. *Id.* at 1101 (Trial Transcript, Opening for Plaintiff).
30. *Id.* at 1102 (Trial Transcript, Opening for Plaintiff).
31. *Id.* at 1104 (Trial Transcript, Opening for Plaintiff).
32. *Id.* at 1104 (Trial Transcript, Opening for Plaintiff).
33. *Id.* at 1102 (Trial Transcript, Opening for Defendant).
34. *Id.* at 1108, 1110–11 (Trial Transcript, Opening for Defendant).
35. *Id.* at 1106 (Trial Transcript, Opening for Defendant).
36. *Id.* at 1106 (Trial Transcript, Opening for Defendant).
37. *Rhinelanders Flee Glare of Publicity,* N.Y. Times, Nov. 15, 1924, at 6.
38. *Rhinelander Bride Fears He Is Captive,* N.Y. Times, Nov. 30, 1924, at 14 [hereinafter *Captive*].
39. *Rhinelander's Wife Denies She Is Negro,* N.Y. Times, Nov. 29, 1924, at 15 [hereinafter *Denies She is Negro*].
40. *Id.* Judge Swinburne's understanding of Alice's race may have come from old southern laws that declared a child to be the race of his or her mother in order to preserve the children of black slave women and their white masters as slaves. *See* Robert S. Cope, Carry Me Back: Slavery and Servitude in Seventeenth-Century Virginia 11 (1973); Adele Hast, *The Legal Status of the Negro in Virginia, 1705–1765,* 54 J. Negro Hist. 217, 220 (1969).
41. *Denies She Is Negro, supra* note 39, at 15.
42. *See* Court Record, *supra* note 3, at 11 (Answer to Amended Complaint); Court Record, *supra* note 3, at 10 (Amended Complaint).
43. *Plea by Mrs. Rhinelander,* N.Y. Times, Jan. 5, 1925, at 23. George indicated "that his mother was white and that he knew little about his father." *Rhinelander Bride Fights for Alimony,* N.Y. Times, Dec. 27, 1924, at 4. He is reported to have said the following: "My mother . . . was a Caucasian of pure English descent. The only information I have about my father is that he was a native of one of the British colonies." *Id.*
44. *Rhinelander Suit May Not Be Tried,* N.Y. Times, Mar. 29, 1925, at 16.
45. This term is borrowed from the work of Ariela Gross, Professor of Law and History at the University of Southern California. *See* Ariela J. Gross, *Litigating Whiteness: Trials of Racial Determination in the Nineteenth-Century South,* 108 Yale L.J. 109, 118–21 (1998); *see also* Ariela J. Gross, What Blood Won't Tell: A History of Race on Trial in America 3 (2008).
46. *Captive, supra* note 38, at 14.
47. *Id.*
48. Court Record, *supra* note 3, at 1109 (Trial Transcript, Opening for Defendant).
49. *Id.* at 1109–10 (Trial Transcript, Opening for Defendant).
50. *Id.* at 1122–23, 1130–31 (Trial Transcript, Opening for Defendant) (emphasis added).
51. *Id.* at 1117–18 (Trial Transcript, Opening for Defendant).
52. *Id.* at 1112–13 (Trial Transcript, Opening for Defendant).

53. *Id.* at 1112 (Trial Transcript, Opening for Defendant).
54. *Id.* at 1113 (Trial Transcript, Opening for Defendant).
55. *Id.* at 1121–22 (Trial Transcript, Opening for Defendant).
56. *Id.* at 1119 (Trial Transcript, Opening for Defendant).
57. *Id.* at 1114, 1116 (Trial Transcript, Opening for Defendant).
58. *Id.* at 1128 (Trial Transcript, Opening for Defendant).
59. *Id.* at 1125, 1131 (Trial Transcript, Opening for Defendant).

Chapter 3. Testimonies

1. *Rhinelander Loses; No Fraud Is Found; Wife Will Sue Now,* N.Y. Times, Dec. 6, 1925, at 1 [hereinafter *Rhinelander Loses*].
2. Association of the Bar of the City of New York, New York Supreme Court: Appellate Division—Second Department, Leonard Kip Rhinelander *against* Alice Jones Rhinelander, Transcript of Record at 50, 73–74, Rhinelander v. Rhinelander, 219 N.Y.S. 548 (N.Y. App. Div. 1927, at 1082) [hereinafter Court Record] (Trial Transcript, Direct and Cross-Examination of L. Pierce Clark).
3. Court Record, *supra* note 2, at 134 (Trial Transcript, Direct Examination of J. Provoust Stout).
4. *Id.* at 135 (Trial Transcript, Cross-Examination of J. Provoust Stout).
5. *Rhinelander's Wife Admits Negro Blood,* N.Y. Times, Nov. 11, 1925, at 1.
6. *Rhinelander Tells Story of Courtship,* N.Y. Times, Nov. 12, 1925, at 1.
7. Court Record, *supra* note 2, at 176 (Trial Transcript, Direct Examination of Leonard Kip Rhinelander).
8. *Id.* at 231 (Trial Transcript, Direct Examination of Leonard Kip Rhinelander). One claimed suitor, Edward Holland, denied that he ever kept company with Alice, gave her a ring, or suggested to her that they live together in an apartment. *See id.* at 302–3 (Trial Transcript, Direct Examination of Edward Holland). Alice, also at times, spelled "know" as "no" and "have to" as "after."
9. *Id.* at 260, 313 (Trial Transcript, Direct Examination of Leonard Kip Rhinelander).
10. *Id.* at 434 (Trial Transcript, Direct Examination of Albert Jolson).
11. *Id.* at 434–36 (Trial Transcript, Direct and Cross-Examinations of Albert Jolson).
12. *Id.* at 186 (Trial Transcript, Direct Examination of Leonard Kip Rhinelander); *see also id.* at 216 (Trial Transcript, Direct Examination of Leonard Kip Rhinelander). In numerous letters, Alice spoke longingly of their time in the Hotel Marie Antoinette. *See,* for example, *id.* at 186–240, 274–78, 326–28, 360–62.
13. *Id.* at 216 (Trial Transcript, Direct Examination of Leonard Kip Rhinelander).
14. *See id.* at 192–93 (Trial Transcript, Direct Examination of Leonard Kip Rhinelander); *see also id.* at 209 (Trial Transcript, Direct Examination of Leonard Kip Rhinelander): "I am going, to make you the happiest man, you have ever been, when you tell me the day, when you are going to be mind [*sic*]."
15. *Id.* at 317–19 (Trial Transcript, Direct Examination of Leonard Kip Rhinelander); *see also id.* at 333, 335–37 (Trial Transcript, Direct Examination of Leonard Kip Rhinelander) (reading from similar letters).

16. *Id.* at 170 (Trial Transcript, Direct Examination of Leonard Kip Rhinelander). According to Leonard, Alice continued her deception about her race after news of their marriage broke on Nov. 13, 1924, proclaiming, "It is not true, I am white, and I shall sue the newspapers through my attorney, Judge Swinburne." *Id.* at 174 (Trial Transcript, Direct Examination of Leonard Kip Rhinelander). Leonard also claimed that Alice told Jacobs that she was white when he first arrived at the Jones family home in mid-November. *See id.* at 175.

17. *Id.* at 250 (Trial Transcript, Direct Examination of Leonard Kip Rhinelander).

18. *Id.* at 760, 785–86 (Trial Transcript, Direct and Cross-Examinations of Miriam Rich). Miriam had also seen Alice's father, too, but claimed to believe that he was of English, Spanish descent because "he dropped his h's in his English" and "[h]e told [her] he is Spanish, of English descent." *Id.* at 790–91 (Trial Transcript, Cross-Examination of Miriam Rich).

19. *Id.* at 761–62 (Trial Transcript, Direct Examination of Miriam Rich).

20. *Id.* at 725 (Trial Transcript, Direct Examination of Joseph Rich).

21. *Id.* at 284–86 (Trial Transcript, Direct Examination of William L. Lawby).

22. *Id.* at 902 (Trial Transcript, Cross-Examination of Elizabeth Jones); *see also id.* at 625–26 (Trial Transcript, Cross-Examination of Leonard Kip Rhinelander) (stating that George Jones told Leonard that he was "pure white," that he was a pure English man suffering from jaundice, and that Leonard believed him).

23. *See id.* at 914–19, 924–29 (Trial Transcript, Cross-Examination of Elizabeth Jones).

24. *Id.* at 1303 (Trial Transcript, Summation for Plaintiff).

25. *Id.* at 883–84 (Trial Transcript, Cross-Examination of Grace Marie Miller).

26. *Id.* at 467 (Trial Transcript, Cross-Examination of Leonard Kip Rhinelander); *see also id.* at 467, 471.

27. *Id.* at 428–30 (Trial Transcript, Cross-Examination of Leonard Kip Rhinelander).

28. *Id.* at 513 (Trial Transcript, Cross-Examination of Leonard Kip Rhinelander).

29. *Id.* at 649 (Trial Transcript, Cross-Examination of Leonard Kip Rhinelander).

30. *Rhinelander's Wife Cries under Ordeal*, N.Y. Times, Nov. 24, 1925, at 3 [hereinafter *Ordeal*].

31. Court Record, *supra* note 2, at 696 (Trial Transcript, Cross-Examination of Leonard Kip Rhinelander).

32. *Id.* at 697 (Trial Transcript, Cross-Examination of Leonard Kip Rhinelander).

33. Renee C. Romano, Race Mixing: Black-White Marriage in Postwar America 167 (2003).

34. Court Record, *supra* note 2, at 486–89 (Trial Transcript, Cross-Examination of Leonard Kip Rhinelander).

35. *Id.* at 822–23 (Trial Transcript, Direct Examination of Barbara Reynolds).

36. *Id.* at 936 (Trial Transcript, Direct Examination of Ross Chidester).

37. *Id.* at 897 (Trial Transcript, Direct Examination of Elizabeth Jones).

38. *Id.* at 433, 437 (Trial Transcript, Cross-Examination of Leonard Kip Rhinelander).

39. *Id.* at 439 (Trial Transcript, Cross-Examination of Leonard Kip Rhinelander).

40. *Id.* at 439 (Trial Transcript, Cross-Examination of Leonard Kip Rhinelander).

41. *Id.* at 439 (Trial Transcript, Cross-Examination of Leonard Kip Rhinelander).
42. *Id.* at 444–45 (Trial Transcript, Cross-Examination of Leonard Kip Rhinelander).
43. *Ordeal, supra* note 30, at 3.
44. Court Record, *supra* note 2, at 681, 685 (Trial Transcript, Cross-Examination of Leonard Kip Rhinelander).
45. *Id.* at 1077 (Exhibits) (emphasis in original).

Chapter 4. A Verdict against the Heart

1. Earl Lewis and Heidi Ardizzone, Love on Trial: An American Scandal in Black and White 231 (2001).
2. *Id.* at 225.
3. *Id.* at 223 (quoting the wife of juror Fred Sanford in a Dec. 6, 1925 *N.Y. World* article).
4. *Rhinelander Loses; No Fraud Is Found; Wife Will Sue Now,* N.Y. Times, Dec. 6, 1925, at 1, 27 [hereinafter *Rhinelander Loses*].
5. Association of the Bar of the City of New York, New York Supreme Court: Appellate Division—Second Department, Leonard Kip Rhinelander *against* Alice Jones Rhinelander, Transcript of Record at 1134, Rhinelander v. Rhinelander, 219 N.Y.S. 548 (N.Y. App. Div. 1927) [hereinafter Court Record] (Trial Transcript, Summation for the Defendant).
6. Court Record, *supra* note 5, at 1133–34, 1140 (Trial Transcript, Summation for Defendant).
7. *Id.* at 1173 (Trial Transcript, Summation for Defendant).
8. *Id.* at 1176 (Trial Transcript, Summation for Defendant).
9. *Id.* at 1177 (Trial Transcript, Summation for Defendant).
10. *Id.* at 1199 (Trial Transcript, Summation for Defendant).
11. *Id.* at 1242 (Trial Transcript, Summation for Defendant).
12. *Id.* at 1190 (Trial Transcript, Summation for Defendant).
13. *Id.* at 1260 (Trial Transcript, Summation for Defendant).
14. *Id.* at 1274 (Trial Transcript, Summation for Defendant).
15. *Id.* at 1268 (Trial Transcript, Summation for Defendant).
16. *Id.* at 1276 (Trial Transcript, Summation for Plaintiff).
17. *Id.* at 1277 (Trial Transcript, Summation for Plaintiff).
18. *Id.* at 1287–88 (Trial Transcript, Summation for Plaintiff).
19. *Id.* at 1299 (Trial Transcript, Summation for Plaintiff).
20. *Id.* at 1437 (Trial Transcript, Summation for Plaintiff).
21. *Id.* at 1350, 1417 (Trial Transcript, Summation for Plaintiff); *see also id.* at 1357, 1364.
22. *Id.* at 1413 (Trial Transcript, Summation for Plaintiff).
23. *Id.* at 1290 (Trial Transcript, Summation for Plaintiff).
24. *Id.* at 1319 (Trial Transcript, Summation for Plaintiff); *see also id.* at 1421.
25. *Id.* at 1433 (Trial Transcript, Summation for Plaintiff).

26. *Id.* at 1429 (Trial Transcript, Summation for Plaintiff).

27. *Id.* at 1431–32 (Trial Transcript, Summation for Plaintiff).

28. *Id.* at 1442. In 1929, a publication, *From Negro to Caucasian; or, How the Ethiopian Is Changing His Skin,* asked provocatively, "Are You Positively Sure That You Are Not Part Negro?" The author of this publication asserted that thousands of colored people were knowingly passing as white and "still more thousands who are Negroes . . . believe themselves to be white." Lewis and Ardizonne, *supra* note 1, at 107–8 (quotations and citation omitted).

29. *Jones Interrupts Rhinelander Trial,* N.Y. Times, Dec. 4, 1925, at 3.

30. Court Record, *supra* note 5, at 18–19 (Issues as Amended During Trial and Submitted to the Jury).

31. *Id.* at 1005, 1049 (Charge of the Court).

32. *Calls Rhinelander Dupe of Girl He Wed,* N.Y. Times, Nov. 10, 1925, at 1, 8.

33. Court Record, *supra* note 5, at 1057 (Case).

34. *Rhinelander Loses, supra* note 4, at 27. *See also* Lewis and Ardizonne, *supra* note 1, at 221–22 (quoting a Dec. 6, 1925 *N.Y. World* article): "The filthy testimony that was introduced had very little to do with the finding of the verdict, or I might say, in the answering of the questions. We did not think very much of the testimony of the man Chidester. . . . The testimony of Mrs. Reynolds was probably the greatest single factor in favor of the defendant. It was the testimony of Mrs. Reynolds that finally decided the jury on the answer to question No. 6. This question puzzled the jurors more than any other." What may explain the jury's rejection of Chidester's testimony was evidence that showed him to be a father who had impregnated an unmarried woman and was delinquent on his support. *See* Court Record, *supra* note 5, at 1322 (Trial Transcript, Summation for Plaintiff).

35. *Rhinelander Jury Reaches a Decision after Twelve Hours,* N.Y. Times, Dec. 5, 1925, at 1.

36. *Rhinelander Loses, supra* note 4, at 1.

37. *Rhinelander Told the Worst Is Over,* N.Y. Times, Nov. 27, 1925, at 3.

38. *Rhinelander Loses, supra* note 4, at 1.

39. *Rhinelander's Suit May End Wednesday,* N.Y. Times, Nov. 28, 1925, at 8.

40. *Rhinelander Loses, supra* note 4, at at 27.

41. *Id.*

42. *Id.*

43. *Id.*

44. *Id.*

45. *Id.*

46. *Mrs. Rhinelander Is Not in Florida,* N.Y. Times, Dec. 16, 1925, at 20 [hereinafter *Not in Florida*].

47. *Rhinelander Loses, supra* note 4, at 27.

48. *Rhinelander's Wife Away with Mother,* N.Y. Times, Dec. 8, 1925, at 14.

49. *Rhinelander Spent $50,000,* N.Y. Times, Apr. 2, 1926, at 21.

50. Lewis and Ardizzone, *supra* note 1, at 247–48.

51. *Kip Rhinelander Dies of Pneumonia*, St. Louis Globe Democrat, Nov. 21, 1936, at 2A.
52. *Id.*
53. *Id.*
54. *Annoyer of Mrs. Rhinelander Insane*, N.Y. Times, Dec. 9, 1925, at 54.
55. *Klan Watches Florida Hotels, Seeking Mrs. Kip Rhinelander*, N.Y. Times, Dec. 15, 1925, at 1; *see also Klan Searches Hotels*, N.Y. Times, Dec. 16, 1925, at 20.
56. *Not in Florida, supra* note 46, at 20.
57. *Intercolor Marriage Ban*, N.Y. Times, Feb. 27, 1926, at 2.
58. *Mrs. Rhinelander to Sail*, N.Y. Times, July 16, 1926, at 2.
59. Lewis and Ardizzone, *supra* note 1, at 252, 259.
60. *Fights Haste in Suit by Rhinelander*, N.Y. Times, May 19, 1925, at 14.
61. Jamie L. Wacks, *Reading Race, Rhetoric, and the Female Body in the* Rhinelander *Case, in* Interracialism: Black-White Intermarriage in American History, Literature, and Law, at 163–64 (Werner Sollors ed. 2000).
62. Joanna Grossman, *Shifting the Terrain of the Trial: What Did the Husband Know?* Findlaw, Aug. 5, 2002, http://writ.news.findlaw.com/books/reviews/20020805 _grossman.html (last visited Oct. 9, 2012).
63. Ferrall v. Ferrall, 69 S.E. 60, 62 (N.C. 1910).
64. *Id.*
65. White v. Tax Collector, 31 S.C.L. (3 Rich) 136, 136, 140, 137 (S.C. Ct. App. 1846).
66. *Id.* at 137.
67. *Id.* at 136–37, 140 (quotation omitted).
68. *Id.* at 137.
69. *Id.* at 141.
70. Ferrall v. Ferrall, 69 S.E. 60, 62 (N.C. 1910).
71. White v. Tax Collector, 31 S.C.L. (3 Rich), at 140.
72. Ozawa v. United States, 260 U.S. 178, 195, 197 (1922) (emphasis added).
73. United States v. Bhagat Singh Thind, 261 U.S. 204, 210, 213–15 (1923).
74. *Id.* at 213.
75. *Id.* at 209, 215.
76. *See* Sunseri v. Cassagne, 196 So. 7, 7–9 (La. 1940). Similar holdings with respect to sex have prevailed in state's regarding the sex of a transsexual person. *See* Littleton v. Prange, 9 S.W.3d 223, 231 (Tx. App. 1999) (noting that if the birth certificate of a person accurately identifies his or her sex at birth, that is his or her sex for life regardless of any sex-altering operations); *see also* Ian Haney López, White by Law: The Legal Construction of Race 66 (2006) (noting that holdings in U.S. Supreme Court cases like *Ozawa* and *Thind* demonstrated that "the Court was committed to socially supposed races and racial hierarchies, not to a search for subtler truths").
77. Hopkins v. Bowers, 16 S.E. 1, 2 (N.C. 1892).
78. *See* Lewis and Ardizzone, *supra* note 1, at 107: "The phenomenon of racial 'passing' was at its height in the 1920s, if not in actual numbers then certainly in the level of awareness and concern on the part of Americans."

79. Cheryl I. Harris, *Whiteness as Property*, 106 Harv. L. Rev. 1709, 1736, 1739 (1993).
80. *Rhinelander Says He Pursued the Girl*, N.Y. Times, Nov. 18, 1925, at 4.
81. Court Record, *supra* note 5, at 419 (Trial Transcript, Cross-Examination of Leonard Kip Rhinelander).
82. *Id.* at 697 (Trial Transcript, Cross-Examination of Leonard Kip Rhinelander).
83. *Rhinelander Loses, supra* note 4, at 27 (emphasis added).
84. Court Record, *supra* note 5, at 443–44 (Trial Transcript, Cross-Examination of Leonard Kip Rhinelander).
85. *Id.* at 411–13 (Trial Transcript, Cross-Examination of Leonard Kip Rhinelander).
86. *Id.* at 478 (Trial Transcript, Cross-Examination of Leonard Kip Rhinelander).
87. *See* Phillip Brian Harper, Are We Not Men?: Masculine Anxiety and the Problem of African-American Identity 136 (1996).

Chapter 5. Understanding the Black and White of Love

1. *See, e.g.*, Catherine E. Smith, *Equal Protection for the Children of Gay and Lesbian Parents: Challenging the Three Pillars of Exclusion—Legitimacy, Dual-Gender Parenting, and Biology*, 28 Law & Ineq. 207 (2010) (analyzing the inequalities that the children of same-sex couples "face because of discrimination against their gay and lesbian parents").
2. *See* Jill Elaine Hasday, *The Canon of Family Law*, 57 Stan. L. Rev. 825, 855 (2004) (noting how "[s]cholars use the example of interracial marriage to stress how family law no longer draws distinctions between families").
3. Heather M. Dalmage, Tripping on the Color Line: Black-White Multiracial Families in a Racially Divided World 2 (2000).
4. Erica Chito Childs, Navigating Interracial Borders: Black-White Couples and Their Social Worlds 6 (2005).
5. *Id.* at 3.
6. In this book, I identify Latinos as a racial group, even though the U.S. Census identifies Latinos as an ethnic group.
7. Rachel F. Moran, Interracial Intimacy: The Regulation of Race and Romance 165–66 (2001): "While most Asian-Americans, Latinos, and Native Americans now have at least a distant white relative through marriage, blacks are much less likely to report a kinship relationship to any other group"; Randall Kennedy, *How Are We Doing With* Loving?: *Race, Law, and Intermarriage*, 77 B.U. L. Rev. 815, 819 (1997) [hereinafter *Doing with* Loving]; Kevin R. Johnson, *Race in America: Strom Thurmond's Daughter and the Enduring Taboo on Black/White Marriages*, S.F. Chron., Jan. 4, 2004, at D5: "The legacy of the deep-seated animus toward African Americans in U.S. society inhibits whites from marrying blacks. Anti-black sentiment, as well as residential and school segregation, makes it much less likely that whites will interact socially with, much less marry, African Americans. Black/white relationships still are taboo in some circles."
8. 388 U.S. 1, 2, 10–11 (1967). In *Loving*, Mildred and Richard challenged the constitutionality of the state of Virginia's anti-miscegenation statutes. *See Loving*, 388

U.S. at 2. After marrying and then living in Washington D.C. for a short period, the Lovings returned to their home state of Virginia, where they found themselves arrested, charged with leaving the state to evade the law, charged with unlawfully residing as an interracial couple, and threatened with the enforcement of a one-year prison sentence unless they left the state without returning for twenty-five years. *See id*. Ruling in favor of the Lovings and striking down Virginia's antimiscegenation statues, *see id*. at 11–12, the Supreme Court rejected Virginia's argument that its antimiscegenation statutes did not violate the Equal Protection Clause because they applied equally to whites and nonwhites. The Court reasoned that such a claim could not legitimate statutes that had no purpose other than to discriminate against racial minorities and promote white supremacy. *See id*. at 10–11. The Court further reasoned that the statutes violated the Due Process Clause because marriage was a fundamental right that rested with the individual, which the State could not restrict by invidious racial discrimination. *See id*. at 11.

9. Association of the Bar of the City of New York, New York Supreme Court: Appellate Division—Second Department, Leonard Kip Rhinelander *against* Alice Jones Rhinelander, Case on Appeal, at 761–62 (Nov. 26, 1924–Dec. 5, 1925) [hereinafter Court Record] (Trial Transcript, Direct Examination of Miriam Rich).

10. Moran, *supra* note 7, at 17.

11. *Id*. at 6, 103; *see also* Randall Kennedy, Interracial Intimacies: Sex, Marriage, Identity, and Adoption 127 (2003).

12. The intermarriage rate for blacks with whites was approximately 6 percent while the intermarriage rates for Japanese-Americans and Chinese-Americans with whites were 55 and 40 percent, respectively. Christine B. Hickman, *The Devil and the One Drop Rule: Racial Categories, African Americans, and the U.S. Census*, 95 Mich. L. Rev. 1161, 1164 n. 9 (1997).

13. Jeffrey S. Passel et al., Pew Research Ctr., A Social and Demographic Trends Report, Marrying Out: One-in-Seven New U.S. Marriages Is Interracial or Interethnic 1–2 (June 15, 2010), available at http://pewsocialtrends.org/files/2010/10/755 -marrying-out.pdf (last visited Oct. 10, 2012); *see also* Kevin D. Brown and Vinay Sitapati, *Lessons Learned from Comparing the Application of Constitutional Law and Federal Anti-Discrimination Law to African-Americans in the U.S. and Dalits in India in the Context of Higher Education*, 24 Harv. BlackLetter L.J. 3, 39 (2008).

14. Kennedy, *Doing with* Loving, *supra* note 7, at 819.

15. *Id*.

16. Jeffrey S. Passel et al., Pew Research Ctr., A Social and Demographic Trends Report, Marrying Out: One-in-Seven New U.S. Marriages Is Interracial or Interethnic 1–2 (June 15, 2010), *available at* http://pewsocialtrends.org/files/2010/10/755-marrying-out.pdf (last visited Oct. 10, 2012).

17. *Id*. at 5.

18. *See* Vincent Kang Fu, *How Many Melting Pots? Intermarriage, Pan Ethnicity, and the Black/Non-Black Divide in the United States*, 38 J. Comp. Fam. Studs. 215, 218 (2007); *see also* Brown and Sitapati, *supra* note 13, at 39 nn. 248 and 249.

19. Ralph Richard Banks, Is Marriage for Black People? How the African American Marriage Decline Affects Everyone 33–48 (2011); Renee C. Romano, Race Mixing: Black-White Marriage in Postwar America 218 (2003).

20. Brown and Sitapati, *supra* note 13, at 40.

21. Passel et al., *supra* note 16, at 2.

22. R. Richard Banks and Su Jin Gatlin, *African American Intimacy: The Racial Gap in Marriage*, 11 Mich. J. Race & L. 115, 131 (2005); *see also* Banks, *supra* note 19, at 33–38.

23. I acknowledge that Alice may not have identified as a black woman.

24. Kevin R. Johnson, *Taking the "Garbage" Out in Tulia, Texas: The Taboo on Black-White Romance and Racial Profiling in the "War on Drugs,"* 2007 Wis. L. Rev. 283, 295: "The truth of the matter, however, is that interracial intimacy has long been a part of the American experience. In the days of slavery, intimate liaisons—often involuntary—were common between white men and black women."

25. Kevin Noble Maillard, *The Color of Testamentary Freedom*, 62 SMU L. Rev. 1783, 1793 (2009) (providing a quotation from Winthrop D. Jordan, White over Black: American Attitudes toward the Negro, 1550–1812, at 145 (1968)).

26. Annette Gordon-Reed, The Hemingses of Monticello: An American Family (2008).

27. Alexis de Tocqueville, Democracy in America: Abridged Edition 358 (J.P. Mayer ed., George Lawrence trans. 2007) (1835).

28. Maillard, *supra* note 25, at 1797–1815. *But see* Adrienne D. Davis, *The Private Law of Race and Sex: An Antebellum Perspective*, 51 Stan. L. Rev. 221, 279-82 (1999) (discussing a case in which a transfer to an illegitimate, biracial child of a slave owner was upheld). *See generally* Bernie D. Jones, Fathers of Conscience: Mixed-Race Inheritance in the Antebellum South (2009).

29. Romano, *supra* note 19, at 230. *But see* Ernest Porterfield, Black and White Mixed Marriages 32 (1978) (indicating the opposite—that black male–white female marriages overwhelmingly outnumbered black female–white male marriages between the period of 1897–1964).

30. Romano, *supra* note 19, at 230–31.

31. Banks and Gatlin, *supra* note 22, at 119.

32. *Id.* at 130.

33. Cynthia Feliciano et al., *Gendered Racial Exclusion among White Internet Daters*, 38 Soc. Sci. Res. 39, 40–52 (2009).

34. *Id.* at 46.

35. *Id.* at 47.

36. *Id.* at 45.

37. *Id.* at 46 (emphasis in the original).

38. Christian Rudder, *How Your Race Affects the Messages You Get*, OkTrends (Oct. 5, 2009), http://blog.okcupid.com/index.php/your-race-affects-whether-people-write-you-back/ (last visited Oct. 10, 2012) (providing dating research from OkCupid).

39. *Id.*

40. *Id.* (emphasis in original).

41. *Id.* (emphasis in original).

42. *Id.*

43. *Same-Sex Data for Race vs. Reply Rates,* OkTrends, http://blog.okcupid.com/index.php/same-sex (last visited Oct. 10, 2012) (providing dating research from OkCupid).

44. *Id.*

45. *Id.* (emphasis in original).

46. *Id.*

47. Isabel Wilkerson, *Hollywood Shuffle,* Essence, Mar. 1997, at 71, 129, 132.

48. Latoya Petersen, *Dear John: It's Impossible to Have "A Bennetton Heart" and a "White Supremacist Dick,"* Jezebel, Feb. 11, 2010, at 2:00 p.m., http://jezebel.com/5469484/its-impossible-to-have-a-benetton-heart-and-a-white-supremacist-dick (last visited Oct. 10, 2012) [hereinafter *Dear John: It's Impossible*].

49. *Id.*

50. Survey 10 (Edith and Stephen).

51. *See* Camille A. Nelson, *Lovin' the Man: Examining the Legal Nexus of Irony, Hypocrisy, and Curiosity,* 2007 Wis. L. Rev. 543, 562–63 (2007).

52. *See* Court Record, *supra* note 9, at 1096 (Trial Transcript, Opening for Plaintiff).

53. For an example of a purity test, *see The Unisex Experience Test,* http://www.thepurplehouse.net/purity/purity/purity.225.txt (last visited Oct. 10, 2012).

54. Erica Chito Childs, *Listening to the Interracial Canary: Contemporary Views on Interracial Relationships Among Blacks and Whites,* 76 Fordham L. Rev. 2771, 2776 (2008) (emphasis in original).

55. *John Mayer: Playboy Interview, supra* note 48.

56. Chito Childs, *supra* note 54, at 2781.

57. *Id.* at 2780–81.

58. Catherine E. Smith, *Queer as Black Folk?,* 2007 Wis. L. Rev. 379, 380 (2007).

59. Survey 11 (Carla and Janice).

60. *See Young Rhinelander Sues for Annulment: Poor Girl to Fight Hubby's Parents,* Chi. Defender, Dec. 6, 1924, at 1.

61. *Id.* at 3.

62. *Rhinelander's Wife Denies She Is Negro,* N.Y. Times, Nov. 29, 1924, at 15.

63. *See* Court Record, *supra* note 9, at 895 (Direct Examination of Elizabeth Jones).

64. *Rhinelander Faces Thorough Quizzing,* N.Y. Times, Nov. 15, 1925, at 14.

65. I acknowledge that Alice and/or Leonard may have viewed themselves as a white couple, not a black female–white male couple.

66. Erin Edmonds, *Mapping the Terrain of Our Resistance: A White Feminist Perspective on the Enforcement of Rape Law,* 9 Harv. BlackLetter L.J. 43, 49–54 (1992); Kevin R. Johnson, *The Legacy of Jim Crow: The Enduring Taboo of Black-White Romance,* 84 Tex. L. Rev. 739, 751, 756–57 (2006); Emma Coleman Jordan, *Crossing the River of Blood between Us: Lynching, Violence, Beauty, and the Paradox of Feminist History,* 3 J. Gender, Race & Just. 545, 566–68 (2000).

67. Peggy Pascoe, What Comes Naturally: Miscegenation Law and the Making of Race in America 10 (2009).

68. Charles Frank Robinson II, Dangerous Liaisons: Sex and Love in the Segregated South 51–70 (2003); *see also* Ariela R. Dubler, *From* McLaughlin v. Florida *to* Lawrence v. Texas: *Sexual Freedom and the Road to Marriage,* 106 Colum. L. Rev. 1165, 1176 (2006): "To be sure, as Martha Hodes has documented, there were always black men having sex with white women, but this coupling inspired far more cultural anxiety. In particular, Hodes documents that white alarm about sex between white women and black men increased dramatically in the years following the Civil War. In the post-Reconstruction South, images of 'the purity of white women' rested on complementary images of 'black men as bestial.'"

69. *See, e.g.,* Reginald Oh, *Regulating White Desire,* 2007 Wis. L. Rev. 463, 482–85 (2007).

70. Romano, *supra* note 19, at 4.

71. Trina Jones, *Shades of Brown: The Law of Skin Color,* 49 Duke L.J. 1487, 1503–4 (2000); Marie-Amélie George, *The Modern Mulatto: A Comparative Analysis of the Social and Legal Positions of Mulattoes in the Antebellum South and the Intersex in Contemporary America,* 15 Colum. J. Gender & L. 665, 674 (2006) (citing *id.* at 1504); Carter G. Woodson, *The Beginnings of Miscegenation of the Whites and Blacks, in* Interracialism: Black-White Intermarriage in American History, Literature, and Law 42, 47 (Werner Sollors ed., 2000).

72. *See* Jones, *supra* note 71, at 1503–4; *cf.* Moran, *supra* note 7, at 21 (2001): "As slavery hardened the lines between whites and blacks, the racial tax on mulattoes increased. Their curtailed privileges clearly identified them as nonwhite."

73. Romano, *supra* note 19, at 2.

74. *See* Johnson, *supra* note 24, at 293–307.

75. Feliciano et al., *supra* note 33, at 41; *see also* Suzanne C. Miller et al., *Perceived Reactions to Interracial Romantic Relationships: When Race Is Used as a Cue to Status,* 7 Group Processes Intergroup Relations 354, 355 (2004) (contending, based on their studies, that the greater hostility felt by black men and white women in couples can explained by parental investment theory and social structural theory). Based on their studies, the authors asserted that "according to non-White males involved with White females, the parents of White females were more disapproving of their daughters dating non-White males than were the parents of any other combination of race and sex." *Id.* at 360, 365. They further noted, "[I]n fact, they were the only group for whom there was perceived to be more disapproval from their partner's family and friends compared to their own." *Id.* at 362.

76. Miller et al., *supra,* note 75, at 365.

77. Romano, *supra* note 19, at 259.

78. *Your Letters,* Essence, Mar. 2010, at 15.

79. *Id.*

80. *Id.*

81. *Id.*

82. Jamilah Lemieux, *If I Were Your Woman,* Essence, Mar. 2010, at 107–8.

83. *Your Letters,* Essence, June 2010, at 25.

84. *Id.*

85. Survey 1 (Cameron and Don).

86. Survey 14 (Becca and Darren).

87. Survey 21 (Julie and Barry).

88. *Id.*

89. Survey 3 (Margaret and Geoffrey).

90. Survey 19 (John and Vernon).

91. Survey 2 (Bryan and Sam).

92. Michelle L. Turner, *The Braided Uproar: A Defense of My Sister's Hair and a Contemporary Indictment of* Rogers v. American Airlines, 7 Cardozo Women's L.J. 115, 143–44 (2001).

93. Phillip Atiba Goff et al., *"Ain't I a Woman?" Towards an Intersectional Approach to Person Perception and Group-Based Harms*, 59 Sex Roles 392, 392 (2008).

94. *Id.* at 397–98.

95. Romano, *supra* note 19, at 133–34.

96. The phrase *essence of marriage* is to be distinguished from the phrase *essentials of marriage,* which include factors such as "[t]he duty of support and services and the duties of cohabitation, sexual access, and monogamy." Twila L. Perry, *The "Essentials of Marriage": Reconsidering the Duty of Support and Services,* 15 Yale J.L. & Feminism 1, 3–4 (2003).

97. D. Wendy Greene, *Determining the (In)Determinable: Race in Brazil and the United States,* 14 Mich. J. Race & L. 143, 168 (2009).

98. Marshall v. Marshall, 212 Cal. 739, 740 (1931). *See, e.g.,* In re Marriage of Johnston, 18 Cal.App.4th 499, 22 Cal.Rptr.2d 253 (1993); V.J.S. v. M.J.B., 592 A.2d 318, 320 (N.J. Super. 1991); Di Pillo v. Di Pillo, 184 N.Y.S. 2d 892, 894 (1959).

99. *See, e.g.,* Marshall v. Marshall, 212 Cal. 736, 737–38 (1931); *see also* Williams v. Williams, 118 Atl. 638, 639 (Del. 1922) (noting that misrepresentations as to wealth or social position do not justify annulment). In this sense, had Leonard alleged that Alice had lied about her social position as opposed to her race—a factor that also was reported to be objectionable to his father, Philip Rhinelander, that claim likely would not have survived because such misrepresentations could have been determined to be outside of the "essence of marriage."

100. *See, e.g.,* People v. Godines, 62 P.2d 787, 788 (Cal. Dist. Ct. App. 1936): "In view of the declared policy of this state that a white person and a Filipino may not marry, it seems clear that a misrepresentation by a Filipino that he is a Spaniard is a fraud that touches a vital spot in the marriage relation and constitutes, therefore, a cause for annulment." Notably and importantly, fraud as to a spouse's fanatic racism or prejudice has been held to go to the essence of marriage. *See* Kober v. Kober, 16 N.Y. 2d 191, 196–97 (N.Y. Ct. App. 1965) (granting an annulment where the husband had concealed that he was fanatically anti-Semitic).

101. Palmore v. Sidoti, 466 U.S. 429, 433–34 (1984).

102. *Palmore,* 466 U.S. at 431 (quoting App. to Pet. for Cert. 26–27).

103. *Id.* at 433.

104. *Id.*

105. J. Jeffrey Gunn, Statute Note, *Utah's Annulment Statute: Are Annulments Underused as a Result of Liberal "No-Fault" Divorce Laws?*, 6 J. L. & Fam. Stud. 385, 385 (2004).

106. *See id.* at 385, 387; *see also* In re Marriage of Liu, 197 Cal. App. 3d 143, 156–57 (Cal. Ct. App. 1998) (not granting the wife any property under community property law because the marriage had been annulled due to her fraud based on the desire to obtain a green card).

107. *See Kober*, 16 N.Y. 2d at 196–97 (N.Y. Ct. App. 1965) (granting an annulment where the husband had concealed that he was fanatically anti-Semitic).

108. Moran, *supra* note 7, at 191; *see also* Russell K. Robinson, *Structural Dimensions of Romantic Preferences*, 76 Fordham L. Rev. 2787, 2803 (2008) (noting "race structures our relationships, even when we think we have transcended it").

109. Rudder, *supra* note 38.

110. *Same-Sex Data for Race vs. Reply Rates, supra* note 43.

111. *White Couple Sue Fertility Clinic for Mixed Race Baby Mistake*, AmericanRenaissance.Com (June 14, 2009), http://amren.com/news/2009/06/white_couple _su/ (last visited Oct. 10, 2012).

112. *Id.*

113. *Couple Sue New York Fertility Clinic Over Use of Wrong Sperm in IVF Treatment*, WayOdd, http://www.wayodd.com/couple-sue-new-york-fertility-clinic-over-use -of-wrong-sperm-in-ivf/v/6872/ (last visited Oct. 10, 2012); *White Couple Sue Fertility Clinic for Mixed Race Baby Mistake*, news.scotsman.com. June 14, 2009, http://www.scotsman.com/news/white-couple-sue-fertility-clinic-for-mixed-race -baby-mistake-1-1353673 (last visited Oct. 10, 2012).

114. *See* R. Richard Banks, *The Color of Desire: Fulfilling Adoptive Parents' Racial Preferences through Discriminatory State Action*, 107 Yale L.J. 875, 881–914 (1998).

115. Kennedy, *supra* note 11, at 400–401.

116. Solangel Maldonado, *Discouraging Racial Preferences in Adoptions*, 39 U.C. Davis L. Rev. 1415, 1457–62 (2006).

117. *Interracial Couple Denied Marriage License*, MSNBC (Oct. 15, 2009), http://www .msnbc.msn.com/id/33332436/ns/us_news-life/t/interracial-couple-denied-mar riage-license/ (last visited Oct. 10, 2012).

118. *Judge Crawls out of Medieval Times, Denies Marriage License to Mixed-Race Couple*, TheRoot.Com (Oct. 16, 2009), http://www.theroot.com/buzz/judge-crawls-out -medieval-times-denies-marriage-license-mixed-race-couple (last visited Oct. 10, 2012).

Chapter 6. Living in Placelessness

1. Peggy McIntosh, White Privilege: Unpacking the Invisible Knapsack, excerpted from Peggy McIntosh, White Privilege and Male Privilege: A Personal Account of Coming to See Correspondences through Work in Women's Studies (Working Paper 189, 1988).

2. *Id.* at 1–2.

3. *Id.* at 5.

4. As noted earlier in the book, my use of the phrase *because of interraciality* concerns more than just mistreatment based on one's involvement in an intimate, interracial relationship—marriage or a committed, nonmarital relationship. Generally speaking, the phrase encompasses mistreatment based on one's being part of an interracial family unit, which includes sibling relationships and parent-child relationships. It does not extend to mistreatment based on platonic friendships, however.

5. *See* McIntosh, *supra* note 1, at 4: "I began to count the ways in which I enjoy unearned skin privilege and have been conditioned into oblivion about its existence. . . . My schooling gave me no training in seeing myself as an oppressor, as an unfairly advantaged person, or as a participant in a damaged culture." *See also* Stephanie M. Wildman and Adrienne D. Davis, *Language and Silence: Making Systems of Privilege Visible*, 35 Santa Clara L. Rev. 881, 890 (1995): "First, the characteristics of the privileged group define the societal norm, often benefiting those in the privileged group. Second, privileged group members can rely on their privilege and avoid objecting to oppression. Both conflicting privilege with the societal norm and the implicit choice to ignore oppression mean that privilege is rarely seen by the holder of the privilege."

6. *See* Darren Lenard Hutchinson, *Identity Crisis: "Intersectionality," "Multidimensionality," and the Development of an Adequate Theory of Subordination*, 6 Mich. J. Race & L. 285, 303 (2001): "[B]ecause sexual orientation remains an unprotected category in federal statutory and constitutional civil rights law, discriminators may willingly concede sexual orientation discrimination when some evidence of discriminatory action exists, but deny racial or gender discrimination."

7. This list closely tracks portions of Professor McIntosh's list in her paper "White Privilege: Unpacking the Invisible Knapsack" and Professor Allan Johnson's list of privileges based on a variety of identity categories in his book *Privilege, Power, and Difference*. *See supra* note 1 and accompanying text; Allan G. Johnson, Privilege, Power, and Difference 25–33 (2d ed. 2006).

8. *See* McIntosh, *supra* note 1.

9. Kimberlé Williams Crenshaw, *Panel Presentation on Cultural Battery, Speaker: Kimberlé Williams Crenshaw*, 25 U. Tol. L. Rev. 891, 892 (1994): "Intersectionality generally functions as a metaphor for capturing the different dimensions of race and gender as they converge in the lives of women of color." *See also* Devon W. Carbado and Mitu Gulati, *The Law and Economics of Critical Race Theory*, 112 Yale L.J. 1757, 1775 (2003) (reviewing Crossroads, Directions, and a New Critical Race Theory [Francisco Valdes et al., eds. 2002]) (asserting that intersectionality is a "concept that conveys at least the following two ideas: [1] that our identities are intersectional—that is, raced, gendered, sexually oriented, etc.—and [2] that our vulnerability to discrimination is a function of our specific intersectional identities").

10. *See* Kimberlé Crenshaw, *Mapping the Margins: Intersectionality, Identity Politics, and Violence Against Women of Color*, 43 Stan. L. Rev. 1241, 1242–43 (1991) (explaining that women of color are at the intersection of race and gender oppression).

11. *Id.*

12. Jeannine Bell, *Hate Thy Neighbor: Violent Racial Exclusion and the Persistence of Segregation,* 5 Ohio St. J. of Crim. L. 47 (2007).

13. Jeffrey S. Passel et al., Pew Research Ctr., A Social and Demographic Trends Report, Marrying Out: One-in-Seven New U.S. Marriages Is Interracial or Interethnic 1 (June 15, 2010), *available at* http://pewsocialtrends.org/files/2010/10/755 -marrying-out.pdf (last visited Oct. 10 2012).

14. Joseph Carroll, Most Americans Approve of Interracial Marriage; Blacks More Likely Than Whites to Approve of Black-White Unions, Gallup (Aug. 16, 2007), http://www.gallup.com/poll/28417/most-americans-approve-interracial-marriages .aspx (last visited Oct. 10, 2012); Passel et al., *supra* note 13, at 5.

15. What Would You Do? Interracial Couple Harassed (ABC television broadcast May 20, 2011), *previously available at* http://abcnews.go.com/WhatWouldYouDo/ (last visited Aug. 21, 2012).

16. *Id.*

17. Passel et al., *supra* note 13, at 13.

18. Survey 15 (Janet and Sam).

19. Heather M. Dalmage, Tripping on the Color Line: Black-White Multiracial Families in a Racially Divided World 2 (2000).

20. *See* Rachel F. Moran, Interracial Intimacy: The Regulation of Race and Romance 155 (2001); *see also* Angela Onwuachi-Willig, *A Beautiful Lie: Exploring* Rhinelander v. Rhinelander *as a Formative Lesson on Race, Identity, Marriage, and Family,* 95 Cal. L. Rev. 2393, 2458 (2007).

21. Multi-Ethnic Placement Act, 42 U.S.C.A. § 622 (2006). For a general discussion of the difficulties interracial couples face in the adoption process, *see Interracial Couple Say They Were Denied Adoption Because They Had Not Suffered Enough Racism,* Jet, Aug. 16, 1999, 23.

22. *See generally* Angela Onwuachi-Willig, *There's Just One Hitch, Will Smith: Examining Title VII, Race, and Casting Discrimination on the Fortieth Anniversary of Loving* v. Virginia, 2007 Wis. L. Rev. 319 (analyzing the dearth of black-white interracial couples in film and television as a result of casting discrimination based on perceived audience preferences).

23. *See* Camille A. Nelson, *Lovin' the Man: Examining the Legal Nexus of Irony, Hypocrisy, and Curiosity,* 2007 Wis. L. Rev. 543, 549 (2007) (footnote omitted).

24. *Id.*

25. Survey 17 (Raven and Jim).

26. Survey 21 (Julie and Barry).

27. *Id.*

28. Survey 8 (Amy and Carrie).

29. Survey 2 (Bryan and Sam).

30. Survey 19 (John and Vernon); Catherine E. Smith, *Queer as Black Folk?* 2007 Wis. L. Rev. 379, 380–81 (2007): "Today, the way I navigate the world in a same-sex interracial relationship as a black lesbian is different than the way a black heterosexual man in an interracial relationship navigates it. My experiences as a black

lesbian are not the same as the experiences of a black heterosexual man, and to make the assumption of sameness marginalizes the unique experiences of black women and men and perpetuates racist, sexist, and heterosexist norms."

31. Other interracial couples have documented similar experiences. *See*, for example, Erica Chito Childs, Navigating Interracial Borders: Black-White Couples and Their Social Worlds 40 (2005); and Paul C. Rosenblatt et al., Multiracial Couples: Black and White Voices 127 (1995).

32. Survey 6 (Jane and Ted).

33. *See* Darren Lenard Hutchinson, *Ignoring the Sexualization of Race: Heteronormativity, Critical Race Theory, and Anti-Racist Politics*, 47 Buff. L. Rev. 1, 9–10 (1999) (discussing multidimensionality, which contends that essentialist equality theories invariably do not reflect the "interlocking sources of advantage and disadvantage").

34. *Compare* Peggie R. Smith, *Regulating Paid Household Work, Class, Gender, Race, and Agendas of Reform*, 48 Am. U. L. Rev. 851, 915–16 (1999) (noting how service work increasingly became synonymous with black women), *and* Pamela J. Smith, *Part II—Romantic Paternalism—The Ties That Bind: Hierarchies of Economic Oppression That Reveal Judicial Disaffinity for Black Women and Men*, 3 J. Gender Race & Just. 181, 196–205 (1999) (describing the linkage between the image of black women and service workers), *with* Richard Delgado, *Rodrigo's Corrido: Race, Postcolonial Theory, and U.S. Civil Rights*, 60 Vand. L. Rev. 1691, 1720 (2007): "[T]he dominant stereotype of the Asian male is sexless: Nerdy. No body hair. Thick glasses. Good at math and science. Bad at sports." Cynthia Kwei Yung Lee, *Beyond Black and White: Racializing Asian Americans in a Society Obsessed with O.J.*, 6 Hastings Women's L.J. 165, 190 n. 120 (1995) (noting that "one common set of racial images portrays the typical Asian American as someone with a heavy accent, who works in a laundry or as a gardener, practices karate, and studies fastidiously").

35. Rashmi Goel, *From Tainted to Sainted: The View of Interracial Relations as Cultural Evangelism*, 2007 Wis. L. Rev. 489, 516–17 (2007).

36. Survey 12 (Fred and Deanne).

37. Survey 17 (Raven and Jim).

38. Survey 3 (Margaret and Geoffrey).

39. *Id.*

40. Follow-up Interview with Janice.

41. Survey 6 (Jane and Ted).

42. Survey 1 (Cameron and Don).

43. Survey 6 (Jane and Ted).

44. Survey 9 (Susan and Ethan).

45. Angela Onwuachi-Willig & Jacob Willig-Onwuachi, *A House Divided: The Invisibility of the Multiracial Family*, 44 Harv. C.L.-C.R. L. Rev. 231, 240 (2009); *see also* Dalmage, *supra* note 19, at 48.

46. Veronica Chambers, *I'm Her Mother, Not Her Nanny*, Essence, June 2010, at 106.

47. Survey 7 (Amber and Caleb).

48. Survey 18 (Shondra and Michael).

49. *Id.*

50. What Would You Do? White Father with Black Daughter (ABC television broadcast, Jan. 28, 2011), *previously available at* http://abcnews.go.com/WhatWouldYou Do/ (last visited Aug. 21, 2012).

51. Angela Nissel, Mixed: My Life in Black and White 19–21 (2006) (emphasis in original).

52. Jennifer Gordon and R. A. Lenhardt, *Rethinking Work and Citizenship*, 55 UCLA L. Rev. 1161, 1169–70 (2008) (defining citizenship as belonging).

53. *4 Ark. Men Indicted on Race Crime Charges*, TodaysTHV.com (Apr. 7, 2011), www.todaysthv.com/news/article/152489/2/4-Ark-men-indicted-on-race-crime -charges (last visited Oct. 13, 2012).

54. Survey 18 (Shondra and Michael).

55. Survey 21 (Julie and Barry).

56. *Id.*

57. *See generally* Richard Wright et al., *Where Black-White Couples Live*, 32 Urb. Geography 1, 14 (2011).

58. Survey 10 (Edith and Stephen).

59. Survey 4 (Darcy and Charlie).

60. Survey 20 (Stephanie and Kirk).

61. Nissel, *supra* note 51, at 107.

62. Pub. L. No. 90-284, 82 Stat. 73 (codified as amended at 42 U.S.C. § 3604 [2000]).

63. *See* I. Bennett Capers, Policing, Race, and Space, 44 Harv. C.R.-C.L. L. Rev. 43, 72 (2009) (citing John Iceland et. al, U.S. Census Bureau, Racial and Ethnic Residential Segregation in the United States: 1980–2000, at 72 (2002)).

64. Lewis Mumford Ctr. for Comparative Urban and Reg'l Research, Ethnic Diversity Grows, Neighborhood Integration Lags Behind 1 (2001), *available at* http://mum ford1.dyndns.org/cen2000/WholePop/WPreport/MumfordReport.pdf (last visited Oct. 10, 2012).

65. John R. Logan et al., *Segregation of Minorities in the Metropolis: Two Decades of Change*, 41 Demography 1, 8 (2004).

66. Survey 19 (John and Vernon).

67. Survey 21 (Julie and Barry).

68. Capers, *supra* note 63, at 46, 66–72; *see also* Sheryll D. Cashin, *Middle-Class Black Suburbs and the State of Integration: A Post-Integrationist Vision for a Metropolitan America*, 86 Cornell L. Rev. 729, 747–49 (2001) (contending that middle-class to upper-middle-class blacks may choose to live in black neighborhoods in order to avoid daily racial hostility and microaggressions).

69. Herbert J. Hovenkamp, *Social Science and Segregation before* Brown, 1985 Duke L.J. 624, 635 (1985); *see also* Jill Elaine Hasday, *Protecting Them from Themselves: The Persistence of Mutual Benefits Arguments for Race and Sex Inequality*, 84 NYU L. Rev. 1464, 1514–28 (2009) (analyzing how racial segregation arguments, including those against amalgamation, were argued to be mutually beneficial to both blacks and whites).

70. Reginald Oh, *Regulating White Desire*, 2007 Wis. L. Rev. 463 (2007).

71. *Id.* at 472–73; *see also* Elizabeth F. Emens, *Intimate Discrimination: The State's Role in the Accident of Sex and Love,* 122 Harv. L. Rev. 1307, 1311 (2009): "Moreover, even aside from its express requirements, law shapes whom we meet and how. It determines the accidents of sex and love, because it controls the infrastructure of our lives—our neighborhoods, schools, workplaces, public spaces, and more—in ways that affect affiliations along the lines of race, disability, and sex."

72. Survey 4 (Darcy and Charlie); *see also* Renee C. Romano, Race Mixing: Black-White Marriage in Post War America 257 (2003) (describing how some interracial couples have "relocate[d] from less friendly areas to those they perceive to be more tolerant").

73. Survey 10 (Edith and Stephen).

74. *See generally* Wright et al., *supra* note 57, at 1.

75. *Id.* at 16, 18.

76. *Id.* at 5 (citing Avery M. Guest et al., Heterogeneity and Harmony, Neighboring Relationships among Whites in Ethnically Diverse Neighborhoods in Seattle, 45 Urb. Stud. 501 (2008)).

77. *Id.* at 2.

78. *See* Dalmage, *supra* note 19, at 78–79.

79. Survey 9 (Susan and Ethan).

80. Wright et al., *supra* note 57, at 4 (citation omitted).

81. Romano, *supra* note 72, at 131–32.

82. Civil Rights Act of 1968, tit. 8, Pub. L. No. 90–284 § 804, 82 Stat. 73, 83 (codified as amended at 42 U.S.C. § 3604 (2000)). Subsequent amendments have expanded the list of protected characteristics to include sex, familial status, and handicap, but the statute's protection is still limited to the characteristics specifically enumerated in its text. 42 U.S.C. § 3604 (2000).

83. 411 U.S. 792 (1973).

84. *McDonnell Douglas,* 411 U.S. at 802–4; *see also* Reeves v. Sanderson Plumbing Prods., Inc., 530 U.S. 133, 143 (2000).

85. *See, e.g.,* Holcomb v. Iona Coll., 521 F. 3d 130, 139 (2d Cir. 2008); *see also* Parr Woodmen of the World Life Ins. Co., 791 F. 2d 888, 889–92 (11th Cir. 1986); Rosenblatt v. Bivona & Cohen, P.C., 946 F. Supp. 298, 300 (S.D.N.Y. 1996); Whitney v. Greater New York Corp. of Seventh-Day Adventists, 401 F. Supp. 1363, 1366 (S.D.N.Y. 1975).

86. 42 U.S.C. § 3602(k) (2000).

87. County of Dane v. Wisconsin, 497 N.W.2d 714, 715 (Wis. 1993); *see also* N.D. Fair Hous. Council, Inc. v. Petersen, 625 N.W.2d 551, 560 (N.D. 2001) (asserting "status with respect to marriage" means "whether a person is divorced, widowed or separated").

88. Bryant v. Automatic Data Processing, Inc., 390 N.W.2d 732, 735 (Mich. Ct. App. 1986).

89. *See* Richard H. Pildes and Richard G. Niemi, *Expressive Harms, "Bizarre Districts," and Voting Rights: Evaluating Election-District Appearances After* Shaw v. Reno, 92

Mich. L. Rev. 483, 506–7 (1993) (defining expressive harms as harms that "result[] from the ideas or attitudes expressed through a governmental action, rather than from the more tangible or material consequences the action brings about"); *see also* Christopher A. Bracey, *Dignity in Race Jurisprudence*, 7 U. Pa. J. Const. L. 669, 676 (2005): "[D]ignity is (and always has been) a central area of concern in the struggle for racial justice, and that current Supreme Court jurisprudence indulges in delusional and counterfeit thinking when it chooses to undervalue, distort, or evade entirely core dignitary concerns in the context of racial disputes."

Chapter 7. Collective Discrimination

1. As noted earlier in the book, my use of the phrase *because of interraciality* concerns more than just mistreatment based on one's involvement in an intimate, interracial relationship—marriage or a committed, nonmarital relationship. Generally speaking, the phrase encompasses mistreatment based on one's being part of an interracial family unit, which includes sibling relationships and parent-child relationships. It does not extend to mistreatment based on platonic friendships, however.
2. Kevin M. Clermont and Stewart J. Schwab, *Employment Discrimination Plaintiffs in Federal Court: From Bad to Worse?*, 3 Harv. L. & Pol'y Rev. 103, 127 (2009) (noting that "[o]ver the period of 1979–2006 in federal court, the plaintiff win rate for jobs cases (15%) was much lower than that for non-jobs cases (51%)"); *see also* Angela Onwuachi-Willig and Mario Barnes, *By Any Other Name? On Being "Regarded As" Black, and Why Title VII Should Apply Even if Lakisha and Jamal Are White*, 2005 Wis. L. Rev. 1283 (explaining and critiquing the failure of courts to recognize racial discrimination through proxies or factors other than skin color that are used to construct and define race); Devon W. Carbado and Mitu Gulati, *The Fifth Black Woman*, 11 J. Contemp. Legal Issues 701, 718–20 (2001) (analyzing courts' failures to acknowledge the harm of working one's identity in the workplace); Kenji Yoshino, *Covering*, 111 Yale L.J. 769, 892 (2002) (defining and describing the harm of covering or downplaying disfavored traits); Barbara J. Flagg, *Fashioning a Title VII Remedy for Transparently White Subjective Decisionmaking*, 104 Yale L.J. 2009, 2009–29 (1995) (revealing the discrimination that can occur through forced racial identity performances and analyzing how courts fail to understand such dynamics in their decisions).
3. Survey 2 (Bryan and Sam).
4. Reginald Oh, *Regulating White Desire*, 2007 Wis. L. Rev. 463, 482–84 (2007) (citing to the work of historian Charles Robinson); Randall Kennedy, *The Enforcement of Antimiscegenation Laws, in* Interracialism: Black-White Intermarriage in American History, Literature, and Law (Wernor Sollors ed., 2000), at 140, 144–45.
5. *See* Charles Frank Robinson II, Dangerous Liaisons: Sex and Love in the Segregated South 67–70 (2003); Barbara Holden-Smith, *Lynching, Federalism, and the Intersection of Race and Gender in the Progressive Era*, 8 Yale J.L. & Feminism 31, 31–40 (1996).

6. *Rhinelander Loses; No Fraud Is Found; Wife Will Sue Now,* N.Y. Times, Dec. 6, 1925, at 1.
7. *Id.*
8. Earl Lewis and Heidi Ardizzone, Love on Trial: An American Scandal in Black and White 247–48 (2001).
9. *Id.* at 252, 259.
10. Angela Onwuachi-Willig, *A Beautiful Lie: Exploring* Rhinelander. v. Rhinelander *as a Formative Lesson on Race, Identity, Marriage, and Family,* 95 Cal. L. Rev. 2393, 2451, 2454 (2007): "Therefore, Leonard . . . had become a race traitor. He had crossed an unforgivable line, and there was no coming back. In essence, he would have to be *punished.* . . . In fact, actions occurring after his loss at trial demonstrated as much, showing that the only way to protect the lines between the colored and white worlds was to *'punish'* Leonard for choosing to cross such a boundary" (emphasis added). *See also id.* at 2403 (noting that "the verdict [in *Rhinelander*] also may be read as Leonard's punishment for failing to meet expectations regarding his race, gender, and class identities"). In our society, people have not just been punished for the type of marriages that they have entered into. They have experienced marriage as a tool of punishment. *See* Melissa Murray, *Marriage as Punishment,* 112 Colum. L. Rev. 1 (2012) (discussing how courts used forced marriage to punish those men who seduced women through a false promise of marriage).
11. *Rhinelander Dropped from Social Register,* Detroit Free Press, Nov. 25, 1925, at 2.
12. *Id.*
13. *To Drop Mrs. Rhinelander,* N.Y. Times, Social Notes, Mar. 16, 1925, at 19.
14. Renee C. Romano, Race Mixing: Black-White Marriage in Postwar America 268 (2003).
15. Heather M. Dalmage, Tripping on the Color Line: Black-White Multiracial Families in a Racially Divided World 53 (2000).
16. *See, e.g.,* Ripp v. Dobbs Houses, Inc., 366 F. Supp. 205, 208–9 (N.D. Ala. 1973).
17. Adams v. Governor's Committee on Postsecondary Educ., No. C80–624A, 1981 WL 27101, at *8–9 (N.D. Ga. Sept. 3, 1981).
18. *Id.*
19. *Ripp,* 366 F. Supp at 208–9: "The employment practices which plaintiff attacks in his complaint are practices which result in disparate treatment of black employees. Plaintiff avers that he is a white citizen. The employment practices, subject to challenge in this action, have no impact upon the plaintiff."
20. *Id.* at 210.
21. *See, e.g.,* Parr v. Woodmen of the World Life Ins. Co., 791 F. 2d 888, 891–92 (11th Cir. 1986): "Title VII of the 1964 Civil Rights Act provides us with a clear mandate from Congress that no longer will the United States tolerate this form of discrimination. It is, therefore, the duty of the courts to make sure that the Act works, and the intent of Congress is not hampered by a combination of a strict construction of the statute in a *battle with semantics*" (emphasis added).

22. *See, e.g.,* Holcomb v. Iona College, 521 F. 3d 130, 138–39 (2008) (deciding the question for the first time); *see also* Parr v. Woodmen of the World Life Ins. Co., 791 F. 2d 888, 889–92 (11th Cir. 1986); Rosenblatt v. Bivona & Cohen, P.C., 946 F. Supp. 298, 300 (S.D.N.Y. 1996); Chacon v. Ochs, 780 F. Supp. 680, 682 (C.D. Cal. 1991); Gresham v. Waffle House, Inc., 586 F. Supp. 1442, 1445 (N.D. Ga. 1984). These cases are to be distinguished from cases based on a denial of the right of association. In these cases, the plaintiff argues that he or she has been denied the benefits of associating with those "who would have been included in the relevant context had they not been excluded because of a racially discriminatory selection process." Palmer v. Occidental Chem. Corp., 356 F.3d 235, 236 (2d Cir. 2004); *see also* Trafficante v. Metropolitan Life Ins. Co., 409 U.S. 205, 209–10 (1972) (recognizing, for the first time, the viability of a claim for denial of interracial association).
23. Rosenblatt v. Bivona & Cohen, P.C., 946 F. Supp. 298, 299 (S.D.N.Y. 1996).
24. *Id.* at 299–300.
25. *Id.* at 300; *see also* Whitney v. Greater New York Corp. of Seventh-Day Adventists, 401 F. Supp. 1363, 1366 (S.D.N.Y. 1975): "Manifestly, if Whitney was discharged because, as alleged, the defendant disapproved of a social relationship between a white woman and a black man, the plaintiff's race was as much a factor in the decision to fire her as that of her friend. Specifying as she does that she was discharged because she, a white woman, associated with a black, her complaint falls within the statutory language that she was 'discharge[d] . . . because of [her] race.'"
26. Madison v. IBP, Inc., 330 F. 3d 1051 (8th Cir. 2002).
27. *Madison,* 330 F. 3d at 1054.
28. *Id.* at 1053.
29. *Id.*
30. *Id.*
31. *Id.*
32. *Id.*
33. *See* Erica Chito Childs, Navigating Interracial Borders: Black-White Couples and Their Social Worlds (2005).
34. Survey 10 (Edith and Stephen).
35. Loving v. Virginia, 388 U.S. 1, 2–3, 10–11 (1967).
36. Mackey v. Children's Medical Ctr. of Dallas, No. 3:05-Cv-043-L, 2006 WL 2713788 (N.D. Tex. Sept. 22, 2006).
37. *Mackey,* 2006 WL 2713788, at *2.
38. *Id.*
39. *Id.* at *4.
40. *Id.* at *15.
41. *Id.* at *15 and n. 13.
42. U.S. Const., Art. II, Sec. 1.
43. The American President (Universal Pictures 1995).

44. 997 F. 2d 898, 904–5 (D.C. Cir. 1993).

45. *Imagine If Obama's Wife Was White, Asks African-American Author,* Thaindian News, Nov. 24, 2008, http://www.thaindian.com/newsportal/uncategorized/imagine-if-obamas-wife-was-white-asks-african-american-author_100122795.html (last visited Oct. 10, 2012).

46. Renee Graham, *In Casting Film Couples, Race Is Still a Black-and-White Issue,* Boston Globe, Mar. 8, 2005, at C1.

47. Jacob Bernstein, *The Woman behind Harold Ford,* Daily Beast, Feb. 10, 2010, http://www.thedailybeast.com/articles/2010/02/10/the-woman-behind-harold-ford.html (last visited Oct. 10, 2012).

48. Erica Chito Childs, *Listening to the Interracial Canary: Contemporary Views on Interracial Relationships among Blacks and Whites,* 76 Fordham L. Rev. 2771, 2780–81 (2008).

49. Lawrence Otis Graham, Member of the Club: Reflections on Life in a Racially Polarized World 41 (1995).

50. *See* Leonard M. Baynes, *The Diversity among Us,* 19 W. New Eng. L. Rev. 25, 27 (1997); *see also* Barbara Flagg, *Whiteness as Metaprivilege,* 18 Wash. U. J. L. & Pol'y 1, 9 (2005) (noting that "[w]ishing away racial injustice, as in the 'I don't think of you as Black' strategy, is not a meaningful antiracist option").

51. Angela Nissel, Mixed: My Life in Black and White 5 (2006).

52. Debra J. Dickerson, *Colorblind,* Salon.com, Jan. 22, 2007, http://www.salon.com/news/opinion/feature/2007/01/22/obama/ (last visited Oct. 10, 2012).

53. *Imagine If Obama's Wife Was White, supra* note 45.

54. *The Woman behind Harold Ford, supra* note 47.

55. *Blog Asks "If Michelle Was White." More Like Could Harold Ford Jr. Get Elected Dogcatcher in Blackland?,* Zimbio, Dec. 8, 2008, http://www.zimbio.com/Emily+Threlkeld/articles/19/Blog+Asks+Michelle+White+More+Like+Harold (last visited Oct. 10, 2012).

56. *The Woman behind Harold Ford, supra* note 47 (emphasis in original).

57. *UI President Says Husband's Deal Made on Handshake, San Francisco,* SFGate.Com, May 24, 2012, at http://www.sfgate.com/news/article/UI-president-says-husband-s-deal-made-on-handshake-3583199.php (last visited Oct. 13, 2012).

58. *University of Iowa President's Spouse is Paid, But ISU President's Wife Is Not; Fair?* Ames Patch, May 10, 2012, at http://ames.patch.com/articles/is-it-fair-that-iowa-presidents-husband-is-paid-to-support-fundraising-when-isu-presidents-wife-is-not (last visited Oct. 13, 2012). Ken Mason "is required to support the university and 'participate in frequent fundraising activities and events both on and off campus' . . . for an average of '20 hours per week.'" Clark Kauffman, *U of I President's Husband Gets Unique Pay Deal,* Des Moines Register, May 5, 2012, at http://www.desmoinesregister.com/article/20120506/NEWS/305060099/U-president-s-husband-gets-unique-pay-deal (last visited Oct. 13, 2012); *see also* B. A. Morelli, *Tell Us: Would Spouse of University of Iowa President Get Fundraising Pay If He Was a Woman?* Iowa City Patch, May 9, 2012, at http://iowacity.patch.com/articles/would

-spouse-of-university-of-iowa-president-get-fundraising-pay-if-he-was-a-woman (last visited Oct. 13, 2012). ("UI says it did not pay a fundraising fee to Robin Davisson, the spouse of former UI president David Skorton, or Carol Fethke, the wife of former interim president Gary Fethke. Those are Mason's two most recent predecessors.")

59. *University of Iowa President's Spouse Is Paid, supra* note 58.
60. *University of Iowa President's Spouse Is Paid, supra* note 58. According to the Des Moines Register, the Board of Regents President, Craig Lang, defended the decision to pay Ken Mason as a fundraiser, "writing that being the spouse of a university president is 'effectively a full-time job, and one that requires their attention, commitment, and presence 24 hours a day, seven days a week,'" noting "that Ken Mason 'attends most if not all athletic events, including networking and entertaining donors and alumni at hundreds of other university events throughout the year,'" and finally highlighting "that paying presidential spouses was common at universities." Clark Kauffman, *Of State's Universities, Only U of I Has Spouse of President on Payroll,* Des Moines Register, May 10, 2012, at http://www.desmoine sregister.com/article/20120510/NEWS/305100034/Of-state-s-universities-only -U-has-spouse-president-payroll (last visited Oct. 13, 2012).
61. Devon W. Carbado and Mitu Gulati, *The Law and Economics of Critical Race Theory,* 112 Yale L.J. 1757, 1772 (2003):"The less stereotypically black she is, the more palatable her identity is. The more palatable her identity is, the less vulnerable she is to discrimination. The relationship among black unconventionality, racial palatability, and vulnerability to discrimination creates an incentive for black people to signal—through identity performances—that they are unconventionally black."
62. As I note earlier in the book, I am using pseudonyms for all of the survey participants.
63. Survey 2 (Bryan and Sam).
64. Survey 9 (Susan and Ethan).
65. Survey 4 (Darcy and Charlie).
66. *Id.*
67. Survey 6 (Ted and Jane).
68. Survey 9 (Susan and Ethan).
69. Survey 12 (Deanne and Fred).
70. Holcomb v. Iona College, 521 F. 3d 130 (2d Cir. 2008).
71. *Id.* at 132.
72. *Id.* at 132.
73. *Id.* at 134.
74. *Id.* at 132.
75. *Id.* at 132–33.
76. *Id.* at 133.
77. *Id.*
78. *Id.*

79. *Id.* at 134.
80. *Id.* at 134–35.
81. *Id.* at 135.
82. *Id.* at 132, 135.
83. *Id.* at 135.
84. *Id.*
85. *Id.* at 136.
86. *Id.* at 132.
87. *Id.* at 140.
88. *Id.* at 141.
89. *Id.* at 134.
90. *Id.* at 134.
91. *Id.*
92. *Id.* at 142–43.
93. *Id.* at 143–44.
94. *Id.* at 144.
95. *See* Holning Lau, *Transcending the Individualist Paradigm in Sexual Orientation Antidiscrimination Law*, 94 Cal. L. Rev. 1271, 1272 n. 4 (2006) (critiquing the antidiscrimination paradigm of rights, "in which rights are accorded only to individuals and individuals are the analytical units among which differentiation is proscribed by antidiscrimination laws").
96. *See id.* at 1285–1302.
97. *Id.* at 1273.
98. *See generally* Tobias Wolff, *Political Representation and Accountability under Don't Ask, Don't Tell*, 89 Iowa L. Rev. 1633 (2004).
99. Angela Onwuachi-Willig, *Undercover Other*, 94 Cal. L. Rev. 873, 890 (2006).
100. Dalmage, *supra* note 15, at 59.
101. *Id.*
102. Survey 3 (Margaret and Geoffrey).

Chapter 8. Reflections in Black and White, and Where We Go From Here

1. *Rhinelander Bride Flays N.Y. Society*, Chi. Defender, Mar. 21, 1925, at 1.
2. Annulment Survey, Introduction.
3. *Id.*
4. *Id.*
5. I wrote: "Dissolution, or the ending, of marriage can occur through one of two legal procedures: divorce or annulment. Typically, annulments are granted when there has been a fraud or misrepresentation that 'goes to the essence of the marriage.' A factor goes to the essence of marriage if it is an issue that is so material and central to marriage that it justifies court declaration that the marriage never existed. An annulment is distinct from a divorce in a number of ways. First, the factor or the defect leading to annulment exists before the wedding ceremony

while the factor or defect justifying divorce, usually just a desire to divorce in our no-fault divorce world, occurs after it. Second, an annulment is a declaration by a court that the marriage was never valid. In the eyes of the law, when an annulment is granted, no valid marriage ever existed. An annulment is granted when the person seeking the annulment proves that grounds for annulment—here, the fraud—existed at the time of the marriage ceremony. On the other hand, a divorce is granted when the marriage was valid when performed and persisted for a finite period of time but is being severed or terminated by legal action: a petition or complaint for divorce by one party."

6. Annulment Survey, Hypothetical 6 Responses.
7. Annulment Survey, Hypothetical 2 Responses.
8. Annulment Survey, Hypothetical 2 Responses.
9. Annulment Survey, Hypothetical 2 Responses.
10. Annulment Survey, Hypothetical 1 Responses.
11. Annulment Survey, Hypothetical 7 Responses.
12. Annulment Survey, Hypothetical 3 Responses.
13. Annulment Survey, Hypothetical 4 Responses.
14. Annulment Survey, Hypothetical 4 Responses.
15. Annulment Survey, Hypothetical 5 Responses.
16. Annulment Survey, Hypothetical 5 Responses.
17. Annulment Survey, Hypothetical 5 Responses.
18. Annulment Survey, Hypothetical 5 Responses.
19. Annulment Survey, Hypothetical 5 Responses.
20. Survey 9 (Susan and Ethan).
21. Survey 16 (Fiona and Peter).
22. Survey 2 (Bryan and Sam).
23. Survey 16 (Fiona and Peter).
24. Survey 7 (Amber and Caleb).
25. Survey 6 (Jane and Ted).
26. Survey 15 (Janet and Sam).
27. Survey 17 (Raven and Jim).
28. Survey 4 (Darcy and Charlie).
29. Survey 10 (Edith and Stephen).
30. Survey 20 (Stephanie and Kirk).
31. Survey 17 (Raven and Jim).
32. Survey 5 (Karen and Evan).
33. Survey 21 (Julie and Barry).
34. Survey 7 (Amber and Caleb).
35. Survey 2 (Bryan and Sam).
36. Survey 11 (Carla and Janice).
37. Survey 19 (John and Vernon).
38. Survey 8 (Amy and Carrie).
39. Carol Shepherd McClain, *Family Stories: Black/White Marriage during the 1960s,*

35 W. J. of Black Studs. 9, 13–20 (2011) (discussing the different experiences of black-white couples during the 1960s).

40. Survey 4 (Darcy and Charlie).

41. Survey 6 (Jane and Ted).

42. Survey 12 (Deanne and Fred).

43. Survey 4 (Darcy and Charlie).

44. Survey 2 (Bryan and Sam).

45. Survey 3 (Margaret and Geoffrey).

46. Survey 12 (Deanne and Fred).

47. *Id.*

48. Survey 21 (Julie and Barry).

49. Survey 13 (Mandy and Liz).

50. Survey 16 (Fiona and Peter).

51. Survey 7 (Amber and Caleb).

52. Survey 4 (Darcy and Charlie).

53. Survey 8 (Amy and Carrie).

54. Survey 16 (Fiona and Peter).

55. Survey 20 (Stephanie and Kirk).

56. Survey 21 (Julie and Barry).

57. Survey 1 (Cameron and Don).

58. Survey 18 (Shondra and Michael).

59. *Id.*

60. Shepherd McClain, *supra* note 39, at 15–20.

61. Survey 1 (Cameron and Don).

62. Survey 21 (Julie and Barry).

63. *Id.*

64. Survey 19 (John and Vernon).

65. Survey 10 (Edith and Stephen).

66. Survey 9 (Susan and Ethan).

67. Survey 16 (Fiona and Peter).

68. Survey 3 (Margaret and Geoffrey).

69. Survey 7 (Amber and Caleb).

70. Shepherd McClain, *supra* note 39, at 9, 16.

71. Barack Obama, Dreams from My Father: A Story of Race and Inheritance 20–21 (1995).

72. Survey 3 (Margaret and Geoffrey).

73. Survey 19 (John and Vernon).

74. Survey 18 (Shondra and Michael).

75. Angela Onwuachi-Willig, *Another Hair Piece: Exploring New Strands of Analysis under Title VII*, 98 Geo. L. J. 1079, 1115–16 (2010).

76. Survey 18 (Shondra and Michael).

77. *Kip Rhinelander Dies of Pneumonia*, St. Louis Globe Democrat, Nov. 21, 1936, at 2A.

78. Barbara J. Flagg, *"Was Blind, but Now I See": White Race Consciousness and the Requirement of Discriminatory Intent*, 91 Mich. L. Rev. 953, 969 (1993).

79. *Id.* at 970.

80. Heather M. Dalmage, Tripping on the Color Line: Black-White Multiracial Families in a Racially Divided World 18 (2000); Paul C. Rosenblatt et al., Multiracial Couples: Black and White Voices 217–28 (1995) (describing how whites in interracial couples learned about racism from their partners).

81. Dalmage, *supra* note 80, at 21.

82. EEOC v. Mississippi College, 626 F. 2d 477, 482 (5th Cir. 1980).

83. Blanks v. Lockhead Martin Corp., 568 F.Supp. 2d 740, 743 (S.D. Miss. 2007).

84. Leibovitz v. N.Y.C. Transit Auth., 252 F. 3d 179, 184–85 (2d Cir. 2001).

85. Camille Gear Rich, *Marginal Whiteness*, 98 Cal. L. Rev. 1497, 1499–1503 (2010) (arguing for a "radical rethinking of how some whites' attempts to maintain white privilege adversely affect other whites' interests").

86. Gibbons v. Demore, No. 2:05-CV-00787-LDG (GWF), 2008 WL 3875271 (D. Ne. Aug. 19, 2008).

87. *Id.* at *2.

88. *Id.*

89. *Id.* at *3.

90. *Id.*

91. Meritor Sav. Bank, FSB v. Vinson, 477 U.S. 57, 64 (1986); *see also* Harris v. Forklift Sys., Inc., 510 U.S. 17, 21 (1993). *Meritor* involved sexual harassment, but hostile environment racial harassment claims are reviewed under the same standard. Nat'l R.R. Passenger Corp., 536 U.S. 101, 116 n. 10 (2002).

92. Survey 18 (Shondra and Michael).

93. Ramsey v. Henderson, 286 F. 3d 264, 268 (5th Cir. 2002).

94. Faragher v. City of Boca Raton, 524 U.S. 775, 786–87 (1998); Burlington Industries, Inc. v. Ellerth, 524 U.S. 742, 751 (1998).

95. *Faragher*, 524 U.S. at 787–88.

96. *Demore*, 2008 WL 3875271, at *12.

97. *Id.* at *9.

98. *Id.* at *9.

99. *Id.* at *12 (emphasis added).

100. *Id.* at *12–13 (emphasis added).

101. EEOC v. Mississippi College, 626 F. 2d 477, 483 (5th Cir. 1980); *see also* Stewart v. Hannon, 675 F. 2d 846, 850 (7th Cir. 1982) (holding that a white woman had standing to sue under Title VII due to her employer's discrimination against minorities in promotion because "the exclusion of minority persons from a work environment can lead to the loss of important benefits of interracial association").

102. *See* Richard H. Pildes and Richard G. Niemi, *Expressive Harms, "Bizarre Districts," and Voting Rights: Evaluating Election-District Appearances after* Shaw v. Reno, 92 Mich. L. Rev. 483, 506–7 (1993) (defining expressive harms as harms

that "result[] from the ideas or attitudes expressed through a governmental action, rather than from the more tangible or material consequences the action brings about").

103. Christopher A. Bracey, *Dignity in Race Jurisprudence,* 7 U. Pa. J. Const. L. 669, 676 (2005) (arguing "that dignity is (and always has been) a central area of concern in the struggle for racial justice, and that current Supreme Court jurisprudence indulges in delusional and counterfeit thinking when it chooses to undervalue, distort, or evade entirely core dignitary concerns in the context of racial disputes").

104. *See generally* Nancy Leong, *Judicial Erasure of Mixed-Race Discrimination,* 59 Am. U. L. Rev. 469 (2010).

105. *See, e.g.,* Survey 7 (Amber and Caleb).

106. Survey 17 (Raven and Jim).

Afterword

1. *See* Daniel J. Sharfstein, *The Secret History of Race in the United States,* 112 Yale L.J. 1473, 1503 and n. 174 (2003).

2. Ferrall v. Ferrall, 69 S.E. 60, 62 (N.C. 1910)

3. *Id.*

4. Association of the Bar of the City of New York, New York Supreme Court: Appellate Division—Second Department, Leonard Kip Rhinelander *against* Alice Jones Rhinelander, Transcript of Record at 1284, Rhinelander v. Rhinelander, 219 N.Y.S. 548 (N.Y. App. Div. 1927) [hereinafter Court Record] (Trial Transcript, Summation for Plaintiff).

5. Court Record, *supra* note 4, at 1108, 1109 (Trial Transcript, Opening for Defendant).

6. Court Record, *supra* note 4, at 1159 (Trial Transcript, Summation for Defendant).

7. Elizabeth Bartholet, *Private Race Preferences in Family Formation,* 107 Yale L.J. 2351, 2351 (1998).

8. Survey 4 (Darcy and Charlie).

9. Survey 1 (Cameron and Don).

10. Ruth Frankenburg, White Women, Race Matters: The Social Construction of Whiteness 93 (1993): "Interracial relationships frequently presented an affront to family unity, and an interracial child an affront to cultural belonging."

11. *Interracial Couple Denied Marriage License in La.,* Breitbart, Oct. 15, 2009, http://www.breitbart.com/article.php?id=D9BBNUJ80 (last visited Aug. 21, 2012).

12. *Interracial Couple Express Shock over Marriage Denial,* The Grio, Oct. 16, 2009, http://www.thegrio.com/news/governor-calls-for-the-outster-of-official-who-halted-interracial-marriage.php (last visited Oct. 10, 2012).

13. *Imagine If Obama's Wife Was White, Asks African-American Author,* Thaindian News, Nov. 24, 2008, http://www.thaindian.com/newsportal/uncategorized/imagine-if-obamas-wife-was-white-asks-african-american-author_100122795.html (last visited Oct. 10, 2012).

14. *Id.*
15. Elizabeth M. Smith-Pryor, Property Rites: The Rhinelander Trial, Passing, and the Protection of Whiteness 54–55, 61 (2009).
16. Kerry Ann Rockquemore and David Brunsma, Beyond Black: Biracial Identity in America (2002); *see also* Matthew J. Taylor, *Sociohistorical Constructions of Race and Language: Impacting Biracial Identity, in* The Psychology of Prejudice and Discrimination: 2, Ethnicity and Multiracial Identity 95 (J. L. Chin ed. 2004).
17. Survey 20 (Stephanie and Kirk).
18. Survey 17 (Raven and Jim).
19. *Id.*
20. Susan Donaldson James, *Halle Berry Cites One-Drop Rule in Battle over Whether Her Daughter Is Black or White,* ABCNews.com, Feb. 8, 2011, http://abcnews.go .com/Health/halle-berry-cites-drop-rule-daughter-black-white/story?id=12869 789 (last visited Oct. 10, 2012).
21. Matthew J. Taylor and John T. Nanney, *An Existential Gaze at Multiracial Self-Concept: Implications for Psychotherapy,* J. Humanistic Psych. 195, 198 (2011) (quoting Matthew J. Taylor, *supra* note 16, at 95).
22. Survey 5 (Karen and Evan).
23. *Id.*
24. Survey 7 (Amber and Caleb).
25. Survey 1 (Cameron and Don).
26. Survey 17 (Raven and Jim).
27. Survey 13 (Mandy and Liz).
28. Survey 1 (Cameron and Don).
29. Jennifer Parker, *On The Daily Show Tonight, Obama Jokes His White Half Will Be Confused of Who to Vote For,* ABCNews.com, Oct. 29, 2008, http://abcnews.go .com/blogs/politics/2008/10/on-the-daily-sh/ (last visited Oct. 10, 2012).
30. *See* Roland G. Fryer Jr. et al., The Plight of Mixed Race Adolescents, NBER Working Paper 14192, July 2008 (emphasis added).
31. Survey 11 (Carla and Janice).
32. *Id.*
33. Survey 17 (Raven and Jim).
34. Survey 7 (Amber and Caleb).

INDEX

Names in quotation marks are pseudonyms. Page numbers in **boldface** refer to illustrations.